Christopher Norris
RESOURCES OF REALISM
Prospects for 'Post-Analytic' Philosophy

Michael O' Pray
FORM AND FANTASY IN AVANT-GARDE FILM

Denise Riley and Jean-Jacques Lecercle
THE FLESH OF WORDS

Moustapha Safouan
SPEECH OR DEATH?
Language as Social Order: a Psychoanalytic Study

Moustapha Safouan
JACQUES LACAN AND THE QUESTION OF PSYCHOANALYTIC TRAINING
(Translated and introduced by Jacqueline Rose)

Stanley Shostak
THE DEATH OF LIFE
The Legacy of Molecular Biology

Lyndsey Stonebridge
THE DESTRUCTIVE ELEMENT
British Psychoanalysis and Modernism

James A. Snead, edited by Kara Keeling, Colin MacCabe and Cornel West
RACIST TRACES AND OTHER WRITINGS
European Pedigrees/African Contagions

Raymond Tallis
NOT SAUSSURE
A Critique of Post-Saussurean Literary Theory

David Trotter
THE MAKING OF THE READER
Language and Subjectivity in Modern American, English and Irish Poetry

Geoffrey Ward
STATUTES OF LIBERTY
The New York School of Poets

Language, Discourse, Society
Series Standing Order ISBN 0–333–71482–2
(outside North America only)

You can receive future titles in this series as they are published by placing a standing order.
Please contact your bookseller or, in case of difficulty, write to us at the address below with
your name and address, the title of the series and the ISBN quoted above.

Customer Services Department, Macmillan Distribution Ltd, Houndmills, Basingstoke,
Hampshire RG21 6XS, England

The Language, Discourse, Society Reader

Edited by

Stephen Heath, Colin MacCabe and Denise Riley

First published 2004 by
PALGRAVE MACMILLAN
Houndmills, Basingstoke, Hampshire RG21 6XS and
175 Fifth Avenue, New York, N.Y. 10010
Companies and representatives throughout the world

PALGRAVE MACMILLAN is the global academic imprint of the Palgrave
Macmillan division of St. Martin's Press, LLC and of Palgrave Macmillan Ltd.
Macmillan® is a registered trademark in the United States, United Kingdom
and other countries. Palgrave is a registered trademark in the European
Union and other countries.

ISBN 0–333–76371–8 hardback
ISBN 0–333–76372–6 paperback

This book is printed on paper suitable for recycling and made from fully
managed and sustained forest sources.

A catalogue record for this book is available from the British Library.

Library of Congress Cataloging-in-Publication Data
The language, discourse, society reader / edited by Stephen Heath,
Colin MacCabe, and Denise Riley.
     p. cm.
   Includes bibliographical references and index.
   ISBN 0–333–76371–8–ISBN 0–333–76372–6 (pbk.)
     1. Philology. I. Heath, Stephen. II. MacCabe, Colin. III. Riley, Denise, 1948–

P49.L22 2003
400–dc22

                                                    2003053650

10   9   8   7   6   5   4   3   2   1
13   12   11   10   09   08   07   06   05   04

Printed and bound in Great Britain by
Antony Rowe Ltd, Chippenham and Eastbourne

For Paul Hirst (1946–2003)

Contents

Notes on the Contributors

Stanley Aronowitz is Distinguished Professor of Sociology and Urban Education at the City University of New York Graduate Center and Director there of the Center for the Study of Culture, Technology and Work. His most recent book is *How Class Works: Power and Social Movement* (2003). In 2002 he stood as the New York State Green Party's candidate for Governor of New York.

John Barrell is Professor of English in the Department of English and Related Literature at the University of York. His books include *The Political Theory of Painting from Reynolds to Hazlitt: The Body of the Public* (1986), *The Infection of Thomas De Quincey: A Psychopathology of Imperialism* (1991) and *Imagining the King's Death: Figurative Treason and Fantasies of Regicide, 1793–1796* (2000).

Mary Ann Doane is George Hazard Crooker Professor of Modern Culture and Media and of English at Brown University. Her most recent book is *The Emergence of Cinematic Time: Modernity, Contingency, the Archive* (2002).

Peter Gidal is a filmmaker, writer and critic whose books include *Materialist Film* (1989) and whose recent essays include 'The Polemics of Painting' in *Gerhard Richter: Painting in the Nineties* (1995). A retrospective of his films was shown at the Centre Pompidou in 1996; his latest experimental film is *Volcano* (2002).

Paul Hirst (1946–2003) was Professor of Social Theory at Birkbeck College in the University of London and Academic Director of the London Consortium. Among the most recent of his numerous books are *Globalization in Question: The International Economy and the Possibilities of Governance* (1996) and *War and Power in the 21st Century: The State, Military Conflict and the International System* (2001).

Ian Hunter is an Australian Professorial Fellow in the Centre for the History of European Discourses at the University of Queensland. His most recent book is *Rival Enlightenments: Civil and Metaphysical Philosophy in Early Modern Germany* (2001).

Jean-Jacques Lecercle is Professor in the Department of English at the Université de Paris X. His books include *Philosophy of Nonsense: The*

Intuitions of Victorian Nonsense Literature (1994) and *Le Dictionnaire et le cri* (1995).

Patrizia Lombardo teaches French, Film, and Comparative Literature at the University of Geneva, Switzerland. She is the author of *The Three Paradoxes of Roland Barthes* (1989) and numerous articles.

Colin MacCabe is Distinguished Professor of English and Film at the University of Pittsburgh and is also a Professor of English at Exeter University. His most recent book is *Godard: A Portrait of the Artist at Seventy* (2003)

Laura Mulvey is Professor of Film and Media Studies at Birkbeck College in the University of London, and is herself a filmmaker. Her most recent film, co-directed with Mark Lewis, is *Disgraced Monuments* (1994). Her books include *Citizen Kane* (1992) and *Fetishism and Curiosity* (1996).

Christopher Norris is Distinguished Research Professor in Philosophy at the University of Cardiff, Wales. Recent books include *Quantum Theory and the Flight from Realism: Philosophical Responses to Quantum Mechanics* (2000) and *Minding the Gap: Epistemology and Philosophy of Science in the Two Traditions* (2000).

Douglas Oliver (1937–2000) was a poet, novelist, lecturer, and critic, author of numerous books and poetry collections. *A Salvo for Africa* (2000), his last book, written in alternate sections of prose and poetry gives a highly original analysis of Africa's problems and Europe's relation to them. His papers are deposited in the Albert Sloman Library of the University of Essex.

Arjuna Parakrama is a Senior Consultant at the Centre for Policy Alternatives in Colombo, Sri Lanka.

Michel Pêcheux (1938–1983) was a philosopher and linguist with a particular interest in discourse analysis. His publications include *Analyse automatique du discours* (1969) and *La Langue introuvable* (1981, with Françoise Gadet).

Denise Riley is Reader in English Literature in the School of English and American Studies at the University of East Anglia. Recent books include *The Words of Selves: Identification, Solidarity, Irony* (2000) and *Denise Riley: Selected Poems* (2000).

Jacqueline Rose is Professor of English in the English and Drama Department of Queen Mary College in the University of London. Her books include *The Haunting of Sylvia Plath* (1991) and *Why War? Psychoanalysis, Politics and the Return to Melanie Klein* (1993). She translated and edited Moustapha Safouan's *Jacques Lacan and the Question of Psychoanalytic Training* (2000) for the LDS series.

Kristin Ross is Professor of Comparative Literature at New York University. Her most recent book is *May '68 and Its Afterlives* (2002).

Brian Rotman is Professor of Comparative Studies at Ohio State University. His books include *Mathematics as Sign: Writing, Imagining, Counting* (2000) and *Ad Infinitum – The Ghost in Turing's Machine: Taking God Out of Mathematics and Putting the Body Back In* (1993).

David Saunders is a Professor in the Division of Humanities at Griffith University, Australia. His most recent book is *Anti-Lawyers: Religion and the Critics of Law and State* (1997).

Stanley Shostak is Associate Professor in the Department of Biological Sciences at the University of Pittsburgh. He is the author of *Evolution of Sameness and Difference: Perspectives on the Human Genome Project* (1999) and *Becoming Immortal: Combining Cloning and Stem-Cell Therapy* (2002).

Lyndsey Stonebridge is Senior Lecturer in English in the School of English and American Studies at the University of East Anglia. Her most recent book is *Reading Melanie Klein* (with John Phillips, 1998).

Raymond Tallis is Professor of Geriatric Medicine at the University of Manchester and Consultant in Health Care of the Elderly at Salford Royal Hospital Trust. He has published over 150 medical research papers, articles and textbooks, as well as a number of critiques of post-structuralism and explorations of the philosophy of mind. *The Raymond Tallis Reader* was published in 2000.

David Trotter is King Edward VII Professor of English Literature at the University of Cambridge. His most recent book is *Paranoid Modernism* (2001).

Cornel West is Class of 1943 University Professor of Religion at Princeton University. He is the author of many books, including *Prophetic Fragments: Illuminations of the Crisis in American Religion and Culture* (1988) and *Race Matters* (1993). *The Cornel West Reader* was published in 1999.

Dugald Williamson is Associate Professor of Communication Studies at the University of New England at Armidale, Australia. He has published on film theory, mass media and media/communications pedagogy.

Peter Womack is Senior Lecturer in English Literature in the School of English and American Studies at the University of East Anglia. His books include *Ben Jonson* (1986) and (with Simon Shepherd) *English Drama: A Cultural History* (1996)

Introduction

The Language, Discourse, Society series (LDS) was launched some 25 years ago, in 1978, with the publication of Colin MacCabe's *James Joyce and the Revolution of the Word*, an exploration of the terms of a political understanding of literary writing. It was followed a year later by Paul Hirst's *On Law and Ideology*, a slim volume that provided a rigorous critical account of the new theory of ideology being developed by Louis Althusser and those around him, before proceeding to consideration of the shortcomings of the conventional Marxist analysis of the law of property. The initiators and editors of the series were Stephen Heath and Colin MacCabe, with Denise Riley joining them as an editor in 1984. All three had been students at Cambridge in the late 1960s and there was a certain appropriateness in the fact that the first of the series books was to be a catalyst soon after its publication for the 'MacCabe affair', an initially local matter of refusal of academic promotion which, in the ideological climate of the early Thatcher years and fuelled by the media, spilled over from parochial Cambridge to become a national concern. 'Traditionalists' were pitted against 'marxists' or 'structuralists' in a controversy as to the nature of English and English studies, the conditions of academic discipline and standards, the establishment of values, and the place and implications of new theoretical approaches – issues that were indeed central to LDS.

The ambition of the series was signalled in the title 'Language, Discourse, Society' and made explicit in the short programmatic statement of aims which appeared in the first books: 'Working from recent advances in linguistics, semiotics, psychoanalysis and the theory of ideology, this series is committed to forwarding an adequate account of the effective reality of meaning, sign, and subject in the relations of signifying practices and formations. That such an account must have implications and repercussions for the current terms of cultural and political understanding is the constant edge of the series.'

That statement and the first two books indicate clearly enough the beginnings of the series in the context of a set of debates with particular theoretical – and cultural–political – concerns. Importantly, those debates placed theories of language and discourse largely taken from French thinkers such as Derrida and Foucault against more traditional Marxist positions which saw discourse as merely the instantiation of ideology, the latter itself determined more or less mediately by the economic relations of production. Running counter to both these positions but attempting to develop from them, the series was also indebted to the work of Raymond Williams (with which and with whom the series editors had been involved as students). The objectives defined were strongly influenced by Williams's *The Long Revolution* (1961) and his attempt in that and subsequent writings to understand the development of forms of communication with reference both to the economic development of capitalism and to the struggle for a meaningful socialist democracy. The work across Marxism, semiotics and psychoanalysis on which the series drew and which it was concerned to develop had points of contact with Williams's project of 'cultural materialism', not least in the need recognised in both for a materialist account of the problems of subjectivity – this being an area in which, in Williams's words, 'Marxism had been generally weak.' Our mutual involvement in these points of contact, Williams ruefully commented, was such that 'we forgot that the older paradigm was still there and still institutionally powerful'; forgot, that is, until the MacCabe affair brought it sharply back to our attention.

The series was shaped, then, from what was seen as the necessity to take language, discourse and society as its complex object, to grasp them *together* in an interdependence and interaction within which they were neither to be held separate nor run into one another regardless of their specificity. The social was not to be subsumed into the discursive through some idealisation of discourse as simply productive of subject and society, at the same time that there was to be no appeal to given facts of the social – or some given fact of the subject – which discourse was taken merely as representing; nor again, was there to be containment of the productivity of language within the set orders of discourse, and *a fortiori* no reduction of language to ideology. Discourse was to be grasped as a work in and on – an ordering of – language, which latter could not itself be merely instrumentalised, reduced to the operations of discourse, even as it was not to be conceived of as some abstract formal entity. The books that followed immediately after those of MacCabe and Hirst further underlined such emphases and, along with theirs, indicated something of the range of the series: Jane Gallop's *The Daughter's Seduction: Feminism and Psychoanalysis*, Christian Metz's *The Imaginary Signifier: Psychoanalysis and Cinema*, Michel Pêcheux's *Language, Semantics and Ideology*. The first, a book commissioned for LDS, took on a number of theoretical texts of the time to give a lively critical account of the uses and abuses of psychoanalysis in varieties of feminist theory; the second made available in translation work that was recasting the understanding of cinema through its description of the institution of a 'cinematic apparatus' effecting a certain disposition of subjectivity and subject meanings (and by its example suggesting the necessity of such descriptions for other socio-cultural technologies); the third, again a translation, examined the assumptions informing current accounts of language and the subject, demonstrating the need to grasp how meanings are produced and received within determinate discursive formations that give specific 'subject forms', specific conditions of subjectivity. Subjectivity, indeed, was, the central concern of the series whose task was that of understanding the interaction of psychic and social in the construction of individuals as agents, identities, subjects. The overall conception of the reality of the individual as that of a subject-process in language was taken up from the work going on in France and was the founding premise for the series.

It should be noted here that when the series began, work influenced by theoretical writings and debates in France had difficulty in finding a space within which to be published and one purpose of LDS was to offer a such a space for original new work in English. At the same time, it sought to play a substantial role in the making available of translations of key texts concerned with particular areas of the language, discourse, society conjunction (the case with the books by Metz and Pêcheux), as too of works that were opening up significantly new areas (the case, for example, with Pierre Legendre's work on law and the unconscious). Often, the LDS volumes were the first book-length translations in English of the authors concerned (the translations of Pêcheux and Legendre are examples).

The series can be situated in the context of a British cultural marxism very much on the agenda in the late 1970s and in relation to the development of which the foregrounding of theory was explicitly made. Two of the editors had been centrally involved with the journal *Screen*, while the third was active in the feminist movement. The assumption made by the series was that theoretical work underway in France was critically important and could be put to use politically (this was the assumption driving the introduction of such work in *Screen*, as it was of the turn to it made by many feminists – Laura Mulvey, for example, in an essay published in *Screen* and reprinted in her LDS volume stressed the appropriation of psychoanalytic theory 'as a political weapon'). Cultural critique was to realise the necessary articulation of intellectual enquiry with the project of political emancipation.

The commitment to the use of theory was caught up by, and itself inescapably contributed to, the eventual establishment of an academic object 'Theory', in a period in Britain in which the gap widened between intellectuals and the political left, with Thatcherism followed by New Labour's politics of skilful news management, abandonment of socialism, and contempt for any intellectual work not readily to be smoothed into its third-way mould ('Labour needs intellectuals' but 'the intellectuals of Britain have nothing to say', as the current Minister for Europe once put it). Theoretical work was reflected back as an end in itself, whose success – significant in Britain and massive in the United States where it now offers a powerful professional academic identity – went along with its delusion of radicalism (the more theory, the less 'complicity'; but then the less commitment to anything other than more theory, leaving nothing but the constant negation of political choices, of political vision; this giving a modicum of unfortunate point to the Minister's remarks). The professional identity, the institutional profit, is indeed the current reality of 'Theory' and the marketing catalogues of the big Anglo-American publishing houses provide a ready expression of what has now become a self-sustaining orthodoxy, complete with its set texts and formulaic repetitions. Not that to say this is to wish in any way to deny the useful and significant theoretical work that has gone on, including within the institutional spaces of 'Theory', with regard to particular areas (that of gender provides a clear example).

Similarly, and linked with 'Theory', the series years have been those too of the development of cultural studies as a major site of academic growth and investment, into which some of the initial cultural–political preoccupations of the series came too easily to settle. As Perry Anderson's classic 1968 *New Left Review* analysis 'Components of the National Culture' underlined, it was literary studies which in Britain had provided the arena for the development of forms of cultural critique that elsewhere had been fostered by sociology but that the academic version of the latter in Britain had eschewed. The key figures in the development of cultural studies – Richard Hoggart, Raymond Williams, Stuart Hall (the list could be started earlier, with F.R. Leavis, Denys Thompson and the work of *Scrutiny*) – indeed came from literary studies, which they drew on and challenged through critical attention to culture and its social forms, assumptions, judgements. Against the professional field of a narrowly defined 'English' and the passive empiricism of much of the British sociology of the time, cultural studies in its initial moments was elaborated not as an academic discipline but as a critical project implicated in a constant construction of and reflection on its objects, as on its own conceptualisations of and positions in relation to those objects, challenging the very understanding of culture and society. The inevitable movement against 'English' and its alignment with an enforced identity of a certain canonical literature gave way to the apprehension of culture as an extensive and heterogeneous field of significant practices to be critically understood and valued.

In the wake of this movement, questions of understanding and value were themselves acutely posed: on the one hand, cultural studies effectively took up a critical distance from its objects; while on the other, refusing the established culture-value and seeking to take in a plurality of other, non-valued cultures and cultural practices, it fell too often into description-cum-celebration of 'popular' cultural practices and 'other' cultures. The political struggle of cultural studies against the received versions of 'culture' and its attempts to derive cultural–political practice from that study – the latter moreover conceived precisely in terms of such a practice – turned into frequent self-satisfaction, with cultural studies, taken as in itself authentically political. Cultural studies, that is, could and did come to substitute for what had been its founding project, that of the provision of a 'marxist critical perspective' (Stuart Hall's phrase): it found its justification in its objects of study as such and – the delusion – the study of hitherto non-academic objects was taken as ipso facto a radical act.

At the same time, the development and expansion of cultural studies had powerful effects and provided crucial impetus and context for forms of cultural recognition and valuation which worked against the projection and protection of any homogeneous unity of 'culture'. Breaking the limits of the latter (stepping outside of 'English' and opening out English Departments institutionally to a heterogeneity of texts and values across the contemporary range of media), cultural studies found plural cultures, a multiplicity of identities, in a process that put cultural studies itself in crisis (the identity of the 'itself' was always the problem). The realities of different social, sexual, ethnic, national groups and of groups within those large categories were taken up in important discourses of identity and difference that forged significant representations with cultural-political force. Thus Cornel West, an LDS author, can value a 'new cultural politics of difference', consisting of 'creative responses to the precise circumstances of our present moment especially those of marginalised First World agents who shun degraded self-representations'. In its contribution to such a politics, cultural studies was a matter neither of study simply nor of immersion simply but of the production of representations, of the establishment of forms of represented experience.

The development of cultural studies – of the academically capitalised Cultural Studies – quickly brought with it an all-embracing extension of culture: *everything is culture*. Such an extension, however, renders 'culture' meaningless as intellectual concept and analytic tool. It encourages, moreover, exactly the celebratory immersion mentioned earlier, the flip side of which is the collapse of the cultural–politically calculated production of representations into assumptions of identity on the basis of the given cultural forms and indeed on the basis of their academic validation in Cultural Studies (a corollary of this is the all-too-common practice, acknowledged or not, of the validation of work produced by reference to its author's identity – grasped as his or her belonging to some recognised, accredited category – which, in an immediately expressive relation, authorises him or her in the particular area of the work, guarantees it as a *legitimate* representation). There is need to think too in this context of the degree to which the creation of identity groups has been utilised by capitalism and to which the turning out of Cultural Studies graduates has provided agents for the economic and ideological support of that utilisation.

* * *

The fundamental concerns and problems of the series can be seen, therefore, as issues of *representation, identity, value*.

As has been suggested above, LDS books have been concerned with representations not just in terms of what is represented by them, the representation given, but also in those of their production and of the specific relations of subjectivity they engage, with subjectivity understood as a complex psychic-social process carried through in specific practices and institutions of representation. To grasp representation in this way is to counter the assumption that any representation produced can be guaranteed by virtue of its provenance (as though the representation made exhausted the process of its making, its represent-ing, which would thus be no more than the reflection or expression of some pre-given identity outside of representation). To ask whether a representation is correct or valid is to ask a question whose substance is socio-cultural, a matter of the calculations and choices and frameworks within which the representation is made and judged for its correctness and validity. The series has been based on the recognition of this and has stressed in one way or another through its different books that there is a *politics of representation*, with which any politics is of necessity always bound up.

The issues of identity and identification are related to such a recogni-tion. The LDS years have seen the powerful development of 'identity politics', a development in which cultural studies with its frequent turn to celebration of 'otherness' and 'other cultures', has had its important part. The significance of this development has lain in the critique it brings of unproblematic assumptions of some generalised political subject. At the same time, that critique has often then been overridden in the passage nevertheless from an identity *politics* (a poli-tics of representation) to an identity *culture* (representations hardened into a fact of identity, a fact of 'otherness'). The theoretical dissolution of terms of identity brings the critical question of the necessary definition of identities (no politics without terms of identification) which then, breaking the political recognition, can be taken as fixed, as of an essence available for representation. Contrary to which, the series has stressed that there is no identity given directly to representation; representation *is* the identification – the establishment – of identities. So, for example, to represent a culture, be it with concern for 'other-ness', is just such an act of identification, the truth of which is not in the culture itself (assuming there were some such available entity 'the culture itself') but in the negotiated understanding of representation and world to make the identification. What is at stake in this making is a socio-historical production of a (provisional) unity of meaning posi-tioned in – cutting across – a complex multiple process; which is where the politics of representation has its necessity and its struggle.

The series books have approached this directly or indirectly in various ways, dealing with a range of topics across a range of histori-cal periods (where the cultural materialism proposed by Raymond Williams was conceived as necessarily involved in historical under-standing, including the historical understanding of the present, Cultural Studies has largely given up on such understanding and confined itself to present-day culture grasped in an ahistorical – 'post-modern' – contemporaneity). Together indeed, they point up the need to think about the extent to which identity is itself anyway a modern form. This is not, of course, to suggest that identities and identifications of people, externally and internally, have not always been part of any society or human group; it is to stress that there is a particular conception and experience and expectation in the modern world (the modern world of Western democracies) which demands on 'identity' come powerfully to focus (and which the postulation of 'the other' can reflexively serve to confirm). That identity is a matter of representations-identifications, not of some self-evident inner determination (of individual, group, or culture) is the continual *crisis* of identity characteristic of our societies and which is a capital point of investment, of their very economy – all the labour of imaging and the providing of images: a whole *therapy* of images in magazines, film and television, advertisements, popular photography, home videos, and so on; and, of course, generally in therapy itself, which with its all-permeating ideas of self-image and self-realisation – of 'finding oneself' – has become today's moral imperative, an imperative that versions of identity politics can at times appear unproblematically to espouse.

'Because it has always already started, representation has no end'. The Derridean emphasis is not to be converted into the idea that there is nothing but representations and that there is nothing much to be said beyond this, that questions of value and truth fall before the inescapable fact of representation. One fundamental task continues to be that of the negotiation of values. 'Theory' has been taken to confirm an impossibility of making judgements of value: everything is open to deconstruction, there are no grounded grounds and any grounds asserted are a metaphysical mystification, with the imperialism of the West not far behind. It can be agreed that everything is open to deconstruction. But that as such gets us nowhere; the need is to work out the terms on which we can negotiate and derive and make grounds. The same problem emerges with the psychoanalytic turn of 'Theory'. Psychoanalysis is different from deconstruction: it works with a system of truth, even if the truth is paradoxical, difficult, only realisable in the analytic situation; it knows a truth that stems from and informs a practice which has clear effects that can be seen to be useful, positive (and far from dependent on simple appeals to 'identity'). But if one stays with current versions of psychoanalytic theory, the bedrock of its truth is, in Lacanian terms, the impossibility of 'the real', in relation to which everything can be read as a symptom, a way of dealing with, holding off, covering up this traumatic impossibility constitutive of the human subject, which nevertheless, of course, is continually, disturbingly there, precisely in the symptom. Deconstruction and psychoanalysis in these theoretical forms, however, cannot be allowed to bring issues to a halt, whether in the endless deferral of the former (everything can be deconstructed) or the structuring inevitability of the latter ('there is nothing true but castration', as Lacan succinctly put it). The notion that values and grounds are only ever constructions or symptoms or whatever other undercutting terms are asserted does not remove the necessity for negotiating the terms of grounds and values. On the contrary, if anything it only exacerbates that necessity. The context in which this now becomes crucial and gets raised and confronted most powerfully is that of cultural identity and multiculturalism, the whole practical politics of culture and value. Which is where 'Theory' has been so damaging: cross the certitudes of deconstruction with the idea of multiculturalism, throw in a dash of liberal guilt and a fair sprinkling of academic isolationism, and you have a recipe for a self-justified giving up – multiculturalism then just means everything is cultural, everyone has their culture, there are no grounds for assent to anything more and awareness of this is the only moral stance, everything else is 'Western' moralising (but that stance could itself hardly be more Western). Contributing to this, cultural studies has precisely been ready to give up its project of critique and cast itself as a kind of culturalism which leaves no space for – no rationality of – critique (one can note here the symptomatic disappearance of ideology as concept and concern). Of course, this way of thinking, on its own terms, can only be just another cultural position, though this either goes unacknowledged or is somehow asserted as what Stanley Fish calls 'antifoundationalist theory hope' (if we realise that it's all a matter of discourse, things will somehow get better).

In this context, it can be stressed that the series has gone against the now commonplace disclaimers of any possibility of truth and objectivity, such concepts regarded as no more than fictions, leading to a relativism arrested only by fiats of 'power', of which truth and objectivity are no more than the strategic tools (the belief that such ideas are self-evidently progressive is a damaging fallacy – no one, it might perhaps be remembered, was more explicitly and vehemently relativist than Mussolini). Of course, to continue to place value on truth and objectivity does not depend on imagining these are somehow separate from the human reality within which they are achieved and that they are not produced in the language–discourse–society conjunction (the very concern of the series). There is a world we seek to represent, within which we are included, and which can control the success of our representations; not because these can be correlated with something – 'raw reality', outer or inner – that in itself takes the form of objects representable in discourse but, adapting a formulation proposed by the philosopher Hilary Putnam, precisely because representation and world together make up representation and world and *it is their interrelation that is originary*, not one or the other (a dichotomy which always ends up in the either/or impasse of the stand-off between textualism – it's all just discourse – and realism – discourse just follows reality); *and* that the matter of the success of representations is bound up with political questions of intent, effect, value, and so on, that there are always social–historical specifications of knowledge, in which exactly the politics of representation can be grasped. That account can also be read in reverse: questions of truth and value produced within representation are necessarily to be worked through with reference to, and in respect of, a constantly envisaged horizon of human objectivity for which the recognition of the historical–social, interpretative–representational construction of objects, identities, knowledge, is crucial, *not* disabling. Such a recognition, that is, does not put paid to objectivity and the production of knowledge on its terms; on the contrary, it is their very condition inasmuch as it holds to any such construction as, and only as, a provisionally enabling negotiation of interpretation and world, that can be judged not just for its usefulness but equally for its understanding, or not, of the terms and effects of its forms as exactly such a – particular cultural-representational – negotiation. If the work of Foucault has been important for the series, Foucauldian and sub-Foucauldian insistence on an unremitting equation of knowledge with power or on individuals as effects of power has been critically resisted.

In this respect, a model example of the problems with which the series is concerned might be provided by Edward Said's influential book *Orientalism* in which he gives an account of the West's construction of the Orient over the last centuries. 'Orientalism' names the system of representation through which this construction was effected and of which Said is critical for its exteriority – Orientalist representation is *exterior* to what it describes. He also, however, has a Derridean textualist idea of there being no outside of representation in the sense of some presence not already taken up in representation, just there immediately to be described, and this in theory negates his criticism of exteriority: 'exteriority' and representation go hand in hand inasmuch as 'what is described' cannot be given in some kind of interiority of itself – there is no inner identity of the represented. So that people representing themselves cannot mean that they will not be implicated in an 'exteriority' of representation. What is important in the book however – the exemplarity – is the way in which Said wants, tries, *has* to hold these two conceptions together around representation. What kind of knowledge does representation produce? Neither reflection (record of some presence) nor invention (creation of what it describes), it is a *demonstration of reality* (around which latter term there is no need for the now obligatory quotation marks; or rather, the need is simultaneously to put and not put them). The elaborated understanding of the world through representations is a process of identifications that the collapse into reflectionism or inventionism reductively, imperatively distorts: the former holding representation to an essential identity (this is what it is); the latter to a voluntarism of identity (this is what it is is going to be).

Said's own fundamental questions to himself – expressing the underlying ethical preoccupations of his book – are significant and important here: 'how can one study other cultures and peoples from a libertarian, or a nonrepressive and nonmanipulative, perspective?'; and, 'how does one *represent* other cultures?'. Inevitably, rightly, this is cast as an issue 'in discussing the problems of human experience' but then that, equally inevitably, makes the question as much one of '*other* cultures' – and of other cultures' in the context of '*human* experience' – as of representation. There can be no side-stepping of the question of representation by appeal to some authentic site – some interiority – of meaning (a kind of positive version of the reversal of the relativist notion that nothing said is anything but the solipsistic expression of cultural forms of the speaker: the 'other culture' is necessarily the authentic expression of itself as such). Discussing the problems of human experience involves a struggle in and for meanings which appeals to 'the human' as the excessive limit on and horizon for its effective constructions, as the commitment of what Said calls 'the critical consciousness' and of which *Orientalism* provides an example precisely in its theoretical difficulties and contradictions, in its constant humanist edge.

The critique of the oppressive and exclusionary uses to which appeals to the 'human' and the 'universal' have been put historically has been fundamental and right. The necessary universalism of the Marxist project of human freedom remains however, and the negotiation of particular and universal has become ever more necessary (ecological movements, to take just one example, have forced the realisation of this). If Cultural Studies and 'Theory' have gone against any reference to the universal in the name of particularities, this movement should be no less subject to critical analysis than the appeal to universalism. The value of the opening up of new sites of representation, grasping new particularities, cannot be allowed to fall into particularism as closure (which, again, can fit well with a capitalism that has grasped the increasingly developing market value of groups identified in terms of 'their' cultural particularity); the necessary commitment to pluralism, depending exactly on reference to values of the human is not to be conflated with the confusions and disavowals of theoretical relativism.

* * *

This *Reader*, then, marks the twenty-fifth anniversary of the series, offering 25 pieces taken from the almost 70 titles that have appeared so far. Together they give an idea of its range, as too of the diversity of its work within the overall project of the study of language, discourse, society. That project remains valid today and the aim of the series is to continue to carry it forward, in new directions across new areas, in relation to the issues outlined briefly above (briefly and without illusion as to the difficulties this outline has raised) – they are, precisely, *issues* that the series must confront)

It should be said finally that the series owes much to the help given us by a succession of Palgrave Macmillan editors who have found themselves allotted to the not invariably easy task of working with us. Special thanks must go to John Winckler and Tim Farmiloe. It was they who gave the initial agreement for the series, at a time when our proposal for it fell quite outside the then available publishing norms; their time and effort, skill and enthusiasm were all-important.

The death of Paul Hirst occurred as this *Reader* was going to press. As indicated above, he was one of the very first LDS authors and his work had a substantial influence on the setting up and subsequent development of the series. He was a friend and colleague of the editors who will greatly miss the generosity of his commitment to ideas, to politics, to people.

Stephen Heath
Colin MacCabe
Denise Riley

1

Colin MacCabe, *James Joyce and The Revolution of the Word* (1978)

In 1968, Jacques Derrida announced in a footnote to a lengthy essay on 'Plato's Pharmacy' in the avant-garde journal *Tel Quel* that, 'of course', the essay 'was only a reading of *Finnegans Wake*' and from the early 1970s *Tel Quel* itself began publication of a series of significant pieces on Joyce's work; pieces that then prompted Jacques Lacan to turn his attention to Joyce (indeed, Lacan was to deliver the opening lecture at the 1975 International Joyce Symposium in Paris). *James Joyce and The Revolution of the Word* was written in the context of this French interest which stressed the force of Joyce's project, the revolutionary nature of his writing. The book provided an account of Joyce's significance (and of his significance *today*) that served to introduce into 'Joyce studies' and the wider English-speaking academic milieu many of the theoretical concepts and issues being raised in France at the time. Welcomed by many of the Joyceans, whose close encounters with Joyce's writing no doubt left them open to its theses, the book was received more generally by members of the British academic literary establishment as a threat to their certainties of tradition and criticism – not least because of its emphasis on *Finnegans Wake* as *fundamental* text (the *Wake* had long been cast far beyond the pale of that tradition and criticism).

As the following extract makes clear, MacCabe's aim was further to explore the terms of a political understanding of writing. If writing was understood as a condition of political transformation (no economic and social revolution without symbolic revolution, as *Tel Quel* unfailingly stressed), it remained to specify why and how, to demonstrate the nature of its transforming practice and establish the relations of politics and language. It is this that MacCabe began here to explore in relation to questions of subjectivity: there is a heterogeneous material reality inscribed in the subject's production in and through textuality that is at once social and psycho-sexual and it is this that the excessive literary practice of Joyce demonstrates, implicating us in a radical experience of limits, against given orders of 'subject' and 'reality', political orders included. It is with the consequences of this that the book as a whole and the concluding pages of this extract in particular are concerned.

A political reading of *Finnegans Wake*

Along with a lack of interest in Joyce's politics, there has been a general failure by linguists or literary critics to deal seriously with Joyce's use of language. Since Margaret Schlauch's fascinating article in the magazine *Science and Society* in 1939, there have been very few articles on this topic produced within the considerable academic framework of Joyce studies.[1] Politics and language are what lie buried beneath the endless studies on the symbolic correspondences, on the autobiography, on myth, on the meaning of the works. It is to questions of the relations between politics and language in *Finnegans Wake* that I wish to devote this chapter but before turning to these substantial questions I want to indicate the importance of a consideration of Joyce's politics at the most *evident* level.

Emblematically one could recall the critical reception afforded to the metaphor which Joyce used to illuminate his progress around Europe. Hundreds of thousands of words have been devoted to glossing this *exile*. It has been construed as the artist holding himself away from his people, as the sensitive soul escaping the provincial deadness of Ireland, as the heretic fleeing the Catholic Church. But what is never investigated is the real basis of this imaginary figure: the economic subservience in which Ireland was held by the imperial power of England. This subservience has ensured that since the famine, exile has been the normal condition of the Irish man and woman:

> although there were some parts of Ireland – most notoriously, Mayo – where there was enough inferior land available for the population actually to increase after the famine, in the more fertile areas often the only alternative to pauperism for the landless man was emigration. Emigration, therefore, there had to be, emigration which in one form or another was to form part of the very fabric of Irish society during the succeeding hundred years (Lyons, 1973, p. 45).

The difficulty of getting a job in Ireland was one of the crucial factors in Joyce's decision to leave and that he was aware of how he shared this fate with his countrymen and women is made clear by the words he addressed to his fellow Triestinos on this subject:

> Finally, in the field of practical affairs this pejorative conception of Ireland is given the lie by the fact that when the Irishman is found outside Ireland in another environment, he very often becomes a

respected man. The economic and intellectual conditions that prevail in his own country do not permit the development of individuality. The soul of the country is weakened by centuries of useless struggles and broken treaties, and individual initiative is paralysed by the influence and admonitions of the church, while its body is manacled by the police, the tax office, and the garrison. No one who has any self-respect stays in Ireland, but flees afar as though from a country that has undergone the visitation of an angered Jove.

From the time of the Treaty of Limerick, or rather, from the time that it was broken by the English in bad faith, millions of Irishmen have left their native land. These fugitives, as they were centuries ago, are called the wild geese . . . even today, the flight of the wild geese continues. Every year, Ireland, decimated as she already is, loses 60,000 of her sons. From 1850 to the present day, more than 5,000,000 emigrants have left for America, and every post brings to Ireland their inviting letters to friends and relatives at home. The old men, the corrupt, the children, and the poor stay at home, where the double yoke wears another groove in the tamed neck; and around the death bed, where the poor anaemic, almost lifeless body lies in agony, the rulers give orders and the priests administer last rites (CW, 171–2).

It is only through a consideration of the economic basis of Joyce's exile that we can understand the uncertainty and irony which is generated around Stephen Dedalus's appeal to exile as the solitary way. An added autobiographical joke has Stephen confiding this to Cranly. For Joyce's friend Byrne, on whom Cranly is based, was also to choose exile when he emigrated to America, six years after Joyce had left Ireland.

It is not only the understanding of such a major theme in Joyce's work that suffers because of the general lack of interest in Joyce's politics. The constant references to politics in Joyce's texts have generally received less attention than those to religion or literature. But these references can add to a given text's connotations in a variety of ways. In the Aeolus section of *Ulysses*, for example, we are treated to the spectacle of the political paralysis of Ireland as the old Parnellites bemoan the speech of the night before. The decline of the papers founded to help the nationalist cause and the windbags that have replaced Parnell are two symptoms of the spread of the disease. But the chapter is interesting in that it moves briefly outside the normal petit-bourgeois world of *Ulysses* and, in that move, it demonstrates a surprisingly clear awareness of the nature and extent of the conservatism that afflicts Ireland. Nannetti, the foreman with whom Bloom discusses the question of the Keyes' advertisement, is one of the few members of the unionised working class who figures in *Ulysses*. He was an MP for the nationalist party and was constantly cited as the example of how the nationalist cause embraced all classes. Indeed Nannetti was appointed as liaison officer between the Irish TUC and the nationalist party, and his was a powerful voice within the trade-union movement against the setting up of a separate working-class party. In addition it may not be farfetched to see an anachronistic political allusion in the prominent place assigned to the newspaper boys and the trams of Dublin. In 1913, in an attempt to break the growing power of the Irish Transport and General Workers' Union, which Larkin and Connolly had been so successful in establishing in the previous five years, the Dublin employers organised a lock-out. The Dublin Lock-Out (which provided the bitterest and longest industrial struggle of Irish history and which was the occasion for the foundation of the Irish Citizen Army) turned around the unionisation of the trams and the newspaper delivery boys. The employers were led by William Martin Murphy, a former nationalist MP.

What I want to suggest by indicating these facts is that the political analysis implicit in the Aeolus section is far more complex than a simple statement that Parnell is dead and gone. The resonances and allusions indicate that the paralysis of Irish politics is a result of the illusions about class antagonisms that were fostered by the nationalist ideology. That this was the political analysis arrived at by the young Joyce and that the later literary works imply a similar position is what I wish to argue in these closing chapters. Both the early political analysis and the later literary works were produced within a certain political conjuncture and they can both be understood in political terms. Such an understanding, however, implies a serious concern with both Irish and Italian politics of the time and it is this concern which is lacking in almost all the standard work on Joyce. Ellmann's biography, magnificent achievement that it is, is sadly wanting in its descriptions of Joyce's political beliefs. Joyce's comments are constantly reduced to the ramblings of a great artist: 'Trieste resembled Dublin, too, in its Irredentist movement; the similarity here was so striking that Joyce found he could interest his Italian friends in Irish political parallels, *though no doubt he would have compelled them to listen in any case*' (Ellmann, 1959 p. 203; my emphasis). The trivialisation of this last phrase distracts attention from the real political similarities between

Ireland and Italy at the turn of the century, similarities so striking that James Connolly learned Italian in America because 'he thought their problems resembled those of the Irish' (Greaves, 1972, p. 185).

If, in later works, Ellmann has taken Joyce's political position more seriously, his general disinterest in politics remains constant. In the article on Joyce's politics in *The Consciousness of Joyce*, Ellmann argues that the use of the slogan 'Sinn Fein' in *Ulysses* indicates that Joyce was a supporter of Arthur Griffith in 1922. Joyce's anachronistic use of the slogan (it was formulated about a year after 16 June 1904) and his fictional claim that Bloom had suggested it to Arthur Griffith confer, in a book which is otherwise remarkable for its meticulous accuracy, great significance on the phrase. But to argue that it demonstrates particular support for Griffith is to ignore the particular history of these two words. Griffith's movement, which had known some success in the years 1905–8 (and which Joyce, at the time, had critically supported as the alternative to the traditional nationalist party), was a spent force two or three years after that. The slogan came back to prominence when it became identified with the Easter Rising. But the major components of the Rising, insurrectionary nationalism and revolutionary socialism, had nothing to do with Griffith's movement, nor its policies of abstentionism and protectionism. After 1916 (during the period that Joyce was writing *Ulysses*), 'Sinn Fein' was not to be identified with Griffith but rather with the political heirs of the Easter Rising, heirs who declared war on the state that Griffith, in 1921, had helped to negotiate into being.

The purpose of these remarks is not to create another context for Joyce in which the texts will finally body forth their true meaning (at long last the political one that those with left-wing sympathies have waited for all along). Rather these considerations are designed to disrupt expectations of the non-political nature of Joyce's writing and to allow some new considerations of *Finnegans Wake*. The *Wake* insists constantly on the relations between language and sexuality; on the secrets about the father's encounters in Phoenix Park that the letter will reveal. What has not been sufficiently understood is the political consequences of these considerations of sexuality.

If Stephen in *A Portrait* still considers himself a 'fosterchild' who may find a father worthy to bear the name of Dedalus, the split between bearer and name is made absolute in *Finnegans Wake* as the father becomes the simple permutation of a set of letters. It is the divorce between bearer and name which allows language to signify, but this divorce is necessarily unconscious in any normal use of language.

Finnegans Wake disrupts any such normal use in order to insist on the divorce. In the imaginary world of the child there is a simple correspondence between sign and referent; the two are magically linked together in a one to one relation. But the word gains its meaning through the differential relations into which it enters on the phonological and semantic levels and not through any relation to its referent. It is the recognition of the systematic nature of language (that names are defined through a set of substitutions; that they find their definition in a nexus of differences rather than a plenitude of being) which is the condition of the use of language. What Joyce offers us in his writing is an experience of what Freud was teaching contemporaneously: that the determining moment in this process is the recognition that the father is no more than a name but that this recognition is buried in an effort to control a possible riot of words.

One can restate this paradox in slightly different terms. As I write, each word finds its sense and meaning through the differential oppositions that define it within the English language. I retain, however, the impression that I am conferring the meanings on the words in the act of writing. This division is the constitutive feature of language and subjectivity and it is a condition of the division that Freud categorised in terms of the conscious and the unconscious, the ego and the id, the 'I' and the 'it'. In the 'I' of the enounced I can locate a secure position but in the enunciation the passage along the material of language offers an endless set of substitutions rather than a fixed position. Thus the importance of the lapsus for Freud because it is at that moment when the subject loses control of his or her discourses that something else can be heard: 'it' speaks there where 'I' have lost control.

The *Wake* is a continuous lapsus. It declares itself to be the 'lapse not leashed' (63.24) and it is the mechanism of the lapsus which allows the work to progress. The lapse is that moment in the world of communication when another subject speaks to another addressee across the phonetic and semantic levels of language. The lapse reveals us in our discourse and out of position, not placed in the comforting 'I' but displaced in the wake of our progress through language. Thus *Finnegans Wake* hesitates between a minimal control which takes us from line to line and a riot of meanings which invoke relations along a heterogeneous set of levels (phonetic, semantic, inter-linguistic). One consequence of recognising the importance of the lapsus is that it implies that *Finnegans Wake* is written in *English*. The answer to the question 'Are we speachin d'anglas landadge' (485.12/13) must be 'yes' because if there was not some continuity within the text then the lapsus would be impossible. It is necessary that we follow both the syntax and the major semantic concerns of any particular passage of the text lest it become a simple collocation of letters which offers no initial opposition to our passage through it.

Finnegans Wake is 'nat language at any sinse of the world' (83.12). Which is to say language which goes beyond meaning (sense) and time (since) in an attempt to understand and abolish the sin involved in language: the guilt inherent in the very act of speaking or writing. It is in the second section of Book 2 of *Finnegans Wake*, the Nightlessons of the children, that we find this concern pushed to the very limit. This section caused Joyce almost more trouble than any other and he was forced, most unusually, to abandon some of the material that he wished to use. 'The Muddest Thick That Was Ever Heard Dump' was the initial title that Joyce gave to the geometry lesson and it is the geometry lesson which provides the central focus of the kaleidoscope of the book. Nightlessons of a 'nightynovel' (54.21), they are the essentials of the NIGHTLETTER. (308.20). It is the section where Dolph, the Shem figure, describes to Kev, the Shaun figure, what is underneath the mother ALP's skirts. Kev secure in a male narcissism thinks that the results will be 'like pah' and 'as plane as a poke stiff' (296.28/30) he refuses to accept the possibility of difference. For it is at the moment that such a difference is accepted that the father ceases to be a full presence as he is articulated in the nets of difference.

What Joyce demonstrates in this section is that it is the phallus which is the determining term within the symbolic order and that it is the acceptance of this term which is crucial in the access to language and writing. It must be re-emphasised that the phallus-must not be confused with the penis – the anatomical reality – but must be understood as the signifier of sexual difference, the possibility of the presence or absence of the object. It is with this possibility that the father becomes a term within the symbolic order, that the name becomes separated from the bearer. But if this rupture guarantees language, it is constantly annealed in the exigencies of communication, exigencies of meaning and identity. How far the claims of sense repress the movement of difference is determined by the social possibilities. Within *Finnegans Wake* it is nationalist politics which serves as the constant image of a new secure position for the subject from which the trauma of difference can be ignored. Kev can disavow what he has seen beneath the mother's skirts by fixing on another model of a full presence: on the heroic struggle for national liberation. But Dolph is intent on driving home the lessons of difference and of the secrets of writing. He urges Kev to 'Pose the pen, man, way me does' (303.2/3) for the activity of writing will allow him to see that 'This is brave Danny weeping his spache for the popers. This is cool Connolly wiping his hearth with brave Danny. And this, regard! how Chawleses Skewered parparaparnelligoes between brave Danny boy and the Connolly. Upanishadem! Top. Spoken hath L'arty Magory. Eregobragh. Prouf' (303.8/4)

It is at this moment, as Dolph ridicules the three great heroes of Irish nationalism: Daniel O'Connell, Charles Stewart Parnell and James Connolly, that Kev finally attacks his brother and knocks him down. To take up the position of writing, to allow absence to make itself felt is unthinkable for him. At all costs meaning and the father must be preserved against the onslaughts of Dolph, against the mocking of *Erin Go Bragh*. The proof that Dolph outlines is that the mother reveals the insufficiency of the father. It is this insufficiency that Kev cannot support and when the refuge that he has taken in nationalism and its heroes is threatened with dissolution by writing, he reacts in the only way possible – with violence. The mechanisms at work here are the same as those at work in the Cyclops episode when the Citizen attacks Bloom. Confronted with the reality of difference and the impossibility of definition (Bloom is both Irishman and Jew, the name is separated from the bearer), the secure ego reacts with violence. The threat of displacement must be resisted.

To speak is to have accepted a symbolic castration; to have accepted difference and absence. To enter into language is thus to have denied to the father his self-sufficiency and it is this denial which constitutes the guilt associated with language. The Shauns attempt to disavow this guilt and to concentrate simply on language as meaning but are thus excluded from the world of desire and writing; the Shems wallow in the guilt, become 'Shame's Voice' (one of Joyce's pseudonyms) but are exiled from the world of communication. If only Shem can write the letter, only Shaun can deliver it. The two are different elements of the same structure and it is for this reason that one can turn so easily into the other throughout the text. System is always likely to solidify into the position it upholds and position is constantly threatening to dissolve into the system that upholds it. The dissolution of Shaun in 111.iii provides an enactment of this process.

The *Wake* makes of the father only a name as he is 'variously cata-logued, regularly regrouped' (129.12) in a play of language that turns him into a set of 'normative letters' (32.18) such that he becomes an 'apersonal problem, a locative enigma' (135.26/27). We are no longer engaged in a search for *the* father, for an origin, but in a study of the 'paradigmatic ear' (70.36) which is the place produced for the father by our forms of address, by our orders of discourse. One of the major metaphors for that place is Howth head. The mountain remains unchanged as the water takes its different forms around it: river, sea, vapour, rain. If the 'masculine monosyllables' (190.35) serve as the fixed point around which the rhythm flows, it is the feminine stream which provides the movement. Language is a constant struggle between a 'feminine libido' which threatens to break all boundaries and a 'male fist' which threatens to fix everything in place:

> who thus at all this marvelling but will press on hotly to see the vaulting feminine libido of those interbranching ogham sex upandinsweeps sternly controlled and easily repersuaded by the uniform matteroffactness of a meandering male fist (123.06/9).

Anna Livia breaks with all forms of law be they secular or religious (139.25/28) but in so far as language depends on law, on a series of exclusions and oppositions, Anna cannot use language; she cannot write down her secrets. Symmetrically Shaun, who is the law-giver and embodies the law, is so fixed by its oppositions that he cannot create enough movement to let the symbols operate. For him, letters are 'tame, deep and harried, in my mine's I' (425.25) and the consequences of his ego's dominance of language is that, despite all his protests in 111.i, he cannot read the letter. If Anna Livia refuses to pay the necessary attention to sexual difference which would enable her to write, Shaun attempts to identify himself with the phallus, to make himself a 'letter potent' (419.24) as a means of avoiding the recognition that his brother has insisted on. Shaun's strategy of disavowal banishes him from the world of writing. Carried along by the river, he ignores its flow and thinks himself the master of his own destiny. It is Shem who provides the point of intersection between the male and female which allows the possibility of writing. It is Anna Livia's tones that break through Mercius' speech and it is Shem's ability to articulate the mother's voice which is his ability to make the 'dumb speak' (195.5).

Through its constant demonstration of the differences and absences with which language is constituted, writing allows a constant openness to the feminine. *Finnegans Wake* lets the unconscious speak by investigating the very act of writing; it tells us the mother's secrets. But the mother speaks only in the position of the male, of the son, and in *Finnegans Wake* there is the suggestion of another discourse which would find the mother speaking through the daughter. Joyce's last text suggests that there are two fundamentally different attitudes to language which are articulated along sexual divisions. But this suggestion brings us to the limits of both *Finnegans Wake* and this book. So far I have been content with explaining how Joyce's writing breaks with that relation between the subject and language which is exemplified by Shaun. The question of the other relation to language has been defined negatively in terms of this 'normal' relation. *Finnegans Wake* demands, however, a more positive definition for it suggests that there is a totally different attitude to language which can be characterised as female.

Within the text Issy, the daughter, functions as an insistent reminder of a different attitude to language. During the Night-lessons she regards the twins' struggles as an irrelevance. While the 'jemmijohns' will cudgel each other, she will not give a damn ('her tootpettypout of jemenfichue') because she has had an opportunity of studying 'gramma's grammar (268.17). Grandma's grammar insists on the dialogic basis to language and draws attention to the consequent reflexivity of both language and desire which makes of 'mind your genderous' an appropriate warning to anyone who attempts to speak (268.29). It is the lack of the knowledge of grandma's grammar which leaves the twins obsessed by the independent Cartesian ego – Kev wallowing in it and Dolph/Jerry attempting to write his way out of it (304.31). Grandma's grammar serves as the term to distinguish a language in which the experience of loss and absence is not determined by the reaction to sexual difference; a relation to the experiences of absence and loss which finds no unification in the articulation of the phallus. In an attempt to indicate what such a language and such an experience might be, a final reflection on the entry to the world of the symbol, of language, is necessary. This reflection must, however, be offered tentatively because the attempt to analyse Grandma's grammar takes us beyond the contemporary limits of psycho-analysis. Freud himself recognised these limits when, at the end of his life, he posed the famous question 'What does a woman want?' Here Joyce's practice remains in excess of any theoretical development. Here Joyce is still writing in our future.

I have attempted to explain how it is a submission to a central lack in being, a gap in the letter, that is the condition of the existence of desire and language. While, in an original moment, an identity of being is presumed, the correlation of alternative states of being with certain sounds entails the recognition of a set of differences which, from the undifferentiated world of being, pluck an object. The object is immediately already a possible absence, a lack in being, and its correlation with any given word depends on a set of differential relationships rather than on some divinely ordered one-to-one correspondence. The indeterminacy of these differential relationships (there are always more words, the system is inherently unstable) is what ensures that the letter has a gap in it, even in the moment of its discovery. This process of separation, which constitutes word and world in the same movement, is constant throughout the small child's life but it is the phallus which takes up metaphorically all these previous separations and thus becomes the privileged signifier, the key term around which all differential oppositions function. It is in terms of certain relations to the phallus that we can understand the terms of the entry of the subject (an entry which is its constitution) into language and desire.

The central role of the phallus is not determined by anatomical difference but by the way that the child understands it to be articulated within the mother's own desire, the evidence of her submission to the world of difference and language. It is thus the maternal grandfather who is the determining term in the child's entry into the symbolic. However, behind the mother's relation to the maternal grandfather, there rests her attachment to her own mother – the maternal grandmother. It is in the availability of the relation to the maternal grandmother that we might try to sketch the central differences in the formation of the male and female unconscious. These differences, which find no explanation within psycho-analytic theory, are, I believe, essential to any explanation of the language of *Finnegans Wake* which affords to the text the importance it deserves.

Joyce indicates that 'gramma's grammar' is available to girls but not to boys. This assymetry can be explicated in psychoanalytical terms by the fact that before the little girl can take up her symmetrical Oedipal relation with her father, she must separate herself from her mother. In one of his last attempts to deal with this problem, the essay entitled 'On Female Sexuality', Freud wrote of this first relation to the mother in the following despairing terms:

> Everything in the sphere of this first attachment to the mother seemed to me so difficult to grasp in analysis – so grey with age and shadowy and almost impossible to revivify – that it was as if it had succumbed to an especially inexorable repression (Freud, 1931, 21: p. 226).

Some reflection on this first attachment and separation should convince us that it is impossible for the phallus to take up previous separations for the little girl in the same way that it does for the little boy. In the separation from the mother the small boy suffers a fundamental wound to his narcissism, a wound which ensures access to language but also a defence against the recognition of this wound. This double action results in a relation to language which we have seen exemplified in such as Buck Mulligan. The little girl's separation from the mother receives no such single determination. While the recognition of sexual difference must eventually function as the recognition of a possible loss, the little girl's first reaction is Issy's 'Funny spot to have a fingey!' (144.35). It is only after the little girl has taken up a position as inferior that the phallus can come to occupy the central symbolic position. What is important to notice is that in so far as the little girl's first identification proves correct, her narcissism is fundamentally different from the male's. Shaun's narcissism is always a defence involving aggression. Issy, like Alice, just looks in the mirror. But in so far as this fundamental narcissism is not challenged so the girl's grasp of language is not so sure, for there is no one term which takes up and stabilises the separations. One might ask what kind of discourse this organisation would produce and the answer might well be *Finnegans Wake*. Or, rather, it is the impact of this discourse on the phallocentric male discourse which produces *Finnegans Wake*. These alternatives present a difficult problem. Can we categorise the text as a feminine discourse despite its articulation by a male pen or must that pen be accounted for? The answer provided by psycho-analysis is ambiguous. On the one hand we have Freud's theory of bisexuality in which every position already implies every other and male and female confront one another as the constantly dividing term of an infinite regress. On this view any specific feature of the female constitution is always already inscribed in the male. On the other hand one might recall Freud's famous comment that 'Anatomy is Destiny' which, in its very phraseology, might seem to allow an effectivity to the body over and above the representations it receives in the symbolic world. These two positions may not in fact be incompatible. If we temporalise the process then we can postulate that every new term will include the features of the preceding terms but also features specific to itself which will be passed on to further terms in the series. This solution has the advantage of ensuring that the infinite regress cannot be translated into imaginary unities. It has the further advantage that it squares with what we know of the construction of *Finnegans Wake*. The original draft of the

Nightlessons section was abandoned after much agony and its content scattered through the final version as Issy's footnotes. The attempt to render Issy's voice defeats Joyce who must rest content with speaking the mother through the pen of Shem.

If we lack the theoretical concepts needed to develop these consider-ations fully, we can say that in the *Wake* the women function as the constant excess of any limits prescribed by the male and an excess which demonstrates those limits as limits. For the father the daughter embodies the last possibility of a being who will believe in him as cause of his own desire. As Anna Livia drifts towards death she remem-bers her husband's wish for a daughter, 'what wouldn't you give to have a girl!' (620.26/7) But the mother reveals the father's inadequacy as she spells out 'my yearns to her' (620.36) because this lesson destroys the myth of the father's omnipotence. Anna Livia gets the opportunity to instruct her daughter when the father has taken the son out fishing and is impressing him by spinning 'yarns to him on the swishbarque waves' (620.35). The oppositions posed her provide a resumé of Joyce's themes: 'If you spun your yarns to him on the swish-barque waves I was spelling my yearns to her over cottage cake.' On the one hand you have the story-telling father promising identity and position and on the other you have the mother dividing language into its constituent parts to let desire speak. Into the oppositions male and female, position and desire *Finnegans Wake* introduces writing: desire in position and position in desire, an ineradicable and inexhaustible bisexuality, a constant process, 'The seim anew' (215.23).

This acceptance of movement and process, coupled with the aware-ness of identity as a constant effect of the passage of language, has profound political implications for a society based on a notion of the individual as an independent and self-sufficient entity. It is only by the acceptance of the most reductive account of the relation between pol-itics and literature that. Joyce's texts can be dismissed as non-political. Traditionally we are accustomed to understand questions concerning the political nature of literature in terms of the specific political posi-tions that are espoused or rejected within a work. But Joyce's writing renders such a criterion obsolete. Given the refusal of any hierarchy of discourses within a text, the political discourses inscribed within it lack any of those determinations which would enable the reader to correlate them as true or false against a given reality. Of course, the temptation may be to read them within the framework of classical irony and to presume that we are merely being shown the emptiness of all politics. Such a strategy of reading, however, must rely on the existence of a meta-language which Joyce's texts refuse. A refusal which can be read throughout his texts but particularly in the Cyclops section of *Ulysses* and 'Ivy Day in the Committee Room'.

Rather than engaging in the direct espousal of political positions, Joyce's work poses new questions about the relation between reader and text in ways that I have attempted to explicate. What remains to be discussed is the politics of this relation and the consequences of a practice of writing which subverts traditional political discourse. I have suggested that the crucial difference for the reader of Joyce lies in the position allocated him or her by the text. Instead of a traditional organisation of discourses which confer an imaginary unity on the reader, there is a disruption of any such position of unity. The reader is transformed into a set of contradictory discourses, engaged in the investigation of his or her own symbolic construction. What is subverted in the writing is the full Cartesian subject and this subversion is a political event of central importance. For with the loss of the punctual subject, it is no longer possible to indicate discrete areas in which the punctual subject is represented. Instead one is confronted with the problem of understanding the individual as a set of overlapping and contradictory practices which produce a plurality of contradictory subjects. To understand the subject as plural and contradictory is to abandon a conception of politics as a determinate area with its specific discourses and organisation. When Lenin called for a 'new kind of party', he was challenging the assumption that those who wished to transform social relations could organise in a discrete area called 'politics'. Lenin's emphasis on 'style of work' and on 'self-criticism' can be understood as an attempt to find an organisational structure which would allow for the articulation of other practices within the area of representational politics and vice versa. The fact that the history of Leninist organisations is all too often the history of the total subordination of other practices to the political (and the political understood in the narrowest of bourgeois senses) should not obscure the revolutionary nature of Lenin's call. And it is in terms of the desire for 'a new kind of party' that one can understand Joyce's texts as revolutionary in their commitment to the overthrow of the possibility of contemporary (both his and still ours) political discourse. Though it is also important to explain the relation between their subversive force and their profound political ineffectiveness.

To understand this contradiction it is necessary to consider the relation between form and politics. It is obvious that Joyce's texts produce a multitude of breaks with previous literary forms and in this book I hope to have demonstrated that these breaks can be articulated in terms of the allocation of contradictory positions to the reading subject. Crucial to this process is the production of a separation between the signifier and the signified and the consequent de-naturalisation of signification. But in so far as one makes a merely formal claim for separation it would seem that the ideal text would be a simple collocation of letters. Such an abstract formalism is untenable and it is through a consideration of the lapsus that one can theorise the necessity for the text to produce enough unity for the separation to be effective as process. For in so far as the text remains totally resistant to any practices of reading it can only be experienced as boredom; it is the extent to which a text subverts a practice from within that it submits the reader to the experience of separation.

It is to Brecht, for whom form and politics were indissolubly linked, that we must return in order to understand the politics of separation within a text. Brecht's calls for an epic theatre were above all calls to break the unity that works of art conferred upon the spectator and to transform the passive consumption of meanings into the active appropriation of knowledge. Rather than a text compact with its own meaning, a text which confers a unity and gives a position to the subject, Brecht demands a text whose fissures and differences constantly force an activity of articulation on the subject; an articulation which in its constant changes and contradictions makes known, demonstrates, the contradictions of the reader's position both as reader and, in consequence, as agent in the world. But in order to achieve this work of separation (the work that *Finnegans Wake* constantly forces on us) it is necessary to begin where there is an identity. If we think back on those constitutive moments which produce us as sexed human beings then we can recognise a regularity whereby each psychic stage is the transformation of an identity – with the breast, the faeces, the phallus – into a separation. What is remarkable about each of these transformations is that they involve the fall from pleasure into desire and from belief to knowledge. For in so far as there is unity and identity the subject is a founding source, secure in its own self-sufficiency. The production of an object defined through its differences changes all this. For it allows both the possibility of knowledge (the studying of sets of differences which find their determination independently of their relation to the subject) and the possibility of desire because the object (in the very fact of its recognition) becomes a possible absence. It is this possibility of absence that condemns us forever to a world of unfulfilled desire because there can be no total enjoyment of an object.

Consciousness, however, is irrevocably bound up with a world of belief in which subject and object merge in intentionality. In so far as the object exists for consciousness; it has been plucked forth from the undifferentiated mass of existence; it is defined through a set of differences. But consciousness, in its concern to maintain life, must studiously ignore this set of differences which are the conditions of the object's existence. Freud's discovery of the unconscious was formulated in terms of this contradiction when he recognised that the defining chain of differences constantly threatens to break and disrupt the necessarily homogeneous world of consciousness. Caught in the homogeneous state of consciousness, the object finds itself trapped in a unity of belief, conferred an identity. In order for there to be knowledge, there must be separation so that an identity can be displaced into its constitutive relationships. On the one hand we find identity and there we discover pleasure and belief and, on the other, we can produce separation and there we will find desire and knowledge.

The political question becomes the question of locating the identity which can be dissolved and appropriated as knowledge. The concept which enables us to pose this question is the central concept of epic theatre – the gest. Benjamin, writing of epic theatre, defined the gest in terms of interruption, the freezing of a moment so that an imaginary vision of obviousness is replaced by a set of relationships to be examined:

> The damming of the stream of life, the moment when its flow comes to a standstill, makes itself felt as reflux: this reflux is astonishment. . . . But if the stream of things breaks against this rock of astonishment, then there is no difference between a human life and a word. In epic theatre both are only the crest of the wave. Epic theatre makes life spurt up high from the bed of time and, for an instant, hover irridescent in empty space. Then it puts it back to bed (Benjamin, 1973, p. 13).

Benjamin's characterisation of a word and a human life as the same for epic theatre serves to emphasise that epic theatre breaks with that identity given to a life in the course of experience, or a word in the flow of speech, in order to make clear that their identity can only be defined through a set of differences – the relationships that define them. The gest, then, is a set of relationships revealed by an interruption and one can see how usefully this concept could be used to characterise Joyce's work where it is often a question of interruptions which reveal a set of relationships (one could use the gest to define the structure of

Dubliners). But in order for astonishment to be generated it is necessary that an obvious identity must subsume the relationships which are revealed by the interruption. In other words it is only when the world of pleasure and belief is interrupted that desire and knowledge become possible. The starting point must always be a recognised identity.

We can now understand how the political question for any specific text is not whether the text 'contains' the correct political line as part of its content but whether it addresses a specific identity or identities and whether it confirms these identities in an imaginary exchange or whether it transforms them into a network of relations which thus become available for knowledge and action. In so far as any individual is a contradictory set of these imaginary identities, it is not a question of addressing an individual in his or her totality but of isolating one of those images, that of husband or wife, mother or son, intellectual or worker, and attempting, by means of that action of 'freezing' which Benjamin describes, to demonstrate that identity as a set of social relations, a demonstration which does not take place either *in* the text or *in* the reader's head but in the active relation between both. The political question to be posed in relation to Joyce's texts is whether the constant fragmentation of the imaginary is determined in terms of particular identities. If the question is asked in these terms then an answer will necessarily include an analysis of a particular political situation.

Considerations like these make it evident that Joyce's texts are politically ineffective because they lack any definite notion of the audience to which they are addressed. It is obvious from Joyce's disappointment at the reaction to *Ulysses* and *Finnegans Wake* that he entertained some notion of the common reader to whom his texts would be available. But this purely imaginary audience did not exist and the real audience to whom the texts are thus necessarily addressed is an isolated individual and the only possible individual: Joyce himself. It is this resurrection of the notion of the individual at the limit of texts dedicated to the subversion of that notion which has allowed Joyce to be so easily recuperated by literary critics. In so far as Joyce addresses an individual he can be read as an investigator of an essential human nature and this reading can find further evidence in his use of theorists like Vico and Bruno. It is important to stress both that Joyce's practice of writing moves beyond any notion of an immutable individual human nature to investigate the very processes of that nature's variable construction *and* that the fact that he is the only audience inscribed in the text resurrects that immutable and individual human nature. If the effort of reading Brecht or Eisenstein is the effort of understanding the political conjunctures in which their texts were produced (and many of the elements in those conjunctures remain contemporary), the effort of reading Joyce is one of imaginary identification. In order to place ourselves in the position from which the processes of separation in *Finnegans Wake* can be experienced, it is necessary to have a commitment to Joyce. The only section of society that shares an imaginary identity with Joyce are the Joyce scholars and it is they who form his only audience.[2]

Notes

1. It is the introduction of the reader into the systematic order of discourse in *Finnegans Wake*, which has made the book so intractable to linguists. Recently Strother Purdy has made an admirable effort to come to terms with the *Wake*'s language in 'Mind your genderous: toward a Wake Grammar' (Purdy, 1972). Purdy's interesting researches are, however, doomed to partial failure in so far as he is committed to a philosophy of language as communication and to using a theory of language which ignores the subject's positioning in discourse. Any account of *Finnegans Wake* must explain the effect that F. G. Asenjo tried to specify in an idealist vocabulary in his article 'The General Problem of Sentence Structure: An Analysis prompted by the loss of subject in *Finnegans Wake*' (Asenjo, 1964). Asenjo tried to explain how each word within the sentence could take up the role of subject with regard to the rest of the sentence but his account is held back by an ideology of expressivity that runs through his account. Margaret Schlauch's article 'The Language of James Joyce' made the point that personal connections of the reader were permitted by the language structure: 'Joyce demands more active participation from his public than any other writer I can recall' (Schlauch, 1939, p. 490). Lacking a linguistics of discourse it is not yet possible to give a theoretical account of how language works in *Finnegans Wake*. What is certain is that it will never be a question of *applying* linguistic theories to the *Wake*. Rather it is a question of using Joyce's experiments to elaborate methods for the analysis of discourse. It is not impossible to envisage a time when *Finnegans Wake* will be an essential part of any linguistics course. Any future advances in this area will lean heavily on the insights, if not the vocabulary, of Anthony Burgess's *Joysprick*, a work produced outside any academic framework.
2. In another context it might be necessary to draw distinctions between the different sections of this audience, for example between the professional and amateur Joyce scholars. However, what is important for the general political argument is that Joyce's audience do not share a political or social identity which is figured centrally in the text.

References

Asenjo, FG., 'The general problem of sentence structure: an analysis prompted by the loss of subject in *Finnegans Wake*', *Centennial Review of Arts and Sciences*, vol. VIII, 1964.

Benjamin, Walter, *Understanding Brecht* (London, 1973).

CW *The Critical Writings of James Joyce*, (London, 1959).

Ellmann, Richard, *James Joyce* (Oxford, 1966).

Ellmann, Richard, *The Consciousness of Joyce* (London, 1977).

Freud, Sigmund, 'Female sexuality' (1931), *The Standard Edition of the Complete Psychological Works of Sigmund Freud*, vol. XXI (London, 1964)

Greaves, Desmond, *The Life and Times of James Connolly* (London, 1972).

Joyce, James, *Finnegans Wake* (London, 1975); references to page and line numbers are given in brackets in the text.

Lyons, F. S. L., *Ireland since the Famine* (London, 1973).

Purdy, Strother, 'Mind your genderous: toward a *Wake* grammar', in Fritz Senn (ed.), *New Light on Joyce from the Dublin Symposium* (Bloomington, Indiana, 1972).

Schlauch, Margaret, 'The language of James Joyce', *Science and Society*, vol. 3, 1939.

2
Paul Hirst, *On Law and Ideology* (1979)

It is difficult to remember today, and more difficult still for younger generations to imagine, the explosive effects of Althusser's re-reading of Marx. In a world where the Communist tradition generally, and the Western European Communist parties in particular, seemed a necessary reference, it was difficult to grasp ideological effects other than as the representation of class forces. As the civil rights and women's and ecological movements gathered force (along with others), the inadequacy of traditional Marxist readings became ever more apparent. Althusser's political importance lay in his careful analysis of the idea of the economic as determining 'in the last instance' and his account of the 'relative autonomy' of the ideological. In this, his work seemed to promise both the possibility of engagement in political struggles whose class character was not determined in advance and that of ideological work which which would take seriously new intellectual developments.

Nowhere in Britain was Althusser's work given closer consideration than in the group associated with the small – but influential – magazine *Theoretical Practice*. That consideration showed, however, that 'relative autonomy' was an oxymoron and that determination 'in the last instance' reproduced, albeit in a highly sophisticated way, the concept of 'social totality' which entailed that all social practices could finally be read off from a fundamental economic analysis. Hirst's *On Law and Ideology* developed this critique in a particularly acute form around the notion of law. For classic Marxism, law is simply an effect of property relations but Hirst clearly demonstrated how such 'basic' property relations cannot be understood independently of legal practices whose variety cannot be reduced to a prior and separate economic realm. In the opening chapter of the book, reprinted here, Hirst gives a powerful critique of Marxist theories of ideology, building on the work accomplished in two earlier co-authored books: *Marx's Capital and Capitalism Today* (1977; with Anthony Cutler, Barry Hindess and Athar Hussain) and *Mode of Production and Social Formation* (1977; with Barry Hindess). This chapter and *Law and Ideology* overall proposed a new understanding of Marx's work for today: still a necessary reference but no longer an automatic answer.

On ideology

Ideology has developed a significance and centrality in Marxist theory in the last decade which it had never possessed before. This change represents an attempt to come to terms with pressing political problems and struggles in modern capitalism. The Women's Movement, the struggles around the character and content of education, movements among Blacks and anti-racist struggles, questions of welfare state practices, the political role and effects of the mass media, and so on, have forced Marxists to recognise a complex field of social relations inadequately comprehended by the classic Marxist theories of the economy and politics. Louis Althusser's work is the primary means by which these problems, inadequately signalled under the notion of 'ideology', have been thought through in this country and in France. The three essays on ideology published here are different stages of my attempt to come to terms with and to criticise Althusser's work. This criticism is no mere dismissal; it attempts to take up and extend certain of Althusser's innovations in relation to Marxist theory. These innovations made possible a new kind of attention to certain political questions, and yet at the same time his concept of the 'ideological instance' closed-off an adequate theoretical response to those questions, restoring the theoretical continuity with classical Marxism which they had disturbed. It is this continuity that I began to challenge. Althusser's incorporation of this field of institutions, practices, discourses and struggles into his concept of social totality as the 'ideological instance' set serious limits on the forms of politics which could be considered appropriate within this field.

My criticism of Althusser has proved unacceptable to many Marxists because it has dismembered the prevailing general theory of the 'ideological' and makes no attempt to replace it with another. They see this criticism as merely negative. And so it would be if the only possible objective of theoretical work in this area was to unify the social relations in question in a general concept and locate them as an element in a social totality, an element which both serves to reproduce it as a totality and which in turn is subject to the logic of its reproduction. But it is precisely this objective that I am attacking.[1] Except as part of a totality, an entity governed by a principle of unity and necessary limits, these relations exhibit no *necessary* homogeneity. This means they cannot be represented in a general concept of their character and effects. It is not only questions of theoretical adequacy that lead me to challenge this objective. The consequences of a theory like Althusser's

for the conception of the politics appropriate to this area of social relations are the main reasons for my opposition to this type of work.
Clearly, the alternative I have offered cannot produce the same type of
theoretical results. In rejecting a general theory of the 'ideological
instance', insisting on the heterogeneity of 'ideological' social relations
and their effects, I have tried to indicate the space for specific theorisa-
tions and questionings of institutions, practices and discourses in this
area. The nature of this work cannot be legislated for in advance of its
products, nor can it have an easy and unambiguous relation to Marxist
theory.

There can be no doubt that the main effect of my criticisms is to
challenge the pretensions of previous Marxisms, to radically limit the
claims and competencies of Marxist discourses in relation to what are
called 'ideological' social relations. Challenging the Marxist notion of
totality means challenging Marxism's claims to competence as a
general science of social relations. It means being prepared to accept
that in questions of sexuality, family forms, methods of training and
social control, and so on, conventional Marxism may have little that is
positive to say and the classic prescriptions of socialist ideology may be
at best irrelevant. This preparedness is essential if the socialist movement is to be able to ally itself with, to learn from, to draw strength
from and to unify in practice a whole complex of movements, practices and struggles. In a sense Marxists and others have been coming to
terms in their practice with this radical limitation for some time. Just
as many people concerned in struggle in a particular area, such as, for
example, welfare policy, have turned to Marxism and to socialism to
gain a wider comprehension and ideological basis, so Marxists are
increasingly being forced to take hitherto 'alien' discourses like psychoanalysis or the work of Foucault and his collaborators seriously for
want of any adequate means within Marxism to come to terms with
the problems they face.

This radical limitation of the claims and competencies of Marxist
theories is part of a much wider challenge to previous conceptions of
the relation of theory and practice. Barry Hindess and I have argued
in *Mode of Production and Social Formation* (*MPSF*) that Marxism is not
a 'science' but a 'political theory', a medium of political calculation.
That is, it is one of the means by which political situations of action
are constructed and definite actions in relation to those situations
determined. A 'political theory' serves calculation in two ways: it provides criteria of appropriateness of political actions (objectives, principles, 'ideology') and it provides discursive means for characterising

the situation of action. The means employed in political calculation are not confined to political theory. The means of calculation are conditioned by and involve political apparatuses, practices and struggles and their effects. Theory has no necessary privilege in relation to this complex of means, it is in no sense necessarily primary in the construction of situations of action. Such modes of calculation have conditions of their operation in and are therefore limited by the practices for which they calculate. They are also, through these practices and their effects, conditioned and limited by the situations which they construct in calculation.

Discourses about politics, 'political theories', have a crucial organising and directing role in certain forms of politics. Marxism postulates such a role for discourse, claiming itself to be the 'unity of theory and practice'. This unity follows from the application to Marxist practice itself of its theory of social knowledge, historical materialism. Social being determines social consciousness, but the adequate apprehension of social being ('science') demands a specific form of social consciousness (Marxism). Marxism is both product of and a scientific guide to the situation of action; it thus makes possible the transformation of social reality because its practice conforms to the nature of that reality. This double connection, central to the claims of classical Marxism, must be challenged. Marxism links its theory of social causality and its theory of knowledge. Its conception of the relation between calculation and the situation of action is an epistemological one. Calculation appropriates the situation as object of knowledge, and that situation – as social being – ultimately determines that process (social causality assures the knowledge being relation). Political calculation is knowledge of an object. In *MPSF* we argued that calculation *constructs* the situation of action, that that situation always exists to political practice in the form of a construct. Calculation cannot appropriate the situation of action as if it were an object of knowledge.[2] Among our general criticisms of epistemological discourse we argued that, in positing a necessary and general knowledge being relation, epistemologies are forced to constitute being as a class of objects with attributes appropriate to the knowledge process by which it is corresponded to or appropriated. A necessary form of knowledge relation requires a reality appropriate to that relation. Marxism conceives social being to be a totality, its phenomena forming a unity of effects. Social being is therefore capable of representation as totality, of appropriation as a singular 'reality'.

Once we step outside of epistemological discourse then we must abandon the concept of 'knowledge'; with it we abandon the concepts of a unitary knowing subject and 'object' of knowledge, the latter a realm of being with general attributes assimilated or appropriated by the subject. The consequences of our critique of epistemology are reinforced by our challenge to the Marxist conception of social relations as forming a totality. It follows, if we do not conceive social relations as subject to a hierarchy of necessary determinations and articulations, that political situations and practices in a particular country or conjuncture can differ radically. There is no single point of reference for all practices. Political situations of action will differ with the types of arenas involved and the practices engaged in, with the contending forces and issues. It does not follow from this that we must therefore consider the political situations as the mere products of the outlooks and 'wills' of their participants. These situations and the nature of the participants themselves depend on definite conditions, but these conditions do not form a totality. Practices encounter obstacles and opposed forces which differ from their calculative constructions, practices do not determine their own conditions of existence. But these obstacles and forces have no necessary general attributes, they do not form a unitary 'reality' which confronts all practices. These obstacles and forces are assessed by the agents of practice in terms of definite forms of calculative construction; calculation is the continued adjustment of constructions to the conditions of practice.

It is an error to differentiate calculation and the situations it constructs in the same way as knowledge and its object. The situation is itself composed of anticipated states of affairs and the intersection of political practices. But calculative discourse does not exhaust political practice, nor is political practice itself unconditional. The construction of situations of action refers to conditions with effects. But the effectivity of the situations calculated on the practice of calculation is not that of a reality, they have no single origin and no necessary pattern of effects. The situations calculated in no sense add up to a single 'political reality'. They are differentiated not least by the types of political practice adopted. This radically effects the conditions of construction. These practices are not merely given in conditions anterior to them, ideology and the construction of strategies play an important part in the political mode adopted. I will attempt to illustrate this non-unity of the situations of calculation. Take a particular Marxist party, say a western European communist party: at any given time it may be involved in a number of practices, intra-party struggles over ideology and programme, parliamentary campaigns, competition with other groups to lead, annex or even stifle social struggles and mass movements; each of these offers distinct conditions for applying criteria of what should be done and the characterisation of the situation for that type of action. These diverse calculations of situations do not sum up to form a 'reality'. What they do when they are brought together is to generate conflicts as to the priority of forms of struggle and the criteria for constructing a hierarchy of such forms. This extends the circle of calculations and conflicts over criteria but does not close it. Marxism is not a 'science' (equally it is not a 'non-science', science-ideology is an epistemological distinction), it has no privileged knowledge (independent of political practice) of the nature and movement of social relations or of the adequacy of political actor's constructions of those relations.

The paradox is that as a 'political theory' Marxism has derived much of its power and appeal from the claim to be a science, to be able to determine the nature and development of social relations and to act according to the objective dictates of that knowledge. It has thereby solved problems of the criteria of appropriateness of action and the means for characterising the situation of action in one and the same operation, knowledge. In its claim to be a science it has been able to eschew questions about the objectives of its practice and the content of its political programme. Both are drawn from the necessities of social development and the realities of the class struggle. In terms of this claim Marxism has staked the whole content of its ideology on the postulated necessity of certain states of affairs. This claim has radically weakened its capacity to respond to conditions of struggle other than those outlined in the texts almost everyone agrees to be simplistic or problematic and yet is forced to adhere to, Marx's '1859 Preface' or Lenin's *State and Revolution*. The reason for this is that Marxism's criteria of appropriateness are contained in constructions of certain anticipated states of affairs. Thus the key Leninist criterion for evaluating political practices in relation to the state, the thesis of its 'withering away', is posulated as a necessary process rather than as an objective to be pursued in struggle. If 'withering' were not thought of as an objective necessity of the process of transition to communism then the problems of its nature as an objective of practice and criterion of evaluation might lead to some critical reformulation of socialist ideology. 'Withering' has come to appear a hollow notion as a result of our experience of socialist regimes; the general effect of that experience is to discredit Marxism. The category is either abandoned, rejected by 'democratic socialists' as a cynical claim made to facilitate Marxist rule, or made a matter of faith on the assumption that things will work out differently in more favourable conditions. As a result political ideology withers into something to forget, or dogma. Non-authoritarian social relations cease to be thought through as a political objective and a guide to political practice.

The content of Marxist political theory, 'ideology' (in the sense of a system of political ideas), cannot be rethought or reconstructed to meet new conditions of calculation and practice without challenging the claims of science, and without questioning one of Marxism's most compelling claims *as a political ideology*. Marxism is threatened by any radical accommodation to new conditions of calculation precisely because it has claimed to have established the *possible* conditions and determined at the most general level the necessary states of affairs. Given the concept of social totality and its movement Marxism has abolished for itself the space to mutate in relation to new political circumstances, if these circumstances are not compatible with its postulation of the effects of capitalism as totality then they threaten its existence by threatening its claim to truth. To the extent that politics has diverged from Marxism's constructions, notably the sustained development of capitalist economies and the continued survival of parliamentary democratic regimes with mass support in certain key capitalist countries, it has been disarmed in relation to those situations. The modes of accommodation made by Marxists are revealing. The withdrawal into the prediction of crises and revolutions to come, a withdrawal from current politics, or the acceptance, *without theoretical reconstruction*, of these political conditions, adaptation by making concessions in ideology, have been the parallel responses. Marxism has frozen into 'anti-revisionism' or melted into a political 'realism' which fails to consider what it means to fight for socialism under conditions set by parliamentary democracy. Scientism has crippled our capacity to think through and adapt our ideology to different political conditions. Our challenge to pretensions, and our insistence upon limits, are not conducted in the interests of reducing Marxism. Marxism in western Europe, despite its immense intellectual popularity, has reduced itself *as political theory* to virtual political irrelevance. The *political* irrelevance of an orthodoxy waiting for its postulated future. The irrelevance to politics of a Marxism which, mutilated by accommodation to conventional suppositions of the conditions of parliamentary success, represents the nominal ideology of the main European communist parties.

These remarks are not directed against 'political theory' or 'ideology'. To deny theory the role of 'knowledge', to challenge the pretensions to 'science', is not to deny the crucial organising and directing role that political discourse can and must have in socialist political practice.

Socialism is nothing if it is not a political theory: a discourse which directs politics toward the construction of definite forms of social relations and in definite ways; a discourse which can construct and evaluate political situations (relative to definite objectives). Marxism has been the dominant form of socialist ideology. Its immense popularity is because it has formulated the objectives and content of socialist ideology. It prevailed in and took its character from opposition to the rationalism and moralism of Utopian socialism, and necessarily so. Socialist ideology has in consequence been carried by Marxist theory, entangled with the scientific pretensions and limits of that theory. Marxism has in consequence been inescapable *as theory*, unsupplantable because of what it carried and supported. Political practice cannot dispense without calculation, and calculation, beyond the politics of preservation of established and opportunist cliques, demands criteria of appropriateness: in a word, 'ideology'. For this reason socialists have held on to Marxism despite its defects. Modern socialism requires a revolutionary transformation in its political theory and the mode of constituting and presenting its political objectives. Theory that is limited neither by scientism, which fuses political objectives with certain necessary states of affairs, nor by the rationalism of moralism which reduces those objectives to 'goals'. Only the broadest recognition and discussion of the need for change and of its content can achieve this; recognising the limits of classical Marxism is merely a start. Ideology can only be reconstituted on a mass basis, learning from failures and innovations in forms of socialist struggle, attempting to adapt these forms to current political conditions, and from struggles, outside the ideological orbit of conventional Marxism, which have the objective of constructing co-operative, non-authoritarian social relations. The development of a 'political theory' broad enough to contain these elements is a crucial condition for uniting and multiplying these various struggles. A unity which is crucial to the restoration of the political strength and content of modern socialism. This implies no rejection of what Marxist theory has sought to attain, rather it is the reconstruction of the means of presenting those objectives and the means of constructing political situations of action.

Theories of 'ideology' such as have hitherto prevailed in Marxism can make no contribution to this reconstruction and development of socialist political ideology. The position presented in *MPSF* and in my essays radically extends the destruction of the pretensions of Marxist theories of ideology which Althusser began. It extends criticism to the foundations of those theories in theories of knowledge. It challenges the claims of those theories to scientificity and to 'knowledge', includ-ing Althusser's own. It is important to remember that Althusser's ques-tioning of what had passed for 'obvious' in post-war Marxist theory, the claims of empiricism, humanism and historicism, made this much more radical challenge to and reconstruction of Marxist theory possi-ble. In denying ideology was 'false consciousness' Althusser broke with the classic claim within Marxism to be able to differentiate between *forms of social consciousness* as true or false representations of social reality. He challenged the sociologisation of political ideology. Marxism could no longer be considered as it so often has been within 'orthodox' Marxism as basically the world outlook of a class raised to the level of science. But he did so by making Marxist *science*, historical materialism, a practice with a decisive atonomy from the social forma-tion. In this way knowledge of social relations could direct mass prac-tices based on an *imaginary lived relation* to those relations. Marxism appropriated the real in the realm of abstraction and returned to the real the knowledges thus gained by guiding the practice of politics. Politics required theoretical practice because social consciousness could never attain to knowledge of the social formation. Strategy was the political extension of the knowledges produced by theory. Althusser defined theoretical practice by means of a construction of Marx's con-ception of method in *Capital* and at the same time severed Marxism's connection with all sociologistic conceptions of knowledge as the reflection in consciousness of social being; something Marx did not do (as the theory of 'fetishism' stands witness).

Althusser has been in retreat from the implications and impossible pretensions of this position ever since the 'Foreword' to the Italian edition of *Reading Capital*. But he has never theoretically come to terms with them. *Theoretical Practice* took these implications as a necessary and valuable part of the theory and tried to develop on this basis the theoretical conditions for a political strategy appropriate to modern Britain. It failed, as it necessarily must have. Althusser's theory, for all its challenge to certain elements of orthodox Marxism, served as the philosophical underpinning for a traditional Marxist–Leninist concep-tion of politics. But this failure made starkly obvious the problems of classical Marxism's claims to be a political knowledge. Both the con-ception of ideology as socially conditioned consciousness and as the imaginary representation of the structure to its agents involve the con-ception of a knowledge adequate to social relations: in the first case, the social consciousness of the class which represents the revolutionary nature of reality, and in the second, historical materialism, a practice without a subject, which appropriates the concrete in thought. Theories of ideology in Marxism have always been the realisation in social relations of theories of knowledge. The concept of ideology as part of an epistemological discourse has always involved the distinction of true and false (ideological) knowledges of reality. Althusser tried to break with this sociologisation of epistemological discourse, the attributing of truth to certain forms of social consciousness, but only by withdrawing questions of the adequacy of knowledge from the consciousness of social agents.

It is in this context that our insistence that Marxism as a political theory is neither *independent* of the situations which it calculates (these situations condition calculation in and through political practice) nor a *representation* of those conditions must be understood. The notion of a relation of 'knowledge' is challenged in this insistence, but not in the interests of scepticism (a position with vested interests in the continuation of the effects of epistemological discourse). The sociologisation of epistemological categories has rendered questions of the sources and content of socialist ideology unproductive; it has reduced them to what can be permitted in terms of answers based on class experience and the necessary effects of social relations. Althusser returns to this kind of sociologism in his paper on ideological state apparatuses (ISAs), as I have shown in Chapter 3, postulating a given 'ruling-class ideology'. Breaking the notions of the *autonomy* of theoretical knowledge and the *representational* nature of socially conditioned experience can actually help us to approach questions of political 'ideology' and calculation in a new and more constructive way. We can begin to investigate the conditions and limits of forms of political calculation. This investigation can aid political practice in sensitising it both to the role of calculation and to the effects of the conditions of calculation upon its means and its constructions. But this investigation can never itself step outside of the conditions of calculation. It can be no master knowledge of how to know, but the partial and problematic construction of the limits of political calculation. There can be no equivalent of the epistemological distinction between ideology and science. The effect of the absence of this criterion need not be a reckless disregard for analysis or the content of political claims. Nietzsche long ago showed that the effect of the decomposition of absolutes (or rather the fictional substitutes for them, for such there cannot be) is not nihilism. The recognition that everything is permissible was for him the foundation of a new sort of morality. Accepting the limits of political calculation and the absence of any necessary foundation for socialist ideology means that we must devote more care to assessing the conditions of and means of analysis, and to establishing what it is socialists make claim to and why it is so.

Our critique of the Althusserian theory of the social totality and of ideology involves the deconstruction of the field of 'ideological' social relations. This deconstruction has positive consequences in that it states certain of the terms on which socialists engage in political practice in this non-unitary area. What is insisted on in the criticism is the complexity and non-homogeneity of these social relations. In terms of the position advanced here, there can be no equivalent unifying concept to ISAs. The pertinence of the notion of 'ideology' to considering those relations is denied because the grip of a certain concept of totality over them is rejected; 'ideology' in its classical Marxist sense *means* categories which represent and organise the social actions of subjects in a certain necessary way, but which, in order to function in this way within social relations, must not constitute an adequate knowledge of those relations. Althusser's concept of 'ideology' retains these problems of functionality and misrecognition. However much he attacks the notion of the 'falsity' of ideology, because he retains the distinction between ideology and science (even in the paper on *ISAs*) he must retain its equivalent (the 'misrecognition' effect of the 'imaginary relation'). Denying the epistemological problem of the validity of knowledge in terms of correspondence or non-correspondence to a 'real' object and the concept of totality as unity of being leaves no place for the theoretical problem of 'ideology'. A general theory of ideology has particular theoretical conditions of existence and is not an inevitability.

This positive reorientation in theory toward the heterogeneity of these relations parallels attempts in political practice to get beyond the workerism and essentialism of existing Marxist and socialist theories. In particular we are coming to and are being forced to realise that many important struggles cannot be aligned in terms of capitalism and anti-capitalism. Political issues and forces with a specificity which challenges this categorisation of alternatives force us to change our practice and our claims. Two contemporary examples should be sufficient here. The broadly based anti-racialist movement increasingly treats racism as a specific issue to be fought and won with all the allies and forces possible. The Women's Movement rightly refuses to be an auxiliary in the anti-capitalist struggle, its potential for generating far-reaching political and social change would be restricted if it were to do so. The Marxist *theoretical* response to movements such as these has been dismal (which is not to say non-Marxist responses are any better). The theories of racism as a product of imperialism and as ruling-class ideology, or of modern family forms as necessary to capitalist reproduction, attempt to place these questions within the confines of conventional socialist analysis, to subordinate them to a causality governed by the economic. As phenomena of capitalism they can be placed under the hegemony of socialist struggle. The problem is that as questions of political practice they obstinately refuse to resolve themselves in that way.

Althusser's central theoretical advance was to treat 'ideology' *as social relations*, to displace the notions of 'ideas' and 'consciousness' which had hitherto reduced ideology to a *representation in thought of social relations*. Althusser's central theoretical failure to break with classical Marxism was, paradoxically, an innovation within it: the theory of the 'ideological instance' as composed of 'ideological state apparatuses'. His advance was a massive one and he must be given due credit for it. The critique of ideology as 'consciousness' or 'ideas' effectively challenged the rationalism of conventional economistic positions. 'False consciousness' in the exploited class, a happy excuse for all sorts of political difficulties, such as racism, could always be posited as being overcome by some appropriate mixture of revolutionary propaganda and the evolution of the material conditions of class experience, such as an economic crisis. Ideology as a representation in consciousness of social relations removed its specificity effectivity, it could always be displaced by the movement of social relations themselves. Ideology conceived as the effects of definite institutions and practices, as a form of organising and conducting social relations which cannot be dispensed with, could not be dealt with by classical economism. Its transformation could only be possible on the basis of specific practices directed at countering its effects. This conception appealed to socialists struggling in education, in or around social welfare institutions, against family forms and modes of subordination of women, etc., precisely because it freed them from the constraints of a certain form of economism. The object of their struggles ceased to be merely a *consciousness* of reality or the secondary effects of the primary economic contradiction. This is the main and progressive basis of Althusser's immense popularity. His work in this area was accepted by people hitherto ignorant of or hostile to the positions advanced in *For Marx* and *Reading Capital* a few years before.

Althusser also provided a theory of the location of these struggles in ISAs. This unified and attached a revolutionary strategic significance to those struggles, another major reason for his immense popularity. The

ISAs were a means of reproducing capitalist relations of production, securing the conditions of existence of the capitalist mode of production by constituting subjects with attributes appropriate to its division of labour. The notion of reproduction thus explained the necessarily *capitalist* character of these social relations and that this character was necessary to the existence of capitalism as a totality; thus it posed class struggle at the level of the ideological instance as *revolutionary*. This has been a powerful legitimation against economism. It is also the source of the main political limitations in this theoretical position. It is wide open to ultra-leftism and excludes certain political practices which may enable socialists to make headway in European capitalist countries. ISAs are *state* apparatuses and unified by the ideology of the ruling class. Class struggle within and against them is possible but as such these apparatuses are confined within necessarily capitalist limits. In challenging the concept of totality which sustains Althusser's position we are also challenging its implications for the conception of politics. Our criticism challenges the basis for his characterisation of ISAs as *state* apparatuses and as forming a unity, a unity given in the ideology of the ruling class. The field of ISAs as the components of a unitary 'ideological instance' serving to reproduce capitalist relations of production is thus decomposed.

This decomposition has positive theoretical–political consequences. It follows from the criticism that all the institutions called ISAs (school, family, media, etc.) are not *necessarily* capitalist in character and effects. Nor are they 'state' apparatuses, dominated by ruling-class ideology. Whether constitutionally part of the state or not, they can be reformed and changed through state action, institutional initiatives and mass practice. The effect of such reforms and changes on wider social relations is not given and could be very radical indeed. Likewise particular institutions can possibly be transformed without radical change in other social relations as a concomitant or pre-condition. In the ISAs thesis legislative reform and state action to change institutions can only be within capitalist limits, apparatuses are merely differentiated parts of the state system subject to the necessities of reproduction. Reforms will merely be within the terms of and in order to serve that primary function. The ISAs thesis sharpens the reform/revolution dilemma by extending it to virtually all social relations.

Revolution or reform is a dilemma produced by essentialist theories of social relations. An index of Althusser's essentialisation of social relations is the identification (criticised in Chapter 3) of *occupational structure* and *social division of labour*. Radical changes in the composition of tasks, work skills and the organisation of work are possible within relations operating through wage labour and commodity forms. Struggles for equality for women, for workers' participation in management, the creation of workers' co-operatives all offer radical prospects for changing the composition of the work-force and the position of workers within enterprises. These changes threaten oppositions considered essential to capitalism by many Marxists such as the division of mental and manual labour: 'opening the books', for example, would provide vital information and means of control to workers' representatives and trade unionists, but it only does so on condition that they and their organisations acquire competence in accountancy. This process is already under way as a result of changes in disclosure provisions. To be effective, workers' participation in decision making (whether as part of legislation or an agreement forced on the enterprise by advanced trade union struggle) involves the acquisition of managerial skills and the formulation of policies for direction of the enterprise by a substantial number of employees. Changes of this kind can clearly react upon workers' attitudes to education and upon educational provision and make for changes in its character. Thus the clear implication of such a campaign for supervision and control of enterprises by the Labour movement would be a change in further education provision by the state, in trades unions, WEA and other sources. Women's struggle for equality, workers' demands for participation, producers' cooperatives, these struggles and forms are by no means fully developed; their full effects and implications lie in the future and are conditional on political practice. The Marxist left in this country has so far been hostile (with the exception of equality for women) because it has been such struggles as reformist. (It should be noted that the essay on Law included in this volume examines the sources of this hostility and argues for a new approach to questions of company law and organisation.) Althusser's theory ultimately reinforces this opposition. Whilst workers' participation in no sense solves all problems of the 'managerial administration of enterprises, and it is certainly true that decisions at enterprise level are not sufficient to transform the economic relations in which enterprises operate, this is to miss the point. What these examples show is that capitalist economies can continue to exist with very different occupational structures and practices of enterprise management than those hitherto supposed necessary by Marxists. Althusser sets the ISAs to guard and secure the conditions of capitalist production, but they are like blind bulldogs at the door of an empty fortress. The conditions of capitalist production are far more complex and flexible. ISAs which did constitute a labour force conditioned as Althusser supposes would require social relations of production as limited as their (ideological) conditions of existence. Wage labour and the production of commodities by enterprises for profit are compatible with a wide range of educational systems, management and occupational structures, family forms, etc. Our politics has to be capable of taking account of this.

By sharpening the reform/revolution dilemma and extending it to a broad and complex area of social relations the tendency of Althusser's position is to disarm the left. ISAs serve to reproduce capitalist relations and can only be opposed by revolutionary class struggle. In western Europe we face a protracted struggle under political conditions set by parliamentary democracy. Socialist parties and groups will need to use all possible sources of change and locations of struggle, not least because their prospects of forming effective administrations committed to socialist construction are limited in the foreseeable future. Reforms are not reformist if they create new grounds for struggle and new sources of strength. Because its effect is to minimise the possible forms of change within capitalist and commodity relations Althusser's position reinforces traditional conceptions of revolutionary socialist struggle and is an obstacle to innovations in political practice on the left. The left badly needs such innovations, forms of politics other than the competition for parliamentary majorities. These forms are vital because they offer the prospect of a mass base on which such a parliamentary majority could be built. The left needs to outflank its enemies, moving into areas and forms of struggle where the opposition is relatively unprepared and weak. The complex, inadequately denoted by the notion of 'ideological social relations', presents the primary example of such an opportunity. To seize it, changes in Marxist and socialist theory, ideology and conceptions of political struggle are necessary.

Notes

1. The tendency to suppose that social relations must be conceived as a totality with a necessary structure, composed of certain 'instances' in definite relationships, is evidenced by Stuart Hall's remarks about the essay which now forms Chapter 3 (*Ideology and Consciousness*, 3, 120). Hall contends that the logic of my position is the 'necessary non-correspondence' of the instances of the totality. In that essay I argue that political forces and issues cannot be interpreted in terms of some postulate of their necessity of correspondence with the given 'interests' of classes of economic agents. What Hall does is to read this challenge to class essentialism, the insistence that there are no given class 'interests' against which politics can be measured, as a doctrine

about the relation of *instances* in the totality. The notion of a 'non-corre-spondence' of instances in this sense is impossible and absurd, to think of 'instances' is to conceive their articulation into a totality. But what I and my co-authors are arguing for is the rejection of the concept of totality itself, and, therefore, the rejection of the problems of the relations of the political, economic, and other 'instances' in terms of heirarchy of causal effectivity, relative autonomy, etc. In our position political, economic and other social relations are not unified into 'instances', that is, definite sectors of the total-ity governed by their place in the whole and subject to its limits. Hall is adopting a practice analagous to those who charge us with arguing for the 'autonomy of the political'. Autonomy from what? This charge assumes that we retain the instances as entities but disentangle their relations, in effect promoting each to the status of an autonomous entity. How then is it possi-ble to retain the concept of totality and how can those autonomous entities exist? The absurdity is not of our making, it results from the persistence of reading in terms of a certain social topography. Clearly, we do not think that political forces, apparatuses and issues are unconditional. What we *are* arguing is that those conditions cannot be specified in a general concept, as stemming, say, from the necessities and effects of the capitalist mode of pro-duction. This imposes on the instance thus conditioned a necessary general form, limits, and range of effects. Such a position is challenged in Marx's *Capital and Capitalism Today*, primarily because of its consequences for polit-ical analysis. To those who argue that the result is a 'Weberian' or 'neo-Kantian' pluralism we answer that in the first volume (Chapter 4, especially pp. 128–32) the field of contest of monism and pluralism is general doctrines of historical causality. It is precisely this field which we reject. General doc-trines of historical causality require the privilege of their chosen categories of causation to be grounded in some way, secured against 'chance' and rival causal privileges. Thus Marxism does this by incorporating all social relations within a totality governed by the economic, and Hegelianism ultimately refers historical 'causation' to the internal development of a unitary and self-subsistent spirit. There is no necessity for the analysis of social relations to be predicated upon patterns of historical evolution, whether of the 'develop-ment of the forces of production', or Weber's 'rationalisation'. General doc-trines of causality serve as the supports of these patterns but are not otherwise necessary to the analysis of specific forms of conditionality and connection between social relations. These patterns are an incubus whose parasitic grip has long enslaved and enfeebled Marxism as a political theory.

2. Gregor McLennan (*Economy and Society*, vol. vii, no. 2) argues that the posi-tion of *MPSF* on calculation and epistemology is ambivalent and inconsis-tent: either we maintain a consistent relativism, insisting that the calculated exists only as and in discourse, or if we reject this consistent but sterile posi-tion, we are forced to recognise a non-discursive object of calculation, in effect to accept a 'reality' to which discourse refers and, therefore, the perti-nence of epistemological categories. What McLennan does is to construct for us an option *within epistemological discourse*. Despite its sophistication the criticism refuses to come to terms with our criticism of epistemology as con-structing a general relation between the categories of knowledge (discourse) and being (the object of knowledge). He distinguishes between two distinct

realms, discourse and non-discourse, and thereby in effect restores the structure of the knowledge–being relation (and the options within it). Our objective was to *dissolve* this distinction. Knowledge and being are differentiated as distinct classes of categories and given general attributes as elements of a discourse which has as its object the posing of the possibility of a relation of *correspondence* between these two terms. We see no reason to retain this differentiation of categories in the absence of this problem. What is subject to calculation in our position is certainly not purely discursive. But what is calculated has *no necessary attributes*. The situations constructed in different calculations have no necessary and common reference point. To suppose this would be to ascribe common properties to the referents different discourses constitute and to suppose the parallel and autonomous existence of those referents to discourse (to restore 'being'). Further, the situations calculated and the referents' discourses speak of do not *exclude* calculations or discourses. Calculative discourses have no common 'referent (distinct from discourse): political situations differ radically between forms of political practice and condition the calculations engaged in differently.

In *MPSF* we argue that there is no single 'situation' external to calculations and yet which is capable of being represented in such a way that it serves as the measure of those calculations made of it. Such a 'situation' presupposes political practices have a common referent and a common location. Such a 'situation' would be both *independent of calculative practice* (outside of and parallel to calculative discourse), and yet *capable of being represented*, capable of being intelligible as itself in relation to the calculative constructions made of it. This auto-intelligibility of the 'real' its capacity to be counterposed to the claims of knowledge of it, is the locus of a certain form of epistemological privilege: the source of this intelligibility is a *non-discursive representation of the real*, the source of the categories of 'experience', 'consciousness' and their analogues. Once such a locus is challenged the category of 'being' as an intelligible unity external to 'knowledge' is challenged (rationalist epistemologies are capable of coping with this: identifying real and rational or unifying existence and knowledge as spirit). Discourses then become interpretable and intelligible only in terms of their own or other discourses' constructions and the categories of adequacy which they apply to them. One has in the absence of a privileged level ('experience', or 'reason' which imposes form on discourse) to accept *the difference* of the referents of discourse, the potential infinity of referents.

Epistemological discourses attribute definite forms of unity to the objects known, and this unity mirrors the definite and general form of the knowledge process. Thus, for example, empiricism involves the reduction of all objects existent to knowledge to those appropriable in 'experience'. Thus the 'objects' to which botany and physics are supposed to correspond have common attributes, existence to experience. The empiricist is forced to argue in the case of subatomic physics that the instruments which both produce and register certain types of particles are extensions of experience, means of 'seeing' an independent reality. Outside of epistemology what it is discourses and practices construct and refer to has no necessary common attributes; equally these constructions and referents are unintelligible except in and as discourse. This does not mean we have abolished the 'non-discursive', merely that we deny general attributes attached to this category and that we deny any non-discursive level of 'experience' or 'consciousness'. Let us take as an example of those practices discourses where the category of 'experience' appears most appropriate: botany, anatomy, and so on. These involve definite practices of observation and visual representation of plants, bodily structures, etc. But these practices can in no sense be said to be exemplifications of knowledge through 'experience'. 'Experience' as an epistemological category reduces these practices to the unity of interiorisation of the sensible reality of the objects by a subject. It supposes moreover a subject appropriate to 'experience' whose sensory faculties are receptive to the intelligibility of the objects. Discourses must interdict and distort experience and access to this intelligibility. But processes of observation and visual representation are specific; they involve discourse, definite technique and training. It is well-established in the history of the sciences that the seventeenth and eighteenth centuries produced a revolution in the observation and depiction of plants and animal structures. This has often been interpreted as an awakening of 'experience', the product of a new openness of mind and a willingness to discard dogmas. Central in the revolution in botany is the production of new classificatory systems which organise the vegetable kingdom as a homogenous space of relations and differences between forms: observation is placed within a new type of order and a distinct, primarily classificatory, practice. Observation is transformed in its technologies; the systematisation of representational technique to rendering differences and relations between aspects of plants, and its stabilisation through plates of a new standard of accuracy. What separates Linnaeus from the 'herbals', the collections of lore and observations about plants so popular in the sixteenth century, is not attention to experience (the herbals reveal a wealth of attention to plants, their effects and uses) but a new machine of observation, a new gaze-in-discourse. Wat is observed is not merely sign, nor are observational practices reducible to the texts which organise them. Foucault brilliantly demonstrated in *The Birth of the Clinic* that the clinical gaze is a complex socio-discursive event, but that, within the institution of the hospital and upon the new discursively constituted space of the body: it is a *gaze* none the less. Its radical specificity and its difference as gaze from the desire-in-the-eye of the voyeur, or the languid contemplation of the window shopper are hidden from us by the category of 'experience'.

Rudolf Wittkower in a brilliant essay on the representation of 'monsters' demonstrated that the fantastic beings depicted in mediaeval and early modern texts represent no failure of 'observation' in the face of credulity and dogma. 'Monsters' are unintelligible except in terms of the status accorded to the texts of antiquity. Thus certain forms of visual 'representation' are hegemonised by verbal descriptions and are their semblance. They are the illustration of reports, and follow certain common discursive hemes established in antiquity. The changes in the zoological, anatomical and botanical practices of observation and depiction which abolished *these* monsters (it did not prevent the installation of *others*, as the history of depiction of human races stands witness) is a mutation in discourse and technique and not the installation of an originary 'experience'.

To those who reply that monsters did not 'really' exist I reply that 'monsters' never do, they are always the fallacies of ancestors and fears of children. The real question is the 'monsters' we cannot see because we believe in them. The potentiality of *difference* in the constructs of practices and the referents discourses speak of explodes the 'non-discursive' as a unitary category. What is constructed and referred to has no necessary unity and the attributes of constructs and referents differ with the type of operations involved. The obvious riposte to this is the change of 'relativism'. But relativism is only possible and pernicious *within epistemology*, as a general doctrine about the knowledge-being relation. The relativist argues that all statements and practices are equivalent relative to an (impossible or unattainable) concept of adequate knowledge, that is, correspondence to or appropriate of its objects. There are no general criteria of adequacy or truth. Hence the question – how do we know that statement is true? – and the paradox of relativism as epistemological doctrine. We would argue that discourses and practices *do* employ the criteria of appropriateness or adequacy (not of epistemological validity) but these are specific to the objectives of definite bodies of discourse and practice. None will pass muster as a general criterion of validity, but there is no knowledge process in *general* and, therefore, no necessity for such a criterion. Techniques of criticism of biblical texts are of no use in garage mechanics. Questions of priority and relation in the Gospels, of the state of wear of a gearbox elicit different types of tests and disputes about them. The referents and constructs, Gospels, motor cars, depend on conditions which differ, so do criteria and tests. Tests, etc., develop within the discourses and practices to which they relate and are subject to dispute. *As tests* they are radically different, they seek to establish or challenge different things according to the objectives and circumstances of the practice in question. The equivalence of relativism is not the problem. Adequacy or appropriateness is always a determinate question with determinate and variable means of its posing. It is a general question only for epistemology.

References

Hall, Stuart, 'Some problems with the ideology/subject couplet', *Ideology and Consciousness* no.3, Spring 1978.

Hindess, Barry and Hirst, Paul, *Mode of Production and Social Formation* (London, 1975).

McClennan, Gregor 'On Mode of Production and Social Formation', *Economy and Society*, vol.7, no.2, 1978.

3
Michel Pêcheux, *Language, Semantics and Ideology* (1982)

Published in French in 1975, *Language, Semantics and Ideology* was intended as a contribution to a materialist theory of discourse. Fundamental for such a theory was the recognition and analysis of *non-subjective effects of meaning*, with 'non-subjective' marking the necessary break to be made with all illusion of the subject as source of meaning. The 'evidentness' of assumptions regarding 'the subject and language' had to be critically refused and properly recast for theoretical understanding, this being the point of Pêcheux's extended argument with linguistics whose various accounts of language were seen as remaining dependent on just such pre-theoretical 'evidentness'. 'Semantics', Pêcheux's central concern, had thus to involve the study of how meanings are produced and received within determinate discursive formations that include specific 'subject forms' themselves produced within such formations as the condition of subjectivity (of the individual as subject).

The immediate framework for *Language, Semantics and Ideology* was the Marxist theoretical work of Louis Althusser (Pêcheux's teacher at the Ecole Normale Supérieure); in particular, the account of ideology given in his paper 'Ideology and Ideological State Apparatuses' (direct reference to which is also made in the extract from Paul Hirst's *On Law and Ideology* in the present volume). Like Althusser, Pêcheux was concerned to combat psychologising assumptions of the subject, including those current within Marxism itself. The 'Ideological State Apparatuses' paper (indeed, Althusser's work in general) said very little on language and *Language, Semantics and Ideology* sought to rectify this with its emphasis on the reality of language in – as – social practices of discourse and the relation of discursive formations to ideological formations (Pêcheux talks of their 'intrication'). In so doing, however, it considerably developed *and challenged* Althusser's formulations as to the construction of the subject and the modes of realisation and functioning of ideology, demonstrating the need for an account of the relations of the subject in language.

In the following 'Postscript', written for the book's LDS publication, Pêcheux reflects on some of the limitations of his account and notably on the difficulties of his own treatment of the subject, his maintenance of a certain unifying power of consciousness in the subject of ideological interpellation. Here he comes back on his limited use of insights from Lacanian psychoanalysis. Where Althusser makes subject and individual correspond in his description of ideology and its functioning (ideology *is* the constitution of the subject), Lacan stresses that the individual is not the subject. The subject is a complex articulation of instances and, first and foremost, a symbolic production, never a unity, a simple effect of ideology. Lacan's emphasis is on the primacy of the signifier in the constitution of the subject such that there is no individual as a given to be converted into a subject in ideology; rather, subjectivity is a fact of the human individual as a being in language, which subjectivity cannot be contained or subsumed any unity of the (individual as) subject in ideology (Althusser's version of the imaginary assumes the very ideological fiction of such a unity which it purports to explain). It is with the implications of this for his own account that Pêcheux is here concerned.

The French political winter: beginning of a rectification (postscript for English readers)

To intervene in Marxism on the question of ideology, interrogating its relationship to psychoanalysis and linguistics, is *ipso facto* to touch on the kind of 'Triple Alliance' in theory concluded, in France at least, between the names of Althusser, Lacan and Saussure during the 1960s. As you will no doubt be aware, today more than ever, the future of this 'Triple Alliance' is highly problematic, and the parties to it have themselves become the object of a real theoretical *and* political shake-up, in which everything is reopened to question.

The reason the triple field of linguistics, Marxism and psychoanalysis is undergoing this shake-up today is fundamentally that something was *wrong* (and hence, no doubt, simultaneously *only too convenient*) in that 'Triple Alliance', with its claim to 'articulate' these three disciplines together and to control the traffic between the three continents of History, the Unconscious and Language: there is no smoke without fire.

And the reason this shake-up has produced the clouds of smoke that are spreading wider and wider today (towards a 'sexology' beyond Freudianism, a concern with language beyond linguistics, a 'new philosophy' beyond Marxism) is also that this shake-up is following its line of least resistance politically and taking shape blindly as the necessary effect of the causes determining it: there is no smoke without fire.

Of course, the two things marked here by the repetition of a single aphorism are but one and the same political contradiction at work in the philosophical element: this can be expressed by saying that the errors, deviations, 'oversights', etc., that took up residence at the heart of the 'Triple Alliance' and played a sometimes fatal the idea of a theoretical relationship between Marxism and certain psychoanalytic concepts (on terms like subject, ego, unconscious conscious, imaginary, identification . . .), on the lines of his 1964 article, 'Freud and Lacan' (Althusser, 1971a).

But more important he was *revealing politically*, in the workers' movement, the urgent need to develop, in unprecedented proportions, the 'fusion' of theory and practice on the terrain of the ideological class struggle in its relationship to the question of the state; and he was implying, from within the practices of the workers' movement, the extent to which the evident propositions and injunctions of the ruling ideology can blind and deafen.

The *political* intervention was probably so unbearable that, in the rebound of a theoreticism willing to recognise in the Ideological State Apparatuses the horror of its own image inverted much more than it found in them its real 'source', 'Ideological State Apparatuses' was read most often and by all sorts of readers as a purely *theoretical* intervention, to be precise as a functionalist thesis, either in order to reproduce it or to condemn it. And despite all Althusser's rectifications, which they regard as null and void, some today are not afraid to go so far as to claim that 'Althusserianism' is a theory of Order and the Master instituted by the dual foreclosure of History (encapsulated in Reproduction) and the Subject (reduced to the automaton that 'works all by itself'). It had to be done!

As if *resentment* would not forgive Althusser for having pointed out politically, and attempted to call by its name theoretically, the plague of subjection, and avoided the unbearable by denouncing him pure and simple as complicit in what he had named and pointed out . . . Others in history before him have suffered from the same resentment, in different forms: Spinoza, for example, a real companion in heresy for Althusser, who also knew the art of taking unforgivable questions to extremes.

Oddest of all, here and there (and especially where one would have least expected it!) the same provocative question arose immediately: 'What have you done with the class struggle, M. Althusser?' One way of signifying to him: 'You've gone over to the class enemy who conducts the class struggle in the forms of silence or denegation in the name of Eternity!' A quite natural response, really, for all those Althusser's interpellated individuals and agent-supports had dispossessed of the famous 'political subject' who, in the self-education of the 'attainment of consciousness', of the 'lessons of experience', etc., 'makes politics' and thereby escapes, surely, from interpellation by the ruling ideology as he struggles, if not for the revolution, at least for 'change'. . . . What is to be done, if men are only 'supports'?!

Some of us were weak enough to take this provocative question seriously, despite the malevolence of those who asked it, and I still have this weakness, for the risk of a *politically functionalist* interpretation of the Ideological State Apparatuses is indeed too great (the line of least resistance!) for us to neglect the question; and recent studies of ideology and the state (e.g., Santiago Carillo appealing to Gramsci and Althusser in order to preach the 'democratisation of the state apparatus') are not likely to prove me wrong.

So, for my part, I undertook to develop the notion of the ideological class struggle in *Language, Semantics and Ideology* on the basis of Althusser's article and starting from its final remarks characterising the Ideological State Apparatuses as the *seat* and *stake* in a class struggle: it seemed to me at once that it was more correct to characterise the ideological class struggle as a process of the *reproduction – transformation* of existing relations of production in such a way as to inscribe there the very mark of the class contradiction constituting that struggle (and I hold firmly to this point today).

In my enthusiasm, and in response to attacks against the 'apolitical eternalism' of the Ideological State Apparatuses, I went further and tried to discover how, in that circle of absurd evidentness constituted by interpellation, 'subjecthood was produced' which was capable historically – on certain conditions, essentially linked to the appearance of Marxist–Leninist theory – of turning against the causes determining it, because it could grasp them theoretically and practically: as a result, at the end of *Language, Semantics and Ideology*, whatever my intentions, I eventually outlined the ghost of a strange materialist subject achieving 'the subjective appropriation of proletarian politics'; and despite all the theoretical precautions I surrounded myself with (in particular the notion of 'disidentification', to which I shall return elsewhere), I finished up with a paradoxical subject of proletarian political practice whose tendential symmetry with the subject of bourgeois political practice went unquestioned!

For, faced with the full subject identified in the interpellation of the dominant bourgeois ideology, bearer of the evidentness that makes everyone say 'That's me!', I found support in a *radical exteriority of Marxist–Leninist theory* to reveal the point at which the absurd reappears beneath the evident, thus making possible a kind theoretical part there, designated the unrecognised presence of the adversary even *inside* the theoretical citadel supposedly organised to resist that adversary's assaults *from without*.

To intervene philosophically one has to take sides: I take sides *for* the fire of a critical work which is only too likely to destroy the 'Triple Alliance' itself, but in which there is at the same time the possibility that something new will be born – and *against* the incinerating fire that produces nothing but smoke.

In order to take sides in this way, it is essential to discern the points in the philosophical battlefield which urgently need to be abandoned and those it is more important than ever to occupy and defend, on condition that they are occupied and defended *differently*. This is a question of precision: the philosophical struggle, a class struggle in theory, is an endless process of co-ordinated rectifications sustained by the urgency of a position to be defended and reinforced in the face of what could be called adversity in thought. It is by going back up that 'line of least resistance' that philosophy makes its specific contact with the real.

I want here to present to English readers a fragmentary sketch of this attempt at adjustment by seizing on one precise point in it and restricting myself to it for now. In the conclusion to the 1975 text (cf. p. 191) there appears the following condensed formulation: 'The subject-form of discourse, in which interpellation, identification and the production of meaning coexist indissociably, realises the non-sense of the production of the subject as cause of himself in the form of immediate evidentness'. Let me emphasise that it is no accident that, in its very formulation, this thesis, which tries to encapsulate a fundamental point of the Althusserian project, sounds odd, recalling both English 'nonsense' humor and the German 'absurd' (to be found in the adventures of Baron Munchausen, for example) as well as, on the other hand, the self-ironising tautologies of the jokes French tradition calls '*lapalissades*' after Monsieur de La Palice: it is no accident because it is precisely at this limit point in Marxist reflection that, 'ideology interpellating individuals as subjects', we run into the impossible fact of a 'subject-form' in History as a 'process without subject or goal(s)'.

It was originally the fact that this materialist point is quite simply incomprehensible to pure 'rationalism' that drew my attention and literally caught my interest. Yet Marxists had long since specifically recognised and expressed this point in a thousand perfectly reasonable common-sensical and obvious ways, when they said, for example, that the material conditions of existence of men determine the forms of their consciousness without the two ever coinciding, that men make history but not the history they want to make or think they are making, etc. These formulations clearly expressed the fact that 'men' are determined in History so that they freely think and do what they cannot not do and think, but always expressed it in the eternal repetition of something *descriptively evident* which ultimately threatened to lock proletarian politics into the dilemma of quietism (the idea that within the revolutionary movement itself time and experience are working for the revolution) and the voluntarist leap (the idea that revolutionary theory has to be imported into the workers' movement to 'put it on the right track').

One could not but realise that at this point reasonable, clear, evident explanations (the 'attainment of consciousness', the 'lessons of experience', the 'penetration of ideas' and even the 'proof of practice') finally marked the site of a long theoretical *and* political blockage. A blockage entailing (among other consequences) the present glaciation of French left-wing politics.

But it was on this in many ways unbearable point in historical materialism that Althusser dared to touch (with the theory of the 'extra-economic' conditions of the reproduction of the relations of production) in order to give this famous singular point a chance to work in Marxism–Leninism: when he said that subjects 'work all by themselves' because they are subjects, i.e. individuals interpellated as subjects by ideology, he was allowing something new to be *heard* within the workers' movement, in both senses of the term.

He was *stating theoretically* vis-à-vis the subject of ideology something which, from outside the workers' movement, played with of *education by breaking with the imaginary identifications in which the subject is caught*, and hence an 'interpellation in reverse' at work in proletarian political practice: the theoreticist exteriority was thus necessarily accompanied by an inverted didacticism; which led to a typically Platonic bent consisting of posing in theoretical succession

(1) the ideological mechanism of interpellation–subjection
(2) the erasure ('forgetting') of any registrable trace of this mechanism in the full subject produced by it
(3) the theoretical remembering of the said mechanism and its erasure, in a kind of Marxist–Leninist-style anamnesis, the notion of 'subjective appropriation' being the practically effective result.

The reader will perhaps be surprised by this insistent self-criticism, to which I reply that an error can never be left to sleep in peace with impunity; what is jarring must be discerned, not so as to guarantee one's definitive location in the true (!) but so as to attempt to go as far as one can in the direction of accuracy.

What is jarring here, with respect to Marxism–Leninism, is, as we have seen, the idealist return of a primacy of theory over practice. But the didacticism which went with this return rebounds to designate another impediment on another scene: there is also something jarring in psychoanalysis, in the reference made to its concepts, and it condenses around the relation between *the ego* and *the subject*. In *Language, Semantics and Ideology*, it is just as if what is said there *about the subject* tended to be confused with the proposition that the *ego* is the 'subject-form' of legal ideology, to the point that functionalism, expelled politically from the door, had managed, despite all denegations, to slip back in through the psychoanalytic window, in the form of a kind of genesis of the ego, by dint of taking the illusions as to the unifying power of consciousness far too seriously.

To allow the installation of such a *Jacobinism of consciousness*, locked up in the evident character of its own control over its acts, speeches and thoughts and with nothing jarring within it (on the pretext of isolating the subjection effects of ideological interpellation), was to let the adversity off too lightly while remaining in a way its prisoner: to take the illusion of a full-ego-subject in which nothing jars far too seriously, there precisely is something jarring in *Language, Semantics and Ideology*!

Thus was evaded, with the utmost philosophical obstinacy, the fact that the nonsense of the unconscious, in which interpellation finds a point of attachment, is *never entirely* covered or obscured by the evidentness of the subject-centre-meaning which is produced by it, because the moments of production and product are not sequential as in the Platonic myth, but inscribed in the simultaneity of an oscillation, of a 'pulsation' by which the unconscious nonsense endlessly returns in the subject and in the meaning which is supposedly installed in it.

There is no cause save for something jarring (Lacan). It is at this precise point that Platonism radically misses the unconscious, i.e. the cause that determines the subject at the point at which it is grasped by the interpellation effect; what is missed is that cause insofar as it is constantly 'manifested' in a thousand forms (the slip, the päräpraxis) in the subject itself, for the unconscious traces of the Signifier are never 'erased' or 'forgotten' but work without intermission in the oscillation between sense and nonsense in the divided subject.[1]

It is just this that ultimately disconnects the psychoanalytic concept of repression (*verdrängung*) from the philosophical (Platonic) idea of forgetting or erasure. Hence it remains true that 'some sense' is produced in 'nonsense' by the origin-less slide of the signifier – whence the installation of the primacy of metaphor over meaning – but it is indispensable to add immediately that *this slide does not disappear without leaving traces* in the subject-ego of the ideological 'subject-form', identified with the evidentness of a meaning. To grasp ideological interpellation as *ritual* in all its implications presupposes recognition that there is no ritual without disruptions, lapses and flaws: 'one word for another', that is the definition of metaphor, but it is also the point at which a ritual fractures in the slip (and the least one can say is that there is no lack of examples, whether in the religious ceremony, legal proceedings, the educational lecture or the political speech).[2]

In this respect, does not the analytical series dream–slip–parapraxis – *Witz* intersect obliquely with something constantly infecting the dominant ideology, even from within the practices in which it tends to be realised? 'Whoever says class struggle of the ruling class says resistance, revolt and class struggle of the ruled class,' wrote Althusser at the end of his article on the Ideological State Apparatuses. . . . The slip and the parapraxis (disruptions in the ritual, impediments for the ideological Order) might well have something very precise to do with this always-already existent point, this unassignable origin of resistance and revolt: fleeting forms of appearance of something 'of a different order', minute victories that for a flash thwart the ruling ideology by taking advantage of its faltering.[3]

To retrace the outcome of the slip and the parapraxis in the disruptions in ideological interpellation does not imply that I am now making the unconscious the source of the dominated ideology, having failed to make it the super-egoic spring of the dominant ideology: the order of the unconscious does not coincide with that of ideology, repression in the psychoanalytic sense (*Verdrän gung*) can be identified neither with subjection nor with (political) repression, but ideology cannot be thought without reference to the unconscious register. Hence I am not suggesting that the slip or the parapraxis are as such the historical bases constituting dominated ideologies; the real precondition for the latter's disjunction from the dominant ideology lies in the class struggle as a motor historical contradiction (one divides into two) and not in One world unified by the Power of a Master.

On this question certain of Michel Foucault's analyses provide the possibility of a correction of the Althusserian distinction between ideological interpellation and repressive violence by their revelation of the process of individualisation – normalisation in which different forms of state violence subject the bodies and materially guarantee the submission of the ruled – *but only on the express condition that Foucault himself is corrected on one essential point* – concerning precisely his relation of foreclosure to both psychoanalysis and Marxism: by patiently dismantling the many mechanisms by which the training and regimentation of individuals is achieved, the material devices that guarantee their operation and the normalisation disciplines that codify their performance, Foucault, whether he will or not, has made an important contribution to the revolutionary struggles of our day, but at the same time he has concealed it, making the resistance points and bases of class revolt ungraspable. It is my hypothesis that this concealment lies in the impossibility from Foucault's strict point of view of making a coherent and consistent distinction between the processes of material subjection of human individuals and the procedures of animal domestication. This masked biologism, which without realising it he shares with various currents of technocratic functionalism, does indeed make revolt strictly unthinkable, because there can be no 'revolt of the beasts' any more than there can be any extraction of surplus labour or language in what is normally called the animal kingdom.

The reason revolt in human history is coeval with the extraction of surplus labour is that the class struggle is the motor of that history.

And the reason, on quite another plane, that revolt is coeval with language is that its very possibility rests on the existence of the division of the subject inscribed in the symbolic.

The specificity of these two 'discoveries' will not allow them to be fused in any theory whatsoever, even a theory of revolt. But a glance at the price paid for their foreclosure forces us to admit that they have something to do with each other politically.

There is perhaps a thread that it would be interesting to follow in the historical study of repressive and ideological practices in order to begin at last to understand the resistance-revolt-revolution process of the ideological and political class struggle, without making the dominated ideology the eternal repetition of the dominant ideology or the self-education of an experience progressively discovering the truth behind the curtain of illusions held up by the ruling class, or the theoreticist irruption of an external knowledge alone able to break the enchanted circle of the ruling ideology.

It seems to me today that *Language, Semantics and Ideology* touched on these questions, but in a strangely abortive manner, in a false-sounding recurrent symptom: I mean the systematic, compulsive (and, at the time, incomprehensible for me) pleasure I took in introducing the largest possible number of jokes – something which, to my knowledge, irritated more than one reader.

As I now realise, this was the only means I had to signify, by the steering of nonsense in the joke, what the moment of a discovery has basically in common with the faltering of a certainty: the joke is a determinant fulcrum, for, while structurally analogous with what goes amiss in the parapraxis, it represents at the same time the maximum form of negotiation with the 'line of least resistance', the instant of a victory of thought in its moment of birth, the purest figure of its emergence. This marks the fact that thought is basically unconscious ('it, the id, ça thinks'!), and theoretical thought to begin with (the 'materialism of our day' cannot, without serious risks, remain blind to this). To put it another way: the *Witz* represents one of the visible points at which theoretical thought encounters the unconscious; the *Witz* grasps something of this encounter, while presenting the appearance of mastering its effects.

Althusser's text on the Ideological State Apparatuses, whose analytical range of reference systematically avoided the series dream-slip – parapraxis, remained prudently noncommital here, while pointing towards the *Witz*.

The 'Munchausen effect' is in its turn aimed in this direction, but again prolongs the non-commitment by 'theoreticising' it. Hence, three years later, this little foot-path that I am trying to trace during our political winter, taking my bearings from two fixed landmarks:

There is no domination without resistance: the practical primacy of the class struggle, which means that one must 'dare to rebel'.

Nobody can think in anybody else's place: the practical primacy of the unconscious, which means that one must put up with what comes to be thought, i.e. one must 'dare to think for oneself'.

Notes

1. Cf. Paul Henry (1977, p. 144):
    The subject cannot be thought along the lines of the unity of an interiority as connected. He is divided as the dreamer is between his position as 'author' of his dream and that of witness to it. As Moustafa Safouan remarks (1974, p. 18), 'only by doing violence to one's intelligence can the dream, considered from a Freudian point of view, impose the distinction between the subject who *truly* speaks (the one that works in the dream)

and the one that could be called the "locutor" or the "word-mill", the one that relates this same dream to us when awake'. He is divided like someone who has made a slip: he didn't say it, it was his tongue that slipped, etc. . . . But dreams, slips of the tongue, blunders, neurosis or psychosis are necessary if this is to appear. Otherwise, I spontaneously think myself the source of my thoughts, my actions and my words.

2. In this perspective, cf. Gadet and Pêcheux (1981).

3. This *impossible degree* of perfect subjection, in the labour process imposed by the capitalist mode of production, is revealed in these lines from the autobiographical account of an intellectual militant who worked for a year as a manual worker in a Citroën factory. He is speaking of work on the assembly line.

'And suppose you said to yourself that nothing is important, just get used to doing the same thing, always in the same way, always at the same pace; hope for nothing more than the placid perfection of the machine? Death tempts you. But life flickers and resists. The organism resists. The muscles resist. The nerves resist. Something in the body and in the head braces up to fight against the repetition and the emptiness. Life: a faster movement, a burst of irregularity, a mistake, a "speed-up", a "slow-down" – all so many tactics on the job: anything by which, in this pathetic corner of resistance against that empty eternity the work point, there are still events, however minimal, there is still time, however monstrously drawn out. That awkwardness, that extra journey, that sudden acceleration, that mis-welding, that hand that has to have two goes, that grimace, that "I've had enough" – they are life itself grabbing on. Everything that in every assembly worker screams silently "I am not a machine!" (Linhart 1978, p. 14).

References

Althusser, Louis (1971) 'Freud and Lacan' [1964], in *Lenin and Philosophy and Other Essays*, trans. by Ben Brewster (London: New Left Books).

Gadet, Françoise and Pêcheux, Michel (1981) *La Langue introuvable*, Collection 'Théorie' (Paris: François Maspero).

Henry, Paul (1977) *Le Mauvais Outil: Langue, sujet et discours* (Paris: Editions Klincksieck).

Linhart, Robert (1978) L'Etabli (Paris: Editions de Minuit).

Safouan, Moustafa (1974) *Etude sur L'Oedipe*, Le Champ freudien (Paris: Editions du Seuil).

4

Jacqueline Rose, *The Case of Peter Pan or The Impossibility of Children's Fiction* (1984)

Jacqueline Rose's *The Case of Peter Pan* is an exemplary work of cultural and literary history. It takes J. M. Barrie's *Peter Pan*, one of the most obvious and evident of cultural products, and 'makes it strange' by taking us back through the multiple determinations that have informed its production. Rose demonstrates the impossibility of locating *Peter Pan*'s origins either in the 'author' J. M. Barrie or in any one of the numerous manifestations of the *Peter Pan* texts she discusses. Instead, her book sketches how *Peter Pan* finds its existence in relation both to commercial imperatives and educational standards. In both cases what determines the form of the text are certain conceptions of the child; it is in the question of the child and how the child is conceived by adults that Rose's analysis finds its unifying theme. The subtitle of the book, 'the impossibility of children's fiction', indicates her central argument here: that the child in 'children's fiction' is always an adult fantasy.

The Case of Peter Pan was first published in 1984 at at a time when children's literature was beginning to establish itself as a recognisable academic field. Rose raised a fundamental problem for that new area of study by questioning the existence of the 'child' for whom this literature was written. Reading Freud through Lacan, she stressed that for every adult childhood and childhood sexuality are unfinished business and that attempts to 'figure' the child are to be located in adult insecurities and anxieties. The book's striking originality lay in the way in which these theses were examined through the detailed textual and institutional history of *Peter Pan* as, precisely, a classic of childhood.

Introduction

Peter Pan offers us the child – for ever. It gives us the child, but it does not speak *to* the child. In fact so rarely has it spoken to the child throughout its history, that it led me to ask whether there might not be some relation between this all-too-perfect presence of the child and a set of problems, or evasions, in the very concept of children's fiction itself. Children's fiction rests on the idea that there is a child who is simply there to be addressed and that speaking to it might be simple. It is an idea whose innocent generality covers up a multitude of sins. This book will attempt to trace the fantasy which lies behind the concept of children's fiction, and will base its case on *Peter Pan*.

Peter Pan stands in our culture as a monument to the impossibility of its own claims – that it represents the child, speaks to and for children, addresses them as a group which is knowable and exists for the book, much as the book (so the claim runs) exists for them. Where or how such a claim originates in the first place will be one of the questions asked here, but the question will be focused on *Peter Pan* in so far as *Peter Pan* is the text for children which has made that claim most boldly, and which most clearly reveals it as a fraud. *Peter Pan* has never, in any easy way, been a book for children at all, but the question this throws back to us is whether there can be any such thing.

Children's fiction is impossible, not in the sense that it cannot be written (that would be nonsense), but in that it hangs on an impossibility, one which it rarely ventures to speak. This is the impossible relation between adult and child. Children's fiction is clearly about that relation, but it has the remarkable characteristic of being about something which it hardly ever talks of. Children's fiction sets up a world in which the adult comes first (author, maker, giver) and the child comes after (reader, product, receiver), but where neither of them enter the space in between. To say that the child is inside the book – children's books are after all as often as not *about* children – is to fall straight into a trap. It is to confuse the adult's intention to get at the child with the child it portrays. If children's fiction builds an image of the child inside the book, it does so in order to secure the child who is outside the book, the one who does not come so easily within its grasp.

There is, in one sense, no body of literature which rests so openly on an acknowledged difference, a rupture almost, between writer and addressee. Children's fiction sets up the child as an outsider to its own process, and then aims, unashamedly, to take the child *in*.

None of this appears explicitly inside the book itself, which works precisely to the extent that any question of who is talking to whom, and why, is totally erased. We do see something of it in the expanding industry of children's book criticism, but mostly in the form of a disavowal – the best book for children is a book for adult *and* child, or else in the form of a moralism (another version of the same thing) – the best book is the book which does the child most good, that is, the book which secures the reader to its intent and can be absolutely sure of its effects.

Let it be said from the start that it will be no part of this book's contention that what is for the good of the child could somehow be better defined, that we could, if we shifted the terms of the discussion, determine what it is that the child really wants. It will not be an issue here of what the child wants, but of what the adult desires – desires in the very act of construing the child as the object of its speech. Children's fiction draws in the child, it secures, places and frames the child. How often has it been said recently that what is best about writing for children is that the writer can count absolutely on the child's willingness to enter into the book, and *live* the story? (Townsend, 1971, p. 13).

This is to describe children's fiction, quite deliberately, as something of a soliciting, a chase, or even a seduction. *Peter Pan* is certainly all of these. Recently we have been made at least partly aware of this, as J. M. Barrie's story has been told and retold, as the story of a man and five small boys, whom he picked up, stole and possessed (Dunbar, 1970; Birkin, 1979). Barrie eventually adopted the Llewellyn Davies boys around whom he built the story of *Peter Pan*, staking a claim to them which he had already acted out symbolically by drawing them into his tale. But in the case of *Peter Pan*, knowledge of this has taken longer to surface than it did, say, in the case of *Alice*, whose underworld journey was long ago traced to, its author's fantasied seduction of a little girl. Charles Lutwidge Dodgson (*alias* Lewis Carroll) wrote his classic for children on condition that the child remain a little girl, held to him by the act of telling the tale. A sexual act which we can easily recognise now, despite (or because of) the innocence and youth of its object. But then, it is argued, Dodgson was a 'schizophrenic', both a mathematician and a writer for children (as if mathematics and verbal play were somehow incompatible), and the worst thing he did was take pictures of little girls (as if the visual image were not the ultimate fetish). *Alice* has been saved as a classic for children, and the question of what we mean by that '*for*' – the question of its more difficult implications – remains unasked.

In the case of *Peter Pan*, the problem is more delicate. Behind *Peter Pan* lies the desire of a man for a little boy (or boys), a fantasy or drama which has only recently caught the public eye. Thus just at the moment when we are accepting the presence of sexuality in children's fiction (which we believed – wrongly – that the Victorians had repressed (Marcus, 1966)), we are asked to recognise it in a form which violates not only the innocence of childhood, not just that of children's fiction, but what we like to think of as normal sexuality itself. There is nothing too disturbing about a man desiring little girls – it is, after all, the desire in which little girls are in the end expected to recognise themselves. And the fact has in any case been relegated to a contingent status as far as *Alice*'s position as a classic for children is concerned. But 'men and little boys' is something else, something in which our very idea of what constitutes normal sexuality is at stake. Children's fiction cannot, I will be arguing, be discussed without touching on this question, but it almost invariably is.

Suppose, therefore, that Peter Pan is a little boy who does not grow up, not because he doesn't want to, but because someone else prefers that he shouldn't. Suppose, therefore, that what is at stake in *Peter Pan* is the adult's desire for the child. I am not using 'desire' here in the sense of an act which is sought after or which must actually take place. It is not relevant, therefore, to insist that nothing ever happened, or that Barrie was innocent of any interest in sex (a point which is often made). I am using desire to refer to a form of investment by the adult in the child, and to the demand made by the adult on the child as the effect of that investment, a demand which fixes the child and then holds it in place. A turning to the child, or a circulating around the child – what is at stake here is not so much something which could be enacted as something which cannot be spoken.

The sexual act which underpins *Peter Pan* is neither act nor fantasy in the sense in which these are normally understood and wrongly opposed to each other. It is an act in which the child is used (and abused) to represent the whole problem of what sexuality is, or can be, and to hold that problem at bay. This is something which, we will see, surfaces constantly throughout the history of *Peter Pan* – it is part of the fabric of the work. But the fact is either not known, or else it is displaced (as with Carroll) onto Barrie himself, and then disavowed (Barrie as the innocent of all innocents).

To call *Peter Pan* a fantasy does not, therefore, absolve us of the sexual question. It focuses it more sharply. At the moment when Barrie was writing *Peter Pan*, Freud was making his most crucial (and in this context least known) discovery that sexuality works above all at the level of fantasy, and that what we take to be our sexual identity is always precarious and can never be assumed. Sexuality persists, for all of us, at the level of the unconscious precisely because it is a question which is never quite settled, a story which can never be brought to a close. Freud is known to have undermined the concept of childhood innocence, but his real challenge is easily lost if we see in the child merely a miniature version of what our sexuality eventually comes to be. The child is sexual, but its sexuality (bisexual, polymorphous, perverse) threatens our own at its very roots. Setting up the child as innocent is not, therefore, repressing its sexuality – it is above all holding off any possible challenge to our own.

The problem is not, therefore, J. M. Barrie's – it is ours. Ours to the extent that we are undoubtedly implicated in the status which *Peter Pan* has acquired as the ultimate fetish of childhood. All Barrie ever did was to write *Peter Pan*, and even that can be disputed, as we will see. But it is we who have recognised *Peter Pan* ('recognised' in both senses of the term), and given it its status. *Peter Pan* has been almost unreservedly acclaimed as a children's classic for the greater part of this century. Its presence in our culture is in fact so diffused that most of the time we do not even notice it. We take it for granted as something which belongs to us and to children, without there being any need for us to ask the question of the relation between the two. Like all children's classics, *Peter Pan is* considered to speak for everyone – adult and child (which in itself neatly disposes of the whole issue of what we mean by fiction for children). The child and the adult are one at that point of pure identity which the best of children's books somehow manage to retrieve. Time and again in its history, *Peter Pan* has been set up as the very emblem of that purity and identity. But this, I would say, has only been possible (and desirable) because it reveals so crudely the travesty on which any such notion rests.

It is, therefore, no part of my intention to analyse Barrie, to try to produce a psychobiography which would diagnose the author so as to set *Peter Pan* free as a myth. *Peter Pan* is a myth, but its status as such rests on the very difficulty which most commentaries refuse to recognise, or else recognise in order to diagnose and remove. *Peter Pan* is a classic in which the problem of the relationship between adult and child is unmistakably at the heart of the matter.

Peter Pan was not originally intended for children. It first appeared inside a novel for adults, J. M. Barrie's *The Little White Bird* (Barrie, 1902), as a story told by the narrator to a little boy whom the narrator was trying to steal. In order for it to become a work for children, it was extracted from its source, transformed into a play, and sent out on its own. *Peter Pan* emerges, therefore, out of an unmistakable act of censorship. The book which it leaves behind is one of the most explicit accounts to date of what it might mean to write fiction for the child. *The Little White Bird* is the story of the difficulty of that process – the difficulty of the relation between adult and child, and a question about the sexuality of each. What is the sexuality of the narrator? What is the origin of the child? What is *going on* between them? Questions which are never quite answered in the book, but which provide the basis for the telling of *Peter Pan*. The rest of *Peter Pan's* history can then be read as one long attempt to wipe out the residual signs of the disturbance out of which it was produced. *The Little White Bird* is an origin of sorts, but only in the sense that no origin is ever left behind, since it neces- sarily *persists*. *The Little White Bird* shows what cannot, or must not, be allowed to get into fiction for children, but the problems to which it so eloquently bears witness do not go away. They remain in such a way as to undermine, finally, any simple notion of children's fiction itself.

Thus the result of that first act of censorship was that *Peter Pan* was both never written and, paradoxically, has never ceased to be written. Barrie himself certainly couldn't manage it. He did not write the play until twenty-four years after its first production. The publication had nothing to do with children, since it was the only children's text in a volume of collected plays (this was the main publication although in the same year it was printed on its own). The story from *The Little White Bird* was eventually published separately, but it cannot be described as a book for children. It was released onto the fine art collec- tor's market, at a time when a whole new market for children's books was developing, a market which it completely by-passed and to which it never belonged. Barrie persistently refused to write a narrative version of the play, and, when he did, it was a failure, almost incom- prehensible, and later had to be completely rewritten along the lines of a new state educational policy on language in the early part of the century (Barrie, 1915). During this time. Barrie authorised *Peter Pan* to a number of different writers, which means that its status as a classic for children depends at least as much on them as it does on Barrie himself. Barrie may well be the source of the play, but this constant dispersion of *Peter Pan* challenges any straightforward idea of origin or source. Above all it should caution us against the idea that things can simply be traced back to their beginning, since, in the case of *Peter Pan*, what followed is at least as important as what came before.

What has followed has been a total mystification of all these forms of difficulty and confusion. Barrie *is Peter Pan*, despite the fact that he could not write it. *Peter Pan* is a classic for children, despite the fact that they could not read it – either because it was too expensive, or because it was virtually impossible to read. Nowhere has it been recog- nised that there might be a problem of writing, of address, and of lan- guage, in the history of *Peter Pan*. *Peter Pan's* dispersion – the fact that it is everywhere and nowhere at one and the same time – has been taken as the sign of its cultural value. Its own ethereal nature merely sanctions the eternal youth and innocence of the child it portrays, and for which it is most renowned.

The sexual disavowal is, therefore, a political disavowal. A disavowal of the material differences which are concealed behind the category of *all* children to which Peter Pan is meant to make its appeal. That *all* speaks volumes of a further set of evasions: not just why are we speaking to the child, and what is our investment in that process; but to which child are we speaking? For, as *Peter Pan* very clearly demonstrates, if we are talking to one group of children, then the chances are that we will not be speaking to another. More likely, the very idea of speaking to *all* children serves to close off a set of cultural divisions, divisions in which not only children, but we ourselves, are necessarily caught.

There is no children's book market which does not, on closer scrutiny, crumble under just such a set of divisions – of class, culture and literacy – divisions which undermine any generalised concept of the child. And there is no language for children which can be described independently of divisions in the institution of schooling, the institution out of which modern childhood has more or less been produced (Ariès, 1960). How language is spoken – both by and to the child – is subject to strictures which need to be located inside the institution where language is systematically taught. The clash between *Peter Pan*'s status as a cultural myth and as a children's book is nowhere clearer than at the point of its confrontation with educational policy of the state.

When *Peter Pan* was written, educational policy on language was directed towards a rigorous separation of the forms of language to be taught in different sectors of the state schools. A whole new concept of 'synthetic' language was developed in the public elementary schools. It was a language to be based on the impressions of the visible world, as opposed to the classical and literary language which was simultaneously being taught in the secondary schools. This is a division which still affects the way in which we use language today, but it is rarely discussed in relation to children's writing. Recently there has been attention paid to class difference in children's books, but this has been posed exclusively in terms of values, to be identified and then avoided in subsequent children's books. *Peter Pan* is no exception to this, and it can certainly be assessed in this way. But when *Peter Pan* is rewritten in order for it to be accepted into the state schools, class difference can be seen to operate at a more fundamental level – that of the base components of the language which the child is actually allowed to speak.

This is an issue which relates to our understanding of literature as a whole – the fact that language has an institutional history which determines how it is written, spoken and understood. But it is a history which most literary criticism, in its concern to identify creativity and individual expression, makes every effort to ignore. In the case of children's fiction, however, the problem comes much closer, since the child belongs to the very institution through which language is being produced. The failure to discuss the importance of educational policy on language for children's writing is, therefore, the more conspicuous evasion.

The material and sexual aspects of *Peter Pan* have been the vanishing-points of its history. They are there, however, and they can be exposed. But what we have been given instead is a glorification of the child. This suggests not only a refusal to acknowledge difficulties and contradictions in relation to childhood; it implies that we *use* the image of the child to deny those same difficulties in relation to ourselves.

Peter Pan comes at the end of a long history, one which can be traced back to the beginnings of children's fiction. Literature for children first became an independent commercial venture in England in the mid- to late-eighteenth century, at a time when conceptualisation of childhood was dominated by the philosophical writings of Locke and Rousseau. This is a fact which is known, but its implications for thinking about children's fiction have not been fully recognised. It is assumed that children's fiction has grown away from this moment, whereas in fact children's fiction has constantly returned to this moment, repeated it, and reproduced its fundamental conception of the child. Children's fiction has never completely severed its links with a philosophy which sets up the child as a pure point of origin in relation to language, sexuality and the state.

The earliest children's writers took from Locke the idea of an education based on the child's direct and unproblematic access to objects of the real world, an education which would by-pass the imperfections of language. They took from Rousseau the idea that it is sexuality which most totally sabotages the child's correct use of language and its exact knowledge of the world. One of the earliest extended narratives for children, Thomas Day's *The History of Sandford and Merton* (1783–9), was based directly on Rousseau's *Emile* (1762). It shared with Rousseau's tract a conviction that both sexuality and social inequality were realities that the child somehow be used to circumvent. The child is rendered innocent of all the contradictions which flaw our interaction with the world. Above all, for both Locke and Rousseau, the child can be seen, observed and known in exactly the same way as the world can be grasped by a rational understanding.

Children's fiction emerges, therefore, out of a conception of both the child and the world as knowable in a direct and unmediated way, a conception which places the innocence of the child and a primary state of language and/or culture in a close and mutually dependent relation. It is a conception which has affected children's writing and the way that we think about it to this day. We can see it, in differing forms, in such apparently diverse types of writing as the fairy tale and the adventure story for boys. Andrew Lang published his fairy tales in the nineteenth century as the uncontaminated record of our cultural infancy (Lang, 1899) to which, it was assumed, the child had a direct and privileged access (an idea whose purely mythical nature was pointed out by Tolkien long ago (Tolkien 1947)). And the boy's adventure story, which came into its own in the mid to late nineteenth century with writers such as Marryat, Kingston, Henty and Stevenson, was always part of an exploratory and colonialist venture which assumed that discovering or seeing the world was the same thing as controlling it. Both types of writing are present in *Peter Pan* which condenses a whole history of children's fiction into its form. They can also be seen in the works of Alan Garner who is considered by many to be one of the most innovatory writers today. But what I want to stress in both cases is the idea which they share of a primitive or lost state to which the child has special access. The child is, if you like, something of a pioneer who restores these worlds to us, and gives them back to us with a facility or directness which ensures that our own relationship to them is, finally, safe.

I am not, of course, talking here of the child's own experience of the book which, despite all the attempts which have been made, I consider more or less impossible to gauge. What I am describing is how these different forms of writing, in their long and continuing association with childhood, have been thought about *for* children. Again, Freud's concept of the unconscious can be seen as a challenge to this association, for it not only undermines our idea of sexuality; it equally questions the idea of mastery which lies behind the notion that the world is something to which we simply have access, or that language is something which we can control. And yet for all the apparent shifts in the way that childhood and children's writing is discussed, what always seems to return in the analysis, in one form or another, is this idea of mastery, which means by implication securing the child's rationality, its control of sexuality or of language (or both).

Thus, for example, even when a troubling of sexuality is recognised in the fairy tale (Bettelheim, 1976), it is something contained by the cohesion of the narrative, transcended on the path to reality, and resolved in the name of a psychological and sexual identity, which ensures in the end that we can master not only the world, but also ourselves. And although addressed to a very different context of children's writing, a similar demand can be seen in the recent appeal to the coherence of realist writing in children's fiction, against the disintegration of the adult novel form, which can lead such a well-known children's writer as John Rowe Townsend to say without inhibition 'I came to the child because I see in him the last refuge from a literature gone berserk and ready for suicide' (quoting Isaac Bashevis Singer, Townsend, 1971, p. 12).

Peter Pan was written at the time of Freud, and the status which it has been given seems to testify above all to our inability to recognise the dislocation which he operated on our conception of childhood. Not just in the sense of what childhood is supposed to be, but, more crucially, as a challenge to why, in terms of our own relationship to language and sexuality, we attempt to construct an image of the child at all.

What we constantly see in discussion of children's fiction is how the child can be used to hold off a panic, a threat to our assumption that language is something which can simply be organised and cohered, and that sexuality, while it cannot be removed, will eventually take on the forms in which we prefer to recognise and acknowledge each other. Childhood also serves as a term of universal social reference which conceals all the historical divisions and difficulties of which children, no less than ourselves, form a part.

There is no child behind the category 'children's fiction', other than the one which the category itself sets in place, the one which it needs to believe is there for its own purposes. These purposes are often perverse and mostly dishonest, not wilfully, but of necessity, given that addressing the child must touch on all of these difficulties, none of which it dares speak. *Peter Pan* is sometimes scoffed at today for the excessive and cloying nature of its innocence. It is in fact one of the most fragmented and troubled works in the history of children's fiction to date. *Peter Pan* is peculiar, and yet not peculiar, in so far as it recapitulates a whole history of children's fiction which has not yet come to an end. My objective in exposing the difficulties of its history will be to make some contribution to the dismantling of what I see as the ongoing sexual and political mystification of the child.

References

Ariès, P., *L'Enfant et la vie familiale sous l'ancien régime* (Paris: Plon, 1960).
Barrie *The Little White Bird* (London: Hodder and Stroughton, 1902).
Barrie *Peter Pan and Wendy* (London: Hodder and Stroughton, 1915).
Bettelheim, B, *The Uses of Enchantment: The Meaning and Importance of Fairy Tales* (London: Thames and Hudson, 1976).
Birkin, A., J. M. *Barrie and the Lost Boys* (London: Constable, 1979).
Dunbar, Janet, *J. M. Barrie, the Man behind the Image* (London: Collins, 1970).
Lang, A., *The Blue Fairy Book*, (London: Longmans and Green, 1899).
Marcus, S. *The Other Victorians: A Study of Sexuality and Pornography in Mid-Nineteenth Century England* (London: Weidenfeld and Nicolson, 1966).
Tolkien, J. R. R., 'On Fairy Stories'(1938), *Essays Presented to Charles Williams* (London: OUP, 1948).
Townsend, J. R., *A Sense of Story: Essays on Contemporary Writers for Children* (London: Longman, 1971).

5

David Trotter, *The Making of the Reader; Language and Subjectivity in Modern American, English, and Irish Poetry* (1984)

If we assume the demise of the fabled Leavisite 'common reader', for which differently imagined readerships have poets been working? On what terms and how, drawing on what rhetorical and thematic resources, have Wordsworth and Arnold, Hardy and Yeats, Eliot and Pound, Auden and MacNeice sought to identify readers in and for their poems? Moving from the French Revolution to the period of the Second World War and on to 1980s Britain, *The Making of the Reader* offers a far-reaching analysis of the resources deployed and the devices at work in American, English, and Irish poetry, giving weight to the importance for those ambitions and resources of the various poets' historical and political locations. The question of readership is then examined in the new themes and rhetorics that characterise the poetry of John Ashbery, Frank O'Hara, Ed Dorn, Philip Larkin, Seamus Heaney, Ted Hughes, and J. H. Prynne, with Trotter's analysis underlining the significance and effects of the pathos and anti-pathos which marks their shifting poetic stances: each of these poets has doted on the pathos of subjectivity and each has turned away from this to a recalcitrance of theme and idiom, a negotiation of readership in remove from any certainty of voice and feeling and origin even as this anti-pathos itself is – in Hughes and Larkin especially – caught up in *its* pathos and the reader involved in that shifting subject-relation. The book's conclusion, reproduced here, considers the institutional production of a readership today; with its particular focus the teaching of poetry in schools, where an attention to the rhetorics of form has long given way to the reading of poems as documents of the putative 'personalities' of their authors. The isolation of metaphor as the one admired and readily identified device in poetry provides a central instance of the fixing of a particular 'convention of reading'. Alongside which, as against which, the poems of Davie, Larkin and Prynne, in their struggles around subjectivity, offer examples of the invoking of conventions that establish their own conditions for reading and readerships.

Conclusion

Books like this one often cap a morbid account of the defects of the 'contemporary situation' by presenting with magicianly pride the young poet whose work will put things right, or the older poet whose work (if properly understood) might yet help to put things right. This arrangement has not always been to the advantage of the poets concerned. Some have barely had time to mumble their thanks before disappearing without trace. For example, Leavis's *New Bearings in English Poetry* proclaimed Ronald Bottrall, whose plummet into relative obscurity was immediate and lasting. 'Mr Bottrall's work,' Leavis had written, 'clinches felicitously the argument of this book, and sanctions high hopes for the future' (1971, p. 211). The mistake so often made, and made with such majesty here, is to suppose that a poem is improved by the way it clinches the critic's argument. In any case, it seems unlikely that readers are much moved by the exercise: either they know more about the poet in question than the critic does, or they assume that the fondness of the one for the other is a sure sign of the imminent demise of both.

I want to take a different course myself, although not just in order to avoid polemic and controversy. (Diffidence always seems a lost cause; if you try to make a book unobjectionable, that is what people will object to.) The 'felicitous' end to my own argument will not involve specific poets so much as the conditions under which poetry is read today. I shall concentrate on England, partly because it is the country I know best, and partly because the situation in America seems more fluid. You do not have to like John Ashbery's poems to be glad that an uncompromising and idiosyncratic writer should have found a readership. In England, by contrast, the conditions under which poetry is read threaten to become so specialised and so rigid that certain kinds of writing will not reach even the relatively small number of people who might take an interest in them.

I have described in Chapters 9 to 11 the rhetorical orientation of various contemporary poems, the play between a declarative voice and its opposites; and I have argued that these poems either abandon the selective and identifying strategies found in poems from the first half of the century, or arrange them by means of a different imperative. The only explanation I have been able to advance is that the growth of institutional audiences of one kind or another has shifted the responsibility for making readers *away from* the rhetorical and thematic layout of the poems themselves. Thus my remarks about the language of recent poetry have tended towards practical criticism; they have been remarks about the coherence of a poem, about significant form, rather than about the way it invokes its secret complement. And they could not perhaps have done otherwise, since practical criticism is now one of the most important of the conventions we use to make sense of poems; a convention devised with the disappearance of the Common Reader in mind, elaborated in schools and academies, and absorbed by the poets who pass through those schools and academies. To put it crudely, if you are aware that a sizeable part of your potential audience will scan your poem in search of significant form and in search of the subjectivity which authorised the significance of that form, then you may not bother with the selective and identifying strategies of a Yeats or an Eliot or an Auden; you may simply ensure that the poem can be practically criticised and that a certain subjectivity can be seen to articulate it.

The shift in the balance of power between poem and reader has important consequences. 'The next event,' Jane Tompkins reports:

> in the drama of the reader's emergence into critical prominence is that instead of being seen as instrumental to the understanding of the text, the reader's activity is declared to be *identical with* the text and therefore becomes itself the source of all literary value. If literature *is* what happens when we read, its value depends on the value of the reading process (1980, p. xvi).

Once the reader's activity has been recognised in theory as 'the source of all literary value', then literary value becomes the product of the specific ways in which that activity is controlled by the institutions which now make readers. Of course, there has been much debate about whether the reader of a text produces or consumes its meaning. What concerns me here is the power acquired by institutions which openly admit that their business is to produce meaning, and thus literary value. If it is a matter of power, then it is a matter of dispute, and we surely need to examine the rules under which the game is played. We must ask how and why it is that some kinds of writing have found a readership, while others have not. The answer will of course have a lot to do with the energy and fortitude of the individuals concerned. But it may also have something to do with circumstances under which they operate. I suspect that it now takes an institution rather than a way with words to create 'high hopes for the future'.

* * *

Despite the power of the institutions, Common Readers – readers identified by assimilation into a 'homogeneous culture' rather than by their response to a segregating rhetoric, or by membership of an academy – have not altogether disappeared. However heterogeneous the culture in question, however segregated it may always have been and may still be, it does make readers. Unfortunately, it has proved more and more difficult to attract the attention of those readers, and the very few poets who do manage to attract it (notably John Betjeman and Philip Larkin) have sometimes been put to strange antics; at least, they have been put to the cultivation of 'personality'.

When Seamus Heaney, in his essay on the language of contemporary English poetry, comes to discuss Larkin, his argument alters for the first time from a preoccupation with tonal and mythic resource to a preoccupation with personality:

> He too returns to origins and brings something back, although he does not return to 'roots'. He puts inverted commas round his 'roots', in fact. His childhood, he says, was a forgotten boredom. He sees England from train windows, fleeting past and away. He is urban modern man, the insular Englishman, responding to the tones of his own clan, ill at ease when out of his environment (19??, p. 167).

Unlike Hughes and Hill, Larkin personifies something. 'He *is* urban modern man, *the* insular Englishman . . .' At that an image familiar to every reader of his poems floats into view: an alert and fastidious observer whose anorexic wit has for so long needled the national decline, a will-have-been among has-beens. This image is the convention according to which each new poem will be read. 'From *The Less Deceived* on,' writes Anthony Thwaite, 'the personality is an achieved and consistent one, each poem restating or adding another facet to what has gone before (1978, p. 105)'.

But the personality has also gained a certain currency outside the poems. It is customary for newspapers to pay some attention to poets who have just published a book or won a prize, but Larkin has on occasion been interviewed because he is Larkin (that is, 'urban modern man'). Each occasion restates or adds another facet to what has gone before. Thus an interview with Miriam Gross in the *Observer* of 16 December 1979 warms over all the old tales about uneventful childhood, lack of interest in any literature except novels or biography, xenophobia, and so on. Did Larkin ever dance, as well as listen, to jazz?

'Dance,' he replies incredulously, 'you mean dance?' Would he like to visit, say, China? Hmm, yes, 'if I could come back the same day.' Politics? 'Oh, I adore Mrs. Thatcher . . . Recognising that if you haven't got the money for something you can't have it – this is a concept that's vanished for many years.' Why does he live in Hull? 'I love all the Americans getting on to the train at King's Cross and thinking they're going to come and bother me, and then looking at the connections and deciding they'll go to Newcastle and bother Basil Bunting instead.' A photograph shows him on his haunches in a nest of bicycles, and the piece is entitled 'A Voice for Our Time'. It is that voice, defined here in relation to social and political issues, which we look for behind the poems.

Of course, Larkin is not to be seen climbing through the potted plants which adorn the quarter-deck of a TV chat-show. To suggest that he has cultivated a personality is simply to say that he is one of the few English poets whose readers are made in the way we imagine an eighteenth-century poet's readers to have been made: socially, rather than rhetorically or institutionally. He has certainly claimed as much: 'What I don't like about subsidies and official support is that they destroy the essential nexus between the writer and the reader. If the writer is being paid to read, the element of compulsive contact vanishes (1979, p. 35)'. In Larkin's eyes that element of compulsive (or socially produced) contact is the only right reason for reading. He has therefore disavowed, although he may well benefit from, the institutional readerships upon which other poets depend. A report in *the Sunday Times* of 11 January 1981 suggests that some students choose Hull University because Larkin is Librarian there; they will, we learn, be sorely disappointed, because the Librarian refuses to discuss poetry with undergraduates. For the same reason, he has also spurned the trappings of literary status. 'Nowadays,' he told Miriam Gross, 'you *can* live by being a poet. A lot of people do it: it means a blend of giving readings and lecturing and spending a year at a university as poet in residence or something. But I couldn't bear that: it would embarrass me very much. I don't want to go around pretending to be me'. Larkin's strategy is honest and successful, but it also looks like hard work. To get people to read his poems for the right reasons, he has to do an awful lot of pretending not to be pretending to be a poet. If all those Americans had found their way to Hull, the game would really be up.

However, very few English poets can hope to be enlisted, as a voice for our time. Larkin's poems have evidently made compulsive contact with a large number of readers, but few of those readers seem compelled to read poems by anyone else. It is as though the Common Reader cannot cope with more than (say) three poets at once. The major publishing houses have either provoked, or more likely adjusted to, this tendency (a tendency whose implications are studied in an excellent essay by Blake Morrison, 'Poetry and the Poetry Business'). Some firms publish no poetry at all, some publish nothing but anthologies, while others rely almost exclusively on a single established poet. Only three – Faber, OUP and Secker and Warburg – have what might be described as a poetry list. 'For the rest,' Morrison concludes, 'poetry is left almost entirely to the small presses like Carcanet, Anvil, Bloodaxe, and Peterloo, all of which depend on Arts Council support for their survival; or indeed to smaller presses than these, private operations run by enthusiastic individuals in back-rooms and garden sheds (1981, pp. 100, 102)'. Nowadays it takes more than a handful of definite articles to identify a readership. You need a Certificate of Registration (as required by the Registration of Business News Act. 1916) for your own press, a garden shed to nail it to ('This certificate is required by the Act to be exhibited in a conspicuous position at the principal place of business'), and the temerity to impose your variously-shaped products on booksellers whose shelves were built to hold Penguins and Picadors. Then you can get started.

There are perhaps other, easier ways. But since small presses now produce more books of poems every year than the major publishing houses, they cannot be left out of any account of the audience for contemporary writing. Rather, we cannot leave out those presses which have persuaded people to read the books they produce. For that reason, I shall concentrate here on Carcanet, an intelligently conceived and relatively well-funded operation which sponsors a particular group of poets and critics and is directed at a particular audience. Whatever one thinks of those poets and critics, it is hard to avoid the conclusion that Carcanet has done what has to be done better than anyone else: namely, made and distributed the books it wishes people to read, while at the same time creating an audience which will read those books for the 'right reasons'. 'Carcanet,' Morrison observes, 'set up twelve years ago as a small press, now publishes eighteen to twenty poetry titles a year; it still relies on the Arts Council for about twenty per cent of its income, but is now sufficiently stable to be planning further significant additions – including a fiction list – to its rapidly expanding programme.' The reasons for its success bear thinking about.

One reason is that Carcanet does not simply publish books. It also tries, more strenuously than any other small or smallish press, to define and promote the conventions according to which those books should be read. The process can be glimpsed in the introduction to a recent Carcanet book, *British Poetry since 1970: A Critical Survey*, where someone called the 'serious reader' puts in a first ever appearance on the literary scene. The editors, Peter Jones and Michael Schmidt, begin with a remark about the seventies: 'The overdue recognition of Geoffrey Hill's uncompromising work, the rediscovery of Edgell Rickword, indicate a change in the quality of seriousness of some readers and writers (1980, pp. ix, xi)'. Whatever this 'quality of seriousness' might represent in the abstract, it would seem in the here and now to be not altogether unconnected with the activities of Carcanet Press, which publishes Sisson and Rickword and allows both space in its associated journal, *PN Review*. The press and the journal have together created a 'seriousness', a set of conventions, which enables certain readers to appreciate certain writers. Their 'serious reader' is thus as much of a construct as the various Super-readers and Implied Readers who throng the corridors of the academy.

This construct has recognisable features which do not belong to any reader of any book of poems, and which can be seen in what Jones and Schmidt have to say about the success enjoyed by poets from Northern Ireland: 'The inflation of the "Ulster school" has occurred for quite understandable extrapoetic reasons; but for the serious reader, there is no reason to re-draw the map of English *poetry* around the six counties,' One doubts whether 'extrapoetic reasons' could ever be separated satisfactorily from poetic reasons; and whether, if they could, the result would not be widespread torpor. Still, the serious reader must be assumed to engage continually in such activities. Introducing a Carcanet anthology, *Ten English Poets*, Michael Schmidt took it upon himself to proscribe 'unspeakable epic poets, tearful lyricists, rhetoricians of a political kidney, adolescent angst peddlers, geriatric lovers, spineless satirists, sinless confessional writers, pasticheurs of modernism' (1976, p. 9). All these are tainted by indulgence in extrapoetic reasons. For the serious reader, on the other hand, poetry is an encounter with form, where convention disposes what man proposes. An editorial in the first number of *Poetry Nation* (which later became *PN Review*) announced that the journal would support 'a renewed popularity and practice of clearly formal writing, a common bridling at vacuous public and private rhetoric' (1973, pp. 3, 50). In a supporting essay on 'The Politics of Form', Schmidt attacked poets who seek 'to cajole or bemuse the readers'.

When *Poetry Nation* became *PN Review* in 1976, he returned to the theme from a slightly different angle:

> Among modern English writers we have sensed, and gone some way in our early issues towards defining, a failure of seriousness, a flippancy before formal and social choices, and an unwillingness to examine the human implications of certain ideas expressed as it were casually in particular works of imaginative writing, or in underlying attitudes (1973, p. 1).

Social choices now took their place beside formal choices, a change of emphasis announced by the addition of the term 'Review' to the journal's title. Seriousness had now to be defined in broader terms. Commenting in an editorial on the refusal of booksellers to stock *PN Review*, Donald Davie wrote: 'It's the level of seriousness that is the inexcusable thing, not at all the topics that we choose to be serious about' (1977, p. 1). To Davie this meant the absence of an 'educated electorate' which might purchase such a journal, an audience distinguished from the accidental and temporary among citizens by its response to serious debate about political and literary issues. *PN Review*, he concluded, 'like any other responsible journal at the present time, must have as a main objective the bringing into being of an electorate that shall once again be educated'. As C. H. Sisson, also a joint editor, put it in the next issue: 'Our problem is therefore with an audience which is not there or – less ambitiously – with one which is just beginning to appear, here and there, in a scattered way . . .' (1977, p. 1). Setting out quite consciously to make a readership, the editors of *PN Review* had decided that the level of seriousness demanded by a certain kind of poetry was the same as that demanded by a certain kind of politics.

This decision took shape against the horrors of the sixties, when demonstrators who were also unspeakable epic poets ran riot. 'The critic's task,' Schmidt said:

> is to help direct contemporary literature and the modern reader back into the main-stream, reclaiming for both a little of their lost authority. This it may be able to do if there are creative writers worth serious attention, who have refused, with the contraction of the responsive audience and the retreat of the critics, to chasten the scope of their art (1976, p. 3).

Only those who have authority can set and maintain an appropriate level of seriousness, and authority was something which the demonstrators and/or unspeakable epic poets had all but destroyed. Donald Davie, then Pro-Vice-Chancellor of Essex University, argued in his 1968 articles for the *Listener* that student unrest and the moral cowardice it met with among academics were symptomatic of a widespread fear of authority. He claimed that good writing depends on 'the drive towards authority, the authoritative note and tone,' (1968, p. 365) and that Britain in the sixties had abandoned this note and tone:

> The pastor in his manse didn't wield much power, but he was magnificently an image of authority. And it's just those images that Britain today won't tolerate. . . . What's new with us is that authority is as unpopular with those who deal it out as with those who take it. It's people like me who, because they can't stand being hated, refuse the authority that makes them hateful: 50-year olds determined to be young for ever.

As long as such people remained silent there would be no seriousness, no way of sorting out the accidental and temporary among citizens or among readers of poetry.

At this point, Davie retired to California. But his preoccupation with the authority-shy persisted, developing into (among other things) a critique of Larkin's *Oxford Book of Twentieth-Century English Verse*, which he reviewed for the *Listener* in 1973. In Davie's eyes, Larkin had not provided the rigorous and decisive view of modern English verse which we would expect from 'an anthology backed by the authority of a famous publishing house, and by his own authority as the best-loved poet of his generation' (1973, pp. 420–1). Larkin's choice of poems had been swayed by histrionic considerations; it showed him to be 'a man who thinks that poetry is a private indulgence or a professional entertainer's patter or, at most, a symptom for social historians to brood over'. This pastor has not exactly abandoned his manse, but he has thrown a wild party and invited every rock star and debutante he could think of: teenagers pet heavily in the upstairs rooms, while bearded social workers stand around scrunching plastic cups. The pastor does not exactly enjoy it, but he thinks they might love him for his Led Zeppelin records.

Davie was equally forthright about his own failures. In 1973 he criticised 'Creon's Mouse', a poem he had written twenty years earlier, for advocating loss of nerve:

> What I didn't envisage then, which there is no excuse for not envisaging now, is that there would be people who would think it too

daring of Creon to be a king at all, however self-limited and vowed to consultation and compromise. It is possible, I now have to realise, to think that it is audacious presumption for a man to get into any position of authority over his fellows, to take on any kind of institutionalized responsibility for directing them (pp. 420–1).

When his *Collected Poems* was published in 1972, it became clear that he had answered that failure of nerve by recourse to a particular kind of institutionalised responsibility, scholarship. The recourse has puzzled at least one of his admirers, Neil Powell:

> But the extent and the obscurity of allusion, and the deliberation with which he refuses to be helpful in some recent poems, are new and disturbing. Two long poems at the end of the *Collected Poems*, 'Trevenen' and 'Vancouver', are provided with J. H. Prynne-like notes which would be of little use to anyone outside one of the copyright libraries (1979, p. 77).

But the deliberation with which Davie refused to be helpful was, I think, a political deliberation, a reassertion of the authority implicit in a certain level of scholarly seriousness. The notes to 'Trevenen' help establish a precise historical moment, which can be said to represent 'an age much like our own', an age when few things were as fashionable as 'indignant righteousness'. In talking about this age, Davie is able to talk about ours as well. Brandishing his footnotes, the pastor has stormed back into the manse and kicked out all the groupies and sociologists and unspeakable epic poets. Prynne's Medusa-head had frozen the spectacle of indignant righteousness, anatomising it while holding it in place; Davie sought to abolish it altogether, by a less devious but less incisive moralism.

Of the two rhetorics, Davie's has proved the more successful in gathering a readership. This is partly because the appeal to authority has found a particular language in present-day political journalism, a language which has proved popular and influential. Writing in the *Sunday Telegraph* of 13 September 1981, Peregrine Worsthorne argued that the true reactionary must always be warning people against idealism and high-mindedness, and that such warnings are 'bound often to take the form of a contemptuous sneer, an angry jibe, a deflating rudeness, and a certain verbal brutality, at best witty but at worst merely abusive, simply because these are the most effective corrosives with which to dissolve liberal waffle'. By way of example he cited the Victorian Prime

Minister Lord Salisbury, who defined universal education as 'pumping learning into louts'. Such 'corrosives' are very popular in England today (they have a lot to do with the success of *Private Eye*). We admire them less for their wit, although they are sometimes very witty, than for their sadism: the brutality with which they lay bare pretensions and reassert the authority of self-evident truths.

Literary men have also found a use for these corrosives, as can be seen from a review by Kingsley Amis, which does to Donald Davie's *New Oxford Book of Christian Verse* what Davie did to Larkin's *Oxford Book of Twentieth-Century Verse* (the pastors like to keep each other up to the mark). Reaching for the corrosives, Amis observes that Davie has included a translation of the 'Dream of the Rood' which 'has words like "durst" and "corse" in it and has small letters at the beginnings of the lines. A useful rough rule says that no good poems do that' (1981, p. 44). Thus the true reactionary punctures the pretensions of all the unspeakable epic poets who have abandoned capital letters, and of all those readers who have been foolish enough to admire them for doing so. Although it would be wrong to identify *PN Review* in general, and Davie and Schmidt in particular, with such posturing, there can be little doubt that the journal has benefited from its loose association with the rhetoric of political and literary reaction. For if one had to name the English critic who most forcefully combined Toryism with a witty and brutal commentary on literature, it would be C. H. Sisson. Introducing the latter's collected essays, Schmidt points out that there 'is often a polemical edge to what Sisson says: he does not wish to per-suade us of anything, but to disabuse us – he is impatient that some men so readily misunderstand' (1978, p. 6). And the essays do indeed steam with indignation whenever they encounter such whimsical notions as 'democracy' or 'Stephen Spender'. Their fashionable dis-abusing rhetoric has clearly had some influence on the tone of the journal Sisson helps to edit.

I must confess that the young writers Carcanet publishes seem to me less interesting than the older ones it has re-published. But whatever its virtues and shortcomings, it can be said to represent a Leavisite project for the making of readers, sharpened by the horrors of the sixties and strengthened by a more astute handling of institutional audiences and the excellence of Donald Davie's writing. Like *Scrutiny*, the project is characterised by a tension between liberalism and reaction which usually resolves itself in favour of reaction. It is exemplary because of its success, a success I would attribute in part to its collusion with a certain political posture.

There are of course other small presses and other journals. The Ferry Press, for example, has published books (by Andrew Crozier, John James, Douglas Oliver, J. H. Prynne, Peter Riley) of a high standard with rare consistency. Libraries which take an interest in contemporary English poetry should buy everything it prints, as well as every issue of the *Grosseteste Review*. But these other presses and journals have not been as successful as Carcanet at reaching and identifying those who might want to read the poets they sponsor. Sometimes one of their books does break surface. In 1975 the *Spectator* gave Ashbery and Crozier and James and Prynne what must be about the only favourable reviews they have ever received in the daily or weekly press. 'By refusing to become a readily accessible and intelligible writer,' Peter Ackroyd said of Prynne, 'he has ensured that poetry can no longer be treated as a deodorised museum of fine thoughts and fine feelings; he is creating, instead, a complete and a coherent language' (1975, p. 793). But the *Spectator*-initiative did not last long (revolt in the rectories? blank stares in the Athenaeum?), and in the absence of a sustained effort of exposition it is hard to see how Prynne can be said to have 'ensured' anything. For the success of Carcanet has shown that the making of readers in England today is an arduous business, and one requiring a range of consistent strategies.

* * *

But however sweet the appeal to authority, it can hardly match the real authority vested in the men and women who teach literature in our schools. According to David Holbrook, these people are 'helping train the sensibility of three-quarters of the nation: and they are helping create its capacities for living and its potentialities as an audience for new forms of literary expression' (1961, pp. 7, 64). That was said in 1961, and twenty years later it looks an ambitious claim. But literature is still very much on the curriculum, and we must attempt some analysis of the way it continues to be taught.

Influential commentators like Holbrook and Frank Whitehead have always emphasised the difficulty of clearing a space for poetry among rival attractions. So unaccustomed are we to poetry, Holbrook observes, that we 'have to train ourselves self-consciously to respond'; according to Whitehead, poetry has been relegated to 'the utmost periphery of normal human activity', and we forget that there were times when hearing it spoken or sung 'formed part of the background in which all children grew up' (1966, p. 94). Since the disappearance of the

Common Reader, the reader primed by living in a homogeneous culture, we have had to *make* an audience for poetry, and the classroom now seems like a good place to start. Whitehead argues that the modern teacher should therefore 'supply as far as he can the deficiencies of the environment'.

This understandably defensive view of the role of poetry in modern life has determined to a large extent the way it is taught in schools. Because the process is felt to be a struggle against great odds, it has come more and more to resemble a minimum programme, a programme which teaches people to recognise not so much 'new forms of literary expression' as the place poetry might hold in their imaginative lives, what it has to offer against counter-attractions. We must learn to know the poetic, not as a discourse whose value lies in its autonomy, but as a mode of perception dormant within our daily lives. Poetry is no longer seen as a series of conventions (prosodic, generic, rhetorical) which have been used to produce new versions of subjectivity, but as a capacity to imagine freshly and unconventionally. 'Every new child,' according to Ted Hughes, 'is nature's chance to correct culture's error' (1976, p. 91).

A sign of the shift of emphasis I am talking about can be seen in the thematising approach adopted by anthologies designed for use in schools. 'Throughout the poetry course,' Whitehead suggests, 'we should be looking first and foremost for poems which can make contact, in an intimate way, with the child's most vital experience and interests' (1966, p. 99). This means that the poems must be coded in such a way as to break through any expectations about the kind of discourse they are and 'make contact' with the child's capacity to imagine his or her world. They are therefore classified not according to, say, prosodic convention, but according to the customary disposition of the vital interests they are supposed to make contact with. Maurice Wollman's 1968 anthology, *7 Themes in Modern Verse*, contains the following categories: Work and Leisure; Travel and Adventure; Personal Relationships; Coming to Terms with People and Life; With People and Away from People; Communication; 'The Age of Anxiety'. In 1969, eye-deep in the Age of Anxiety, Rhodri Jones edited for Heinemann Educational a series of anthologies entitled *Themes*: Men and Beasts; Imagination; Conflict; Generations; Sport and Leisure; Men at Work; Town and Country. Not so much the Age of Anxiety, more like the Age of Themes. Of course, anthologies have to be categorised somehow, and classification according to theme has traditionally been one way of doing it. But it may be that what was once a matter of convenience has become an indispensable coding, a way of labelling poems so that they make contact with the vital interests of the pupil.

I have been dealing with a minimum programme for the training of readers. No doubt other kinds of reading, including a study of prosodic conventions and so on, can follow from it. But the minimum programme, with its attention to *the poetic* rather than to *poems*, may take such a firm hold on the habits of young readers that only a powerful counter-argument will dislodge it. Since the majority of readers learn how to read in the classroom, and publishers favour poets who are likely to be read there, this specialisation of reading-habits must eventually have some consequence for literary practice.

Features of the minimum programme for the training of young readers in school are reproduced in the overall context for the writing and reception of poetry. Consider the possible effect of the emphasis placed on creative writing in the schools today. Hughes's influential *Poetry in the Making*, first published in 1967, was intended to encourage ten- to fourteen-year-olds to 'more purposeful efforts in their writing' (1967, pp. 11–12). He argued that 'by showing to a pupil's imagination many opportunities and few restraints and instilling into him confidence and a natural motive for writing, the odds are that something – may be not much, but something – of our common genius will begin to put a word in'. As Whitehead remarks, creative writing fosters 'the acceptance of poetry as something which is neither esoteric nor precious, but a normal and natural facet of human life' (1966, p. 96). The shift from poems to the poetic is achieved by encouraging pupils to write themselves, and by showing them many opportunities and few restraints (that is, few conventions).

As the discipline of teaching English has become more codified, so the emphasis on opportunity rather than restraint (capacity rather than convention) has become firmly established. It governs not only the teaching of pupils, but the teaching of teachers. When in the late sixties the universities took on a greater responsibility for teacher-training, there was some concern that the courses they provided should not be too 'academic'. 'A teacher,' Holbrook wrote, 'who has written at some time or other honest creative work about his inmost self, and who has often been truly moved by word-art, will be able to respond to children's own creative writing' (1967, p. 128). Such honest creative work, Whitehead argued, 'should form part of the in-service training of all teachers of English, whatever their age' (1970, pp. 103–4).

These may well be sensible provisions, and the emphasis given to creative writing by the syllabus may well be amply justified. The problem arises when such specialised activities begin to dominate not only the classroom but the literary world as a whole. This could be happening now. For example, poetry competitions are here to stay, and their immense popularity – anything up to 35 000 entries in some cases – must surely be attributed in part to an educational system which insists that an achieved poem by someone else is simply the stimulus to the poetic capacity in oneself, an incentive to produce more of the same.

The way poetry is taught in schools may have other, more precise consequences for the literary world as a whole, although these are hard to establish. It may perhaps help to determine what kinds of writing are recognised as 'poetic'. If we are to understand how, we must look more closely at particular techniques of reading taught in the schools.

Whitehead has suggested that the teacher needs to devise:

> ways of helping the pupils to give to the words and their meanings the right kind of attentiveness. . . . The process is one of drawing attention (usually by questioning) to some of the key points in the meaning of the poem – those focal points or nodes around which the total poetic meaning is organised and concentrated. In searching, during the preparation of the lesson, for these nodes of meaning it will be found that the 'tip' commended by F. R. Leavis to the critic, 'scrutinise the imagery', holds good for the teacher as well.

The emphasis is on the focal point of a poem, the single detail around which it has been organised; and that focal point will almost invariably be an image. So the first step in our recognition of the poetic will be to isolate within the discourse of the poem a significant detail. This is what we imagine the poet to have done when he scanned the 'discourse' of experience in the first place and isolated the germ of his poem. This is what we ourselves will be attempting to do in our own creative writing. Description, Hughes says, is a matter of picking out and remembering significant details: 'then it is just a matter of presenting those vividly in words (1967, pp. 44, 47)'.

But what is it that makes the detail we pick out of the poem significant? What will render the detail we have picked out of experience vivid? Comparison. 'It is one of those curious facts,' Hughes claims, 'that when two things are compared in a metaphor or a simile, we see both of them much more distinctly than if they were mentioned separately as having nothing to do with each other.'

Comparisons are what we notice in a poem, and what we want to produce in our own writing:

> You are forced to look more closely, and to think, and make distinctions, and be surprised at what you find – and all this adds to the strength and vividness of your final impression. And it all happens in a flash. Just give yourself a few odd similes or metaphors and see how they set your imagination going:
> How is a dragonfly like a helicopter?
>
> How is a tramp-steamer in a rough sea like an old man?
> How is a ball like an echo?
> So, in this business of bringing people to life in words, comparisons can be helpful.

Having scanned experience for significant detail, the poet will reproduce the detail by means of a comparison, which is what the reader will recognise as the poetic part of his activity. Poems are, in the first instance, metaphors or similes. Other instances will follow, other recognitions (of prosody or genre or whatever). But the chances are, particularly if the process of reading is short-circuited by creative writing, that the first instance will remain primary: the indelible mark of the poetic. When we think of poetry, we will think first – and maybe last – of vivid comparisons: 'it all happens in a flash'.

This is certainly the assumption behind *Touchstones*, a series of five anthologies edited by Michael and Peter Benton and widely used in the middle school. *Touchstones* I opens with a discussion of 'word-pictures', using Japanese haiku as a model:

> Imagination is difficult to define but we go some way towards it if we say that it is being able to look at things in a fresh or original way. Comparisons help the poet to do this, for he puts together two things which we do not normally connect and gives us a new and vivid picture of them. Dylan Thomas, for example, describes milk-churns standing at the corner of the village street 'like short, silver policemen'. D. H. Lawrence sees bats flying in the evening air as 'bits of old umbrellas' (1968, pp. 8, 15).

So the Bentons define poetic thinking as an ability to 'look at things in a fresh or original way', an ability to look at bats as though they were pieces of umbrella. They go on to consider other aspects of poetry; but comparison remains for them the primary element, and one they return to again and again. Thus their next topic is the ballad, but even here they remark that 'the ballad composer has stressed a few significant details and kept the picture he wants you to imagine bold and simple'. Generic considerations are less important than seeing familiar things in a fresh or original way; what the reader does in effect is to isolate the haiku (the vivid comparison) within the ballad.

That, at any rate, is the basis upon which the creative writing of the pupils must proceed. Here are a couple of exercises from the third volume of *Touchstones*:

> You may be able to think of comparisons for some of the following and write two or three lines of free verse where you use them: petrol or oil on the surface of a puddle, the surface of your desk, electricity pylons, the London underground. These are only suggestions; find your own subjects if you can.

> Look carefully at your desk lid. Possibly it is new and shiny but it is quite likely that on it there are marks, initials, doodles, 'train lines', blots and stains dating back over many years. What is the texture of the wood like? Why and when were the different marks made? If a minute insect were to make its way across this desk 'landscape' what features would it notice? What obstacles would it encounter? one or two of these questions may suggest ideas for a poem (1969, pp. 28, 147).

In this way familiar objects can be revived by the exercise of comparison, and the poetic faculty vindicated. Comparison, one of the many different ways in which poems signify, has become a sign for poetry itself: for the entire scope and value of the art.

No doubt the *Touchstones* approach works in the classroom. No doubt many teachers supplement it with an emphasis on other aspects of poetic form. But it does predispose one rather heavily towards a certain kind of writing, and if the assumptions which support it were to take root outside the classroom as well as inside, we might have a problem. This could happen directly, through the making of readers in the schools and in teacher training programmes, or indirectly, through the pressure exerted on publishers. (The schools remain the only large market for books of poetry, a market which has determined such ventures as the joint paperback selection of work by Thom Gunn and Ted Hughes, two poets who are usually taught together; Faber have sold well over 100 000 copies.) I want to argue that the assumptions I have described are already taking root outside the classroom, and so determining which poets get to be read.

The establishment of Craig Raine as a popular and respected poet has been, as Alan Hollinghurst points out, 'a conspicuous feature of British literary life during the last three years. . . . And the result of this rapid creation of . . . taste is of course a dangerous over-definition of his skills which any young writer might find restricting and which can easily threaten an atrophy through excessive self-consciousness' (1981, p. 4). Hollinghurst suggests that the taste has been created – in part, at least – by a burst of praise from important people (Peter Porter, John Carey, John Bayley). I think we need to look beyond such factors, to the skills which have been over-defined and the assumptions which have defined them.

On 30 December 1979 the *Observer* said goodbye to the seventies. Christopher Booker recalled the 'gloom and confusion' of the decade in a gloomy and confused manner; someone else decided that sex, apparently an 'invention of the sixties', was now 'in retreat'. But the paper also looked forward to the eighties, and to the young men and women who might be expected to make their mark in the coming decade. Among the young hopefuls were two poets:

> CRAIG RAINE, 35, poet and critic who leapt to fame last year with the publication of his first slim volume *The Onion, Memory*, which earned him the title of founding father of a new school of poetry – the Metaphor Men. A second volume, *A Martian Sends a Postcard Home*, has just appeared.

> CHRISTOPHER REID, 30, a young poet whose first book, *Arcadia*, published last summer, introduced a new note of brilliant stylishness and subtle feeling (1979, p. 24).

The soubriquet 'Metaphor Man' indicates that the popularity of this new school is based on a rhetorical choice, rather than on a choice of subject-matter. Prestige attaches to the exercise of a particular skill. Faber and Faber, who missed out on Raine and Reid, have acknowledged as much by signing up another metaphor-fiend, David Sweetman, and by appointing Raine poetry editor.

The skill defined and over-defined by the work of Raine and Reid is the skill which has become in our society a sign for the entire scope and value of poetry. Readers trained to identify poetry with the art of noting visual correspondences will inevitably favour poets who are better at comparing things than they are at handling genre or rhythm or argument. Several critics have commented on the relative inconspicuousness of genre and rhythm and argument in Raine's writing. His poems are coded by our expectations about what their metaphors will yield, to the point at which we more or less ignore anything else they might have to offer. Thus, like the Bentons' pupils, he has been thinking of things to compare with electricity pylons: in one poem, pylons go for their guns; in another, they pull out their pockets. The basis of these metaphors is almost always visual, and their purpose to demonstrate the enduring validity in everyday life of the poetic faculty. In Raine's world, a packet of cigarettes looks like a miniature organ and a rose has a shark-infested stem. In Reid's world, glasses lie in a lotus position and violinists do a futile side-stroke; his sequence 'The Haiku Adapted for Home Use' even brings the Bentons' favourite form to bear on the domesticity which is one of the favourite subjects of the Metaphor Men. When Ian Hamilton, reviewing *A Free Translation*, observed that 'Raine continues to fish out the flashy similes, as if from a bottomless school satchel' (1981, p. 43), his own simile was perhaps less flashy and more apposite that he knew.

Of course, comparison is not a sin. It only becomes dangerous when a significant number of readers identify it with the entire scope and value of poetry, and use it to distinguish good from bad. The success of the Metaphor Men suggests that this has already happened. I cannot explain why it has happened. But if the identification of poetry with comparison does derive from the way the subject is taught in the schools, then a particular institution can indeed be said to have become responsible for the making of a large number of readers.

On the other hand, Carcanet has shown that it is possible to make a readership for poets who do not necessarily at first appeal to that institutional audience. In doing so, the press has had to collude to some extent with a certain political stance. Not for the first time, dismay at the awfulness of the contemporary world has made a place in our culture for the defence of a particular kind of writing.

I believe it is the responsibility of criticism to sustain a plurality of readerships, if necessary against the monopoly power of any institution or rhetoric. That means tolerance, and something more than tolerance, namely the ability to recognise the different conventions of reading invoked by different poetries and the ability to understand how such conventions find their reason in society.

References

Ackroyd, Peter (1975) 'Verse and worse', *Spectator* (20 December), p. 793.

Amis, Kingsley, (1981) 'Jerusalem and the heavenly aeroplane', *The Sunday Times*, p. 44.

Benton, Michael and Peter (eds) (1968) *Touchstones*, 1, pp. 8, 15.

—— (1969) *Touchstones*, 3, pp. 28, 147.

Davie, Donald (1968) 'Views', *Listener* (21 March), p. 365.

—— (1973) *Listener* (29 March), pp. 420–1.

—— (1973) *Thomas Hardy and English Poetry*, p. 86.

—— (1977) *PN Review*, 2, p. 1.

'Eighty for the eighties' (1979) *Observer* (30 December), p. 27.

Hamilton, Ian (1981) 'View from a backyard in Cumbria', *The Sunday Times* (21 June), p. 43.

Heaney, Seamus (1980) 'England of the mind', *Preoccupation: Selected Prose 1968–1978* (London).

Holbrook, David (1961) *English for Maturity: English for the Secondary School* (Cambridge), pp. 7, 64.

——(1967) *The Exploring Word* (Cambridge).

Hollinghurst, Alan (1981) 'Best Things', *London Review of Books*, 3, p. 14.

Hughes, Ted (1967) *Poetry in the Making*.

Jones, Peter and Schmidt, Michael (eds) (1980) *British Poetry Since 1970: a Critical Survey* (Manchester).

Larkin, Philip (1979) 'A voice for our time', *Observer* (16 December), p. 35.

Leavis, F. R. (1971) *New Bearings in English Poetry*, new edn.

Morrison, Blake (1981) 'Poetry and the poetry business', *Granta*, 4.

Poetry Nation (1973), pp. 3, 50.

Powell, Neil (1979) *Carpenters of Light* (Manchester), p. 77.

Schmidt, Michael (1973) PN Review, 1, p. 1.

—— (1976) *PN Review*, 1. p. 3.

—— (ed.) (1976) Introduction to *Ten English Poets* (Manchester).

—— (ed.) (1978) *The Avoidance of Literature: Collected essays of C. H. Sissoon* (Manchester).

Sisson, C. H. (1977) *PN Review*, 3, p. 1.

Thwaite, Anthony (1978) *Twentieth-century English Poetry* (London)

Tompkins, Jane (1980) 'An introduction', *Reader-Response Criticism* (Baltimore).

Whitehead, Frank (1966) *The Disappearing Dais: a Study of the Principles and Practice of English Teaching* (London).

—— (1970) *Creative Experiment: Writing and the Teacher*.

6

Peter Gidal, *Understanding Beckett: A Study of Monologue and Gesture in the Works of Samuel Beckett* (1986)

Peter Gidal is an independent avant-garde film-maker and critic whose work, in both his films and his writings, has been concerned to combat the conditions of illusion inherent in representation – 'reproduction in any form'. What that work stresses and realises, therefore, is a materialist presentation of the construction of meanings, resisting terms of identification, narrative ordering, metaphorical relation: challenging all coherent *presence* of 'subject'/'reality'.

Understanding Beckett was written in the context of Gidal's political–aesthetic conjunction of theory and practice (there is no separation of the two), a result of his long-standing engagement with Beckett's drama and prose, with Beckett's own lessening of the holds of meaning. Utterly removed from the academic world of 'Beckett studies', the book's writing is itself carried through as a materialist practice in a manner well described by Angela Moorjani in her LDS book *The Aesthetics of Loss and Lessness*:

> In his writing, [Gidal] accomplishes the (partial) obliteration of the writer's first person, the usual deictic centre, by transferring techniques from his experimental film work to critical discourse. Thus, he threads into the chapters of his books (or the paragraphs of his essays) strings of quotes that work with and against one another and the reader. Such echoing intertexual sequences challenge the reader to enter into the production under way. In the sense of patchwork (or montage), writer and reader stitch together, unravel, and redo patterns involving previously worked materials . . . this writerly montage of texts precludes anchoring in a readily available subject of knowledge.

The following extract gives something of the experience of this and indicates one of Gidal's main arguments in the book: that the standard opposition of Brecht's theatre as political and Beckett's as formalist needs to be revised, based as it is on an assumption of some stable givenness of political meaning.

Quote: Malevich on Cubism and Communism
Producing Contradictions in the Spectator/Reader
Analysis of a Sentence
Use of Sounds *vs Gestik*
Use Value *vs* Exchange Value
Quotes from *Capital*
Effects and Causes
Against Implicit Author
Brecht *vs* Beckett/Interpretation/Audience's Desires
Against Psychology

The artist at the stage of Cubism, instead of creating a facial image, has multi-imaged the concrete difference, i.e. has transformed the face into elements and created a new phenomenon which in turn has become an abstraction and has roused the indignation of the vigilant citizen's consciousness. This has happened because existence, the object, for society was in one centre of reflection and, for the artist, in another, and what the former considered understood, ordered, and natural, was, for the latter, disordered, unnatural, and senseless. And then angry society must search either for a photographer, or for an artist not far removed from that photographer. . . . In the stages of Cubism . . . when many associative decisions are taken, hidden from the spectator, [one can see] an object which is understood by the masses, *the objective*, becomes sharply subjective, producing 'astonishment' in society because it is unintelligible to intelligence. . . . The Cubist has carried it from the intelligent into the unintelligent, and has temporarily broken the link with society, only because society has not had time to follow the kinesthetic associative displacement through to the end . . . some artists have taken fright at this break with the masses and have cut short (Malevich, 1976, pp. 283–4).

I have not met a single person who would say that all artistic portraits of Lenin correspond to reality . . . only science can show his true portrait. The greater reality of his portrait is the cinema, it is outer truth, the scientific is inner truth, both together would be a portrait. Therefore the portrait of Lenin does not exist in art, as other portraits in general do not exist; when they enter the sphere of aesthetic painting they depart into the future, into the ideal. . . . Communists too object to non-objectivity, since, for them, existence without an object, like the capitalist without capital, cannot exist. With nonobjectivity disappears their means of reflecting environment and portraits, propaganda through the object, propaganda through capital in the other case. The non-objective is incomprehensible . . . and abstract, the consciousness of society is deprived of its main support, what to see, what to cognise? This function can be materialistic; matter does not have an object-portrait . . . if it is fluid and dynamic. From matter we can make material and from material whatever one pleases: we do not have an authentic portrait of it, we can only create an image of our conjectures, transform the unknown into the known (ibid., p. 322).

Non-objectivity: that the idea does not attain the object except as an image. This non-representational image is the possible, finite form of materialism and reality (ibid., pp. 348–9).

If not disquisition disquiet. That sentence is a descriptive statement in reference to *Not I*'s form, and to the thought that the lack of disquisition (i.e. contradictions) is inbuilt for the viewer-listener producing disquiet. What *If not disquisition disquiet* states is that in *Not I*, the sentences, the repetition structure, the monologue-in time, is disquieting for the speaker and for the listener, producing a sense of disquiet in both. It is not a disquisition, i.e. speech *about* a subject. *If not disquisition disquiet* also means it might or might not be a disquisition, *might* but in any case hasn't become limited to that. This is what the idiomatic usage of 'if not . . .' denotes in current language use. What it means is that in any case disquiet is produced. But the contradiction for the listener comes up because of the beginning word 'if'. 'If' as part of the idiomatic expression 'if not' has an *opposing*, strictly opposing, meaning to 'if' (meaning *when*) as in: 'when there is no disquisition then there is disquiet, *not otherwise*'. Thus the two uses of 'if' force a contradictory motoring of the reader–listener. And this contradictory motoring of the reader-listener in relation to the production of disquiet, and in relation to the production of a disquisition-monologue, forms contradictions which can only be resolved by the reader-listener's position, consciously or unconsciously, in the momentary resolution of (that) contradiction-in-meaning. Taking such a position has nothing to do with truth, but has to do with transformations of meaning through language-forces, and attempting to separate an idea, a thing, etc., from the process of its attempted description. This is not a playing with 'open' language where the reader–listener-as subject can willy-nilly insert him-/herself in idealist play, but rather, the reading, or the play is the work. It is the work of taking a position in meaning and thereby, for that moment, formulating a political solution, not outside ideology and inside truth, but as a position, an acting within the process of contradiction, in language, in meaning, against the natural 'fulfilment' of speech as some pre-given truth or knowledge outside of the work of production and subjective and objective transformations of position. Such motivation of the reader–listener and the viewer–listener is beyond a mere energetics. The above is merely an example of a process that is on-going in *Not I, Rockaby* and *A Piece of Monologue.*

Seven Countenances of Time:

It is said 'the' time. Who wants may read 'our' time. But in no case can it be called 'my time'. Because it isn't *my time* which with brutal openness horrifically grins. My time stands in wild opposition to the times. I have nothing in common with the time which wretchedly hangs about. I am not a *contemporary [Zeitgenosse*, which means time plus comrade].

He who in this form gave countenance to 'the' time thought the drawings stood in stark opposition to the words which followed. I would want them to stand in ten times stronger opposition to the words. But there is no 'stronger' opposition. There is only opposition. Opposition, as I feel it, has no adjective.

If I say 'wild' opposition or 'lazy' opposition, these aren't emphases, but rather adornments. The spirit is freezing and wants to warm itself with the heart's blood. (B. Traven, 'Rut Marut', in *Der Ziegelbrenner* ('The Brickburner'), 21 December 1921), published during the Bavarian Soviet period

Given in Beckett's *Not 1* the broken moments of stuttering speech and speechlessness, the memory, for example, of a previous moment causing moment-to-moment hesitation of the larynx, tone, movement; given such *gestik* of materialist monologue, sound against image (the image of the continuum of a mouth against the non-continuum of speech-production): how are we produced and how are we to make use of such means of production of language and sight, *in* language and sight? And how is such a construction produced against culturally inculcated 'narrative desire', when it is precisely the anti-narrative that materialist sound-and-sight-processes, as described, engage? How is all this put to *use*, rather than commodified for consumption? We can utilise the apparatus, the apparati, of meaning-making and meaning-unmaking as a move, not as an identification but against it, as a figuring of how is what it is what it is.

Cultural, intellectual, sensual (as in: the sense) use-value is important if use-value is to be seen as other than purely economic. The use-value of, for example, sexuality in its concretised form and in terms of sexual meanings (that woman there, rocking, on stage, that mouth speaking, those words, in such and such a way) is still a question of use-value *for whom*, not use-value pure and simple. That is one contradictory placement, as the *for whom* becomes an operative question *specifically in relation to the seeming use-value pure and simple*.

Another contradiction that is operative constantly is that use-value is always already exchange-value.

The third, in fact last-instance, contradiction is that, still, there is a difference between use-value and exchange-value: one is for use, process, productivity, one is for profitability. *At the same time*, the concept *use* is an ideology of use, and the concept *exchange* is an ideology of exchange, both of which can only be disinterred, towards various kinds of uses and exchanges, laboriously. Disinterring such concepts alone requires a materialist process, in endless regress 'towards' a political use and exchange separate from a pre-given 'good' or 'truth'.

> The process disappears in the product; the latter is a use value (Marx, *Capital*, vol. I, p. 176).

> though a use-value, in the form of a product, issues *from* the labour process, other use-values, products of previous labour, enter *into* it as means of production. The same use-value is both the product of a previous process, and a means of production in a later process. Products are therefore not only results, but also essential *conditions of labour*. It is generally by their imperfections as products that the means of production in any process assert themselves in their character (ibid., p. 178):

Human action, or the human voice, etc., with a view to the production of use-values, is 'the appropriation of natural substances to human requirements'.

'Rushed switching of subject matter loosens the relation between speech and person . . . resulting in the detachment of the enunciation from the figure' (Beckett, 1973, pp. 136–6). In Gertrude Stein's *Tender Buttons* and much else, in H.D.'s *Palimpsest* and *Hedylus*, in Beckett's *How It Is*, this is the case. A non-localisability, causelessness, is structuring the reader-listener's imbrications through the text.

Can there be non-metaphysical materiality based on unanswerable (but real) cause and causelessness? Can there be material without theoretical explanation or formulation? The opposite also obtains: *theoretical* models, physically not observable, are no less real for that, though another historical conjuncture is necessary to 'observe' their physicality. Things are true for a time and place, in certain historical epochs, scientific for the specific ideology of each history, perception, conception, of science and the (ostensible) object. The object in its very concept is already redolent with the scientific or anti-scientific ideology of its historical moment; each is produced as an object of knowledge, no finite and static object of knowledge pre-existing.

The placement within the apparatus *theatre* of such a conceptual framework bears upon the matters and manners of effects with, and effects without, cause. In the case of the latter, it can be a matter of cause elsewhere, possibly denying the identifications and gratifications of a narcissism as reassuring as it is absurd. The speaking voice, its larynx-function, is the operation through you as sexed being of conscious and unconscious process in that present rememoration-attempt, a historical moment inseparable from the political relations produced and producing, *or preceding yet decaused*. It is a speaking voice staged *ars ficia*, as in: the artifice/the artificial.

Brecht and Beckett have both been described as producing non-Aristotelian theatre, though the former's hesitation on that score is often no less ambivalent than the latter's, according to interpretations which have as their bases some implicit authorial say-so. The humanisation inveigles itself and is attributed to the author of the 'lonely woman speaking her life' and the 'lonely woman acting her life', the one being Mouth in *Not I*, the other Mother Courage in *Mother Courage*. This attributed humanisation is based on the dual empiricisms: (a) the intentional fallacy, and (b) the reading-off an audience the truth of the piece, the audience thus as the adequate reflection/mirror of the piece's truth as a piece of truth. But what is needed is an analysis that does more (or less) than find in 'the audience' or in the 'implicit' author the rationale for a communication which pre-exists the theatric act as if the latter redoubles a nature outside the theatre.

Material theatric contradictions make Mother Courage a character who walks against the turning stage (as in the Berliner Ensemble production); she is standing, in fact, still. The insight in thought which that can produce, when 'compared' with an audience responding to the 'tragedy of her hopelessness' within only the most general sociality of the play, forms the basic question of interpretation against which all cultural production comes up. Throwing up that problem *outside* of a dialectic (that is, a possibly *useful*) work-process, which could lead to some sort of insight into the social theatrical and other mechanisms which produce the emotional effects a specific scene instigates, means throwing *out* that problem as a problematic and being left with the 'unanswerable', the problem of multiple interpretation. Multiple interpretation gets one nowhere near an 'answer', a position, because it allows for the over-determination by ideology of everything instate. A contract which would imply a willingness by the producer and a willingness by the consumer to provide and work with *a* specific meaning, an agreement as to the desirability of that, its use-value for both the producer and consumer, elides or could elide or does not necessarily *not* elide the question of ideological fabrication: the fabric of the audience's desire as much as the actor's and director's to consciously or not cater for meanings that, *prior to this staging*, have dominant power within the culture and its history. That would be an aesthetic and a politics of leaving well enough alone, whereas Beckett's work (and Brecht's occasionally) manages to leave nothing alone, not even nothing; forgoing the possibilities of satisfaction; leaving you to leave the theatre unsatisfied, dissatisfied, powerfully unassimilated, evicted from the comfort that closure and resolution, an ending, any ending, could supply. The consequent, and consequential, negation or refusal to terminate unpleasure is the aesthetic/political importance of such work, when it works.

That Brecht's ambiguities at the end of each play allow for either socially useful and politically radical possibilities, in the realm of fantasy endings (for example *Threepenny Opera* and *The Caucasian Chalk Circle*), or for more crudely the anticipated correct ending for a politicised consciousness-in-concrete (in both senses!) (for example *St Joan of the Stockyards, Galileo, The Good Woman of Szechuan, The Measures Taken and Arturo Ui*) either through an empirical 'positive event' or with an anti-hero who can, via inversion, be identified with against the naturalistically represented reactionary forces, leaves the space for Beckett's radical solutions which are not solutions, enduring and unendurable (and in that their radicalism is precise).

Shortly after reading *Waiting for Godol*, Brecht wrote, as to his own early works, *Bei Durchsicht meiner ersten Stücke* ('Whilst looking through my first works'):

I see today that my contradictory spirit led me close to the border of the Absurd. They (my first five full-length works) show . . . without regret how the great flood breaks upon the bourgeois world. First there is still land, but with laughter which becomes ruins [*Trumpeln*] and sin; then there is only the vastness of black water, with islands which quickly crumble.

The act of speech is never *in vacuo*, the act of gesture is never *in vacuo*. The marionette-like moves of Didi and Gogo in Beckett's production are a constant rearrangement, a constant attempt at impossible sociality, congruence, synchronicity, of either 'one' with either 'other'. These moves are also a constant attempt at impossible internal synchronicity of the sound/movement/speech /gesture/body's endless moves ending with no physical concretions other than this body, this mind, this hearing, this sight. Through the marionette-like *gestik* (which, though, is never mechanised to the point of illustrating 'industrial mechanisation' or 'alienation' or 'existential dehumanisation'), psychology and individual psychology are evicted and the external givens of a body (its movements, etc.) are not manifestations of character. Thus, nothing is given that can be used as an excuse to infer psychology and its categories of the known (implicit identity) for the audience's self-identifications and projections. The marionette-like *gestik* is thus not a substitute for 'the mechanical' or for a statement: 'people in this condition of identity are like marionettes'. It is, rather, a form of movement which declines to take the human conventions of movement and gesture as natural. It declines the pretence that 'natural actions' are codeless. The figures of Didi and Gogo are vacated of such naturalism; the discourse is as something else. For those who do not accept negation, it is materialism, process, subjectivity, history, position, both before and after *and during* (and always *against*) on-going attempts, by the conventions we know and recognise, at homogenisation. The power and authority of speech and gesture are instituted theatrically against other powers and authorities of the culturally dominant 'natural'.

References

Beckett, Samuel (1973)., *Materialien zu Warten auf Godot* (Frankfurt: Suhrkamp).
Brecht, Bertolt (1954), *Gesammelte Werke* (Frankfurt: Suhrkamp, 1967), vol. 17, p.945.
Malevich, Kasimir (1976) *Unpublished Writings 1922–25* (Copenhagen: Borgens).
Marx, Karl (1974), *Capital*, vol. 1 (London: Lawrence and Wishart).

7
Brian Rotman, *Signifying Nothing: The Semiotics of Zero (1987)*

Brian Rotman's monograph on the semiotics of zero is an unusual work for two reasons. First, it breaks the ever more damaging divorce between science and the analysis of culture by taking mathematics as the key system for its exploration of conceptual changes in the Renaissance: the introduction of the Hindu zero in mathematics, the development of perspective in painting, the development of imaginary money. Second, its characterisation of the fundamental alterations of signifying codes in the Renaissance is conceived not as an historical investigation finding its justification in the realms of influence and tradition but as a genuine semiotic study which links mathematics, painting and money through the tracing of formal similarities in their historical transformations.

In the sections given here from a chapter entitled 'Nothing Zero', Rotman considers the different intellectual traditions which come together in the Renaissance to link meditations on nothing with the mathematical sign zero. In particular, he sketches the problem that the idea of nothing caused for a Christian tradition which drew on two contradictionary accounts: that from the dominant modes of Greek philosophy for which nothing was a frightening impossibility and that from orthodox Jewish theology in which God created the world from nothing.

Rotman ends his chapter with a reading of the famous opening scene of *King Lear*. He points out that Shakespeare was from the first generation of English schoolchildren who would have encountered the sign for zero in their classrooms and shows how Shakespeare's play on 'nothing' as both concept and symbol in Lear gives expression to much of the crisis of the transition to the world of Renaissance capitalism; a world where the zero does not simply facilitate the increasingly complex system of financial transactions but also inaugurates a system in which every human quality has an arithmetical price.

Nothing: Zero

> Nothing is
> But what is not
> (Shakespeare, *Macbeth*)

The iconography of '0'

The thesis advanced so far runs as follows. In each of the written codes of mathematics, painting, finance a fundamental shift occurs with the introduction into that code of a particular meta-sign for the absence of certain signs. Each meta-sign – zero, the vanishing point, imaginary money – disrupts the code in question by becoming the origin of a new, radically different mode of sign production; one whose novelty is reflected in the emergence of a semiotic subject able to *signify* absence. Further, these meta-signs beget others, they engender closures of themselves, secondary meta-signs whose meaning lies in their capacity to articulate a central, and previously implicit, feature of the meta-signs which gave rise to them: namely that the opposition between anterior 'things' and posterior 'signs' (for things) is an illusion, a fiction of representation unsustainable when faced with the inherently non-referential status of a sign for the absence of signs.

These deconstructive movements – zero/variable, vanishing point/ punctum, imaginary/paper-money – from originals to closures declare themselves as a loss of anteriority: a declaration made possible by the emergence of a new self-conscious subject, the meta-subject, able to *explicitly signify* this loss in the discourses of number, vision, and money.

To the written codes of mathematics, painting, finance, and the autobiographical text already discussed, one could add other examples; the written code of Western musical notation for instance. In this the cognate of zero would be the sign for a silence, the meta-note designating the absence of other notes – a blank, a rest – introduced into musical notation in the late medieval period. And the closure of this meta-sign, the musical homomorph of the algebraic variable, would then be the emergence of the well-tempered scale which initiated tonal music in the seventeenth century. But instead of pursuing yet another elaboration of a by now clearly discernable semiotic phenomenon, I want to return to the meaning of the sign 'nothing', in particular the connection between 'nothing' and zero.

The concept of nothing – the void emptiness, that which has no being, the non-existent, that which is not – is a rich and immediate source of paradoxical thought: the sign 'nothing' either indicates something outside itself and thereby attributes the condition of existence to that which has none, or the sign has no referent, it does not ostend, it points to nowhere, it indicates and means no more than what it says – nothing. Paradoxical formulations such as this admit, as we shall see, many different responses. They can be interpreted as mere rhetorical games, word play, idle poetic mirrors, ultimately empty of meaning; or as modes of irony, sites of ambiguity that allow forms of nihilism to be simultaneously accepted and, because of the dangers of heresy, repudiated; or as meta-logical arguments against the referent, against the notion that signs refer to something prior to and outside themselves; or as vehicles of ascetic practice or mystical speculation, iconic tropes which constitute a mimicry in words, of God's mysterious – absent – presence.

In her encomium, *Paradoxia Epidemica*, of paradoxes and the paradoxical mode in Western intellectual and rhetorical discourse, Colie (1966) gives much thought to 'nothing', tracing a path from pre-Socratic debates about the void, through Christian theological disputes concerning the attributes of God and the dialectical opposite to 'nothing' – All, the Cosmos, Infinity – that impinge on questions of individual existence, survival, oblivion, and annihilation, to the *nihil* rhetorical paradoxes of the sixteenth century, the struggle to formulate the concept of a vacuum in seventeenth-century science, and the visual oxymorons for 'nothing' constructed in Dutch still-life painting.

Colie's principal interest in 'nothing', impacted in an almost overwhelming density of historical detail, is its metaphysical fecundity, its endless capacity to generate paradoxical thought. By contrast, the present account is interested in the purely semiotic fecundity of the mathematical sign zero, its ability to serve as an origin, not of paradox, but of sign creation. In some obvious but obscure sense nothing and zero are connected; and, in a narrow formal sense, can be made to look identical. Zero signifying an absence of signs and 'nothing' signifying an absence of things seem to occupy the same space once one denies the illusion that 'things' are anterior to signs. But zero and 'nothing' are manifestly separate, moving in different historical and linguistic terrains, and being carried by very different signifiers: against words – 'nothing', 'rien', 'nihil', and so on – zero, represented by the symbol '0', has a physical shape, a graphic presence independent of particular languages, with its own iconography.

But what can be learned from its iconography? Is not the shape of zero accidental? A mere historical contingency? What, in any case, has its material or geometrical manifestation to do with the *idea* of nothing?

Consider the mathematical, purely notational problem that zero addresses. It arises as a gap, an empty region, within the place notation for individual numerals signifying, in the decimal case, the absence of 1,

2, . . . 9. An iconic, mimetic approach to the writing of this absence – taken for example by Babylonian mathematicians for nearly two millenia – might be the use of an empty space to signify it; so that, for instance

11, 1 1, 1 1, 1 1

would notate eleven, one hundred and one, one thousand and one and ten thousand and one respectively. But the scheme has an obvious defect: the right-hand space merges with the blank surface of writing, making 11 ambiguous between eleven, one hundred and ten, eleven hundred, and so on. Moreover, and for the same reason, an empty space is not transportable: unlike the other numerals it cannot be reproduced, written independently of its syntactical presentation within particular numerals, without it merging with the space used to separate words from each other. Signifying absence by absence is not, then, a stable and coherently interesting option for writing down zero.

On the contrary, one signifies absence by making a (graphic) presence, by writing something down, inscribing an unambiguous, permanent, transportable mark. What sort of mark is suitable to inscribe absence?

There is the minimalist possibility of the pure monotone, the atomic mark: the single irreducible dot, point, stroke. But this carries the meaning of presence and nothing else, since the writing of a dot – an undifferentiated, atomic, ur-mark, a monad – has to mean at the least 'there is a sign here'. To mean more, to be able to signify something other than the declaration of its own signifying presence, would require a mark to have a physical attribute, a graphic characteristic, *other* than that of being a signifying mark. Now there is of course nothing to prevent this ur-sign of presence from signifying *by convention* an absence, and so, in the context of numbers, from being used as a symbol for zero. But though such a usage can be found in early occurrences of the place notation it was not, at least in the Western tradition, the historically preferred solution.

Moreover, there is no pressing need to force the ur-sign of presence into a *conventionally* written representation of absence: the iconic approach of the Babylonians can indirectly be retrieved. Instead of literal mimesis, copying a space by a space, one can *depict* an absence through a signifier that contains a gap, a space, an absence in its shape. The most elemental solution, the urmark of absence, is any instance of an iconographic hole; any simple enclosure, ring, circle, ovoid, loop, and the like, which surrounds an absence and divides space into an inside and an outside. Thus, presumably, the universal recognition of 'o', 'O', '0' as symbols of zero. And thus a circle of associations linking zero and 'nothing'. As Colie observes (1966, p. 226) 'from the "O" to the egg was an obvious step since the egg was the symbol of generation and creation; since, too, it bore the shape of zero, contradictions of all and nothing could be constructed on eggs'; which one can continue through the mystical O of the Kabbalah, the Hollow Crown which served as an icon of *ex nihilo* creation; the great circle of white light signifying infinity for Traherne; the origin and place of birth – 'nothing' as slang for vagina in Elizabethan English; to the icon of de-creation and self-annihilation in the shape of the circle made by a snake swallowing its own tail.

But iconography goes on its own peculiar paths: graphically based metaphors and metonyms for absence and nothing are an inherently limited source of insight. The particular written shape of a signifier and the range of its graphic and kinetic associations seems in the end a capricious and somewhat arbitrary route to its meaning. The signifier for zero, for example, could be other than the symbol '0', and was: later Babylonian mathematicians used a double cuneiform wedge, and the Mayans a figure resembling a half open eye, and so on. The connections, or lack of them, between 'nothing' and zero, if they are to go beyond fortuities of shape, must be located in Western intellectual discourse; within the discussions, arguments, and modes of thought, Greek, Jewish, Christian, which attempted to give, or refuse, a significance to 'nothing'.

Greek–Christian nothing

Orthodox Christianity in Western Europe from St Augustine's moral foundations to the scholastic legacy of St Aquinas took its conception of God as a being knowable or unknowable to man, from Greek theology and metaphysics and its image of God as a maker, the Creator of the world, from Jewish monotheism. In so doing it saddled itself at the outset with a fundamental contradiction, a logical dilemma which it never resolved, about the ontological and eschatological status it was to assign to 'nothing'. Christianity thus inherited two mutually incompatible accounts of the first, original, initiating act of creation. For the Greeks this was the moment whereby God gave form to primitive matter which was itself eternal and uncreated; the world was an artifice of God, God was its architect, not its maker. Against this the God of the Old Testament created the whole universe – its matter, substance, form, design – out of nothing.

Moreover, this insistence that 'something' was always there, that there was never 'nothing', which separates Greek artifice from Hebrew *ex nihilo* creation, is the passive expression of a direct and agonistically fraught confrontation with 'nothing' that runs deep inside Greek philosophical discourse: the metaphysical and theological discussions within which Plato and Aristotle cognised their God are hostile to the very idea of the *void*. This hostility – ultimately a refusal to countenance that emptiness, nothingness, that which is not, was a 'thing' that could be signified – permeated all of Greek thought, with the notable exception of Epicurean atomism to which we return below, from the Eleatic precursors of Socrates onwards.

The Greek refusal of the void was at once a philosophical proposition, a conclusion explicitly and safely debated within the domain of rational discourse. Ontologically it was impossible to attribute being to 'nothing' since 'nothing' is that which *is* not, and epistemologically 'nothing' was without meaning. It could only be known by knowing nothing (a paradox which, as we shall see, Socrates made much ironic play with in relation to his own knowledge). At the same time there was a phobic and terrified reaction by Greek thinkers to emptiness, a shrinking back from the disruption, chaos and anarchy that they feared would issue from granting signification and presence to that which is not. Both the fear and the reasoned argument inseparable from it have their original expression in the picture of an eternal changeless universe given by Parmenides.

Parmenides, like Plato and the Christian theologians after him, separated the universe into the world of appearance, the gross physical habitation of the senses, always in motion, heterogeneous and fragmented, and the world of reality, the world of pure form, God, unchanging Being, which was full, homogeneous, indivisible, timeless and One. To give assent and credence to such a bifurcation it is necessary to be convinced, at least it was so for Greek thinkers, by rational argument. One had to be logically persuaded that change and plurality, however much they *seem* real to us, must be illusions, mere dreamlike phenomena of appearances which seem to *be* but in truth are not and can never be part of Being. Parmenides, and more famously his disciple Zeno, gave many arguments defending his unitary static cosmos. Those that survive are principally in the form of paradoxes which forced their interlocutors into accepting that the ideas of motion and plurality were inherently contradictory and incoherent and were therefore, by a *reductio ad absurdum* argument, not real.

Zeno's celebrated paradoxes (in which a stadium was impossible to traverse, arrows could never arrive at their targets, Achilles could never overtake the tortoise, and a moving body must always fail to pass another body) had a profound effect on the structure of Greek thought

– on its mathematics no less than its theology and cosmology – far beyond their original focus of defending the Parmenidean 'one' from the pluralism of Pythagorean number mysticism with its belief in a Being forever being enlarged from the unreality of the void. Certainly, there is no record of the conclusions argued for by Zeno having been refuted, or any indication that the paradoxes were the subject of disabling criticism, or could be explained away. In particular, Aristotle's description and supposed dismissal of them more than a century after their appearance is cursory, opaque and lacking in appreciation of their dialectical subtlety.

If, for the moment, we focus on mathematics, then it is plausible to hold, on the evidence of Euclid's elements alone that, far from ignoring them, Greek mathematicians were shocked by the Eleatic arguments into a certain kind of silence, an unarticulated mistrust and suspicion of the ideas of motion and of plurality; especially any explicit mention of these ideas within what was supposed to be a valid mathematical argument or legitimate mathematical definition. Thus, in the case of motion, for example, they rejected as invalid a well-known and easily achieved solution to the famous problem of trisecting an angle by ruler and compasses because it rested on a reference to a moving point as an essential part of its argument. Again, in terms of definition, they denied any role to motion. All objects of Greek mathematical thought such as numbers, ratios, points, figures, and so on, were characterised as wholly static fixed entities so that, for example, the figure of a circle was defined as the locus of points equidistant from some given point and not as the path of a moving point. If the paradoxes of motion, then, encouraged a mathematics conformable with Parmenides' static changeless reality, what of his attack on plurality?

For plurality one must read the dialectical opposition which Parmenides extracted from it; namely, that which is limitless, without end, infinite, against that which is nothing, has no being, the void. A typical formulation of Zeno runs:

> If there is a plurality, things will be both great and small; so small as to be infinite in size, so small as to have no size at all. If what is had no size, it would not even be. . . . If there is a plurality, things must be just as many as they are, no more and no less. And if they are just as many as they are, they must be limited. If there is a plurality, the things that are are infinite; for there will always be other things between the things that are, and yet others between those others. And so the things that are are infinite (Zeno, quoted in Kirk and Raven, 1957, p. 288)

What the Zeno-Parmenides interdiction of motion, the void, and infinity engendered within Greek mathematics was a hypostasised literalism and an attachment to visually concrete icons which influenced mathematics from the time of Euclid to the Renaissance (and beyond: a version of Parmenidean stasis is central to the dominant present-day conception of mathematics in which mathematicians are supposed to apprehend eternal truths about entities – 'structures' – in an unchanging, timeless, static, extra-human world, Rotman (in press)). Thus, in cognising mathematical entities in visuo-spatial terms as physically palpable icons, so that for example the number x meant an ideal length x units long, Greek mathematics interpreted x^2 as the area of a square, x^3 as the volume of a cube, and only with great difficulty could give any meaning to x^4, x^5, and so on. Within this form of iconised cognition negative numbers, algebraic abstraction as opposed to geometrical construal and zero as a sign marking an *absence* are impossible to conceive. The idea of infinity either as a completed process or a limitless extension (tainted by the disruptive contradictions of Zeno's arguments but seemingly essential to mathematical cognition) became the source of an uneasy fear witnessed, for example, in Euclid's mistrust and ambivalence to the axiom of parallels with its implicit reference to an infinitely prolonged length.

If the idea of 'nothing', through the opposition void/infinite, was a source of anxiety and unease in mathematics, and if more generally, it was in logic and rhetoric, as Colie (1966, p. 222) puts it,

> technically dangerous, wild, at the loose edge of conceptualisation and of discourse, nullifying – literally – ideas of order and ordination . . . psychologically destructive, threatening the familiar boundaries of human experience . . .

then in the psychologically more vulnerable and fraught regions of ontology and theology it inspired a form of terror. For Aristotle, engaged in classifying, ordering and analysing the world into its irreducible and final categories, objects, causes and attributes, the prospect of an unclassifiable emptiness, an attributeless hole in the natural fabric of being, isolated from cause and effect and detached from what was palpable to the senses, must have presented itself as a dangerous sickness, a God-denying madness that left him with an ineradicable *horror vacui*.

In short, the Greek reaction to the void, characterised by unease, fear, and horror, was one of psychological denial. Within the full indivisible universe of Being there could be no fissure, absence, hole, or vacuum; the void did not exist, it could have no being, it was not. Confronted by the need of the Christian church to accept the Genesis account of creation *ex nihilo* such a denial was no longer sustainable, and Christian theology was forced to recognise 'nothing' as something; a thing which had a presence, an originating but somehow unreal, part in the scheme of things-which-are, and as something which had to be given a sense, equally unreal, in relation to a God who acted upon it in order to create the world.

St Augustine, though he absorbed the God of Parmenides and Plato and their abhorrence of the void through the neo-Platonist writings of Plotinus and not from Aristotle, assigned an eschatological status to 'nothing' – it was the devil – which neatly Christianises the sort of horrific object Aristotle was at such pains to deny. For St Augustine 'nothing' was a kind of ultimate privation, the final and limiting term of that which was absent, lacking, lost, which had been subtracted and taken away from the original presence and fullness of God. To be in a state of sin was to enclose within one's spiritual being an absence of God. Conversely, to be in a state of grace was to be filled with God's presence. Within this dialectic of spiritual absence and presence where goodness was God, and evil – the inevitable fruit of sin – the arena of His absence, 'nothing' is equated with the ultimate evil: the non-being of 'nothing' becomes the being of evil – whose physical incarnation is precisely the devil.

There is in this privative solution to 'nothing' a difficulty that borders on blasphemy, since it would seem that *before* the creation out of nothing there was something missing, lacking, something not yet part of God's being which was to be subsequently supplied by the creation. St Augustine's answer, elaborated ingeniously in his theory of time, was that in creating the world God also created time itself, and so God, being outside of time, could never have lacked what he always had. The issue however – that is essentially what could and could not be ascribed to God, the nature and status of God's attributes – remained a dangerous one within Christian theology. Any attempt to refer too positively or too directly to God's relation to 'nothing' could be easily converted into heresy and unbelief. Hence St Aquinas' ruling, for example, that God could only be described and spoken about in a mediated way through negative affirmation. God was not finite, not specifiable, not mortal, not changeable, not temporal, and so on. Within this Aristotelian-based negativism God, loving everything abhors nothing, and indeed destroys and nullifies 'nothing' in order to create the world.

But this attempt to negate the problem of 'nothing', by a formulaic transfer of Aristotle's horror of the void onto God's transformative overcoming of it, was more an avoidance of the void than any real engagement with a sign signifying no thing. Not only was the destructive impact of *ex nihilo nihil fut* not to be contained, as we shall see when we encounter that which comes from nothing in *King Lear*, but, for two centuries before Shakespeare's play, the double image of 'nothing' and 'everything' was in itself too interestingly subversive and enticing – in rhetoric and mathematics and logic as well as theology – to be kept under doctrinal restraint. Perhaps if zero had not made its appearance within Christian Europe, much of this larger interest in 'nothing' would not have occurred, and 'nothing' might have stayed within the writings of Aquinas and the Schoolmen as a remote theological issue. But this was not the case, and if from the tenth to the thirteenth century the church's hostility to 'nothing' was successful in confining zero to Arab mathematics, and so staving off the threat of nullity it presented, the neo-Aristotelian apparatus of concepts inherited by Christian theology was too fixated against absence to even impinge on the larger issue of zero as a sign. Confronted with the rising surge of attention focused on *nihil* in mathematics, rhetoric, and literature engendered by the impact of zero, Christian theology ignored the source and attacked the nihilistic consequences, the heretical and atheistic dangers of believing in and talking about 'nothing'.

As one would expect, it was mathematics that saw the first attempt to incorporate infinity and nothing into its range of signifieds. Already among the later scholastics in the fourteenth century there is a growing interest in infinity and infinite processes. Indeed, the use of infinite addition – combining infinitely many number signs together – to form finite numbers (as in $1 + 1/2 + 1/4 + \ldots + (<1/2>)^n + \ldots = 2$) or infinite numbers (as in Oresme's demonstration that the sum $1 + 1/2 + 1/3 + \ldots + 1/n + \ldots$ exceeds any finite magnitude) initiated the theory of infinite series which was to give a mathematical escape from Zeno's paradoxes. A century later, the writings of Nicholas de Cusa, a vigilantly orthodox theologian and certainly no heretic, were openly full of the possibilities of the infinitely large and infinitesimally small.

Such fascination with the infinite *omnis* and the vacuous *nihil* that went with it was safe from heresy so long as it was confined to the spiritually neutral domain of mathematical signs; the church could hardly mount an inquisition against all the secular users of Hindu numerals. But if the *nihils* of mathematics were secure from the taint of atheism those of rhetoric and the nihilism they bordered on were another matter.

Colie (1966), in her survey of the *nihil* poems and the *nihil* paradoxes of the fifteenth and sixteenth centuries, points to the mimicry of the divine inherent in such forms as the source of their danger:

> In the Renaissance one can find many such paradoxes, appealing because of their impossible affirmations and opportunities of double negation. All affirmations about 'nothing', it turned out, might be taken as analogues to God's original act of Creation, bringing 'something' out of 'nothing' . . . *nihil* paradoxes aspire to the imitation of God's unique act. In precisely that imitation lay the danger: paradoxes about *omnis*, or all . . . might be regarded as pious imitations of God's plenist Creation, but *nihil* paradoxes were another matter altogether. They were engaged in an operation at once imitative and blasphemous, at once sacred and profane, since the formal paradox . . . parodied at the same time as it imitated the divine act of Creation. And yet, who can accuse the paradoxist of blasphemy, really? Since his subject *is* nothing, he cannot be said to be impious in taking the Creator's prerogative as his own – for nothing, as all men know, can come of nothing. Nor indeed is he directing men to dangerous speculation, since at the very most he beguiles them into – nothing (Colie, 1966, p. 224).

Thus, such beguilements, avoiding blasphemy and the dangers of heresy through disowning what they seem to avow, allow their authors to sport with 'nothing' by playing the fool. And indeed, the *nihil* paradoxes and rhetorical conceits about 'nothing' that burgeoned in the sixteenth century were part of a literature of Folly, an *amphitheatrum sapientiae socraticae joko-seriae* of wise Fools and Doctors of Ignorance that has its origin in Socrates' ironic disavowal of knowledge, runs through de Cusa's celebration of foolishness and Erasmus' *Praise of Folly*, and is ultimately turned in on itself and deconstructed by Montaigne in his *Essays*.

Socrates, in declaring 'all that I know that I know nothing' was ironically allowing 'nothing' to puncture a certain ideal of self-knowledge in which one knows 'all'. His declaration does not, of course, mean what it says. For, to know nothing is to know no thing and in particular not to know the thing which *is* your knowing nothing, and so on. The paradox plays on the simultaneous difference and identity between two I's: he who knows and he who is known. And it forces an oscillation between subject and object which it does not, cannot, resolve. It creates, in other words, a fissure, a hole in the full indivisible knowing 'I' at precisely the point where such an 'I' has to cognise 'nothing' in relation to itself. And it goes no further.

In terms of our earlier discussion of signs Socrates' paradox, though it disrupts an existing sign – the familiar subjective 1 of discourse – initiates no new sign, no meta-sign pointing to the absence of signs at the site of the disruption. Like all paradoxes, and that is the point of them, Socrates' conundrum is self-contained, it cannot transcend the puzzle it establishes: it points to nothing outside itself other than the dissolution of its own terms. Unlike Montaigne's confrontation with the delphic injunction to 'know thyself' which creates a meta-sign for a new self-conscious subject, Socrates' irony has no meta-lingual dimension to it. Nor is this surprising if we understand that Socrates, in playing the Fool, was very specifically playing the Greek Fool: one who, however much he ironised about knowing nothing, was not, because of his prior and unquestioned denial of the void, able to know 'nothing'. In denying emptiness the iconic literalism of Greek thought had necessarily to deny any rational presence to that which is absent. Socrates, while forcing us to recognise that the knowing 'I' cannot be always unfracturedly present, had no means to *signify* – by signs which would necessarily have to refer to the absence of signs – this lack of presence. Thus by nullifying the capacity to know, reducing knowledge to nothing, Socrates' paradox achieves a certain sort of epistemological self-annihilation: the 'I' of discourse, as a sign for a full indivisible unitary self who knows, is ironised out of existence.

If Socrates impaled that which as a philosopher he professed to love – the act of knowing – on nothing, then St Jerome strove to annihilate the act of living within the world, to negate and retreat from that world of mundane sensual everyday reality he had loved. In so doing he legitimised, and became the sanctified model of, the tradition of Christian ascetic self-abnegation and annihilation in the face of the infinitude of God.

Abjuring the world, excising one's presence from it, is not to destroy it or destroy the self (Jerome and his monastic followers did not of course advocate suicide) but to swear permanent absence from it, to nullify being in the world, and see it for what it truly was: an arena of sin, lust, and empty vanity. To achieve this world-negating vision one had to follow the path of ascetic withdrawal, the familiar *via negativa* of opposition, self-denial, renunciation and retreat. One had to absent the love of friends, physical pleasures, spiritual ease and sexual desire through the dialectical negatives of hermetic isolation, fasting, scourging the self and abstinence.

The process of ascetic self-annihilation has to come to an end. When all else is gone God is still present: when the whole world has been renounced sentient physical presence must remain. But physical presence is temporary, a moment in oblivion to be reclaimed at any time by death. And to forget this, to be beguiled by life and be blind to its utter impermanence was not to have escaped the world but be trapped in the vanity of being. Hence the necessity for *memento mori*, those metonymic signs of the passage of time and of universal decay, like hour-glasses and skulls, which serve as prophylactics against vanity, reminders of death, annihilation and the ephemerality of the world.

In Dürer's depiction the saint huddles over the bible, his existence given over to pious contemplation, reading, studying and translating the word of God. When he turns from God's word to the world he confronts an hour-glass reminder of the swiftness of life's passing. When he looks up he sees first a crucifix, an icon of God's death in the world, then, again juxtaposed against the outside world, a skull, an icon of Man's death, and then the lion lying with the lamb, an icon of Paradise: the end and promised reward of physical being. All has been reduced and stripped to a bare and stark duality: God/presence of death, eternal heaven/transient world, infinity/abyss of nothing.

Unlike for the paradoxist, who is forced to equivocate his relation to 'nothing', the heretical dangers of consorting with 'nothing' are obviated for the ascetic precisely because he places it at the centre of his repudiation of the world. To see the world in terms of 'nothing' – vanity and emptiness – becomes the point of that long and arduous route through negation to the final union with God. But the ascetic desire for nothingness is safe from heresy only so long as it adheres to the authority of God's moral law. Whatever else in the world he repudiates the ascetic must remain attached to the moral *presence* of God, to the obligations upon his will and therefore his actions in the world that this presence imposes. Hence the necessity for St Jerome to obey the injunction, in this world, to translate God's word so that men might be saved. To negate this, to claim that Faith alone, without the subjugation of the self that issues from obedience to moral law, was sufficient for salvation was to press the impulse to nothingness into a state of outright heresy.

In the seventeenth century such an heretically extreme form of nihilism known as Quietism, practised by Miguel de Molinos and his followers, was persecuted by the Jesuits. Molinos was a Spanish priest who:

> developed his extreme Quietist outlook and practice in Rome and died in an Inquisition prison; his impulse to supress the will to the

point where God took over and worked His own way led him to accept any sexual temptation or aberration as the work of the Devil upon a passive, and therefore sinless, believer, who was thereby intensified in his quiet repose in God; at his trial he admitted to his antinomianism . . . and, as was natural in a Quietist, in the end offered no defense.

> (Unamuno, note by the editors Kerrigan and Nozick, 1972, pp. 442–3)

Molinos' moral anarchism, reversing Jerome's sexualisation of Man's love of God into a belief that sexual union was ultimately a form of divine love was itself enough to have aroused the Inquisition against him. But beyond this was his attempt to annihilate his will, his desire for *uada*, his longing for self-annihilation, for the embrace of 'nothing' as a form of being: his wish to become and to *be* nothing – for that, within the terms that the inquisition imposed on the nature of 'being', was the sin of spiritual self-destruction.

If the Christian ascetic courted heretical nihilism by pursuing a divine union of self with God beyond the constraints of moral obedience in the world, then Christian mysticism, from Meister Eckhart onwards, by seeking total *oneness* with God represented, for orthodox theology, the extreme nihilistic heresy of divine usurpation, a hubristic assumption by the mystic of the original nothingness of God himself. In his account of Eckhart in *Religion and Nothingness* Nishitani observes how the difference between union and oneness with God issues from the distinction Eckhart made between God as *a* being – the Creator, Love, the Divine Presence, and so on – and God as the godhead, conceived as nothing other than the underlying *ground of being* of God, his 'essence' that transcends all particular modes of actuality that can be imagined of His being and becoming. For Eckhart it was necessary to go beyond a union, a personal joining with a soul on one side and God conceived either as a subject or an object on the other, to an identification with the 'absolute nothingness' that constitutes the godhead itself. In this identity there is no longer any meaning in the separateness of a personal soul and God: 'As God breaks through me, so I, in turn, break through him' (Eckhart, quoted in Nishitani, 1982, p. 63). For Nishitani, interested in placing Eckhart within a tradition that contains Heidegger's writings on Nothing, Eckhart's importance and originality is to be found in his finding of the godhead in the absolute nothingness that lies beyond the 'personal God who stands over against created beings' (Nishitani, 1982, p. 62), a location where, in the nothingness before He created the world *ex nihilo*. He had already uttered *I am that I am*. We shall encounter this terminal/originating nothingness again in what is perhaps Eckhart's source, the *Zohar* Kabbalah of Moses de Leon.

One can say that from whatever direction, whether it be the source of heretical nihilism in Eckhart, the incarnation of evil for St Augustine, the site of terminal self-deprivation for St Jerome, the object of Aristotelean horror for St Aquinas, the vehicle of moral suicide for the Jesuits, responses to 'nothing' within the discourse of orthodox European Christianity characterised it as the locus of what was irredeemably negative and evil; a place where the presence of God was constantly in danger of being emptied out, denied, nullified, repudiated through apostasy, heresy and unbelief; a place of void to be religiously 'a-voided'.

Unsurprisingly, then, the Christian need to graft Hebrew *ex nihilo* creation onto a Greek theogeny filled with *horror vacui* was the source of a certain unease from which orthodox rationality had to psychologically defend itself. It did so either by exercising a form of repressive denial which met what it saw as the destructive potential of 'nothing' by doctrinally surrounding it with silence; or by involving itself in a form of splitting: a falling back into gnosticism that produced an irreconcilable opposition, the Good world in conflict with the Bad world, God's All counterpointed to the Devil's Nothing.

Moreover, in precisely the same way that Socrates' Nothing, by being the agent of an absence in the previously full and indivisible knowing self, marked the place of an epistemological disruption, so 'nothing' allowed within Christian discourse – and this was its heretical danger – the means of a parallel theogenic disruption by introducing the possibility of an *absence of God* a falling short from God's total unfractured omni-presence. And, as with Socrates' nullification, the disruptive hole within God's unitary being caused by 'nothing' was semiotically barren: it did not issue in a meta-sign through which this absence could have been signified, recognised and discursively elaborated.

All this prompts an obvious question. Given that Christian thought inherited the problem of 'nothing' through its need to accept the Hebrew account of creation in Genesis how did *Jewish* theology, unburdened by Greek denials and horrors of the void and forced from its inception to make its own sense of creation *ex nihilo*, cognise 'nothing'? The question needs elaborating and I shall return to it below. Before doing so, I want to fill a hole left in the earlier discussion of Greek thought concerning the void.

Abhorrence of emptiness, though a central element in the thinking of Parmenides, Zeno, Socrates, Plato, and Aristotle, was not universal within Greek thought. The atomists (Epicurus, Leucippus, but principally Democritus) accepted the existence of the void as a rational, coherent concept. The universe in all its manifestations was not, as Parmenides insisted, a plenum – full, indivisible, motionless, and one – but was composed of a plurality of atoms in movement which, though themselves were indivisible and so on, had come together in the void to form the physically real, material, empirical world. Democritus' materialism, permitting reference to 'nothing' and antagonistic to explanations of reality in terms of a God-inspired Purpose or Final Cause postulated by Aristotle, was as a result double anathemised and suppressed by Christian theology as both heretical and atheistic.

It was only late in the Renaissance, when emptiness became a pressing object of materialist investigation, that a recrudescence of Democritean Atomism occurred. In the seventeenth century, two fundamentally new 'nothings' fought for existence against the Aristotelian *horror vacui* and the inevitable Jesuit charge of atheism that defended it: the 'nothing' of a physical vacuum – a hole in the all pervading life-giving plenum of air – theorised by Pascal and others as a real, physically present something; and the 'nothing' of empty space – a place devoid of materiality – with respect to which Newton could distinguish relative from absolute motion.

The historical relevance, importance and intellectual support provided by Democritus' materialism to the establishment of these 'nothings', what Colie calls (1966, p. 221) 'that underground stream [which] turned out to be the sacred river feeding the new physics', seems widely accepted. As indeed is the close connection between such 'nothings' and the mathematical insights and preoccupations of their proponents:

> Blaise Pascal was eminently suited to such experimentation on so paradoxical a subject as *le vide*. His scientific and mathematical interests ran to the paradoxical, the improbable, and the ambiguous: his work on infinitesimals and infinite series and on permutations and combinations led to his remarkable contributions . . . to probability theory. He was concerned . . . with the kind of unsolved problem which is fundamentally irrational, and denies altogether the formulation of conceptual limits. His interest in the vacuum is of a piece with his attraction to such problems as those of infinite series and probability theory. He knew that the vacuum was by

definition an 'impossible' subject, that the establishment of its actual existence implied not only a revolution in physical thought but a revolution in moral and ontological thought as well (Colie, 1966, p. 254).

There is, however, from the standpoint of the present essay, something methodologically unsatisfactory, some misplaced adherence to a model of historical 'influence' and causation, behind such a description. Talk of Pascal's psychological predisposition to be interested in the problem of emptiness and of 'sacred' historical rivers sustaining it ignores the semiotic matrix within which such interest, interpreted in terms of the signs which were to encode such physical 'nothings', could not but occur. Pascal, Torricelli, Newton and other did not, after all, exist in a semiotic void with regard to 'nothing'. They had at their disposal, and were in fact immersed in, the whole practice and mode of discourse about 'nothing' built into the Hindu numeral system. Colie's account of Pascal, which is much alive to his mathematical interests, particularly his fascination with infinity, makes no mention of zero. In a sense this is perfectly understandable: unlike the question of infinity, zero was not problematic for Pascal. It was not, in fact, an explicit item of mathematical concern for him. But, as will be obvious by now, the mathematical infinite was the fruit of the mathematical nothing: it is only by virtue of zero that infinity comes to be signifiable in mathematics. Now Pascal, psychologically driven as he no doubt was to contemplete emptiness, silence, nothing, a vacuum, was nevertheless not unfamiliar with the mathematics of his day. He knew Stevin's work celebrating the decimal notation and had read Vieta's work on algebra. He thus had, to aid his contemplations of *le vide*, two highly articulated meta-signs based on the absence of signs which had, moreover, overturned the anteriority of things to signs that stands in the way of cognising emptiness. In other words, the 'revolution in . . . ontological thought' he looked for had already been instituted in mathematics.

The point, then, is this. The elaboration of the code of scientific discourse in the seventeenth century to accommodate the concepts and reality of 'vacuum' and 'empty space' was a question, not of historical causation to be traced through the supposed influence of Greek atomism, but the completion of an existing semiotic paradigm. Within this discourse the terms 'vacuum' or 'empty space' were obliged to signify the absence of what before them had been conceived as full, indivisible and all-pervasively present: the plenum of breathable air and the plenum of material (as opposed to divine) existence. And, as we have seen, to write the mathematical symbol 0 is to signify the absence of the positive number signs; the absence, that is, of the unit 1 and its iterates 11, 111, 1111, etc. the absence, in other words, of entities perceived as full, indivisible, whole, integer. Democritus' embrace of the void offered seventeenth century thinkers not so much a means of thinking about 'nothing' in a new way as a classical imprimatur to a mode of thinking that they already, unknowingly, possessed.

* * *

King Lear and 'Nothing'

Whatever its role at the centre of Moses de Leon's theosophic scheme, zero's impact on European consciousness from the thirteenth century was plainly not through the Kabbalah, but in an obvious and direct way as a number: as a Hindu numeral in the arithmetic of money, and as the principle of zero balance in the double-entry book-keeping that controlled the expanding market of credit, debt, and commodities engendered by mercantile capitalism.

The disruption and moral disintegration inherent in capitalism's threat to commoditise social reality, its capacity to nihilise fellow feeling and reduce human beings to acquisitive wolves fixated on money and power, is the central theme of two plays, Jonson's *Volpone* and Shakespeare's *King Lear*, written a year of each other in London around 1605.

Both playrights would have learned about numbers at school some thirty years earlier, and were in the first generation of children in England to have learned about zero from Robert Recorde's *Arithmetic*, which bases itself on a strange pedagogical mixture of the new decimal notation and the old abacus manipulations. And they wrote their plays at the historical point of transition between two methods of writing down monetary accounts: when the new Hindu numerals based on zero and the traditional abacus-based Roman ones about to be ousted by them existed, briefly, side by side, until the eclipse of Roman numerals signalled the death of a feudal classical order and the arrival of the accounting practices, and the commoditised reality of mercantile capitalism.

Both plays dramatise reductions to nothing, charting the annihilation of human warmth, the dissolution of social, natural, familial bonds, the emptying of kindness, sympathy, tenderness, love, pity, affection into hollow shells, into substitutes for themselves which take part in the deal, the transaction, the exchange. Jonson's play – a satire rooted in the social immediacy and cultural details of its milieu – confronts 'nothing' as a predetermined moral and social given, the depraved end-point of the moral scale occupied by pure 'inhuman', vulpine, greed. Focusing on the social route to 'nothing' through all the literal and palpable details of gold, money, and the manipulations thereof, *Volpone* does not and does not need to interest itself in the metaphysics of 'nothing', in the nature of annihilation and of being 'nothinged' *per se*. Shakespeare's interest in 'nothing' (like Donne's and like that of the *nihil* paradoxists of the sixteenth century) was more intellectually alert, allusive, and linguistically abstract than Jonson's. And more varied: from the comic play on nothing/vagina in *Much Ado About Nothing* and in Hamlet's savaging of Ophelia in *Hamlet*, to the fixation on Time's nothing – oblivion – and the self's ambitious ascent into nothing, on the 'absence, darkness, death; things which are not' in *Macbeth*, to nothing begetting nothing in *King Lear*, whose *ex nihilo nihil fit*, is given the lie by human love being annihilated and counted out of existence by all that comes from 'nothing'.

The action of the play opens with Lear old, wishing to crawl unburdened to his grave, about to play out a promissory deal, a transactional charade, whose unreal premise involves an exchange of material goods for spoken signs: he will hand over portions of his kingdom – land, goods, the privileges, prerogatives and exercise of royal power – to each of his daughters in exchange for formulaic utterances, set empty speeches of love for him. In this opening scene Lear is contriving to absent himself, to dissolve a certain feudal self, to annihilate the unitary, gothic self of his kinghood, by selling it; transacting it in precisely those terms alien to its

> Lear: . . . which of you shall we say doth love us most that we
>   our largest bounty may extend.
>
> (I (i) 52)

The demand of 'most' for 'largest', the maximum amount of love for a, ceremoniously, measurable portion of the kingdom, reveals that it is in the one-dimensional language of quantity – arithmetic – that Lear has constructed his deal. It is a deal which treats love as a commodity, something to be bought and sold by suitably formulated speech: speech fashioned so as not to 'mar . . . fortunes', speech that had internalised the principle of the deal to become the language of commerce.

Goneral and Regan render him – in language that is obsequious, mechanically filled with comparatives and superlatives of quantity, transparently duplicitous to the audience if not to Lear – the verbal formula he seems to want. He is made to appear satisfied: they immediately get their portions. Cordelia, appalled and emptied by the cynical ease of her sisters' lies, can neither signify her love in this way, nor withdraw and refuse the transaction, nor remain silent:

> *Lear*:   . . . what can you say to draw a third more opulent than
>   you sisters? Speak.
> *Cordelia*: Nothing my lord.
> *Lear*:   Nothing?
> *Cordelia*: Nothing.
> *Lear*:   Nothing will come out of nothing: speak again.
>
> (I(i)90)

No encounter with *King Lear* could miss the force and threat of such a 'nothing,' or avoid the ominous warnings of disruption, the promise of violent explosion it sends echoing through the play. From Cordelia's 'nothing', and its double in the sub-plot uttered by Edmund, the action and the themes of this tragedy bitterly and relentlessly unfold: Kent is instantly nullified, banished. Cordelia is repudiated, robbed, disowned, and ultimately hanged. Gloucester, Lear's aged double, is sadistically blinded. And Lear is riven apart, by a great arc of reason-filled madness, and dies at the very moment he faces his blindness to 'nothing'. The play shows the destruction of a world and a self by a force derived from 'nothing'; a force wearing the mask, as we shall see, of zero.

In forcing Cordelia to outbid her sisters Lear coerces her into the world of exchangeable commodities where, before the play has started, he has trapped himself. Cordelia's attempt at silence comes from the intuition that any answer to Lear's question would make sense only in a world where love, as she has to understand it, is absent. But, unlike the Fool who can make mock of the difference between silence and saying nothing, the moral space she occupies precludes any doubleness. She cannot voice this absence; she can only say 'nothing'.

Cordelia is made to stand for, embody, and, throughout the play, never depart from a conception of natural love as love in *action*, in kinship, in context, in use, in obligation, in mutual responsibility. Shakespeare puts it all into the verbs:

> *Cordelia*: You have begot me, bred me, lov'd me I
>   Return those duties back as are right fit
>   Obey you, love you, and most honour you.
>
> (I(i)98)

These verbs express the domestic pieties of the classic and gothic, pre-Renaissance, world. A world under threat, within which love takes place through lived action; it recreates itself through obligations, duties, promises, and contracts of nurture. Such love is produced, and has meaning only in situ, in the context of its production. practice, which is how Cordelia conceives it, by love neutralised into a *commodity*, an item within a system of measurable values. And in doing so rapes it.

It is this violation, this destruction that *King Lear* relentlessly and obsessively pursues. The play was written in a London of bubonic plague, cheap death, religious burnings, torture; a London given over to the deal: the buy/sell transactions of a risingly brutal capitalism dealing in information through spies and informers, flesh through rampantly exploitative prostitution, liberty and freedom through indentures and slavery. It sets up, and ultimately recoils in horror from, what it conceives to be the terminal transaction: the buying and selling of natural love.

For Cordelia, confronted with Lear's question about love ('how much?') the only response, the only one possible in her moral universe, is silence. Her 'nothing', her failed attempt to remain silent, to stay outside the language of commodities set up by Lear, becomes for him an answer – the arithmetically worst answer – to his question. Obsessed by the need to close his deal Lear converts Cordelia's unarticulated refusal to bid – a meta-sign about deals which she has not the means to express – into a bid.

What Lear, blind to the difference between silence and saying nothing, between a sign and a sign about signs, has to be made to see is the nature of Cordelia's 'nothing'. His education into the meaning of 'nothing' is through numbers. He is given two lessons in the arithmetic of nothing; first by the Fool, who serves as Cordelia's moral and intellectual surrogate, and then by his other two daughters. Both lessons end on zero.

The first reference to Lear's Fool, pining for Cordelia, establishes him as her proxy, her advocate in the case of 'nothing'. He begins by teasing Lear with a piece of doggerel, a commonplace *nihil* skit which, by quantifying the world out of existence and ending on the request for nothing, allusively mocks the whole arithmetical language and fate of Lear's deal.

Fool: Mark it, Nuncle:
Have more than thou showest
Speak less than thou knowest
Lend less than thou owest
Ride more than thou goest

> Learn more than thou trowest
> Set less than thou throwest
> Leave thy drink and thy whore
> And keep in-a-door
> And thou shalt have more
> than two tens to a score.
>
> (I(iv)133)

> *Kent*: This is nothing fool.
>
> (I(iv)134)

Then the Fool twits Lear directly:

> *Fool*: Can you make no use of nothing Nuncle?
>
> (I(iv)138)

Lear, oblivious to the Fool's line of attack, still anaesthetised to the import and significance of Cordelia's 'nothing', repeats his formula from the opening scene:

> *Lear*: Why, no, boy; nothing can be made out of nothing.
>
> (I(iv)139)

Lear's foolish, uncomprehending repetition proves unbearable to the Fool, who explodes into scorn, and taunts Lear into being a bitter fool. Then the Fool returns to 'nothing' tracing its shape from an egg to a coin to a crown to Lear's bald, empty, head. Then, more explicitly, with a growing satirical edge, an emptied place:

> *Fool*: I'd rather be any kind of thing than a fool; and yet I would not be thee Nuncle. Thou has pared thy wits on both sides and left nothing in the middle
>
> (I(iv)192)

And finally, in the terminal and terminating barb:

> *Fool*: Thou art an O without a figure. I am better than thou art now; I am a fool, thou art nothing.
>
> (I(iv)202)

Lear is reduced to a zero and to nothing. And as a last flourish on the difference between a sign for silence and silence, the difference between saying nothing and saying 'nothing', he turns to Goneril:

> *Fool*: Yes, forsooth, I will hold my tongue; so your face bids me
> though you say nothing.

(I(iv)204)

It is now the turn of Goneril and Regan to diminish Lear to zero. Where the Fool was satirical, allusive, allegorical, Goneril is viscious and immediate. She vilifies the remnant of Lear's kinghood – his entourage of one hundred knights and squires – as a brothel rabble and suggests in arithmetically icy language, that he 'disquantity' it. Goneril and Regan start to systematically contract Lear's kinghood, to disquantity it by numerical shrinkage: they halve his train of one hundred to fifty, and then again to twenty-five. At this point Lear perceives, bitterly, for the first time, that he might be a victim of the very language of commodities he has instituted.'

> *Lear*: Thy fifty doth double five and twenty
> And thou art twice her love.

(II(iv)262)

Made to bid for *himself*, to turn himself into an object of commerce, he begins to fear the Fool's *nihil*, the disintegration of himself, the self-dissolution, that lies at the end of this arithmetic reduction. Goneril and Regan leave him in no suspense: from one hundred they move swiftly through fifty, twenty-five, ten, one, and then with

> *Regan*: What need one?

(I(iv)265)

Lear arrives at zero. Thus the language of arithmetic, in which his train of followers is counted down to nothing, and in which the Fool articulates the loss of Lear's kinghood as a thing reduced to zero, becomes the vehicle and image of the destruction of Lear's self and of natural love. Both, by being converted into number signs, are emptied, neutered, stripped of human content. After this Lear knows he will go mad. And when he does, his first release is to rage with demented fixation on the 'need' denied him by Regan, the need for gratitude, for companionship, for justice and the need which he has murdered and cannot ask for, the need for 'natural' human love; needs which now count for nothing in a world where 'What need one?' reduces human beings to dumb creatures, to isolated pre-social nothings.

Cordelia's 'nothing' which detonates Lear's reduction to madness and zero is reproduced – to the word – in the sub-plot of the play, where again it initiates a chain that ends in inhumanity and violence. Edmund, feigning brotherly protectiveness, pretends to conceal a letter he has written, supposedly from his brother Edgar, which reveals Edgar as plotting against their father Gloucester:

> *Gloucester*: What paper are you reading.
> *Edmund*: Nothing my lord.
> *Gloucester*: No? What needed then that terrible dispatch of it into your pocket. The quality of nothing hath not such need to hide itself. *Let's see: come; if it be nothing I shall not need spectacles.*
>
> (I(ii)35)

Indeed he will not need spectacles, for his eyes will be gouged out before he can see the treachery of Edmund's 'nothing'. Edmund is a Machiavel, ruthless, fast, self-made from nothing. His origin is a void: a bastard, conceived òutside sanctioned kin, a whore's son, whose mother, his 'natural' beginning, the play reduces to an empty vaginal hole – a nothing – as 'dark and viscious' as Gloucester's eye sockets will become.

Lear's madness, made hot by the fantasy of revenge, comes to be dominated by an all-devouring obsession with sexual generation. And it rides him on a journey that ends in death and the emptiness of an inhuman, mechanical repetition. His call for revenge is cloaked at first in the language of justice. He sets up a mock trial of Goneril and Regan, but is unable to finish it – to do so would be to visit the origin, the initiating 'nothing' of his own madness. This he cannot do, and so is condemned to go on, reproducing its consequences blindly, without human purpose, until he finds his sons-in-law and has his suitably mechanical, mindless, and repetitive revenge of 'kill, kill, kill, kill, kill, kill'.

Sexual generation starts with copulation:

> *Lear*: I pardon that man's life. What was thy cause?
> Adultery?
> Thou shalt not die: die for adultery. No:
> The wren goes to 't and the small gilded fly

Does lecher in my sight.
Let copulation thrive

(IV(vi)117)

By accusing birds and insects of adultery – patently absurd – Lear is being made to grasp at the distinction between sanctioned, lawful, 'natural' sexuality, and the uncontrolled lust of copulation. But he is unable to separate the two, instead they are joined in the figure of a centaur: half the gods' inheritance, half the sulphorous pit. The image is unstable, the pit swallows the rest, and Lear ends in an invective of disgust and revulsion at the stench of the female part (the smell of nothing) and of mortality. Where earlier, in the sonnets, Shakespeare saw lust, however destructive, as part of the human moral order, an expense of spirit in a waste of shame, he portrays it here as dehumanised and empty. Sexuality, reduced to no more than the urgent quivering of a fly, shrinks to mindless vibration, a blind animal urge to repeat in a world where the loss of human love makes anything else impossible. And procreation is dead, replaced by an unnatural grotesque continuation, replicating ingratitude, hate, and lifelessness. Lear will have no grandchildren, no 'natural' continuation, no issue from a site he has already cursed:

Lear: Into her womb convey sterility
Dry up in her the organs of increase
And from her derogate body never spring
A babe to honour her.

(I(iv)287)

The two great themes of *King Lear*, human blindness to itself, to love, and the horror of *ex nihil*, of that which issues from nothing, are reflected and doubled between the plot and the sub-plot. Cordelia and Edgar, both legitimate heirs, both innocent, both loved, maligned, repudiated, usurped, banished, both witnessing the seeing and unseeing madness of their fathers, are mirror reflections of the same 'natural' love. Likewise Edmund's literal bastardy finds its image, and sexual confirmation, in the unnatural daughterhood, the figurative bastardy of Goneril and Regan. Lear's metaphorical blindness to the literal 'nothing' wrenched from Cordelia, which fills the play, is the invisible double of Gloucester's staged, full view, all too literal, blinding engendered by Edmund's 'nothing'.

Lear's metaphorical blindness is also a blindness to metaphor. He cannot 'see' the ambiguity of Cordelia's 'nothing', he is blind to the difference between a meta-sign whose meaning is to deny the possibility of speaking and the literal spoken sign 'nothing'. Harshly dramatised in his separation from Cordelia and the reduction of his kinghood to zero, this ambiguity returns, inverted and softened, late in the play when Lear is briefly united with Cordelia. He woos her with a strange and moving domestic fantasy:

> *Lear*: . . . come, let's away to prison;
> We two alone will sing like birds i' the cage
> When thou dost ask me blessing, I'll kneel down,
> And ask of three forgiveness: so we'll live,
> And pray, and sing, and tell old tales, and laugh
> At gilded butterflies, and hear poor rogues
> Talk of court news; and we'll talk with them too,
> Who loses and who wins; who's in and who's out;
> And take upon's the mystery of things,
> As if we were God's spies: and we 'll wear out,
> In a walled prison, packs and sects of great ones
> That ebb and flow by th'moon.

(V(iii)19)

The dream Lear offers Cordelia is the presence-in-absence of ghosts. Protected from the ravages of the world, the machinations of power and the passing of time, enclosed in a mythical and benign mutuality, distanced from others and from their selves as spies for an absent God they will exist in an unreal stasis, as ambiguous signs of signs, living by proxy, both in life and at one remove from life – on a meta-level – through the gossip and court news that make up the spoken signs of life.

The play ends with an address:

> *Edgar*:   The weight of this sad time we must obey;
> Speak what we feel, and not what we ought to say.
> The oldest hath borne most: we that are young
> Shall never see so much, nor live so long.

(V(iii)326)

Who are the 'we' here? Read as a conventional tragic coda pointing inwards to the dramatic events, 'this sad time' is the fictional time created by the play, and the 'we' signifies the generation left on stage – those whose lives pale before that of their tragic king.

But there is also an external reading: one can interpret the final address as pointing outwards to make 'this sad time' the early seventeenth century time of its original performance, and 'the young' those that issued from that time; so that the 'we' in the first two lines indicates the remaining characters left to uphold the pieties of natural feeling, while the 'we that are young' points to the unknown future, to those who will never experience these events but must live in the historical wake of those times.

One can, in other words, follow the lead given by the Fool earlier in the play when he 'predicts', as Shakespeare's *contemporary*, that:

> *Fool*: . . . the realm of Albion
>   Come to great confusion:
>   Then comes the time, who lives to see't,
>   That going shall be us'd with feet.
>   This prophecy Merlin shall make; for I live
>   before his time.
>
>   (III(iii)95)

and allow the play to step out of its own mythical time into history. In this case Lear is not a pagan folk king mythologised by Shakespeare, nor some trans-historical figure of nihilism, nor the hero of a Christian epic of Job-like redemption, nor the universal Old Dying Man Goethe took him to be, he is the embodiment of a contemporary, historically unique, social and cultural event. Lear registers, he acts out, he is, the rupture in the medieval world brought about by the transactions of Renaissance capitalism. Read thus, the play is Shakespeare's encounter with the empty doubleness of 'nothing', with the spectre that he saw in those transactions; saw not in terms of abstract meta-signs or some grand metaphysical void but as zero, painfully concretised in the buying and selling of kinghood, self and love through numbers.

References

Colie, R. (1966) *Paradoxia Epidemica* (Princeton: Princeton University Press).

Kirk, G. and Raven, J. (1957) *The Presocratic Philosophers* (Cambridge: Cambridge University Press).

Nishitani, K. (1982) *Religion and Nothingness*, J. Van Bragt (trans.) (University of California Press).

Shakespeare, W. (1969) *King Lear* (London: Methuen).

Unamuno, M. de (1972) *The Tragic Sense of Life* (trans.), A. Kerrigan and M. Nozick (eds) (Princeton: Princeton University Press).

8
Mary Ann Doane, *The Desire to Desire: The Woman's Film of the 1940s* (1988)

With considerable originality, *The Desire to Desire* undertook the detailed study of a particular genre of film at a particular historical moment as the occasion for a critical discussion of issues and concepts central to the semiotic–psychoanalytic film theory developed in the 1970s and early 1980s (the British journal *Screen* – to which Doane herself contributed – played the key role in this development). The book was concerned with possibilities and difficulties raised by the use of that film theory from a feminist perspective, as a means of posing feminist questions of cinema (the major initiating text for that use was Laura Mulvey's 'Visual Pleasure and Narrative Cinema', first published in *Screen* in 1975 and reprinted in her LDS book *Visual and Other Pleasures*). Historical and theoretical, *The Desire to Desire* was also political, engaged in contemporary debates within feminism about women's relations to the mass cultural productions of the given social order of male domination, the understanding of 'female spectatorship', and the problems involved in achieving alternative images and representations.

The term 'woman's film' in Doane's title refers to that group of Hollywood films made in the 1930s/1940s which were directed explicitly at a female audience. With a woman protagonist at their centre, these films treat of matters culturally defined and received as 'female' (those of domestic life, parent–child relations, maternal self-sacrifice, and so on); their tone then tends to the melodramatic and the heavily emotional (within those overall parameters, the 'woman's film' can be divided into a number of sub-groups, as Doane indicates in the following extract). The female spectator is part of the picture, a representation the film makes: it addresses its representation of *her:she* as the point of its desire – the desire it has for her, offers her, and to which it holds her. In a series of analyses, Doane brings out the terms of this representation and shows the involvement of female pleasure in this cinema as being complicit with masochistic constructions of femininity; the films, indeed, activate a pathos which embraces and celebrates loss, reconciling the spectator to the terms of the given social-gender order. This blockage of desire, however, does not exhaust the films which, in their attempts to trace the contours of female subjectivity and desire within the traditional forms and conventions of Hollywood narrative (forms and conventions which cannot easily sustain such an exploration) produce disturbances, 'stress points', as Doane calls them. As is apparent from this extract, she makes no radical claims for these; rather, their demonstration and analysis may be useful as 'a kind of lever to facilitate the production of a desiring subjectivity for the woman – in another cinematic practice'. It is in this context that the discussion at the end of the extract of moments of 'double mimesis' in these 1940s films can be understood. For Doane, what is important is the possibility her analyses may provide for an understanding of 'a political textual strategy' involving the enactment of a 'defamiliarized version of femininity'.

The shadow of her gaze

> And her eye has become accustomed to obvious 'truths' that actually hide what she is seeking. It is *the very shadow of her gaze* that must be explored (Irigaray, 1985, p. 193).
>
> Luce Irigaray

The preceding chapters constitute an attempt to expose those 'obvious truths' of femininity as they are inscribed within the woman's film and to defamiliarize them, to break down and subject to analysis their very obviousness. For this reason, the project may seem too fully to embrace the stereotypes and given images of the 'feminine', to accept those psychical conditions associated with the woman – masochism, narcissism, hysteria, intensification of affect or 'emotionalism', an entire pathology of the feminine – far too readily. And in a sense this is true. These are the culturally constructed positions of femininity which the films represent and re-represent in particularly moving and intense forms. It is a mistake to believe that women have the option of simply accepting or rejecting these positions, a mistake buttressed by a misunderstanding of subjectivity and its relation to discourse. What is far more important than a declared rejection of such familiar tropes is the activity of analysing them in relation to processes of representation and meaning, delineating the positions from which texts become readable and meaningful to female spectators.

The major breakthrough in feminist film theory has been the displacement of its critical focus from the issue of the positive or negative representations or images of women to the question of the very organisation of vision and its effects. This has the decided advantage of demonstrating that processes of imaging women and of specifying the gaze in relation to sexual difference, like most forms of sexism, are far more deeply ingrained than one might initially suspect. From this point of view, it can never be enough simply to reverse sexual roles or to produce positive or empowered images of the woman. It is the constitution of vision as a process both within the filmic text (the representation of the woman seeing) and between text and spectator which most warrants attention. Part of my attempt here has been to demonstrate that the feminine does not exist in a patriarchal society merely as the negation or 'Other' of the male. We are not always dealing with the binary opposition male/nonmale, and the phenomenon of spectatorship is a case in point. As Foucault (1978) maintains, the analysis of power through its negative means, censorship and repression, does not exhaust its effects. Power also works positively to construct the positions which subjects inhabit. Western culture has a quite specific notion of what it is to be a woman and what it is to be a woman looking. When a woman looks, the verb 'looks' is generally intransitive (she *looks* beautiful) – generally, but not always. When the woman looks in order to see, the trajectory of that gaze, and its relation to the otherwise nonproblematic opposition between subject and object, are highly regulated. Her positioning as a very specific kind of spectator lays the groundwork for and dovetails with her activity as a consumer.

The premise of the woman's film as it solicits the female gaze is that this gaze abolishes the distance conducive to voyeurism. The oppositions between 'having' and 'being' and between 'being' and 'appearing' are collapsed in order to produce a desire for the image/commodity which is all the more insistent as it fails to differentiate between the image/commodity as object and the spectator as desiring subject. The association of the woman with sympathy, empathy, and a type of overidentification with the image contributes to the commodification of the body which is so pervasive even, or especially, today. The discourse of psychoanalysis provides the theoretical rationalisation of such a positioning of the woman in its conceptualisation of hysteria. For, as Freud points out, hysterical imitation (which is only the surface manifestation of hysterical identification) is 'sympathy, as it were, intensified to the point of reproduction' (1965, p. 183). The woman's film tends to rely heavily on pathos as the means of activating this type of relation to the screen. Pathos always connotes a loss or fading of individual subjectivity in the process of signification. As Bakhtin demonstrates, 'A discourse of pathos is fully sufficient to itself and to its object. Indeed, the speaker completely immerses himself [sic] in such a discourse, there is no distance, there are no reservations' (1981, p. 394). One might add that the situation of the receiver of the discourse mimics that of the speaker – immersion and loss of a well-defined subjectivity. There is also a sense in which the discourse of pathos purports to be the most mimetic of discourses, presenting itself as an 'unmediated impression deriving from the object itself . . . one unencumbered by any ideological presuppositions' (ibid., pp. 394–8). This is the mechanism by means of which the woman's film claims that it is only a text which speaks no more than the obvious, the already familiar truths of everyday life, the details of intersubjective relations.

Pathos is thus one way of containing the potentially disruptive effects of attributing the gaze to the woman, of delineating a specifically female subjectivity. The decade of the 1940s, with its reorganisation of sexual roles due to the war and the intensity of its very felt need to sustain a consumer perception despite the shortage of commodities, marks a crisis point in the elaboration of female subjectivity. The films align themselves with an entire array of extracinematic discourses; they feel the effect of the introduction of psychoanalysis in the Hollywood cinema as a means of institutionalizing and directing the woman's discourse about herself, together with the necessity for new theories of the mother/child relation which constrain and limit maternal activity to a site which is neither too far from nor too close to the child. In the late 1940s, the paranoia associated with relations between the sexes is evinced in the pervasive influence of the gothic form.

These pressures on filmic representation make it extremely productive to trace and analyse the trajectory of the female gaze, its vicissitudes across the four subgroups of the woman's film. In the films of the medical discourse, more than in any other group, the woman is most nearly the pure object of the gaze. She is deprived of subjectivity through the displacement of the sympathy one might have expected to characterise the relation between spectator and film to the diseased body of the female protagonist. This body is fully in sympathy with the psyche, hence the disease is not accidental or contingent, but essential to her being. The female body is above all symptomatic, and it is the doctor who is therefore endowed with a gaze – a gaze which demonstrates, for the male subject, the compatibility of rationality and desire. The logical outcome of this suppression of female subjectivity is the blindness of Bette Davis in *Dark Victory*. In the maternal melodrama, separation between mother and child is thematised, inducing distance and even voyeurism (as when Stella Dallas watches her daughter from afar). The window is the figure of this separation and of this distance manufactured in the service of the symbolic. But the pathos which plays a dominant role in the maternal melodrama works to close the gap between spectator and text. In the love story the attempted eroticisation of the gaze is turned back on itself to produce the narcissism traditionally associated with the woman, the mirror constituting its most exemplary figure. The narcissistic relation of spectator to screen is transformed into a divided identification with the male character loving the woman and with the woman in the process of being loved. Yet the desire attributed to the female subject in this group of films is often so excessive that the only satisfactory closure consists in her death. When this becomes literally the death of a point of view, as in *Humoresque* and *Waterloo Bridge*, the mechanics of the love story and its failed attempt to contain and constrain female desire are exposed. Finally, it is in the paranoid gothic films that the attempt to attribute the epistemological gaze to the woman results in the greatest degree of violence. Due to the difficulty in localising, confining, and restraining the representation of paranoid subjectivity in the cinema, the cinematic apparatus itself is activated against the woman, its aggressivity an aggressivity of the look and the voice, directed against her.

Despite the many differences between the various subgroups of the woman's film, one can trace a consistency in certain recurrent themes as well as in the dependence on a limited number of spatial and temporal categories. In terms of the representation of time, the woman's film shows a marked preference for a mistiming which facilitates the production of pathos (particularly in the maternal melodrama and the love story) and an expansion of time which simulates the type of time most fully associated with women – the time of waiting and duration. A time which is intensified through suspense and expectation is foreign to most of the films, found only in those of the gothic group and those strongly influenced by film noir such as *Mildred Pierce*. Similarly, space is constricted in the woman's film, usually to the space of the home. The opposition between inside and outside in relation to the house attains a significance which it rarely reaches in other genres. In *Reckless Moment*, the difficulties begin when the outside, in the guise of a figure from the underworld, invades the inside of the family home. The house often becomes uncanny or claustrophobic. In this narrowing of space the most humble of objects signifies, but for that very reason it is often difficult to tell that signification is taking place, that these films witness the transformation of the 'natural' fact or domestic entity (which one usually takes for granted) into the sign. In a patriarchal society, women's genres are characterised by a kind of signifying glut, an overabundance of signification attached to the trivial. In the woman's film there is a hypersignification of elements of the domestic – doors, windows, kitchens, bedrooms. The staircase functions multiply as the site of the woman's specularisation, her pathway from curiosity to terror, and as a symbolic prison (at the end of *Reckless Moment* and in *Beyond the Forest*). In watching a woman's film, one actively senses the contraction of the world attributed to the woman, the reduction of meaning and its subordination to affect.

Such an account of the spatial and temporal coordinates of the woman's film can be depressing insofar as it suggests that even in its deep structure this type of film is ideologically complicit. In feminist film criticism, it often seems that politics and pleasure are absolutely incompatible. This is due to the fact that feminist criticism manifests itself primarily as a work of negation of the given images, the given desires. And what often gets lost in the process is the issue of women's pleasure. This partially explains, I think, the temptation to return to genres specifically demarcated as feminine in order to retrieve something *for* the woman, something which belongs to her alone and escapes the patriarchal stranglehold. This is the logic behind studies such as that of Janice Radway on the paperback romance and its reception. Such studies tend to emphasise the ways in which individual readers or spectators use the texts of mass culture for their own purposes and therefore produce more positive and empowering meanings than critics give them credit for. Another strategy for dealing with women's genres is that of re-evaluation, taking the characteristics attributed to women in these texts and designating them as hierarchically superior to male values and attributes. This is, of course, to implicitly accept these characteristics or attributes as fully adequate definitions of femininity.

The question of pleasure is a difficult one, and it is tempting to advocate the usurpation of pleasure from patriarchal representations wherever that is possible. But it is crucial to remember that textual pleasure is produced primarily through processes of recognition and misrecognition. The texts of mass culture represent to the female spectator those gestures and desires which are purportedly 'feminine', purportedly her own. And what is 'recognised' by the spectator is something quite different from what is stolen – the gestures and desires become the basic elements of a complex signifying structure which reinforces a fairly rigid understanding of sexual difference. In short, we are dealing with a process of *mis*recognition. It is not that women's genres have nothing to do with a marginalised female culture which organises certain experiences and specifies them as the property of women, but that something gets lost in the transition. As John Brenkman points out, mass culture involves a process of 'respeaking'.

> The mass-mediated discourse respeaks and so silences its socially rooted subtexts. . . . On the one hand, the mass communication is effective only insofar as we hear in it some echo of our actual or virtual collective speaking – which is why even the most manipulative examples of mass culture contain a residual utopian or critical dimension. On the otherhand, the mass-mediated public sphere establishes a schism between what I hear and what I speak, such that I receive a message I would not speak and am forced to read in it the figure of my needs, my desires, and my identity – which is why effective resistance does not emerge from the reception situation itself (1979 p. 105).

Femininity is *stylised* through the work of the woman's film. The genre returns to us the familiar scenarios of waiting, giving, sacrificing, and mourning ennobled and made acceptable by the very fact of their narrativisation. What is needed is a means of making these gestures and poses *fantastic*, literally *incredible*.

And it is true that the credibility of these representations is sometimes undermined, in isolated images or scenes. In the process of 'respeaking' the woman's desire something slips through. Or more accurately, perhaps, a 'respoken' femininity is subjected to a respeaking in its turn. Double mimesis renders void the initial mime or, at the very least, deprives it of its currency. There is a slip-page between the two representations. This type of doubling is described by Silvia Bovenschen when she claims, with respect to a recent performance by Marlene Dietrich, '. . . we are watching a woman demonstrate the representation of a woman's body' (1977, p. 129). Or, as Roland Barthes maintains, '. . . the best weapon against myth is perhaps to mythify it in its turn, and to produce an *artificial* myth' (1972, p. 135). In the woman's film, the process of remirroring reduces the mirror effect of the cinema, it demonstrates that these are poses, postures, tropes – in short, that we are being subjected to a discourse on femity.

This 'double mimesis' occurs in the woman's film at moments in the text where the woman appears to produce a reenactment of femininity, where her gestures are disengaged from their immediate context, made strange. In *Stella Dallas* this moment is a scene in which Stella effectively parodies herself, pretending to be an even more exaggeratedly embarrassing mother than she is in the rest of the film. She *exhibits* her garishness and lack of taste through her dress, her manners, her choices in men, music, and language – all in order to convince her daughter Laurel that she should forsake Stella for her father. It is this notion of maternal sacrifice which ultimately recuperates the scene, but for the duration of the pretense, at any rate, the excessiveness of her role is clearly visible. In *Gaslight*, this kind of doubling occurs at the end of the film when Ingrid Bergman acts out the part of the mad wife – a role which her husband had laboriously prepared for her by intensifying her self-consciousness about her looks and her memory. In *Dark Victory*, Bette Davis mimes sight; she pretends to be able to see in order to be the good housewife, packing for her husband, even finding a hole in his sock through the sense of touch. In another Bette Davis film, *Beyond the Forest*, she reenacts in exaggerated form her own narcissism, misapplying makeup and dressing up in a grotesque parody of herself that underlines the absurdity of the woman's status as spectacle.

But the most striking instance of this 'double mimesis' is a scene in *The Gay Sisters* (Irving Rapper, 1942). Toward the middle of the film the eldest sister, Fiona (Barbara Stanwyck), tells her two sisters what she refers to as a 'bed time story'. It is basically a story about how she tricked a man into marrying her so that she could obtain her inheritance. The man, Charles Barclay (George Brent), turns out to be the person who, in the present tense of the film, is attempting to claim for himself the property belonging to the Gaylord sisters. Her flashback account presents, in a distanced form, all the clichés of the love story. It consists of images which bear all the signs of a romance accompanied by Fiona's voice-over, which works to undermine the credibility of the images. In the images, Fiona plays the silent role of a shy and demure young woman. But her voice-over narration is clearly sarcastic, activating the prose of a cheap romance. That narration consists of phrases such as: 'He got that spaniel look in his eyes', 'His manly heart pounding', 'I walked over and sat demurely', 'I threw him a soft and pleading look', 'I expected at any minute an orchestra to start up' and 'I'll never forget the stink of those apple blossom'. The sequence forces a divergence between voice and body in the representation of the woman. Her voice is mocking, distanced, while her body assumes the poses of idealised romance – looking shyly down and away, not allowing the man to hold her hand. In a contradiction of the classical hierarchy of image over sound, the voice is clearly given more truth value here than the image. The image is false, and the woman's voice directs our reading of it. For her own purposes, the woman mimes the gestures and language of the romance. The disruptive effect of the sequence is, however, cancelled by its rather violent ending, in which Barclay essentially rapes Fiona, claiming that it is his right as her husband. Furthermore, Fiona's sisters laugh at the ending of the story, implying that she deserved what she got. And ultimately the image reasserts its claim to truth at the end of the film, when Barclay and Fiona make up and 'really' kiss. Nevertheless, the sequence does posit, if only for a short time, the possibility of a radical distance between the woman and her 'own', fully feminised gestures.

The 'doubling' in these films is particularly crucial in a discourse which is addressed specifically to women, since the prevailing filmic assumption is that female spectatorship is characterised by a closeness to, an affinity with, the image. Fiona's ability to hold the image at arm's length and to analyse it, as well as her ability to enact a defamiliarised version of femininity, bring to mind the strategy of *mimicry* advocated by Luce Irigaray:

> One must assume the feminine role deliberately. Which means already to convert a form of subordination into an affirmation, and thus to begin to thwart it. . . . To play with mimesis is thus, for a woman, to try to recover the place of her exploitation by discourse, without allowing herself to be simply reduced to it. It means to resubmit herself – inasmuch as she is on the side of the 'perceptible,' of 'matter' – to 'ideas,' in particular to ideas about herself, that are elaborated in/by a masculine logic, but so as to make 'visible,' by an effect of playful repetition, what was supposed to remain invisible: the cover-up of a possible operation of the feminine in language (1985, p. 76).

One does not necessarily have to believe in a specifically feminine relation to language in order to agree that it is only through a disengagement of women from the roles and gestures of a naturalised femininity that traditional ways of conceptualising sexual difference can be overthrown. Mimicry as a political textual strategy makes it possible for the female spectator to understand that recognition is buttressed by misrecognition. From this perspective, fantasy becomes the site of a crucial intervention, and what is at issue is the woman's ability to map herself in the terrain of fantasy. The feminist demand of the cinema cannot be to return our gestures to us, nor to make them more adequate to the real (this type of mimesis is always a trap), but to allow for an active differentiation between gesture and 'essence', a play with the signs previously anchored by a set notion of sexual difference. The fascination which the women's films still exert on us can be taken up and activated in the realm of fantasy rather than melodrama – particularly if fantasy is perceived as a space for work on and against the familiar tropes of femininity. Because everything depends, of course, on how one sees oneself. And it is now possible to *look elsewhere*.

References

Roland Barthes (1972), *Mythologies*, trans. Annette Lavers (New York: Hill and Wang, 1972).

M. M. Bakhtin (1981), *The Dialogic Imagination: Four Essays*, trans. Caryl Emerson and Michael Holquist, ed. M. Holquist (Austin: University of Texas Press), p. 394.

Silvia Bovenschen (1997), 'Is there a feminine aesthetic?', *New German Critique*, no. 10 (winter).

Michel Foucault (1978), *The History of Sexuality*, vol. 1, trans. Robert Hurley (New York: Pantheon Books).

John Brenkman (1979), 'Mass media: from collective experience to the culture of privatization', *Social Text*, no. 1 (winter), p. 105.

Sigmund Freud (1965), *The Interpretation of Dreams*, trans. James Strachey (New York: Avon Books, 1965).

——, *This Sex Which Is Not One*, trans. Catherine Porter (Ithaca: Cornell University Press, 1985).

Luce Irigaray (1985), *Speculum of the Other Woman*, trans. Gillian C. Gill (Ithaca: Cornell University Press, 1985).

Jeanne Redcuss *true* Janice Readway, *Reading the Romance: Women, Patriarchy, and Popular Literature* (Chapel Hill and London: The University of North Carolina Press, 1984). See also Andrea S. Walsh, *Women's Film and Female Experience 1940–1950* (New York: Praeger, 1984).

9

Denise Riley, *'Am I that Name?'* *Feminism and the Category of 'Women' in History*, (1988)

Riley's extended essay, devised as an argumentative contribution to the feminist histo-riography of the 1970s and 80s, suggests that the category of 'women' is to be deployed cautiously and strategically since its meanings are rarely straightforward; if used as an ever-reliable foundation, it will continue to produce more problems for con-temporary feminist analysis than it solves. 'Women' as a category has its own elaborate – and profoundly political – history of production and use, is marked with strange tem-poralities, and is hardly more transhistorical than the category of 'the homosexual', the historical emergence of which has been shown by Foucault. The history of feminism is itself endemically vexed by the ambiguity of 'women' on which it is founded. The book reflects on the extent to which the newish 'human science' of sociology and the development of social policy at the turn of the century, in creating those very ques-tions of 'women', posed as perhaps intractable, did not in fact establish forms of thought which, ostensibly in order to investigate 'sexual difference', constructed their own convictions in sexualised terms from the very beginning. The nineteenth-century intimacy between women and 'the social' is discussed as an invention of this kind, while the history of the suffrage in Britain is seen as an instance of past feminism's pro-ductive games with the instability of 'women'. For the present, reliance on 'the body' as the key to confounding modern anti-essentialism is argued to be worse than useless. The problems of 'sexual difference' cannot be resolved within epistemological frameworks inherited from the nineteenth-century human sciences, but must remain eternally smouldering away – in part because the problem of 'sexual difference' was itself at least partly constitutive in forming these very epistemologies

Bodies, identities, feminisms

Instead of interrogating a category, we will interrogate a woman. It will at least be more agreeable.

(E. P. Thompson, *The Poverty of Theory, or An Orrery of Errors*, 1978)

Let it be a care
How man or child
Be called man or child,
Or woman, woman.
(Laura Riding, 'Care in Calling', *The Poems of
Laura Riding*, 1938)

In my first chapter there were allusions to what I called the peculiar temporalities of 'women'. But what are the consequences of this for feminism; what does it mean to insist that 'women' are only sometimes 'women', and wouldn't this suggestion undercut feminism anyway? As part of my argument that it would not, we could start with a fairly straightforward version of what this temporality might be.

That is, that it's not possible to live twenty-four hours a day soaked in the immediate awareness of one's sex. Gendered self-consciousness has, mercifully, a flickering nature. Yet even here there are at once some puzzles; because to be hit by the intrusions of bodily being – to be caught out by the start of menstruation, for instance – is just not the same as being caught up unexpectedly in 'being a woman'. Only at some secondary stage of reflection induced by something else, some ironic juxtaposition perhaps, would your thought about your body's abrupt interruption become, 'Now, maddeningly, I'm pushed into this female gender.' But what about a classic example of another kind of precipitation into a sexed self-consciousness? You walk down a street wrapped in your own speculations; or you speed up, hell-bent on getting to the shops before they close: a car slows down, a shout comments on your expression, your movement; or there's a derisively hissed remark from the pavement. You have indeed been seen 'as a woman', and violently reminded that your passage alone can spark off such random sexual attraction-cum-contempt, that you can be a spectacle when the last thing on your mind is your own embodiedness. But again, the first thought here, surely, is not, 'Now, humiliatingly, I've become a woman', but rather that you have been positioned antagonistically as a woman-thing, objectified as a distortion.

So in both of these examples, the description of 'suddenly becoming your sex' would be too secondary to be accurate. In the first case, the leakage of blood means that the sovereignty exercised by your hormonal cycle has gone and done it again. You might view this badly timed event as your being taken up – or thrown down – into your sex, but you need not do so. In the second case, the mastery not of 'nature' but of 'man' is so leadenly at work that it has pushed you into what leftist sociologists would once have called an alienated self-recognition. Are there, then, any readily available senses in which a simple conception of 'being a woman at times' can hold good? Are there moments when some, as it were, non-ideological kind of woman-ness irrupts, such that you are for that moment a woman unironically and without compromise?

Someone might well retort, against my dark examples, that the experiences of sexual happiness or of childbearing might furnish resonantly optimistic ways of taking up 'being a woman now'. And that these instances can affirm some solidarities among women; that there are such positive elements to being a woman that only a joyless Puritan could miss them; and that it is exaggeratedly pessimistic to characterise the mutual recognition of woman-ness as merely the exchanged glances of those cornered in the same cells by the epithet 'woman'.

There is an obstinate, perhaps intractable, difficulty inherent in this argument, to which I'll return soon. For the moment, it seems to me that even the apparently simplest, most innocent ways in which one becomes temporarily a woman *are not* darting returns to a category in a natural and harmless state, but are something else: adoptions of, or precipitations into, a designation there in advance, a characterisation of 'woman'. This holds true for even the warmest, the most benign congratulation on one's being 'a real woman'. And while there is indeed a phenomenology of inhabiting a sex, the swaying in and out of it is more like ventures among descriptions than like returns to a founding sexed condition.

So to speak about the individual temporality of being a woman is really to speak about movements between the many temporalities of a designation. And as this designation alters historically, so do these myriad possibilities assume different shapes. 'Women' as a collective noun has suffered its changes, as the chapters above have suggested. If we look at these historical temporalities of 'women' in the same light as the individual temporalities, then once again no originary, neutral and inert 'woman' lies there like a base behind the superstructural vacillations. Some characterisation or other is eternally in play. The question then for a feminist history is to discover whose, and with what effects. This constant characterising also generates the political dilemma for feminism, which – necessarily landed with 'women' – has no choice but to work with or against different versions of the same wavering collectivity.

Is 'women', then, an eternally compromised noun? Suppose it is admitted that even the statistician and the anatomist are up to something when they amass 'women' for their purposes; aren't, say, medical discoveries about preventing cervical cancer examples of a valuable concentration on 'women'? Or legislation for equal rights and educational chances, which must name the social grouping that they help? Or feminist invocations of 'women', which, alert to the differences between them, call for courage and solidarity within and between their pluralities? Granted, it would be wildly perverse to deny that there can be *any* progressive deployments of 'women' – all the achievements of emancipation and campaigning would be obliterated in that denial. My aim is different – it is to emphasise that inherent shakiness of the designation 'women' which exists prior to both its revolutionary and conservative deployments, and which is reflected in the spasmodic and striking coincidences of leftist and rightist propositions about the family or female nature. The cautionary point of this emphasis is far from being anti-feminist. On the contrary, it is to pin down this instability as the lot of feminism, which resolves certain perplexities in the history of feminism and its vacillations, but also points to its potentially inexhaustible flexibility in pursuing its aims. This would include a capacity for a lively and indeed revivifying irony about this 'women' who is the subject of all tongues. A political movement possessed of reflexivity and an ironic spirit would be formidable indeed.

To be named as a woman can be the precondition for some kinds of solidarity. Political rhetorics which orchestrate an identity of 'women' or 'mothers' may generate refusals from their ostensible targets. So, to the well-known Lacanian formula – that there's no becoming a subject without having to endure some corresponding subjection – we could add, a little more optimistically, that there's no becoming a subject without the generation, sooner or later, of a contesting politics of that subject. Nevertheless, this revision doesn't get near the heart of the problem introduced at the beginning of this chapter, of the 'positive' aspects of 'women' as a collectivity.

There is a wish among several versions of Anglo-American feminism to assert the real underlying unities among women, and of the touchstone of 'women's experience'. It is as if this powerful base could guarantee both the integrity and the survival of militant feminism. Other schools, sometimes influenced by readings of Luce Irigaray, emphasise their belief in the necessity of a philosophy which includes the distinctiveness of women's bodies. Despite their different genealogies, both this specifying the feminine and the stress on 'experience' share the conviction that there is a real or potential common essence to being a woman, which must not suffer eclipse. The now familiar device for challenging the essentialism from a feminist perspective attacks its false universality in representing the experiences of, usually, middle-class white western women as if they embraced all womankind. But this move to replace the tacit universal with the qualified 'some women's experience' is both necessary yet in the end inadequate. Below the newly pluralised surfaces, the old problems still linger.

There is no gainsaying the forcefulness of the moment of recognition, the 'but that's me!' of some described experience, which, if the political possibilities are there, will pull some women together into a declared feminism. Perhaps it is not so much the 'experience' that is the puzzle which persists after the pluralising correction has been made, but the 'women's experience'. The phrase works curiously, for it implies that the experiences originate with the women, and it masks the likelihood that instead these have accrued to women not by virtue of their womanhood alone, but as traces of domination, whether natural or political. And while these may indeed pertain uniquely to one sex, they can hardly be used to celebrate or underwrite the state of being a woman without many gloomier qualifications. But it is virtually impossible for feminism to unpick 'women's experience' to its own satisfaction. This is because, in its historical analysis, social upheavals produce the experiences; but then, rather than appealing to the altered 'women' who are the constructions or the outcome of these, feminism, a product itself of these revolutionary processes, appeals for solidarity to an embryonic consciousness of women. Because of its drive towards a political massing together of women, feminism can never whole-heartedly dismantle 'women's experience', however much this category conflates the attributed, the imposed, and the lived, and then sanctifies the resulting mélange.

But do we always need the conviction of unifying experience to ground a rallying cry? Donna Haraway has denied this:

> We do not need a totality in order to work well. The feminist dream of a common language, like all dreams for a perfectly faithful naming of experience, is a totalizing and imperialist one. In that sense, dialectics too is a dream language, longing to resolve contradiction.[1]

She pursues her attack on that spectrum of identities and identifications which constitute some contemporary feminist thought:

> Feminisms and Marxisms have run aground on Western epistemological alternatives to construct a revolutionary subject from the

perspective of a hierarchy of oppressions and/or a latent position of moral superiority, innocence, and greater closeness to nature. With no available original dream of a common language or original symbiosis promising protection from hostile 'masculine' separation, but written into the play of a text that has no finally privileged reading or salvation history, to recognise 'oneself' as fully implicated in the world frees us of the need to root politics in identification, vanguard parties, purity, and mothering.[2]

It might be objected that there are marxisms which refuse wholeness, and feminisms which refuse identification – but if we let these qualifications pass, there is still a question as to whether this vivid recommendation to a radical pluralism is able to cope with the fundamental dilemmas lodged in the category 'women'. It vaults over them here, but they must return – or they will do so for as long as sexual division is a bifurcation of the discursive world, a state of affairs that it's hard to envisage withering away. It is that obstinate core of identification, purity, and mothering which helps to underpin the appeal to 'women's experience' – and that core is the concept of the female body.

* * *

Here we are on notoriously difficult ground. Hard, indeed, to speak against the body. Even if it is allowed that the collective 'women' may be an effect of history, what about biology, materiality? Surely, it is argued, those cannot be evaporated into time. And from the standpoint of feminism, what has always been lacking is a due recognition of the specificity of women's bodies, sexual difference as lived. Indeed, Simone de Beauvoir – she who, ironically, has been so often upbraided for paying no attention to precisely what she does name here – wrote in *The Second Sex*:

> In the sexual act and in maternity not only time and strength but also essential values are involved for woman. Rationalist materialism tries in vain to disregard this dramatic aspect of sexuality.[3]

Several contemporary feminisms also set themselves against what they believe to be a damaging indifference to the powerful distinct realities of the body. Here Elizabeth Gross sets out her understanding of the Irigarayan conception:

> All bodies must be male or female, and the particularities, specificities and differences of each need to be recognised and

represented in specific terms. The social and patriarchal disavowal of the specificity of women's bodies is a function, not only of discriminatory social practices, but, more insidiously, of the phallocentrism invested in the régimes of knowledge – science, philosophy, the arts – which function only because and with the effect of the submersion of women under male categories, values and norms. For Irigaray, the reinscription, through discourses, of a positive, autonomous body for women is to render disfunctional all forms of knowledge that have hitherto presented themselves as neutral, objective or perspective-less.[4]

If, for the moment, we take up this conviction about the political–analytic force of women's bodies and lead it towards history, then our question becomes – In what ways have these social and patriarchal 'disavowals' functioned, and how could the subdued bodies of women be restored in a true form? Do the existing social histories of the female body answer that? They do not. We may leaf through voyeuristic and sensational catalogues of revulsion. That is not to deny that, could they escape being charmed by the morbid, the histories of trained, exploited, or distorted flesh – of bodies raped, circumcised, infected, ignorantly treated in childbirth or subjected to constant pregnancies – would carry some moral force.[5] In respect of the developed countries at least, such accounts would suggest that women are less relentlessly caught in physical toils than they were, as pregnancy can be restricted and gynaecological hazards are far less catastrophic – that in this sense, women can spend less of their lives awkwardly *in* their bodies. But even this fragile assumption of progress can be qualified if we recall that contraception was rarely a complete mystery even when the physiology of reproduction was not deciphered, and that medical Whiggishness must be shaken by many examples – the exhaustion of over-used antibiotics, the ascent of new viral strains, the deeply undemocratic distribution of resources, the advancing technologies of international genocide.

So to the history of the body as a narrative of morbidity and its defeats, we could contrast a historical sociology of the body. This would worry about the management of populations, about social policies drawing on demography or eugenics, about malnutrition caused by economic policy in another hemisphere, the epidemiology of industrial and nuclear pollution, and so forth. Yet in all this, both 'the body' and 'women's bodies' will have slipped away as objects, and become instead almost trace phenomena which are produced by the wheelings-about of great technologies and politics. Is this simply the predictable end of that peculiar hypostatisation, 'the body'? Perhaps it must always be transmuted into bodies in the plural, which are not only marked and marred by famine, or gluttony, destitution or plenty, hazard or planning, but are also shaped and created by them. 'The body' is not, for all its corporeality, an originating point nor yet a terminus; it is a result or an effect.

And yet this train of thought doesn't satisfy our original question of the bodies of women in history. Even a gender-specific historical sociology would somehow miss the point. For instance, we could consider what an account of *men*'s bodies would look like; it would include historical descriptions of sex-related illnesses, heart disease, lung cancer and the statistical challenge here from women; the history of soldiery, war slaughter, conscription; of virility as a concept, of Sparta; of the greater vulnerability of the male foetus; of narcissism and its failures; of disabling conditions of work, of mining accidents; of the invention of the male homosexual as a species-being. A history of prostitution but this time written from the side of the clients, of contraception written from the side of the fathers – to add to the histories of bodily endurance, triumphant musculature, or the humiliations of the feebler of frame. All this and more could count up the male body in history, its frailties and its enjoyments, analogously to women's. Yet the sum of the two parts, men and women, would still not produce a satisfying total of 'the body', now democratically analysed with a proper regard to sexual difference.

What would have gone wrong, then, in the search? A chain of unease remains: that anyone's body is – the classifications of anatomy apart – only periodically either lived or treated as sexed, therefore the gendered division of human life into bodily life cannot be adequate or absolute. Only at times will the body impose itself or be arranged as that of a woman or a man. So that if we set out to track the bodies of women in history, we would assume in advance that which really we needed to catch, instead, on the wing of its formulation. Neither the body marked with time, nor the sexed body marked with time, are the right concepts here. For the impress of history as well as of individual temporality is to establish the body itself as lightly or as heavily gendered, or as indifferent, and for that to run in and out of the eye of 'the social'. It's more of a question of tracing the (always anatomically gendered) body as it is differently established and interpreted as sexed within different periods. If female bodies are thought of as perenially such, as constant and even embodiments of sexed being, that is a misconception which carries risks. If it leads to feminist celebrations of the body as female, which intoxicatingly forget the temporality and malleability of gendered existence, at the same time it makes the feminist critique of, say, the instrumental positioning of women's bodies all the harder to develop coherently, because this critique needs some notion of temporality too. It could be claimed that a characteristic of the sadist's gaze is to fix and freeze its object, to insist on absolute difference, to forbid movement.

There is a further reason for unease with the sufficiency of a historical sociology of the body, sexed or not. In a strong sense the body is a concept, and so is hardly intelligible unless it is read in relation to whatever else supports it and surrounds it. Indeed the queer neutrality of the phrase 'the body' in its strenuous colourlessness suggests that something is up. We could speculate that some of the persistent draw of this 'the body' lies in the tacit promise to ground the sexual, to make intimacy more readily decipherable, less evanescent. But then this enticement is undercut by the fact that the very location of 'the sexual' in the body is itself historically mutable. And 'the body' is never above – or below – history.

This is visible in the degree, for instance, to which it is held co-extensive with the person; to which the mind – body distinction is in play, if at all; to which the soul is held to have the capacity to dominate the flesh. If the contemporary body is usually considered as sexed, exactly what this means now is in part the residue remaining after a long historical dethronement of the soul's powers, which in turn has swayed the balance of sexed nature. The modern western body is what the soul has thoroughly vacated (in favour, for some, of the unconscious). But here there is no symmetry between the sexes, because we can show that 'sex' expanded differently into the old fields of soul and body in a different way for 'women'. I suggested earlier that the eighteenth-century remnants of the soul were flooded with the womanly body, preparing the way for the nineteenth-century naturalising of the species Woman. Any history of how far 'the body' has been read as the measure of the human being would have to include this – how far 'the body' has been read as co-extensive with the gender of its bearer.

Some philosophical writings now hint that 'the body' does have the status of a realm of underlying truth, and try to rescue it from medicine or sociology by making it vivid again. Sebastiano Timpanaro attempts this for socialism in his *On Materialism*.[6] And Michel Foucault, at points in his *History of Sexuality*, treats 'bodies and their pleasures' as touchstones of an anarchic truth, innocent brute clarities which are then scored through with the strategies of bio-technical management from on high.[7] But elsewhere in his work there is nothing of a last court of appeal in the body. On the contrary, in the essay, 'Nietzsche, Genealogy, History', he writes:

> The body is the inscribed surface of events (traced by language and dissolved by ideas), the locus of a dissociated self (adopting the illusion of a substantial unity), and a volume in perpetual disintegration. Genealogy, as an analysis of descent, is thus situated within the articulation of the body and history. Its task is to expose a body totally imprinted by history and the process of history's destruction of the body.[8]

The integrity of the body's claim to afford a starting-point for analysis is refused:

> 'Effective' history differs from traditional history in being without constraints. Nothing in man – not even his body – is sufficiently stable to serve as the basis for self-recognition or for understanding other men.[9]

This Foucauldian body is a deliquescing effect; composed but constantly falling away from itself. What if the 'man' attached to it is erased, and 'woman' set there instead? Has history 'totally imprinted' the bodies of women in different ways?

One train of thought must answer yes. That women's bodies become women's bodies only as they are caught up in the tyrannies, the overwhelming incursions of both nature and man – or, more optimistically, that there are also vehement pleasures and delights to offset a history of unbridled and violent subjection. But to be faithful to the suggestion that 'the body' is really constantly altering as a concept means that we must back off from the supposition that women's bodies are systematically and exhaustively different, that they are unified in an integral otherness. Instead we would need to maintain that women only sometimes live in the flesh distinctively of women, as it were, and this is a function of historical categorisations as well as of an individual daily phenomenology. To say that is by no means to deny that because of the cyclical aspects of female physiology, there may be a greater overall degree of slipping in and out of the consciousness of the body for many women. But even this will always be subject to different interpretations, and nothing more radical than the facts of intermittent physiology really holds the bodies of women together.

Where they are dragged together, a sort of miserable sexual democracy may obtain – of malnutrition, for instance – although then they may well move from being starved bodies to being starved sexed bodies as amenorrhea sets in. But these are rare constructions which do produce 'women's bodies' as the victims of shared sufferings. Conditions of deprivation, of sex-specific hard labour, do also pull together the bent backs of women, but then it is the sexual division of labour which has made the partition – not a natural bodily unity. Another kind of massing of potentially maternal bodies belongs to demographic policies, although even here 'nature' is remote. Of course, if women did not have the capacity of childbearing they could not be arrayed by natalist or anti-natalist plans into populations to be cajoled or managed. But the point is that irrespective of natural capacities, only some prior lens which intends to focus on 'women's bodies' is going to set them in such a light. The body becomes visible as a body, and *as* a female body, only under some particular gaze – including that of politics.

So the sexed body is not something reliably constant, which can afford a good underpinning for the complications of the thousand discourses on 'women'. How and when even the body will be understood and lived as gendered, or indeed as a body at all, is not fully predictable. Again this isn't only a function of an individual phenomenology but of a historical and political phenomenology. There is no deep natural collectivity of women's bodies which precedes some subsequent arrangement of them through history or biopolitics. If the body is an unsteady mark, scarred in its long decay, then the sexed body too undergoes a similar radical temporality, and more transitory states.

Then what is the attraction of the category of the body at all? For those feminist philosophies which espouse it, it promises a means of destabilising the tyranny of systematic blindness of sexual difference. It has to be conceded that such philosophies do not have to assume any naturally bestowed identity of women; the female body can be harshly characterised from above. This is demonstrated through Elizabeth Gross's exposition of the Irigayan schema, a clear, sympathetic account of the feminist reception of that work:

> Psychical, social and interpersonal meanings thus mark the body, and through it, the identities or interiority of sexed objects. The female body is inscribed socially, and most often, individually experienced as a lacking, incomplete or inadequate body. . . . Women's oppression is generated in part by these systems of patriarchal morphological inscription – that is, by a patriarchal symbolic order – or

part by internalised, psychic representations of this inscribed body, and in part as a result of the different behaviours, values and norms that result from these different morphologies and psychologies. Irigaray's aim . . . is to speak about a positive model or series of representations of femininity by which the female body may be positively marked, which in its turn may help establish the conditions necessary for the production of new kinds of discourse, new forms of knowledge and new modes of practice.[10]

It is the conclusion here which worries me – that the goal is a fresh and autonomous femininity, voiced in a revolutionary new language, to speak a non-alienated being of woman. Indeed the 'woman' we have available is severely damaged. But for myself – in common with many other feminists, but unlike many others again – I would not seek the freshly conceived creature, the revelatory Woman we have not yet heard. She is an old enough project, whose repeated failures testify to the impossibility of carving out a truly radical space; the damage flows from the very categorisation 'woman' which is and has always been circumscribed in advance from some quarter or other, rendering the ideal of a purely self-representing 'femininity' implausible. A true independence here would only be possible when all existing ideas of sexual difference had been laid to rest; but then 'woman', too, would be buried.

Such reflections undo the ambition to retrieve women's bodies from their immersions beneath 'male categories, values and norms'. The body circulates inexorably among the other categories which sometimes arrange it in sexed ranks, sometimes not. For the concept 'women's bodies' is opaque, and like 'women' it is always in some juxtaposition to 'human' and to 'men'. If this is envisaged as a triangle of identifications, then it is rarely an equilateral triangle in which both sexes are pitched at matching distances from the apex of the human. And the figure is further skewed by the asymmetries of the histories of the sexes as concepts as well as their present disjointedness. If 'women' after the late seventeenth century undergoes intensified feminising, this change does not occur as a linear shift alone, as if we had moved from mercifully less of 'women' through a later excess of them. Other notions which redefine understandings of the person have their influential upheavals: Reason, Nature, the Unconscious, among many. The periodic hardenings of 'women' don't happen alone or in any necessary continuum (as any history of individualism would need to take into account).

* * *

For 'women' are always differently re-membered, and the gulf between them and the generally human will be more or less thornily intractable. One measure of that gulf is the depth of 'women's' resonances. Is it so highly charged, just as a noun, that it is impassably remote from the human? Can it be claimed that the collective 'women' possesses a virtually metaphorical force, in the way that the theatrical Woman does? And if it does, this force would change. Linguistic studies of the 1950s contemplated the ranges of metaphor. William Empson examined I. A. Richards' proposal that all language was indeed radically metaphorical, but found this wanting; 'cat', Empson objected was a hopeless candidate for metaphor status.[11] The 'woman–beauty' equation was one which Empson would allow; and he believed that such a tacit metaphor as 'woman' carried a 'pregnant' use in which the word was full with its own extra weight. The emotive colouring of some words was, as other linguists described it, an integral part of their signification. But where there could be fullness, so there could be contraction; the historical 'hardening of a convention' might narrow the range of a word. Here Empson offered the example of Chastity, which gradually became restricted in its reference to women's conduct. This alteration came about, he thought, because 'what changes in the language are, so to speak, practical policies'. If it were true that 'a word can become a "compacted doctrine" or even that all words are compacted doctrines inherently' then it would be vital to grasp these means 'by which our language is continually thrusting doctrines upon us, perhaps very ill-considered ones'.[12] Perhaps, Empson concluded, this risky power could be caught at its work through those analyses which had interested I. A. Richards – of the interactions 'between a word's Sense and its Emotion or Gesture'.[13]

To adopt Empson's phrase, the evolutions of 'women' must offer a good instance of a changing 'compacted doctrine'. Is the variant with which post-Enlightenment feminism must tangle, woman as almost an anthropological species-being, nevertheless so impacted that it dooms feminism to being a kind of oppositional anthropology to protect its own kin? Or can we look for evolutions of 'women' itself? Rather than this, Julia Kristeva has suggested that modern European feminism, because of its very invocation of 'women', is itself a temporary form which must wither away. She has described this feminism as in some ways 'but a *moment* in the thought of that anthropomorphic identity which currently blocks the horizon of the discursive and scientific adventure of our species'.[14] So, in her account, 'woman' has merely inherited that baggage of drawbacks belonging to the generic 'man'.

European feminism, trading in this debased currency 'women', has turned into a renewed form of the tedious old anthropomorphism – into a gynomorphism which is equally suspect. In the fullness of revolutionary time, it too would have to be transcended.

Meanwhile she characterises two strands of contemporary feminism. One associates women, using spatial references, to the timelessly maternal. Cyclical, monumental temporalities are allied to an idea of femaleness. As with James Joyce's antithesis, 'Father's time, mother's species', these take their distance from linear, historical notions of time. The result, she writes, is that 'female subjectivity as it gives itself up to intution becomes a problem with respect to a certain conception of time; time as project, teleology, linear and prospective unfolding; time as departure, progression, and arrival – in other words, the time of history'.[15]

This tendency is perfectly consonant with the sensibilities of a newer feminism which lacks interest in the 'values of a rationality dominant in the nation state'.[16] Here it departs from its antecedents, the egalitarian feminism which had spoken to the state, especially on family policy matters. Nevertheless this newer philosophy, despite its theoretical unwillingness to be dealing with political history, in practice often tied in with the older strand. A curious eclecticism, as Kristeva describes it, resulted – a theory of timeless sexual difference which was none the less embedded in history, an '*insertion* into history and the radical *refusal* of the subjective limitations imposed by this history's time on an experiment carried out in the name of the irreducible difference'.[17]

This is a good characterisation too of the history which holds that an eternal sexual antagonism will always be re-enacted in changing skirmishes, as if men and women are the same actors wearing different costumes from scene to scene but whose clashes are always the same. Kristeva takes the opposite stance: 'the very dichotomy. man/woman as an opposition between two rival entities may be understood as belonging to metaphysics'.[18] This must be dismantled through 'the demassification of the problem of difference, which would imply, in a first phase, an apparent de-dramatisation of the "flight to the death" between rival groups and thus between the sexes'.[19]

How, though, to carry out this programme of lowering the dramatic stakes? Not, she argues, by aiming at a 'reconciliation' between the warring sexes, but by relocating the struggle in the opposite arena. That would be 'in the very place where it operates with the maximum intransigence, in other words, in personal and social identity itself, so as to make it disintegrate in its very nucleus'.[20] Such a strategy of disintegration would include intensifying aesthetic practices which bring out 'the relativity of his/her symbolic as well as biological existence'.[21] There is a true radicalism in this attempt to undo given identities, to go beyond the policy of creating counter-identifications. It is evident that 'women' do undergo an excessive bestowal of all too many identities, and forcing new content into the old category is a doomed project. But does it follow that a radical policy of harassing tediously entrenched namings must also hold feminism to be a transitional aspect of what is to be attacked? Certainly if all that feminism could ever manage was a parrot-like reiteration of sexual fixity – it has to be admitted that at worst some versions are that – then its dissolution would be a blessing. But in its past and in its present, feminism is infinitely more ambiguous and sophisticated than that parody allows. Only by ignoring the twists and turns of its history can it be seen as a monotonous proponent of a simple sexual difference, or of an unshaded idea of equality.

Julia Kristeva's recommendation is a bold stroke – that the only revolutionary road will slice through the current confusions to bypass 'women' as an anthropomorphic stumbling-block. But this would only follow if you assume that the identity of 'women' is really coherent, so that you are faced only with the options of revering it, or abandoning it for its hopeless antagonistic conservatism, as she proposes. And it would also only follow if you had an extraordinary faith in the powers of 'aesthetic practices' to erode, for example, the sexual division of labour. A policy of minimising 'women' could be more plausibly pursued by going through the instances of the categorisation in all their diversity to see what these effect, rather than longing to obliterate 'women' wholesale, as if this massification really did represent a unity. But such a scrutiny would not be likely to reach some welcome point of termination. For as long as the sexes are socially distinguished, 'women' will be nominated in their apartness, so that sexual division will always be liable to conflation with some fundamental ontological sexual difference. So feminism, the reaction to this state of affairs, cannot be merely transitional, and a true postfeminism can never arrive.

But if feminism can't be fairly characterised as a passing cloud which heralds the dawn of an ultimate sexual translucency, then neither must it be understood to name untroubled solidities of women. It cannot be a philosophy of 'the real'. Given that the anatomically female person far outstrips the ranges of the limiting label 'woman', then she can always say in all good faith, 'here I am not a woman', meaning 'in this contracting description I cannot recognize myself; there is more to this life than the designation lets on, and to interpret every facet of existence as really gendered produces a claustrophobia in me; I am not drawn by the charm of an always sexually distinct universe'.

Nevertheless, modern feminism, because it deals with the conditions of groups, is sociological in its character as it is in its historical development. It cannot escape the torments which spring from speaking for a collectivity. The members of any exhorted mass – whether of a race, a class, a nation, a bodily state, a sexual persuasion – are always apt to break out of its corrals to re-align themselves elsewhere. Indeed, the very indeterminacy of the span of 'being a woman' can form the concealed subject-matter of a political sociology of women which is interested in their 'stages'.

These difficulties can't be assuaged by appeals to the myriad types and conditions of women on this earth. They are not a matter of there being different *sorts of* women, but of the effects of the designation, 'women'. Criticisms of white educated Western feminism for generalising from its own experiences have been strongly voiced, and have had their proper impact. Yet however decisively ethnocentricity is countered, and the diversities of women in race and class allowed, even the most sophisticated political sociology is not going to be concerned with the historical crystallisations of sexed identities. Modern feminism, which in its sociological aspects is landed with the identity of women as an achieved fact of history and epistemology, can only swing between asserting or refusing the completeness of this given identity. But both the 'special needs' of women as different or the desired 'equality' of women as similar may be swamped by the power of the categorisation to defeat such fractures within it.

* * *

Equality; difference; 'different but equal' – the history of feminism since the 1790s has zigzagged and curved through these incomplete oppositions upon which it is itself precariously erected. This swaying motion need not be a wonder, nor a cause for despair. If feminism is the voicing of 'women' from the side of 'women', then it cannot but act out the full ambiguities of that category. This reflection reduces some of the sting and mystery of feminism's ceaseless oscillations, and allows us to prophesy its next incarnations. Yet to adopt such a philosophical resignation to the vagaries of a movement doomed to veer through eternity is cold comfort, perhaps. What does it imply for the practice of feminist politics? And if indeed the label 'woman' is inadequate, that it is neither possible nor desirable to live solidly inside any sexed designation, then isn't that its own commentary on the unwillingness of many to call themselves feminists? It explains, too, the exhaustion with reiterations about 'women' which must afflict the most dedicated feminist. Surely it's not uncommon to be tired, to long to be free of the merciless guillotines of those gendered invocations thumping down upon all speech and writing, to long, like Winifred Holtby, for 'an end of the whole business . . . the very name of feminist . . . to be about the work in which my real interests lie'.[22]

Does all of this mean then, that the better programme for feminism now would be – to minimise 'women'? To cope with the oscillations by so downplaying the category that insisting on either differences or identities would become equally untenable? My own suggestions grind to a halt here, on a territory of pragmatism. I'd argue that it is compatible to suggest that 'women' don't exist – while maintaining a politics of 'as if they existed' – since the world behaves as if they unambiguously did. So that official suppositions and conservative popular convictions will need to be countered constantly by redefinitions of 'women'. Such challenges to 'how women are' can throw sand in the eyes of the founding categorisations and attributions, ideally disorientating them. But the risk here is always that the very iteration of the afflicted category serves, maliciously, not to undo it but to underwrite it. The intimacies between consenting to be a subject and undergoing subjection are so great that even to make demands as an oppositional subject may well extend the trap, wrap it furiously around oneself. Yet this is hardly a paralysing risk, if it's recognised.

Sometimes it will be a soundly explosive tactic to deny, in the face of some thoughtless depiction, that there *are* any 'women'. But at other times, the entrenchment of sexed thought may be too deep for this strategy to be understood and effective. So feminism must be agile enough to say, 'Now we will be "women" – but now we will be persons, not these "women".' And, in practice, what sounds like a rigid opposition – between a philosophical correctness about the indeterminacy of the term, and a strategical willingness to clap one's feminist hand over one's theoretical mouth and just get on with 'women' where necessary – will loosen. A category may be at least conceptually shaken if it is challenged and refurbished, instead of only being perversely strengthened by repetition. For instance, to argue that it's untrue that women workers freely gravitate towards some less-well-paid jobs because these fit their natural inclinations, does indeed leave the annoyingly separable grouping, 'women workers', untouched, but it also successfully muddies the content of that term.[23] And the less that 'women workers' can be believed to have a fixed nature, as distinct from neglected needs because of their domestic responsibilities, the more it will be arguable that only for some purposes can they be distinguished from all workers. Feminism can then join battle over which these purposes are to be. Of course this means that feminism must 'speak women', while at the same time, an acute awareness of its vagaries is imperative. Domestic concerns can easily be rewritten into a separate spheres familialism, as in some European countries in the 1930s; aggressive recuperations are always hovering near. So an active scepticism about the integrity of the sacred category 'women' would be no merely philosophical doubt to be stifled in the name of effective political action in the world. On the contrary, it would be a condition *for* the latter.

To be, or not to be, 'a woman'; to write or not 'as a woman'; to espouse an egalitarianism which sees sexed manifestations as blocks on the road to full democracy; to love theories of difference which don't anticipate their own dissolution: these uncertainties are rehearsed endlessly in the history of feminism, and fought through within feminist-influenced politics. That 'women' is indeterminate and impossible is no cause for lament. It is what makes feminism; which has hardly been an indiscriminate embrace anyway of the fragilities and peculiarities of the category. What these do demand is a willingness, at times, to shred this 'women' to bits – to develop a speed, foxiness, versatility. The temporalities of 'women' are like the missing middle term of Aristotelian logic; while it's impossible to thoroughly be a woman, it's also impossible never to be one. On such shifting sands feminism must stand and sway. Its situation in respect of the sexed categories recalls Merleau-Ponty's description of another powerful presence: 'There is no outstripping of sexuality any more than there is any sexuality enclosed within itself. No one is saved, and no one is totally lost.'[24]

Notes

1. Donna Haraway, 'A Manifesto for Cyborgs: Science, Technology and Socialist Feminism in the 1980s', *Socialist Review*, 80, vol. 15, no. 2, March–April, 1985, p. 92.
2. Ibid., p. 95.
3. Simone de Beauvoir, *Le Deuxième Sexe*, 1949: *The Second Sex*, transl. by H. Parshley (London: Jonathan Cape, 1953), p. 84.

4. Elizabeth Gross, 'Philosophy, subjectivity, and the body: Kristeva and Irigaray', in Carole Pateman and Elizabeth Gross (eds), *Feminist Challenges: Social and Political Theory* (Sydney: Allen & Unwin, 1986), p. 139.

5. See Edward Shorter, *A History of Women's Bodies* (New York: Basic Books, 1982).

6. Sebastiano Timpanaro, *On Materialism* (London: New Left Books), 1975.

7. Michel Foucault, *The History of Sexuality Volume 1: An Introduction* trans. R. Hurley, (London: Allen Lane, 1979).

8. Michel Foucault, 'Nietzsche, genealogy, history', in *Language, Counter-Memory, Practice: Selected Essays and Interviews*, Donald F. Bouchard and Sherry Simon (eds and transl.) (Ithaca: Cornell University Press, 1977), p. 148.

9. Ibid., p. 153.

10. Elizabeth Gross, 'Philosophy, subjectivity, and the body: Kristeva and Irigaray', p. 142.

11. William Empson, *The Structure of Complex Words* (London, 1951), p. 29.

12. Ibid., p. 39.

13. Ibid.; see Empson's discussion of I. A. Richards, *The Philosophy of Rhetoric*.

14. Julia Kristeva, 'Le temps des femmes', transl. as 'Women's Time' by Alice Jardine and Harry Blake, *Signs*, vol. 7:1, Autumn, 1981, p. 35.

15. Ibid., p. 17.

16. Ibid., p. 19.

17. Ibid., p. 20.

18. Ibid., p. 33.

19. Ibid., p. 34.

20. Ibid., p. 34.

21. Ibid., p. 35.

22. Winifred Holtby, 'Feminism divided', *Yorkshire Post*, 26 July 1926, in *Testament of a Generation: The Journalism of Vera Brittain and Winifred Holtby*, (eds and intro.) Paul Berry and Alan Bishop, London: Virago, 1985, p. 48.

23. See Joan Scott, 'The Sears Case', in *Gender and The Politics of History* (New York: Columbia University Press, 1988).

24. Maurice-Merleau-Ponty, *The Phenomenology of Perception*, trans. Colin Smith (London: Routledge & Kegan Paul, 1962), p. 171.

10
Raymond Tallis, *Not Saussure: A Critique of Post-Saussurean Literary Theory* (1988)

Lacan, Barthes and Derrida in the 1950s and 1960s had produced important readings of the linguist Ferdinand de Saussure's concept of the sign. This concept,
according to which the phonic or graphic material of a word (the signifier) is bound
to what the word signifies (the signified) in a complex chain of differences in which
both are defined and meaning is produced, has been fundamental to the development of modern linguistics and the semiology which takes its inspiration from that
linguistics. If the French theorists had read Saussure carefully if idiosyncratically, a
commonplace version of their readings swiftly became unquestioned truth in much
literary and cultural criticism.

The merit of Raymond Tallis's *Not Saussure* is that it submits both those readings
and Saussure's original work to detailed critical examination. Committed to a realist
theory of language, Tallis is more than unhappy at the way in which Saussure's ideas
have been expanded and elaborated into a canonical orthodoxy rather than understood and used as a particular theory. It was because of our concern at the institutional status gained by a questionable appropriation of Saussure that Tallis's book
was welcomed in the LDS series. Significantly, as if to confirm the hold of the new
orthodoxy, American university presses refused to publish a book which did not 'fit
well', left them 'apprehensive' and could thus only be dismissed as 'right-wing'.

Statements, facts and the correspondence theory of truth

The Correspondence Theory of Truth (referred to throughout this
chapter as 'the Theory') has assumed many different forms since
Aristotle, developing an argument in Plato's *Sophist*, first brought it to
the forefront of the debate about the nature of truth. Much of the controversy surrounding the Theory has arisen because its advocates and
opponents have had different ideas about what it is that is supposed to

correspond to or with what. The uncertainty – sometimes a matter of conscious disagreement but more often one merely of confusion – extends to both ends of the correspondence. Is the correspondence between, say, statements and states of affairs, or between perceptions and things, or between thoughts and things, or what? Various permutations are possible, generating numerous variants of the theory. Almost any X may be said to correspond to almost any Y:

The Correspondence Theory of Truth
X corresponds to Y

X	Y
Perceptions	Objects
Thoughts	Things
Knowledge	Facts
Beliefs	The world
Logos	Res
Propositions	States of affairs
Statements	Reality

When, as has often been the case, it is unclear which variant is being advocated or denied, well-heated but poorly illuminated argument is inevitable. In some versions, the Theory applies to knowledge or perception; in others, it is about *statements*. Even where it is made clear that the version of the Theory under discussion is about the truth of statements – rather than of, say, percepts or beliefs – ambiguity about its scope may remain.

We may usefully divide 'statement' versions of the Theory into stronger forms which purport to give an account of the nature of truth; and weaker forms which claim only to provide a criterion for differentiating true statements from false. In the latter case, the Theory holds that a statement is true if and only if it corresponds to a real (historical or current) state of affairs. (We may have to add 'and this state of affairs is or was the one referred to or meant by the person making the statement' to guard against an accidental correspondence between an insufficiently particularised statement and a reality, other than the particular one that was meant, that happens coincidentally to correspond with it.) This weaker version of the Theory will converge with the stronger version if it is additionally maintained that the essence of truth inheres in this correspondence between statements and reality. In the present discussion, the Theory will be taken to be about the truth of statements rather of knowledge or perception. Although my main task will be to defend this weaker version of the Theory, I shall give reasons for supporting a qualified form of the stronger version towards the end of this chapter.

When the weaker version is stated in its contemporary form – that deriving from Tarski – it is difficult to avoid giving the impression that the Theory is inoffensive to the point of triviality. To use Tarski's example, according to the Theory:

(i) 'Snow is white' is true if and only if snow is white.

Or, to generalise:

(ii) 'x' is true if and only if x,

where 'x' is a statement belonging to an object language (in the example given, English) and x is the state of affairs corresponding to it. The entire sentence (i) or (ii) belongs to a meta-language in which the object language to which 'x' belongs can be discussed. If the theory seems non-trivial in the context of Tarski's own paper,[1] it is because he introduces it at least in part to avoid the Russellian paradoxes that always seem to threaten when one is using statements to talk about statements. This latter does not concern us here but it is interesting to discuss briefly why the weak forms of the Theory often seem trivial.

It is difficult to state the Theory non-trivially because, when we are *talking* or *writing* about truth (and in particular about the truth of statements), both statements and the realities to which they are refer are necessarily presented verbally. We therefore remain on the hither side of language. That is why the formulation:

(ii) 'x' is true if and only if x

seems merely to state, rather unhelpfully, an obvious internal truth about language rather than to cast light on the relations between language and reality. The alternative way of presenting the theory:

(iii) 'x' is true if and only if——

where '——' is (rather than merely standing for) a non-verbal act of indicating the state of affairs in question is obviously not possible within the bounds of the printed page.[2] But it is no less impossible outside of the printed page because, as Wittgenstein argued convincingly in

Philosophical Investigations, one cannot show the referents of words, never mind of sentences, by ostension or some other non-verbal mode of signification such as picturing. One cannot give the equivalent in, say, 'Pointish' of an assertion made in English; though if one *were* able to do so, then the quasi-tautological character of the Theory would disappear.[3]

Despite its apparently truistic nature, the Theory has been singled out for particular attack by post-Saussurean literary theorists. As may be imagined, the grounds of the attack are not often explicitly stated and the Theory is often dismissed in disparaging asides thrown off during the course of muddled, impressionistic idea-skating. Comparatively clear accounts of post-Saussurean opposition to the Theory are given by *Eagleton, Belsey and Hawkes*.[4] It will be useful to summarise some of the arguments again to indicate the rough direction from which the attack has been mounted.

The general drift is that after Saussure 'we now know' that language is a system composed of arbitrary signs and that this system has its own internal rules for combining the signs. Because of this, statements do not and cannot genuinely refer outside of themselves. 'A language does not construct its formations of words by reference to patterns of "reality", but on the basis of its own internal and self-sufficient rules. . . . structures are characteristically "closed" in this way.'[5] Eagleton even suggests that the arbitrariness of the linguistic sign undermines the correspondence theory of *knowledge*: 'for if, as Saussure had argued, the relationship between the sign and the referent was an arbitrary one, how could any "correspondence" theory of knowledge stand?'[6]

Since language is inescapably involved in the construction of ordinary reality, the implications of the arbitrariness of the linguistic sign are, for Belsey, even more far-reaching:

> Signs owe their capacity for signification not to the world but to their difference from each other in the network of signs that is the signifying system. Through linguistic difference 'there is born the world of meaning of a particular language in which the world of things will come to be arranged. . . . 'It is the world of words which creates the world of things' (Lacan).[7]

There is no correspondence between our knowledge and reality; or, rather, such correspondence as there is is rigged. The Theory, which assumes a correspondence between statements and extralinguistic reality, is based upon the false premiss of a transparent, referential language and is consequently itself false. 'Il n'y pas de hors-texte'.[8]

In Chapter 3 these views were shown to be false and, furthermore, it was emphasised that they could not be legitimated by an appeal to Saussure. A further reason for rejecting the Theory is the incorrect assumption (analogous to that used to undermine realism in fiction and discussed in Chapter 4) that to subscribe to the idea of a correspondence between statements and reality is also to subscribe to the belief that language is a *mirror* of reality. It would be as well to confront this assumption.

Some versions of the Theory do rest upon the mirror analogy. The most famous – or notorious – modern instance is, of course, to be found in the *Tractatus*. In Wittgenstein's theory there was a correspondence between the configuration of a proposition and that of the state of affairs referred to or asserted in it. A proposition was a concatenation of terms each of which corresponded to objects in the real world. The arrangement of objects that constituted the state of affairs was signified by a corresponding arrangement of the corresponding terms. The correspondence of form was not, however, one of spatial organisation. The proposition expressed the corresponding state of affairs by virtue of the convention linking individual terms with individual objects and the *logical* form it shared with the state of affairs. When Wittgenstein found that he could not give meaning to 'logical form', he rightly abandoned the mirror theory but, unfortunately, also repudiated all correspondence theories as well, thus throwing out the baby with the bathwater.

Identity of logical – or indeed any other – form is not only unintelligible but it also solves nothing. This cup is like another cup; but this fact does not make the one cup a sign of or expression of the other. Wittgenstein hoped that the picture theory would explain how propositions had a definite sense and how a new proposition could make sense to someone who, though he was familiar with its constituent terms, had not come across that particular proposition before. The reader could see what the new proposition meant because in some sense it *looked* like what it meant.

Notwithstanding the example of the *Tractatus*, there is no *a priori* reason why commitment to the Theory should entail acceptance of a mirror theory of language. Truth and isomorphism have no privileged relationship to one another. The reverse may, in fact, be the case: truth may *require* non-isomorphism, a distance which makes the embodiment of explicitness possible.

A much more rigorously argued, and consequently more interesting, expression of doubt about the ability of factual statements to refer to objects outside of themselves derives from Strawson and emerged in his famous debate with Austin about the nature of truth.[9] This debate will occupy an important place in the present discussion.

Consider a statement S^R by or in or through which it is asserted that there is a state of affairs R^S – the reality expressed in the statement. According to the Theory, S^R is true if and only if the corresponding R^S does indeed exist or (in the case of statements referring to the past) did exist at the time stated. A common thread running through many of the arguments against this seemingly inoffensive claim comes from the suggestion that the 'correspondence' between S^R and R^S is spurious in so far as S^R and R^S are not genuinely *external* to one another. Strawson thought that the R^S was 'a fact' and, additionally, that facts were not genuine entities on the surface of the globe: a fact is a pseudo-entity somehow internally related to the statements that 'correspond' to it. The implication is that the Theory naively overlooks the role that language plays in structuring or even creating the facts it is used to speak of: the role of S^R in the genesis of R^S.

In drawing attention to this, Strawson, perhaps unwittingly, uncovered the non-tautological aspect of the Theory, its positive content, and hence its vulnerability. For the force of the Theory – and that which distinguishes it non-trivially from, say, coherence theories – lies in the unspoken implication that the reality which corresponds to a true statement really is *outside* and *independent* of it – or indeed of any other statement. Or, at the least, there is a core or base of statements whose corresponding realities are not internal to language so that R^S is typically, in some sense, and to some degree, extra-linguistic. It is this that lies at the heart of the Theory and this which has been most forcefully attacked by its opponents.

One way of demonstrating that R^S is *not* internal to S^R, that it does not depend upon the latter for its very existence, would be to show that R^S can be accessed without the mediation of language; that it is available, for example, to sensory perception. In the case of material object particulars picked out by uniquely referring expressions, this seems to present no problem. The word (or token-instance) is produced here (or is sitting here, on the page) and the relevant object is over there. The two are independent of one another. I can gain access to the dog Rover either linguistically, via a referring expression, or directly by sensory perception. In such a case, the referent clearly exists independently of the act of reference. Even though it is picked out from its background by reference, it is already a self-contained whole and could have equally well been picked out by a focusing of sensory attention. (Whether such acts of 'pure reference', even to material object particulars, can ever take place without at least implicit predication or without inclusion in a speech act that performs, for example, assertion, is another matter.)

Things become less clear when we consider general referring expressions. Perception may yield experiences of particular dogs but does not give access to 'dog' or 'animal'. There would appear, therefore, to be no extra-linguistic experience corresponding to 'Dogs are fine animals'. This objection could be overcome by arguing, as many of course have done, that general statements relate to extra-linguistic reality only indirectly, via their particular consequences: they are meaningful only in so far as they have particular instantiation – or imply other statements that do – and can consequently be verified. Extra-linguistic access to the R^S corresponding to the S^R 'Dogs are fine animals' is possible through perception of a particular dog or a series of particular dogs. It may additionally be pointed out that, in many cases, the referring expression, though grammatically general, is implicitly particularised by the linguistic or extra-linguistic context of the statement in which it occurs – permitting, respectively, 'story-relative' identification[10] which depends in part upon what the speaker has already said, and 'body-relative' identification, which mobilises deictic co-ordinates.[11]

This will not satisfy everyone; for the further objection may be raised that when a common (i.e. general) noun is used to secure reference to a particular, the referent of the referring expression differs from any object that could be present to the sense. Referring even to a particular dog as a 'dog' conceptualises it in a way that it is not conceptualised when it is given to unmediated perception.

This objection opens up a whole new can of worms. For it raises the question of whether, in fact, perception is ever entirely innocent of conception; whether, more particularly, sensory perception is ever unmediated by, or uncontaminated with, language. It has been suggested – notably by Geschwind – that it is disconnection of sensory association areas from language centres that accounts for those severe disorders of perception called agnosias.[12] Perception without language is highly deficient; indeed, in the absence of language, sensation cannot give rise to what we would count as fully formed perception. There is, that is to say, no purely extra-linguistic perceptual reality and language is conterminous with all human consciousness above the level of brute, uninterpreted sensation.

A new can of worms indeed. Fortunately, we can close it without damaging the credibility of the case we shall put forward for the Theory. For our aim is not to demonstrate that R^S is perceived in a fashion that is independent of all possible formulations of reality but that R^S is in some sense independent of a particular S^R or group of S^Rs and of the language or group of languages from which S^R originated; that it is not internal to a 'closed' linguistic system. Adherence to the Theory in other words does not require that one should overlook the extent to which language is implicated in the structuring of human reality. Nor does it demand that one should believe that the reality 'out there' is extra-human or extra-social; that it is entirely naturally derived rather than being at least in part historically determined.

The independence of R^s seems undeniable when we reflect how the edges of material object particulars are spatial, not semantic. 'Dog' may be bounded by, and contrasted with, 'cat' and so on at the semantic level; but the individual dog referred to has literal spatial edges. It is *not* a bundle of semantic features. 'Dog' may be a concept bounded by other objects; but the dog on my lap is a patch of space-time, three of whose dimensions are fur-lined.

It may be objected that we have so far dodged the cases that present real problems for the correspondence theorist. We have not yet confronted the many abstract objects that populate the world of statements; and – much more to the point – we have dealt only with the referents of referring expressions and not with the *facts* picked out by *statements*. If we are to defend the Theory, however, we must concern ourselves with the realities that are asserted in factual statements. Now the referents of *statements* seem almost impossible to extricate from language. Whereas it is possible to draw a continuous (fur-) line round a dog one cannot do so around 'The dog is sitting on the mat'. It is not satisfactory to circumvent this difficulty by designating the latter, or its referent, 'a complex object'[13] by analogy with a complex material object made up of several components. For the only available complex object is the compound dog-plus-mat. A line that bounded this object would implicitly encircle much that fell outside of the specific reference of 'Rover is sitting on the mat' – for example, the four paws of the dog (or 'The dog has four paws'). The referent of the statement cannot be transformed into a definable patch of space – time by calling it, say, 'dog-mat'.

It would appear, then, that R^s does not enjoy a bounded, independent existence except in so far as it has been picked out by S^R (or one of its synonyms). It has no continuous non-linguistic edges. If this is true of 'The dog is sitting on the mat', how much more obviously true must it be of 'I am getting on in years' or 'The health of the national economy is in decline'.

Strawson denied that facts are real entities or 'objects on the surface of the globe' and, consequently, since the Theory typically asserts a correspondence between statements and *facts*, repudiated the Theory. Facts seem internal to statements: they are apparently inseparable from the statements in which they are asserted; there is a suspiciously snug fit between them. 'What could fit more perfectly the fact that it is raining than the statement that it is raining. Of course fact and state-ment fit. They were made for one another.'[14] As Austin points out, this remark gives (and is meant to give) 'the impression of reducing "facts" to an accusative so deeply and hopelessly internal that their status as entities is hopelessly compromised.'[15] The correspondence between logos and res is neither a lucky accident (requiring perhaps divine intervention to explain) nor a happy achievement: it has been rigged. Fact and statement belong to the same realm – the realm of discourse. The fact is not a res but a semi-linguistic entity in disguise, a quasi-res.

Austin's response is not as helpful as one would wish. He points out that, in ordinary conversation, we often refer to entities that are undoubtedly things-in-the-world as 'facts':

> Phenomena, events, situations, states of affairs are commonly sup-posed to be genuinely-in-the-world, and even Strawson admits events are so. Yet surely of all of these we can say that they *are facts*. The collapse of the Germans is an event and is a fact – was an event and was a fact.[16]

Facts, then, are seemingly out there in the world. That they are *not* inside statements becomes obvious when we consider that the end of a statement does not terminate or eliminate the corresponding fact or that when (to use an example of Strawson's[17] we tear up a written page we may tear up the statements on it but we do not tear up the facts – even if there are no synonyms or copies of those statements stored elsewhere in the world. The facts remain apparently out there, beyond this or any other page, apparently unharmed.

There seem, then, to be equally good cases for believing that facts are *inside* and that facts are *outside* of language. How shall we adjudicate between them? Or is this unnecessary? Is there, perhaps, some way of reconciling Strawson with Austin, of accommodating the observations both sides have made in support of their respective positions?

Strawson's attack on the extra-linguistic status of facts is highly damaging to the Theory, if the latter is seen to assert a correspondence between statements and *facts*. For, if facts were intra-linguistic and the Theory were about the correspondence between *facts* and statements, the criterion of truth furnished by it would seem at best feeble and at worst implausible: S^R is true when there exists a fact F that itself can exist only by courtesy of S^R. The 'correspondence' would be an internal affair of S^R and R^s would seem, at least in part, to be intra-linguistic, 'marsupialised' within S^R. This enfeebled version of the Theory is in danger of collapsing into a coherence theory in which truth resides in the consistency of statements with one another.

It is fortunate for the correspondence theorist, therefore, that the apparent strength of Strawson's case and much of the dispute between him and Austin originates from a failure to recognise that facts are not the same as S^Rs. Once it is appreciated that Austin is talking about R^Ss and Strawson about *one aspect* of facts, the basis of their disagreement disappears.

We shall try to clarify the nature of facts shortly. For the present, let us again think about the nature of R^S and its relation to S^R. Consider the R^S corresponding to the S^R 'The dog is on the mat'. This R^S is not, as we have already noted, merely a complex of objects. It could be characterised in part as a relationship between two objects. The objects themselves are presupposed in the assertion of that relationship; S^R does not assert or state that they exist. It expresses neither the dog nor the mat but the relationship between them. This relationship has been *brought out* by S^R: although it can be perceived directly, it is only by virtue of S^R (or a synonymous statement) that it emerges fully out of the 'reality mass', R, of perceptual experience.

There is a sense, therefore, in which it is true to say that R^S does not entirely pre-exist S^R or that it does not exist *as a definable, determinate entity* prior to the S^R that picks it out. Though the related elements – and, indeed, their relationship – pre-exist S^R the relationship between them acquires separate existence only through S^R. For the relationship does not inhere in either of the objects in question, nor of course in the space between them. It is there to be pre-linguistically perceived but it has to be spoken or written to acquire objective (and even object) status; only when it is embodied in language is it liberated from the nascency of existence in a particular consciousness, freed from the privacy of an individual's view-point and the instability of his attention, to become fully formed and publicly accessible. S^R thus confers upon R^S the objectivity enjoyed by other, self-bounded, parts of

R – that is to say, by material object particulars. S^R uproots R^S out of R and remakes it as, say, one thread in a nexus of facts or one atom of a described situation. S^R in short, does not create R^S but does confer aseity or atomicity or separate existence upon it.

Under this analysis, R^S still remains independent of language inasmuch as it can be accessed non-linguistically. In the case of more general, more complex, more abstract S^Rs, non-linguistic access to the corresponding R^Ss becomes more indirect. Perceptual access is to the consequences, illustrative instances or samples (whichever is appropriate) of R^S and perception is more explicitly verification. Nevertheless, even in the most abstract cases, in so far as S^R is meaningful and true, thus far is R^S extra-linguistic.

This not to imply that we ought to subscribe to an unreformed, or indeed any sort of, verificationism. Meaning, truth and verification remain quite distinct even if they are not totally independent of one another. If an S^R is true, there must be independent access either to the corresponding R^S, or to its components, or to the R^Ss or components of the R^Ss corresponding to the statements implied by S^R.

An R^S on the present analysis, may have two existence conditions; or, rather, an *existence* condition plus an *emergence* condition permitting it fully explicit, bounded existence. In this respect the referent of a general or abstract term or the R^S corresponding to a factual statement will differ from the referent of the proper name or other expression designating a material object particular. Rover exists and exists explicitly without the help of 'Rover' because he comes furnished with his own (furlined) edges. But the smile (on my face), while no less extra-linguistic than Rover, is not so bounded by continuous spatial or spatio-temporal edges and requires the referring expression to separate it from the face whose affective colouring it constitutes. Like the health of the economy or the R^S corresponding to any factual statement, the smile stands in need of an emergence condition to confer separate existence upon it. This condition will be fulfilled by the linguistic expression that is used to refer to it, the statement that asserts that it is the case or that something or other is true of it.

In such cases, R^S requires S^R to bring it out; S^R does not *create* R^S. The latter is not (to use the post-Saussurean term) an *effect* of the former. R^S has an existence condition additional to that of the existence of the appropriate S^R – namely a certain disposition of matter in space and time corresponding to the configuration asserted in S^R. The latter condition is clearly extra-linguistic. R^S remains an independent truth condition of S^R. It is not a puppet owing its existence entirely to S^R.

We are therefore in a position to uphold a non-trivial, non-tautological version of the weaker Theory. It can be stated as follows:

A statement S^R is true if and only if there is a corresponding R^S and false where there is no such R^S.

In a true statement there is a correspondence between a proposed and an actual reality.

So much for S^Rs and R^Ss. But what of facts? Facts are neither statements nor are they purely extra-linguistic realities. If facts *were* identical with statements, no statement could be counter-factual. There would be no call to distinguish a sub-category of 'false statements' or of 'factually true statements'. Nevertheless, facts *do* seem to be inextricably bound up with statements: facts and statements 'fit each other so well' as Strawson said, it is difficult to conceive of a means of gaining access to facts except via the statements through which they are asserted. Are facts, then, intra- or extra-linguistic? Do they belong with S^Rs or R^Ss?

The truth is that they belong entirely with neither: facts are neither entirely inside nor entirely outside of language. A fact is an R^S-picked-out-by-an-S^R. It is the product of the fusion of an S^R and an R^S, of a linguistically encoded meaning and a piece of reality. As such, a fact has two inseparable facets – one corresponding to the S^R and the other to the R^S – standing in relation to one another rather as (to appropriate Saussure's famous metaphor) the recto and verso of a sheet of paper. An S^R without a corresponding R^S is a lie or a mistake or a joke; and an R^S without a corresponding S^R is inchoate or nascent, a percept incompletely crystallised out of the reality mass R.

Those who fail to appreciate the intermediate status of facts are prone to imagine that factual reality must have some kind of sentence-like form and/or to believe that sentences must somehow replicate the structure of the extra-linguistic reality they express. When it is discovered that neither of these is the case, they become suspicious as to whether language can really be open to external reality. Facts, which seem *when discussed* to look like statements, are accused of being intra-linguistic since it is obvious that reality itself does not have a sentential form and statements do not look like the realities they are about. Doubts begin to be expressed about whether or not even factual statements can be true of, or even reach out towards, extra-linguistic reality. Once the intermediate status of facts is understood, however, these doubts are seen to be without foundation.

There are no facts without language and yet facts are not internal to language. So the Theory, in so far as it is concerned with the relationship between statements and extra-linguistic reality, is not about the correspondence between statements and *facts*:[18]

$$S^R : F$$

but between S^Rs and R^Ss. Facts are constituted in this correspondence between S^Rs and R^Ss:

$$\frac{S^R}{R^S} = F$$

In order to be 'fair to facts', one must therefore recognise that they are neither wholly intra- nor wholly extra-linguistic but arise out of the *interaction* between language and external reality. And to be fair to the Theory, it must be appreciated that the R^S picked out by an S^R owes its *explicit* existence, but not its existence, to the S^R. It is not helpful, nor is it necessary, to think, as Russell and Moore sometimes did, of facts as a special (and hence problematic) sort of object in the world.

There can, therefore, be a genuine correspondence, rather than a mere internal relation, between statements and reality, *logos* and *rem*. The Theory, which asserts this external relationship between what is said or written and what is the case, is non-trivially true: it affirms the objectivity of facts, that factual truth is not determined solely by what people happen to say. More importantly, it denies that truth is a mere matter of conformity between one assertion or articulated belief and another: truth is a matter of conformity between statements and a world outside of those statements. Contrary to Derrida, we assert that, for at least part of the time 'il y'a de hors-texte'; and *that is the time when language is earning its keep*.

It is necessary to add this last rider to forestall the criticism that the Theory is naïve because it overlooks how most statements do many other things than merely state what they seem to be stating: they imply, persuade, distract attention from what has not been stated, and so on. The Theory alone would be unable to deal with 'Nice and sunny, isn't it?', a true statement given in response to someone complaining that he had just been badly beaten up. Nevertheless, a significant portion of the truth is encoded in factual statements.[19]

A weaker version of the Theory is thus upheld. But what of the stronger version? In accordance with the latter, correspondence between statements and reality is not merely a criterion for classifying statements as being true or false but truth itself. Truth *is* or inheres in the relation between language and the world.

If 'truth' is taken to mean 'factual truth', then it is easy to see how the weaker version of the Theory could pass over into the stronger. But factual truth is only one mode of the truth. A good deal of truth (and falsehood) lies outside of factual statements; indeed outside of statements altogether. If we think of the different relata in the various versions of the Theory mentioned at the beginning of this chapter, then it will be appreciated that there are widely divergent views about the scope of the concept 'truth'. Truth may be seen variously as residing in the relation between: perception and reality; belief and reality; knowledge and reality; thought and reality (adequation of things and the intellect); and so on. It may even be argued that truth resides in reality itself: that either R^S or R is truth. Why, then, choose the relations between *statements* and reality as the privileged repository of truth?

Most importantly, it is obvious that, in the absence of *any* view-point or consciousness, there is no truth. Material reality in the absence of consciousness is neither true nor false; it simply is. The claim that it (inexplicitly) embodies truth would have the immediate result of rendering the concept of truth redundant and assimilating the category of truth to that of existence.[20] If a rock on a planet unvisited since the beginning of time embodies truth, then the concept of truth adds nothing to that of existence. In fact, truth is inseparable from explicitness: the rock is not of itself true; truth refers to what has been made explicit about the rock. A single consciousness, however, seems insufficient to establish the concept of truth. For truth is essentially a public matter. The question of truth arises only when there are at least two viewpoints or consciousness. In a postulated solitary consciousness (if such a thing were possible), the truth 'of' or 'about' something would be only implicit, nascent or inchoate. It becomes explicit only where there are two or more consciousnesses in communication – informing, or disagreeing with, one another. Truth emerges when there is a public, when *it* becomes public, and so explicit. One could plausibly suggest that a material reality becomes 'true' or 'the truth' only when it is appealed to (picked out, expressed) to arbitrate between conflicting points of view. And it is in *statements* that that which is true of or about reality becomes most fully explicit because in statements it acquires separate embodiment, a place of its own: truth is most fully developed in true statements. So while truth may not inhere *exclusively* in the correspondence between true statements and reality, it achieves its most complete development towards substantiality there. The development of truth is inseparable from the development of explicitness.

That is why Ramsay's account of truth[21] is so seriously misconceived. According to Ramsay, the concept of truth is empty because to assert '*p* is true' is the same as to assert '*p*'. The 'is true' adds nothing. Truth is a redundant category; '– is true' is an empty predicate. It is not, however, the case that to assert '*p* is true' is the same as to assert '*p*'. There is an important difference between asserting that 'The earth is round' and asserting that ' "The earth is round" is true'. Something is made explicit in the second assertion that is not made explicit in the first – namely the truth value of the first. The difference between the assertions may be compared with the difference between '*p*' and ' "*p*" is asserted'. To assert that *p* is asserted does not modify *p* but we do not conclude therefrom that the concept of assertion is empty.

Ramsay's argument illustrates an almost perverse determination to disregard the real tendency of the question 'What is truth?' The question does not imply a search for some object or substance or property which will count as the essence or embodiment of truth. What it really means is: what is the search for truth really aimed at? What, if anything, is there in common between the criteria of truth applicable in different fields of enquiry? What distinguishes truth from falsehood?

But what Ramsay's dismissal of the concept of truth overlooks most importantly is the relationship between explicitness and truth (and falsehood). Most accounts of truth focus upon the distinction between truth and falsehood. (The weak Theory is a good example of this tendency.) Truth, however, cannot be understood entirely in terms of those features or criteria by which it is distinguished from falsehood. Just as a woman is not simply the sum of her differences from a man: she is also composed of that common humanity which woman and man share. Likewise truth is additionally composed of that which truth and falsehood have in common – namely explicitness. Theories and definitions of truth that do not recognise the common basis of both truth and falsehood in explicitness overlook what is essential to it: its basis in and emergence through articulate consciousness.

This is why truth is best seen as *emergent* – beginning with perception (it does, after all, makes sense to speak of true and false perceptions) and developing through judgement and articulation to reach full flower in factual statements. And although there are vital existential truths not unravelled in factual discourse, it seems reasonable to conclude that it is in the correspondence between a statement and extra-linguistic reality that we find truth at its most developed. In this conclusion the weaker form of the Theory converges with the stronger form.

Notes

1. See 'The Semantic Conception of Truth and the Foundations of Semantics', in *Philosophy and Phenomenological Research*, vol. 4 (1944) pp. 341–76.
2. That is what is so odd about G. E. Moore's 'Proof of an External World' (*Proceedings of the British Academy*, 1939):

   > I can prove now that two human hands exist. How? By holding up the two hands and saying, as I make a certain gesture with the right hand 'Here is one hand', and adding, as I make a certain gesture with the left hand 'and here is the other'

   Clearly this is not a proof at all. If it is anything, it is a report of a series of acts that Moore carried out imagining that it might be a proof; or a recipe for carrying out a proof. In either case, it does not appear on the printed page.
3. On this theme, see Roland Barthes's discussion of isologous systems in *Elements of Semiology*, trans. Annette Lavers and Colin Smith (London: Jonathan Cape, 1967), pp. 43–4.
4. Comparatively clear accounts of post-Saussurean opposition to the Theory are to be found in: Terry Eagleton, *Literary Theory* (Oxford: Basil Blackwell, 1983); Catherine Belsey, *Critical Practice* (London: Methuen, 1980); and Terence Hawkes, *Structuralism and Semiotics* (London: Methuen, 1977).
5. Hawkes, *Structuralism and Semiotics*, p. 16.
6. Eagleton, *Literary Theory*, p. 108.
7. Belsey, *Critical Practice*, p. 136.
8. Jacques Derrida, *Of Grammatology*, trans. Gayatri Chakravorty Spivak (Baltimore: the Johns Hopkins University Press, 1976), p. 158.
9. J. L. Austin and P. F. Strawson, 'Truth', *Proc. Aristotelian Society, Supplementary Volume* (1950) pp. 111ff.
10. A term borrowed from P. F. Strawson, *Individuals* (London: Methuen, 1959), p. 18.
11. See, for example, the illuminating discussion in John Lyons, *Semantics* (Cambridge University Press, 1977) vol. 2, pp. 636–724. These points are also touched on in Chapter 4.
12. Norman Geschwind, 'The Development of the Brain and the Evolution of Language', in *Monograph Series on Language and Linguistics*, Georgetown University, Washington DC, vol. 17 (1964) pp. 155–69.
13. So that a sentence becomes (as in Locke, Frege's later works and Wittgenstein's *Tractatus*) a complex proper name.
14. P. F. Strawson quoted in J. L. Austin, *Unfair to Facts*, p. 160. This paper is most readily available in *Philosophical Papers*, J. O. Urmson and G. J. Warnock (eds).
15. Austin, ibid., p. 169.
16. Austin, ibid., p. 156.
17. P. F. Strawson, Editor's Introduction to *Philosophical Logic* (Oxford University Press, 1967), p. 15.

18. That is why Austin's paper is ultimately unsatisfactory as a defence of the Theory. Although the version of the Theory he supported in his earlier paper tried to avoid using 'facts' and 'corresponds', he makes it obvious that he considers that if there is anything that corresponds to statements it is facts.

19. We could define a statement as D. W. Hamlyn does, as 'a form of language that is true or false'. *The Theory of Knowledge* (London: Macmillan – now Palgrave Macmillan, 1970).

20. For a more detailed treatment of these points, see R. C. Tallis, 'As If There Could Be Such Things As True Stories', *Cambridge Quarterly*, xv (1986) no. 2, pp. 95–107.

21. F. P. Ramsay, *The Foundation of Mathematics* (London: Routledge & Kegan Paul, 1931), pp. 142–3.

11
Kristin Ross, *The Emergence of Social Space: Rimbaud and the Paris Commune* (1988)

In *The Emergence of Social Space*, Kristin Ross examines the cultural movement in and on the peripheries of the Paris Commune – an oppositional culture that consists of political language, postures, values and strategies. Employing a close textual analysis, Ross considers Rimbaud's poetry contextually as one aspect among others in the experience of an entire generation of Communards, using it to examine developments in the history of geography, anthropology, worker's culture. political theory and aesthetics. She demonstrates that the very notion of 'social space' emerges as one of the by-products of the Commune and that it leads to a far-reaching rethinking of social and cultural strategies. In so doing she also examines shifts in the conception of work and the role these play as textual operators in significant poetic and theoretical texts of the day and, indeed, of subsequent periods.

The transformation of social space

I

Attempts to discuss Rimbaud in terms of the events of 1871 have for the most part been limited to frenzied interrogations by literary historians and biographers anxious to ascertain his precise physical whereabouts during the months of March to May 1871.[1] Was Rimbaud an active participant in the insurrection? Which informants are to be believed? Even to pose the question in this form reveals the anxiety of the empiricist working in the service of reductivism – a reductivism that most likely has political (recuperative) motivations. Would Rimbaud's absence, definitively proved, from the scene of the crime, in turn definitively silence the social and political repercussions of his work? Would an eyewitness account of his presence on the barricades give a political interpretation of his poetry more validity?

The actual, complex links binding Rimbaud to the events in Paris are not to be established by measuring geographic distance. Or, if they are, it is perhaps by considering Rimbaud's poetry, produced at least in part within the rarefied situation of his isolation in Charleville, as one creative response to the same objective situation to which the insurrection in Paris was another. In what way does Rimbaud figure or prefigure a social space adjacent – side by side rather than analogous – to the one activated by the insurgents in the heart of Paris?

To begin to answer this question I propose postponing for now a discussion of Rimbaud's most explicitly and thematically 'political' poems – poems like 'Les Mains de Jeanne-Marie', which praises the revolutionary actions of women during the Commune, or 'Chant de guerre parisien', announced by Rimbaud under the rubric of a 'contemporary psalm' and featuring verbal caricatures of Favre and Thiers lifted straight from the stockpile of revolutionary imagery used in political cartoons and gravures produced during the early months of 1871. Such overtly political verse is important for an ideological reading of Rimbaud, but no more so, I hope to show, than the early Charleville erotic verse (or, for that matter, than the late 'hermetic' prose poems) – in Rimbaud there is little distance between political economy and libidinal economy. And the significance of the Commune is most evident in what Marx called its 'working existence': in its *displacement* of the political onto seemingly peripheral areas of everyday life – the organization of space and time, changes in lived rhythms and social ambiences. The insurgents' brief mastery of their own history is perceptible, in other words, not so much on the level of governmental politics as on the level of their daily life: in concrete problems of work, leisure, housing, sexuality, and family and neighbourhood relations. Revolutionary struggle is diffuse as well as specifically directed, expressed throughout the various cultural spheres and institutional contexts, in specific conflicts and in the manifold transformations of individuals rather than in some rigid and polar opposition of capital and labour. Taking seriously such a 'displacement of the political' can point us in the direction of certain of Rimbaud's poems thematically at a distance from the turbulence in Paris: the early ironic and erotic everyday Rimbaud of kisses, beer, and country walks.

Like much of Rimbaud's early lyric poetry, 'Rêvé pour l'hiver' (1870) puts forth a particular imagination of the nineteenth-century commonplace of 'the voyage'. The poem opens with the dream of an enclosed, infantile universe:

L'hiver, nous irons dans un petit wagon rose
    Avec des coussins bleus.
Nous serons bien. Un nid de baisers fous repose
    Dans chaque coin moelleux.

[In winter we shall travel in a little pink railway carriage
    With blue cushions.
We'll be comfortable. A nest of mad kisses lies in wait
    In each soft corner.]

The interior of the carriage is created oppositionally to the winter outside; inside is warmth, well-being and comfort (the simplicity of 'Nous serons bien'), repose and restfulness. The muted pastel colours suggest a nursery; the carriage is a nest where the violence and jolts of the voyage are cushioned and where all sensation or sound of moving through space is dulled. The passage will not be noticed.

But if the carriage is a nest, it is also the container of nests – a potential disturbance in the nursery is suggested by the adjective 'mad', whose threat is for the moment attenuated by the verb *repose*. Madness is there, a violence oddly separated and detached from the actors and seemingly part of the environment, but it is, at least at present, a sleeping *folie*:

Tu fermeras l'oeil, pour ne point voir, par la glace,
    Grimacer les ombres des soirs,
Ces monstruosités hargneuses, populace
    De démons noirs et de loups noirs.

[You will close your eyes, so as not to see through the window
    The evening shadows grimacing,
Those snarling monsters, a swarm
    Of black devils and black wolves.]

The second stanza opens out onto the landscape, continuing the childlike tone whereby shadows are frozen into grimaces not unlike the anthropomorphized nature illustrations in the popular children's books (*petits livres d'enfance*) Rimbaud mentions in 'Alchimie du verbe'. Still, it is the gesture of cushioning, or refusing the experience of voyaging, that appears to hold sway. You will close your eyes to the outside, shutting off vision – that which continually makes and undoes relations between the voyager and the outer world. You will believe yourself intact because surrounded by the walls of the carriage. But the refusal of vision is double-edged: it is also a relinquishing of the mastery involved in any viewer/viewed relation, the domination of the look. To stop seeing the horrifying exterior through the window is, by the same token, to shut off the possibility of defining the interior by its contrary. Gone then is the protection of being distanced from the outside world that would remain there, detached, frozen into an illustration. The closing of the eyes makes the illustration come alive and awakens the sleeping madness:

> Puis tu te sentiras la joue égratignée . . .
> Un petit baiser, comme une folle araignée,
>   Te courra par le cou . . .
>
> Et tu me diras: 'Cherche!', en inclinant la tête,
> – Et nous prendrons du temps à trouver cette bête
>   – Qui voyage beaucoup . . .
>
> [Then you will feel your cheek scratched . . .
> A little kiss, like a mad spider,
>   Will run about your neck . . .
>
> And you'll say to me 'Find it!' bending your head,
> – And we'll take a long time to find that creature
>   – Who travels far . . .]

A kiss begins its journey; as a spider, it shares with the outer world the quality of darkness; its threatening aspect is underlined by the repetition of the adjective 'mad'. The outside invades the inside, the nursery is threatened by erotic madness. Closing the eyes awakens the possibility of haptic perception – touch rather than an abstracted and distanced mastery of the scenery. The word *égratignée* signals the movement from *voir* to *faire*: the violence of contact is reminiscent of key moments in many of the poems of *opening*, moments when seams are exposed, the instant of scratching the surface: the fingernails on the child's scalp in 'Les Chercheuses de poux', the *picotement* of 'Sensation', the holes in the pockets and trousers in 'Ma Bohème'; 'A blast of air pierces gaps in the partitions, . . . blows away the limits of homes' ('Nocturne vulgaire'). Rimbaud's poetry as a poetry of transformation is crystallized in this moment: the phenomenon of an absolutely commanding perception of the transformation brought on in us by the event of 'contact', 'opening', 'rupture'. Thus the importance of the reflexive form in many of these moments: 'Puis tu *te* sentiras . . .'.

The adjective *petit* used to describe the carriage in the first verse is repeated apropos of the kiss; the kiss shares with the carriage the properties of motion and time as well. The movement of the poem follows the invisible silent machine, the carriage, tracing its passage through space, and the spider/kiss, tracing its passage along the microgeography of the woman's body. These two transgressive movements become one, and what has initially functioned as a mode of separation, an enclosed module transporting its passengers through space, becomes in the intruding spider/kiss what articulates or breaks down the division between interior and exterior. Roland Barthes, speaking of the more extensive and dramatic play with the boundary between inner and outer space that occurs in Rimbaud's 'Bateau ivre', calls this the move beyond a psychoanalysis of the cavern to a true poetics of exploration.[2] And indeed, the lover's exclamation 'Cherche!' the only sound in the poem, becomes a true *invitation au voyage* – the invitation to conceive of space *not* as a static reality but as active, generative, to experience space as created by an interaction, as something that our bodies reactivate, and that through this reactivation, in turn modifies and transforms us. The space of the voyage, whose unmapped itinerary lies in the dashes and ellipses that crowd the end of the poem, merges with a temporal passage ('And we'll take a long time . . .') that guarantees that the voyagers will not be the same individuals at the end of the trip that they were at the beginning.

The poem, as such, constitutes a movement and not a tableau, a *récit* rather than a map. Instead of the abstract visual constructions proper to the stasis of a geographic notion of space, the poem creates a 'nonpassive' spatiality – space as a specific form of operations and interactions. In the late 1860s the expression 'chercher la petite bête' was prevalent slang for wanting to know the inner workings of a thing, the hidden reasons of an affair – like a child wanting to know what lies beneath a watch face. But it was also a slang expression popular among literati, who used it to signify amusing oneself on the level of stylistics instead of bearing down on serious matters of content.[3] The turns and detours of the spider – ruse, madness, desire, passage – are at once the turns and detours of figures of style, an erotics, and a manner of moving through the world. It is this prefiguration of a reactivated space that in turn becomes transformative that we will take as our point of access to the event or 'working existence' of the Commune.

II

In his *Mémoires*, Gustave-Paul Cluseret, the Commune's first Delegate of War, reflects on the lessons to be learned from the street fighting at the end of the Commune, and, in the process, details the philosophy and strategic use of that topographically persistent insurgent construction, the barricade. The building of barricades was, first of all, to be carried out as quickly as possible; in contrast to the unique, well-situated, and centralised civic monument, whose aura derives from its isolation and stability, barricades were not designed around the notion of a unique 'proper place': street platoons were to set up as many barricades as they could as quickly as possible. Their construction was, consequently, haphazard and makeshift:

> It is therefore not necessary for these barricades to be perfectly constructed; they can very well be made of overturned carriages, doors torn off their hinges, furniture thrown out of windows, cobblestones where these are available, beams, barrels, etc.[4]

Monumental ideals of formal perfection, duration or immortality, quality of material and integrity of design are replaced by a special kind of *bricolage* – the wrenching of everyday objects from their habitual context to be used in a radically different way. A similar awareness of the tactical mission of the commonplace can be found in Rimbaud's parodic 'Ce qu'on dit au poète à propos de fleurs' where standard Parnassian 'tools' are rendered *truly* utilitarian: 'Trouve, ô Chasseur, nous le voulons, / Quelques garances parfumées / Que la Nature en pantalons / Fasse éclore! – pour nos Armées! . . . Trouve des Fleurs qui soient des chaises!' ('Find, O Hunter, we desire it, / One or two scented madder plants / Which Nature may cause to bloom into trousers – For our Armies! . . . Find Flowers which are chairs!') In this poem and elsewhere Rimbaud's paradoxical solution to the sterility of Parnassian imagery is, on the one hand, an unqualified return to the full range of ordinary experience – everyday life at its most banal and on the other hand a breakthrough to a distinctly utopian space. Similarly, anything, writes Cluseret, can serve as building material, anything can be a weapon – 'explosives, furniture, and in general, anything that can be used as a projectile' – and any person can be a soldier:

> Passersby were stopped to help construct the barricades. A battalion of National Guards occupied the area, and the sentries called on everyone passing to contribute their cobblestone willy-nilly to the defense effort.[5]

But perhaps the most crucial point to emphasize concerning the barricades was their strategic use: they were *not*, as Auguste Blanqui also makes clear in his *Instructions pour une prise d'armes*, to be used as shelter. Barricades, writes Cluseret, 'are not intended to shelter their defenders, since these people will be inside the houses, but to prevent enemy forces from circulating, to bring them to a halt and to enable the insurrectionists to pelt them with . . . anything that can be used as a projectile'. Cluseret's remarks are reflections that took place after the event on how the defense should have been carried out; in fact, much of the actual fighting, particularly during the final massacres of the *semaine sanglante*, took the form of traditional hand-to-hand combat. Nevertheless, some of the urban guerilla strategies outlined or prescribed by Cluseret and Blanqui seem to have been followed. In the memoirs he dashed off immediately after the demise of the Commune, Catulle Mendès describes the difficulties experienced by the disciplined Versaillais soldiers in gaining access to certain Parisian *quartiers*:

> But at other points in Paris, military operations were less successful. In the Faubourg Saint-Germain, the army advances very slowly, if it advances at all. The federalists fight with a heroic brutality: from street corners, from windows, from atop balconies ring gunshots, rarely ineffective. This sort of war tires the soldiers, whose discipline does not allow them to respond with similar maneuvers. In Saint-Ouen as well, the forward march of the troops has been halted; the barricade on the rue de Clichy holds strong and will hold for a long time.[6]

The immediate function of the barricades, then, was to prevent the free circulation of the enemy through the city – to 'halt' them or immobilize them so that they, the enemy, could become targets. The insurgents, meanwhile, who have mobility on their side, offer no targets: 'offering them no targets. . . . No one is in sight. This is the crucial point'. To this end Blanqui advocated the strategy known as 'piercing the houses':

> When, on the line of defense, a house is particularly threatened, we demolish the staircase from the ground floor, and open up holes in the floorboards of the next floor, in order to be able to fire on the soldiers invading the ground floor.[7]

Cluseret writes of a 'lateral piercing' of the houses: 'Troops guard the ground floor while others climb quickly to the next floor and immediately break through the wall to the adjoining house and so on and so forth as far as possible.' Houses are gutted in such a way that the insurgents can move freely in all directions through passageways and networks of communication joining houses together; the enemy on the street is rendered frozen and stationary. 'Street fighting does not take place in the streets but in the houses, not in the open but under-cover.' Street fighting depends on mobility or permanent displace-ment. It depends on changing houses into passageways – reversing or suspending the division between public and private space. 'A blast of air pierces gaps in the partitions . . . blows away the limits of homes' ('Nocturne vulgaire'). Walter Benjamin writes that for the *flaneur* at the end of the Second Empire, the city is metamorphosed into an interior; for the Communards the reverse is true: the interior becomes a street.

III

Commentators on the Commune from Marx and Engels on have singled out the Communards' failure to attack that most obvious of monumental targets, the Bank of France:

> The hardest thing to understand is certainly the holy awe with which they remained outside the gates of the Bank of France. This was also a serious political mistake. The Bank in the hands of the Commune – this would have been worth more than 10,000 hostages.[8]

Engels evaluates the 'serious political mistake' by calculating a rate of exchange between bank and hostages. Not surprisingly, his analysis is situated soundly in the realm of political economy. In the early 1960s the Situationists – a group whose project lay at the intersection of the revolutionary workers' movement and the artistic 'avant-garde' – pro-posed another sort of analysis, one that altered the sphere of political economy by bringing transformations on the level of everyday life from the peripheries of its analysis to the centre. To the extent that the Situationist critique of everyday life was inseparable from the project of intervening into, transforming lived experience, the activities of the group can be seen to fall under the dual banner of Engels's 'making conscious the unconscious tendencies of the Commune' and Rimbaud's 'Changer la Vie'. In the failure of the Commune – its failure, that is, in the classical terms of the workers' movement, to produce what later, more 'successful' revolutions produced, namely, a state bureaucracy – in that failure the Situationists saw its success. To view the Commune from the perspective of the transformation of everyday life would demand, then, that we juxtapose the Communards' political failure or mistake – leaving intact the Bank of France – with one of their more 'monumental' achievements: the demolition of the Vendôme Column, built by Napoléon to glorify the victories of the Grand Army. On the one hand, a reticence, a refusal to act; on the other, violence and destruction as complete reappropriation: the creation, through destruction, of a positive social void, the refusal of the dominant organisation of social space and the supposed neutrality of monuments. The failure of the Communards in the 'mature' realm of military and politico-economic efficacy is balanced by their accomplishments in the Imaginary or preconscious space that lies outside specific and directly representable class functions – the space that could be said to constitute the realm of political desire rather than need.

What monuments are to the Communards – petrified signs of the dominant social order – the canon is to Rimbaud:

> Les blancs débarquent. Le canon! Il faut se soummettre au baptême, s'habiller, travailler.
> J'ai reçu au coeur le coup de grâce. Ah! je ne l'avais pas prévu!
> [The whites are landing. The cannon! We will have to submit to baptism, get dressed, and work.
> I have received in my heart the stroke of mercy. Ah! I had not foreseen it!]

This imaginary historical reconstruction, which occurs near the middle of the 'Mauvais Sang' section of *Une Saison en enfer*, depicts a scene in the colonization of everyday life. In his attempt to rewrite his genealogy, to find another history, another language, the narrator has adopted the persona of an African. Precisely at that moment, the colonists arrive. The 'coup de grâce' is also the shot of the cannon: in this context, the word *canon* should be taken, as Rimbaud said elsewhere, *littéralement et dans tous les sens* – not only as a piece of artillery or as a law of the church, but as the group of books admitted as being divinely inspired. The cannon is also an arm that implies an economic investment that only a state apparatus can make.

(The issue of canonisation should play an important role in any discussion of Rimbaud *today*, given the ideologically significant modification of the 'place' of Rimbaud in the literary canon that has occurred over the last twenty years. Dominant methodological or theoretical concerns have always generated a list of chosen texts that best suit their mode of analysis. Literary theory of the last twenty years – from structuralism to deconstruction – is no exception. It has, to a certain extent, brought about a rewriting of the canon that has elevated Mallarmé while visibly neglecting Rimbaud; this rewriting in and of itself attests to Rimbaud's resistance to a purely linguistic or 'textual' reading.

It is, however, the most extended sense of the word *canon* – the set of rules or norms used to determine an ideal of beauty in the Beaux Arts – that dominate *Une Saison en enfer*. Beauty appears in the opening lines of the poem, capitalised and personified, seated on the knees of the narrator and cursed by him: 'Un soir, j'ai assis la Beauté sur mes genoux. Et je l'ai trouvée amère. Et je l'ai injuriée.' ('One evening I sat Beauty on my knees. And I found her bitter. And I cursed her.') It is the transformation of this idealised beauty into a 'decanonized', lowercase form by the end of the narrative – 'Je sais aujourd'hui saluer la *beauté*' – that constitutes, along with the gradual construction of a plural subject, the primary direction and movement of the poem. But the decanonisation of beauty is not just a change in the object; it is a transformation in the relation of the narrator to the object – a transformation signaled by the verb *saluer* (a greeting that is both a hello and a farewell): thus, a relation to beauty that is no longer timeless or immortal, but transitory, acknowledging change and death.

The verb *saluer* appears again near the conclusion in one of the poem's most celebrated passages:

> Quand irons-nous, par delà les grèves et les monts, saluer la naissance du travail nouveau, la sagesse nouvelle, la fuite des tyrans et des démons. la fin de la superstition, adorer – les premiers! – Noël sur la terre!
> [When will we journey beyond the beaches and the mountains, to hail the birth of new work, new wisdom, the flight of tyrants and demons, the end of superstition; to adore – the first! – Christmas on earth!]

Here *saluer* is unambiguous and the poem concludes with the anticipation of, the unmitigated yearning for, the birth of new social relations figured in properly spatial terms: the as yet to emerge revolutionary space of 'Noë sur la terre'. The various geographic synonyms for 'Noël sur la terre' that spring up at the end of the poem, the 'splendid cities', the 'beaches without end', are all situated in a future time, which suggests that 'Noël sur la terre' is to be construed not as the founding of a new 'proper place' but rather as that which, in its instability, in its displacement or deferment, exists as the breakdown of the notion of proper place: be it heaven or hell, Orient or Occident, winter or summer. The dizzying religious or vertical topography of the poem, with its meteoric descents and ascensions ('I believe myself to be in hell, so I am'; 'hell is certainly *below* – and heaven above'; 'Ah! to climb back up into life'; 'It's the flames which rise up with their damned one'), is resolved in the narrative's final sections by a horizontal and social topography ('I, who called myself magus or angel, exempt from all morality, I am given back to the earth, with a task to pursue'), a kind of lateral vision that is not so much a vision as a movement ('The song of the heavens, the march of peoples!'), and not so much a movement as a future movement: 'Let us receive all the influx of vigor and real tenderness. And, at dawn, armed with an ardent patience, we will enter into splendid cities.'

To the extent that the particular revolutionary realisation of the Commune can be seen in its political understanding of social space, we can speak here of an analogous breakdown of the notion of 'proper place'. Class division is also the division of the city into active and passive zones, into privileged places where decisions are made in secret, and places where these decisions are executed afterward. The rise of the bourgeoisie throughout the nineteenth century was inscribed on the city of Paris in the form of Baron Haussmann's architectural and social reorganisation, which gradually removed workers from the centre of the city to its northeastern peripheries, Belleville and Menilmontant. An examination of the voting records in the municipal elections organized by the Commune shows this social division clearly: less than 25 per cent of the inhabitants of the bourgeois *quartiers*, the 7th and 8th, voted in the election; only the 10th, 11th, 12th, and 18th, workers' *quartiers*, and the 5th, the university district, voted at more than half.[9] The workers' redescent into the centre of Paris followed in part from the political significance of the city center within a tradition of popular insurgency, and in part from their desire to reclaim the public space from which they had been expelled, to reoccupy streets that once were theirs.

If workers are those who are not allowed to transform the space/time allotted them, then the lesson of the Commune can be found in its recognition that revolution consists not in changing the juridical form that allots space/time (for example, allowing a party to appropriate bureaucratic organisation) but rather in completely transforming the nature of space/time. It is here that Marx's 'Transform the World' and

Rimbaud's 'Changer la Vie' become, as the Surrealists proclaimed, the same slogan. The working existence of the Commune constituted a critique pronounced against geographic zoning whereby diverse forms of socioeconomic power are installed: a breakdown of a privileged place or places in favour of a permanent exchange between distinct places – thus, the importance of the *quartier*. Lefebvre's work is especially important in emphasising the disintegration of the practical, material foundations and habits that organised daily life during the hardships of the siege of Paris in the fall and winter of 1870.[10] In the midst of this disintegration sprang up new networks and systems of communication solidifying small groups: local neighbourhood associations, women's clubs, legions of the National Guard, and, above all, the social life of the *quartier* – groups whose often avowedly revolutionary aspirations were allowed to develop freely in part because the government lacked both the means and the authority to police the city. The local *arrondissement* gained a considerable degree of autonomy, and the heavily populated popular districts had come close to being self-governing. The siege allowed new ambiences, new manners of encountering or of meeting with one another to develop that are both the product and the instrument of transformed behaviour.

The breakdown of spatial hierarchy in the Commune, one aspect of which was the establishment of places of political deliberation and decision making that were no longer secret but open and accessible, brought about a breakdown in temporal division as well. The publicity of political life, the immediate publication of all the Commune's decisions, and proclamations, largely in the form of *affiches*, resulted in a 'spontaneous' temporality whereby citizens were no longer informed of their history after the fact but were actually occupying the moment of its realisation. If the city and its streets were in fact reappropriated by the Communards, this undoubtedly entailed a Communard reinvention of urban rhythms: white nights and 'revolutionary days' that are not simply certain days marked off on a calendar, but are rather the introduction to and immersion in a new temporal movement. Journals and accounts of everyday life during the Commune written by people active in the insurrection suggest a particular and contradictory movement of time, a duration experienced as being at once more rapid and more slow than usual.[11] We will return to this peculiar temporality at some length in the next chapter; for now, we can describe the sensation as being a simultaneous perception of events passing by quickly, too quickly, and of each hour and minute being entirely lived or made use of: saturated time.

The workers who occupied the Hôtel de Ville or who tore down the Vendôme Column were not 'at home' in the centre of Paris; they were occupying enemy territory, the circumscribed proper place of the dominant social order. Such an occupation, however brief, provides an example of what the Situationists have called a *détournement* – using the elements or terrain of the dominant social order to one's own ends, for a transformed purpose; integrating actual or past productions into a superior construction of milieu.[12] *Détournement* has no other place but the place of the other; it plays on imposed terrain and its tactics are determined by the absence of a 'proper place'. Thus, the *détournement* of churches: using them to hold the meetings of women's clubs or other worker organizations. *Détournement* is no mere Surrealist or arbitrary juxtaposition of conflicting codes; its aim, at once serious and ludic, is to strip false meaning or value from the original:

> When the Club Communal of the Salle Molière took over the church of Saint-Nicolas-des-Champs, 'a public monument that until then had served only a caste, born enemy of all progress,' this was announced as a 'great revolutionary act' by the population of the district.[13]

A similar aim is apparent in Rimbaud's 'Ce qu'on dit au Poète à propos de fleurs', where the literary code of Parnassian aestheticism is 'deturned' by a jarring influx of social, utilitarian vocabulary:

> Ainsi, toujours, vers l'azur noir
> Où tremble la mer des topazes,
> Fonctionneront dans ton soir
> Les Lys, ces clystères d'extases!
>
> [Thus, continually toward the dark azure
> Where the sea of topazes shimmers,
> Will function in your evening
> Lilies, those enemas of ecstasy!]

Here the echo to Lamartine at his most elegiac ('Ainsi toujours poussés vers de nouveaux rivages . . .') coexists with the most mechanistic and technical of jargons: *fonctionneront* and *clystères*. What is the effect of the audacious realism of a word like *fonctionneront*? Rimbaud's insertion of technical vocabulary is purely strategic, and the word takes on significance only in the context of its Parnassian surroundings – of its relations with it and in dynamic criticism of it. Rimbaud's lexical anomalies, in other words, should not be considered as the mutation of isolated elements. We should always bear in mind that change lies in the *relation* of elements to each other: the particular dynamic created by what we might call lexical shock, incest, bastardism, or other such arrangements. Nor should the oppositional dynamic at work in 'Ce qu'on dit . . .' be understood as accidental or haphazard – an arbitrary, extrinsically conceived assemblage of juxtaposed disparate parts or discourses. Rather, the poem produces its own parts by active differentiation that in turn reform themselves into a new unity.

Certainly, the introduction of a jarringly 'nonpoetic' word like *fonctionneront*, placed in such close proximity to 'shimmering topazes', serves to assault the elite enclosure of Parnassian aesthetic isolationism, marooned and cut adrift as it was from the world of working relations and wider social institutions. It lays bare the Parnassian high bourgeois flight from the realm of utility – a flight governed, it would seem, by fear of the very contagion the poem enacts: fear of contact with the popular, fear of industrial 'progress' conceived of as social equality. But Rimbaud's gesture is double-, perhaps triple-edged. For although his use of technical vocabulary allies him with a class culture whose concerns – science, politics, social organisation – are distinct from the aesthetic and metaphysical interests of orthodox Parnassian culture, it does not, on the other hand, imply his entrenchment in some distinct, preconceived, countercultural identity. By the same token, the abrupt shock of lexical juxtaposition manages on a formal level to keep at bay the smooth ideological agenda – the whole reasoned march of progress regulated by instruction, by scientific principles and by the general interest, progress as the dominant explication of the social order, and of a society that thinks itself under the aegis of perfectibility – associated with the vocabulary of utility.

Elsewhere in Rimbaud's poetry, a similar subversion is carried out by the trivial, commonplace nature of the represented object, the introduction of the detail that is neither distinguished nor abject, the detail that has no higher significance than itself: the clove of garlic in 'Au Cabaret-Vert'.

IV

Accounts of the Commune and accounts of the 'phenomenon' of Rimbaud rely on a shared vocabulary:

> Rimbaud erupts into literature, throws a few lightning bolts and disappears, abandoning us from then on to what looks like twilight.

> We had hardly time to see him. . . . This is enough for the legend to be born and develop.[14]

> The seventy-two days from 18 March to 28 May 1871, the length of time Paris was able to hold out against the National Government at Versailles and its army, though too short to carry out any permanent measures of social reform, were long enough to create the myth, the legend of the Commune as the first great workers' revolt.[15]

Brevity, eruption, lightning flash, myth, legend – these are the words that recur. Mallarmé, for example, uses the metaphor of a meteor when speaking of Rimbaud; René Char writes of his 'sudden evaporation'. Qualities of speed, brevity, and brilliance are transferred from the bio-graphical phenomena to the production and reception of the work: anarchist art and literary critic Félix Fénréon, one of the first serious readers of the *Illuminations*, describes these poems in 1887 as having 'suddenly appeared, scattered by shocks into radiant repercussions';[16] Leo Bersani writes of Rimbaud's work as that of someone who wants to ' "stay" in language as briefly as possible'.[17] Neither Rimbaud, 'the first poet of a civilization that has not yet appeared' (Char), nor the Commune, that 'unplanned, unguided, formless revolution',[18] reached maturity. Perhaps it is this joint lingering in the liminal zone of adoles-cence – that Mallarmé, referring to Rimbaud, called 'a perverse and superb puberty' – that tends to create anxiety. For it is striking to see the way in which narratives of both subjects, for the most part, adhere to a traditional developmental model, concluding almost invariably with a consideration of the reasons for the failure of the Commune to become stabilised, of Rimbaud to remain loyal to literature, and ensuing motifs: the silence of Rimbaud, the demise of the Commune. Speculations abound as to what 'fulfillment' or 'adulthood' *might have* looked like: the poems Rimbaud would have written in Africa, the social reforms the Commune would have put through had it been given the time to stabilise.

But such an omniscient theoretical viewpoint gives way to easy proofs that the Commune was objectively doomed to failure and could not have been fulfilled. This viewpoint, as the Situationists point out, forgets that for those who really lived it, the fulfilment was *already there*. And as Mallarmé said of Rimbaud. 'I think that prolonging the hope for a work of maturity would harm, in this case, the exact interpretation of a unique adventure in the history of art.'[19] It is in this sense that Marx should be understood when he says that the most important social measure of the Commune was its own *working existence*.

The Commune, wrote Marx, was to be a working, not a parliamentary, body. Its destruction of hierarchic investiture involved the displacement (revocability) of authority along a chain or series of 'places' without any sovereign term. Each representative, subject to immediate recall, becomes interchangeable with, and thus equal to, its represented.

The direct result of this kind of distributional and revocable authority is the withering away of the political function as a specialised function. Rimbaud's move beyond the idea of a specialised domain of poetic language or even of poetry – the fetishisation of writing as a privileged practice – begins not in 1875 with his 'silence' but rather as early as 1871 with the 'Lettres du voyant'. In these letters, writing poetry is acknowledged as one means of expression, action, and above all of *work* among others:

> I will be a worker: that is the idea that holds me back when mad rage drives me toward the battle of Paris – where so many workers are dying as I write to you!'

The *voyant*, as has been frequently pointed out, '*se fait* voyant'. 'I *work* at making myself a *voyant*.' The emphasis here is on the work of self-transformation as opposed to the Romantic commonplace of poetic predestination. The *voyant* project emerges in the letters as the will to combat not merely specific past or contemporary poetic practices, but the will eventually to overcome and supersede 'poetry' altogether. Like the 'abolition of the state', the process outlined by Rimbaud is a long and arduous revolutionary process that unfolds through diverse phases. The work is not solitary but social and collective: 'other horrible workers will come: they will begin at the horizons where the first one has fallen!' In fact, the *voyant* project can be taken, in its totality, as a figure for nonalienated production in general. Its progress is to be measured. Rimbaud implies, by the degree to which 'the infinite servitude of women' is broken: 'When the unending servitude of woman is broken, when she lives by and for herself, when man – until now abominable – has given her her freedom, she too will be a poet!' An exclamation from the letters like 'Ces poètes seront!' must be placed in the context of the emergence, particularly in Rimbaud's later work, of a collective subject: the *nous* of the concluding moments of *Une Saison* ('Quand irons nous . . .'), of 'A une Raison'; of 'Après le Déluge'. Masses in movement – the human geography of uprisings, migrations, and massive displacements – dominate the later prose works: 'the song of the heavens, the march of peoples' (*'Une Saison'*); 'migrations more enormous than the ancient invasions' ('Génie'); 'the uprising of new men and their march forward' ('A une Raison'); 'companies have sung out the joy of new work' ('Villes').

The utopian resonance of *travail nouveau* – 'to greet the advent of new work' – can be found even in the project of *voyance*: an enterprise of self-and social transformation which implies that poets themselves accept their own uninterrupted transformation – even when this means ceasing to be a poet.

Notes

1. The one notable exception is Steve Murphy, in his 'Rimbaud et la Commune?'. In Alain Borer (ed.), *Rimbaud Multiple. Coloque de Cérisy* (Gourdon: Bedou & Touzot, 1985), pp. 50–65. I came across Murphy's very valuable and erudite research as I was completing this book; although our arguments and findings frequently overlap, Murphy's goal, as I take it, to enhance explications of particular poems by Rimbaud, is more circumscribed than mine.

2. Roland Barthes, 'Nautilus et Bateau ivre', *Mythologies* (Paris: Seuil, 1957), p. 91.

3. Alfred Delvau, *Dictionnuaire de la langue verte* (Paris: Marpon & Flammarion, 1883), p. 87.

4. Gustave-Paul Cluseret, *Mémoires du général Cluseret*, vol. II (Paris: Jules Levy, 1887); citations taken from pp. 274–87.

5. Louis Rossel, *Mémoires, procès et correspondance* (Paris: J. J. Pauvert, 1960), p. 276.

6. Catulle Mendès, *Les 73 Journées de la Commune* (Paris: E. Lachaud, 1871), p. 311.

7. Auguste Blanqui, *Instructions pour une prise d'armes* (Paris: Editions de la tête de feuilles, 1972), 61.

8. Friedrich Engels, introduction to Karl Marx and V. I. Lenin, *The Civil War in France: The Paris Commune* (New York: International Publishers, 1940), p. 18.

9. Pierre Gascar, *Rimbaud et la Commune* (Paris: Gallimard, 1971), p. 66.

10. See Henri Lefebvre, *La Proclamation de la Commune* (Paris: Gallimard, 1965).

11. See, especially, Louis Barron, *Sous le drapeau rouge* (Paris: Albert Savine), pp. 83–7, for one of the best descriptions by an active Communard of the sense of daily life under the Commune.

12. For a description of *détournement*, see especially Guy-Ernest Debord and Gil J. Wolman, 'Mode d'emploi du détournement', *Les lèvres nues*, no. 8 (May 1956); reprinted in Gil Wolman, *Résumé des chapitres précédents* (Paris: Editions Spiess, 1981), pp. 46–53; English version in Ken Knabb (ed. and trans.), *Situationist International Anthology* (Berkeley, Calif.: Bureau of Public Secrets, 1981), pp. 8–14.

13. *Bulletin Communal*, 6 May 1871, cited in Stewart Edwards, *The Paris Commune 1871* (Devon: Newton Abbot, 1972), p. 284.

14. Gascar, *Rimbaud et la Commune*, p. 9.
15. Stewart Edwards (ed.), *The Communards of Paris, 1871*, (Ithaca, NY: Cornell University Press, 1973) pp. 9–10.
16. Félix Fénéon, 'Arthur Rimbaud: *Les Illuminations*', in Joan Halperin (ed.), *Oeuvres plus que complètes*, vol. II (Geneva: Massot, 1970), p. 572.
17. Leo Bersani, 'Rimbaud's Simplicity', in *A Future for Astyanax: Character and Desire in Literature* (Boston: Little, Brown, 1976), p. 247.
18. Edwards (ed.), *The Communards of Paris, 1871*, p. 10.
19. Stephane Mallarmé, *Oeurves complèetes*, ed. Henri Mondor and G. Jean-Aubry (Paris: Gallimard, 1945), p. 518.

12

Peter Womack, *Improvement and Romance: Constructing the Myth of the Highlands* (1989)

In the course of the latter half of the eighteenth century, the Highlands of Scotland were subject to a process of ideological appropriation that turned them from a perceived alien province of no interest into a site of romance, the world of a romantic imagination epitomised at the end of the process by Walter Scott's ballad-epic *The Lady of the Lake* (1810). Womack analyses this cultural construction from its inception after the defeat of the Jacobite clans at Culloden in 1746 and shows how, in 'a covert complementarity', it accompanies 'improvement', the dominant theme of British discourse concerning the Highlands. Though 'romance' and 'improvement' may seem opposites, they prove, in fact, to have been closely related: romance serves to settle the contradictions to which improvement gives rise within 'a kind of reservation in which the values [the latter] provokes and suppresses can be *contained* – that is, preserved, but also imprisoned'.

In the following extract, the particular relationship to place involved in *holidays* is shown as bound up with a new practice central for the romancing of the Highlands and used as a specific demonstration of the complementary interaction of the terms and realities of improvement and romance. What interests Womack here and throughout – it informs the conception and style of his analysis – is, as his subtitle suggests, the Highlands as *myth*. They are romantic *because* they have been romanticised, colonised by a plethora of signs that *give* their nature, precisely what we *see* as 'the Highlands'. It is with the history of this nature, these signs, that Womack is concerned and of which 'going on holiday' is to be recognised as a significant part.

Holidays

Make-believe

In July 1771, an English tourist called Anthony Champion found himself in a remote Highland valley. The farmer who occupied it was away, and his wife, anxious to be suitably hospitable, sent a boy to the hill to fetch 'a lamb and a kid'. Charmed by this pastoral injunction, and clearly a little titillated by his sudden intimacy with the pretty mistress of the isolated holding, Champion recorded the whole encounter in the style of the Authorised Version.[1] For example, it appears that the woman was puzzled by Champion's touristic enthusiasm for the scenery. The account makes her express her reaction in these terms:

> the country from which thou comest . . . is a rich and plentiful country, and the people thereof live in fair dwellings, and eat of the fat of the land; but this country, thou seest, is poor and barren, and the manners thereof are rude and ignorant; thou canst not surely be pleased with such things.

The narrator's comment is:

> The very wildness of the country is pleasing to me, and for the manners thereof, this kindness to the traveller must indeed seem strange to those who come from afar.

It isn't altogether barren in any case: there is a stream, and good pasture, with trees – 'And he cast his eyes around, and the place seemed to him as a portion of Eden.'

The thought here – the contrast between the material assets of the south and the immaterial assets of the poor Highlands – is familiar from Anne Grant; as is the poetic literalism which ties an aesthetic pleasure down to a well-documented Highland fact (the laws of hospitality). These values are gravely, even touchingly enforced. But the biblical pastiche undermines their seriousness in a peculiar way: despite its aptness – or rather, precisely because its aptness is so neat – it has the effect of facetiousness. It's like fancy dress: Champion is playing at being Abraham's servant meeting Rebekah at the well, and it's that tone of make-believe, of walking into literature, that makes everything so delightful. This wilful frivolity affects the treatment of history as well. Champion is aware that the absent husband is a Lowland sheep farmer whose 'flocks multiplied exceedingly, and fed upon a thousand hills' – that is, the pastoralism actually reflects contemporary change. But he chooses to see it as timeless, exclaiming, 'Surely this is the ancient world, and the manners of the times of old.' He is able to indulge in this interpretation because he is a visitor, with no commitments or connections in the neighbourhood – at the end, he looks back, sighs, and bends his way into the hills. In other words, his eccentric form is a stylistic production of a historically new relationship with place, crucial to the Highlands: *going on holiday.*

Although going on holiday is a practice which is clearly related to the Tours and Journeys I've drawn on extensively throughout this book, the similarity of the activities conceals a significant retextualisation. The 'describer of distant regions', as Johnson put it in 1760, 'is always welcomed as a man who has laboured for the pleasure of others, and who is able to enlarge our knowledge and rectify our opinions':[2] that is, travelling comes under the sign of information; it is rather like reading works of history or agronomy or aesthetics, with the added advantage that one is seeing the antiquities, fields, paintings, for oneself. This is the notional status of the Grand Tour which is the model for the lesser tours – it's a part of the tourist's education. A holiday, on the other hand, is a gesture, not of inquiry into the world, but of playful refusal of it; not an extension of one's practical experience but a licensed truancy from it. The literary analogy is not information but fiction (a critical opposition which is exactly contemporary with the invention of holidaying as a social practice,[3] the travelling, to invoke a greater eccentricity from the same moment as Champion's Highland trip, is not so much a Grand Tour as a sentimental journey.[4] In this, the holiday directly picks up the readings, which we have already seen, of Highland scenery and society as literally poetic, and seeks to enact them. Adopting the region as the setting for a pleasurable and circumscribed narrative, one constructs a personal text, a literarisation of a few weeks of one's own real life.

The shift of models is intriguingly visible in Johnson's own journey, which happened two years after Champion's. Johnson's account of it conforms wholly to his own principles for such works, being informative, philosophic and only rarely and uneasily anecdotal. But then it is shadowed, so to speak, by Boswell's *Journal*, whose preoccupation with Johnson as a personality has the unmistakable effect of rewriting the itinerary of the *Journey* as a holiday. The biographical emphasis recurrently turns the Highlands into *décor*: the piquant vignettes – Ursa Major on a horse, the Rambler practising stoicism at a poor inn, the English Tory in a bed once slept in by Prince Charlie, the famous Scotbaiter posing with Caledonian broadsword and blue bonnet, the editor of Shakespeare walking upon the locations of *Macbeth*[5] – have exactly the character of an album of snapshots.

This light-heartedness also retextualises the issue of the patriarchal past: against Johnson's sombre analysis, Boswell sets a curious hilarity:

> My endeavours to rouse the English-bred Chieftain, in whose house we were, to the feudal and patriarchal feelings, Dr Johnson this morning tried to bring him to our way of thinking. – *Johnson.* 'Were I in your place, sir, in seven years I would make this an independent island. I would roast oxen whole and hang out a flag as a signal to the Macdonalds to come and get beef and whisky (p. 256).'

Whatever the tone of Boswell's endeavours, Johnson's are parodic: the picturesque vision of rude hospitality is a fantasy which delights in its own absurdity. At Dunvegan, he reacts with the same high spirits to the playful offer of an island:

> Dr Johnson was highly amused with the fancy. . . . He talked a great deal of this island; – how he would build a house there, – how he would fortify it, – how he would have cannon, – how he would plant, – how he would sally out, and *take* the isle of Muck; – and then he laughed with uncommon glee, and could hardly leave off (p. 327).

The attraction and the absurdity have the same source: the small, inter-personal scale of the imagined polity. It's not only that Johnson knows his plans aren't real; the plans themselves, with their lilliputian princi-palities and naively direct power relations, have a playacting quality; he is imagining *being* an imaginary king. So that when he exclaims, on Raasay, 'This is truly the patriarchal life: this is what we came to find' (p. 268), his delight is partly that of the philosophic traveller, pleased at the chance to learn about a society different from his own; but it is also the pleasure of make-believe, of playing the role of Ulysses among Homeric islets (p. 59).

Another doubled tour, that of William and Dorothy Wordsworth, records the same 'uncommon glee'. Wanting to see the Trossachs, they and Coleridge left their horse and car at Tarbet, crossed Loch Lomond and walked east to Glengyle with no idea of where they would stay. They ended up in the house of the ferryman who took them on Loch Katrine. Their night there thus represented the success of a mildly adventurous departure from the ordinary tourist route from Dumbarton to Inveraray: it was as it were an exclusion from their excursion, a double truancy. Their response is full of that pleasant irresponsibility:

> We caroused our cups of coffee, laughing like children at the strange atmosphere in which we were: the smoke came in gusts, and spread along the walls and above our heads in the chimney, where the hens were roosting like light clouds in the sky. We laughed and laughed again, in spite of the smarting of our eyes.[6]

It's not altogether clear what they were laughing at, until later on, when Dorothy describes herself going to sleep thinking 'of the Fairyland of Spenser, and what I had read in romance at other times, and then, what a feast would it be for a London pantomime-maker, could he but translate it to Drury Lane, with all its beautiful colours!' This is again, intensely, the sense of being on holiday. To be really here, in a sort of pantomime woodcutter's cottage, with smoke, and criss-cross beams, and hens! – the childlike laughter is not so much amusement as *merriment*; a suspension of normal prudence.

Later in their tour, the Wordsworths revisited the same hut by deviating westward from their route south towards Stirling, this time leaving the horse at Callander.[7] This second piece of touristic inventiveness is the context for William's poem 'Stepping Westward': they heard the suggestive phrase in a civil greeting from a woman on the road by Loch Katrine. The incident is a variant of those we looked at in a different context: again, it is an evening encounter on the road, with a native speaker in a lonely place furnishing the mind with an enigmatic text that carries it beyond itself and beyond the material world. But this time, although the intimation of mortality is still felt in the implicit allegory of the westbound road as the course of life, the tone is markedly less elegiac:

> And stepping westward seemed to be
> A kind of *heavenly* destiny:
> I liked the greeting; 'twas a sound
> Of something without place or bound;
> And seemed to give me spiritual right
> To travel through that region bright.[8]

The difference is that the moment of transcendence is not founded on the intense feeling of separation which characterised 'The Solitary Reaper' or the Ossian poem. Instead of the indecipherable Gaelic text, there is just a slightly idiosyncratic English; and the poem's expansive construction of the phrase is consciously and waywardly *chosen* – that is, the imagination is self-delightingly at play. Hence the relaxed tone – 'seemed', 'liked', 'something'. What motivates this pleasant easing up is that by returning to the 'pantomime' hut from a different direction – by knowing that it is waiting for them in 'that region bright' towards the sunset – the travellers have made it into an imaginary home. The 'something without place or bound' is as it were the freedom of the country: it is eternity as mediated, not by any theological category, but by the holiday game of staying somewhere a few days and acting as if one lives there always, always retaining the fresh impressions and uncommitted liberty of the chance visitor.

It was on the same loch, a few years later, that Scott established the shrine of this holiday-cottage Elysium. In a lavish costume dramatisation of Champion's homestay, the lost traveller, who is the King in disguise, is welcomed into the island retreat of the mysterious Lady of the Lake who might be an enchantress and who will not divulge her parentage. The King is wandering in dangerous country for reasons in which political finesse and whimsical pleasure are obscurely mixed; the Lady is hiding on the island because her noble father has been outlawed. Their first meeting, before the determinacies of the plot cut short its possibilities, is thus the encounter of two Shakespearean holiday myths – Prince Hal and Rosalind. For both, to be in the Highlands is to leave behind one's constricting official identity and assume a playful and temporary innocence. The island refuge, then, with its ready music, its rich adornment of trees and flowers, and its weightless 'shallop' the delightfully fragile link with the shore, is a retreat, not just from specific dangers, but from 'life's uncertain main' in general. The lyrics, such as 'Soldier, rest!', 'The lonely isle', 'Ave Maria!',[9] which undercut the rather philistine comedy of the main narrative, reflect in their self-absorbed melancholy the transitory perfection of that withdrawal. Real life is a scene of brutality and self-interest, but before long one must leave the island and go back to work.

The tourist in the text

In the most incompetent literary fictions of the Highland romance, the analogy with going on holiday is naively visible. For example, in *The Romance of the Highlands*, a deservedly forgotten publication of that '*annus mirabilis* of romance',[10] 1810, the hero, Kenneth, is wandering in the mountains one day when he is impressed by a portent we've encountered before, the hollow sound of the wind among the rocks:

'He looked around, expecting to see the majestic form of some ancient bard, seated upon a high rock, musing upon the scene, and now and then striking the strings of his harp.'[11] It's an expectable fancy in an Ossianised tourist. But Kenneth is a medieval Highlander; he plays the harp himself, and a few chapters earlier in another rugged setting, he really did meet with a majestic form – that of an ancient hermit rather than an ancient bard – who told him the secret of his birth. The author has forgotten that his hero is part of the romance, and incongruously made him part of the romanticism too. Something similar is happening in other costume fictions of the Highlands when heroines about to be ravished, and generals marching into battle, nevertheless continue to admire the cataracts and woods around them.[12]

In all these cases it's inadequate to say that the reader is being invited to identify with the character. Rather, the character is identifying with the reader; the romantic associations of the story have won a pyrrhic victory over its practical details; we are reading about lives which are imaginary, not only for us, but also for the people who are supposed to be leading them. What many of these novels need is a preface explaining that the story is really set, not in the fourteenth century, but in the 1790s, and that the characters are all guests at an elaborate fancy-dress weekend party.[13] On such a basis the narrative becomes fairly intelligible.

More sophisticated romancers integrate the holiday-maker in the fiction by the device of *wandering*. By being homeless, or losing his way, the protagonist approximates naturally to the designedly 'truant' condition of the visitor for pleasure exemplified by the Wordsworths. In Ann Radcliffe's first book, for instance – *The Castles of Athlin and Dunbayne* – the noble heir to one of the castles is an enthusiast in the mould of Beattie's 'Minstrel'[14] who goes for long walks amid 'the wild variety of nature'. The story begins when, straying too far in one of his poetic reveries, he finds he is lost.

> He remained for some time in a silent dread not wholly unpleasing, but which was soon heightened to a degree of terror not to be endured. . . . His memory gave him back no image of the past; and having wandered some time, he came to a narrow pass . . .[15]

Through the pass he comes upon a lushly wooded valley where, in a romantically situated cottage, he encounters a peasant of inexplicably noble mien who eventually turns out to be the lost heir of the other castle. The aesthetics of holiday scenery have passed seamlessly over into the mechanics of narrative. But then it's clear from this transition that Radcliffe is really interested, not in the places, which are only differentiated to the extent needed to separate out the romantic, the terrible and the beautiful, and not in the plot, which is a cliché, but in sensibility. The hero's emotional responses to his changing situation are traced with a subtlety that stands out from the crudity of the rest; the narrative is essentially a pretext for the subjectivisation of the landscape, as the mystery which is the plot provides a formula for the *sense* of mystery which is the desired effect of the mountainous setting.

For the definitive version of this formulation, we must return once more to *The Lady of the Lake*. As is well known, the poem was received as a literal invitation to visit its locations. It made the Trossachs into the prime Highland tourist site overnight, spreading prosperity along the banks of the Teith and redundancy along those of Loch Lomond.[16] Sir John Sinclair's carriage in the autumn of 1810 was the 297th of the season; since the previous maximum was about a hundred, he concluded with appropriately statistical wit 'that the effect of praise in verse compared to praise in prose is as 3 to 1'.[17] Scott's appropriation of the place continues to be acknowledged by the Ordnance Survey, which marks 'Ellen's Isle' in the current series.

One result of this extraordinary instance of literary effectiveness is an impression that Loch Katrine was actually discovered by Scott. As is suggested by Sinclair's control figure, itself quite high, the impression is false. As early as 1800, John Stoddart could say that the celebrity of Loch Katrine made him anxious to visit it;[18] this may reflect rhapsodic descriptions in Mrs Murray's *Companion to, Scotland* (1799) and, earlier still, in the Callander entry for the *Statistical Account*, which was written by the minister, James Robertson, in 1791. Robertson records that 'the Trosacks are often visited by persons of taste';[19] so even he was not the pioneer. Scott himself generously drew on (and acknowledged) a local guide book produced in 1806 by the minister at Aberfoyle, Patrick Graham. In short, he chose for his Highland poem a setting which was already well known for its scenery. The poem did not create a tourist attraction inadvertently, as *Hamlet* has done at Helsingør, for example. Its holiday connection with place was part of its making.

At the opening of the poem, when the 'antler'd monarch of the waste' pauses on the slopes of Uamh Mhor to decide whether to make for Loch Ard or Loch Achray, it is surveying the alternative approaches to the Trossachs which make up the two sections of the Revd Graham's booklet – the west road from Callander and the south road by Aberfoyle from Gartmore. The animal chooses the more popular

Callander route, and so leads the hunt up the valley of the Teith through a litany of place names and thumbnail descriptions – Cambusmore, Ben Ledi, Loch Vennachar, Loch Achray, Ben Venue – which exactly rehearses the notable features of the road as they would appear to a user of the guide book.[20] So the ride which occupies the first eight stanzas is like a day trip to the Trossachs, delightfully transformed into a breathless and antique adventure.

As in Radcliffe, the destination of this journey is a pass, on the far side of which the story is waiting. Scott specifies that vague sense of inadvertent admission to an alien world by linking it to the romantic topos of the wild rider who, like Sir Walter in Words-worth's 'Hart-Leap Well' (1800) or Bürger's 'Wilde Jäger' (1778),[21] is separated from his companions and led by his quarry into an encounter with the supernatural. So that by the time the stag reaches the 'darksome glen' of the Trossachs, the place is already charged with magical expectations; and these are fulfilled in literal fashion when it transpires later that the huntsman is expected, his arrival having been foreseen by a second-sighted bard. But the real enchantment is not supernatural: it is scenic.

The noisy vigour of the chase is abruptly cut off by the death of the huntsman's horse. In the strange stillness he sets off on foot to find his 'comrades of the day': clearly that should mean that he follows his own tracks eastwards in the direction of Brig o' Turk. At this point however, the landscape takes over, in four stanzas of virtuoso natural description which refract all the accumulated energy of the ride, so that now it's the path that finds its way, the rocks that shoot up, nature that scatters the flowers and trees which themselves mingle, find their bowers, group, weep, cast anchor and fling their boughs across the sky.[22] The huntsman, now the 'wanderer', loses the initiative: first his eyes and then his steps are passively drawn upward and westward by the brilliant and balletic scenery. His subsequent discovery of Loch Katrine itself is displaced in the same way:

> Onward, amid the copse 'gan peep
> A narrow inlet, still and deep . . .
> Lost for a space, through thickets veering,
> But broader when again appearing,
> Tall rocks and tufted knolls their face
> Could on the dark-blue mirror trace.

The movement denoted by 'onward' and 'veering', and the seeing suggested by 'trace', must literally be the wanderer's, but the syntax avoids having him as subject, and misrelates its participles confusingly in order to keep the objects of his gaze in motion. The effect is like subjective camera: the person vanishes and the text records only the retinal image swaying and scintillating. So one hardly notices that he is walking in exactly the wrong direction. He is unresisting: the picturesque leads him to its mistress like a fairy herald.

Thus, as in the romantic novels but with incomparably greater power, the hero's adventure provides a formula for the affectivity of the setting. The sublimity of the Trossachs contributes directly to his destiny, by half-stealing him from himself and drawing him into the presence of the mystery. Burke's conceptual link between mountain aesthetics and the 'passions belonging to self-preservation', which underpins the whole theory of the sublime, is made dramatic by literally concealing in the precipitous scenery the perils which the plot holds in store. So readers of the poem who then go to Loch Katrine see it, not only highlighted for them by a minute picturesque description, but also bathed in the glow of a narrative aura. In a letter of August 1810, Elizabeth Spence, one of Sinclair's 296 predecessors, describes the locality in terms which are ecstatically soaked in the poem's imagery, but also declares that even Scott's description is inadequate to the beauty of the real thing.[23] This is the poem's unconscious accolade: the readers see its romance, not printed on the page, but inhering in the land.

This triumphant naturalisation, however, is marked by an operating contradiction. Scott's huntsman is an *ideal* picturesque tourist in the precise sense that the ideas suggested by the scenery – solitude, danger, wonder – are practical aspects of his situation. The holiday-makers imitate his extreme experience, but their own practice is in fact organised by considerations – convenience, safety, planning – which specifically negate the terms of the original. The huntsman, after all, finds Loch Katrine by accident: one could hardly arrange to do that. This is the ironic force of Sinclair's calculations: the glamour of the image is measurable by the number of people who come to contemplate it and so render it commonplace. The brighter the aura, the faster it is dispelled. Like the search, in our own time, for 'unspoiled' Mediterranean resorts, the project of actualising the Highland romance is caught in a self-defeating circularity.

The huntsman

Scott was offering one beguiling chance of squaring the circle. The activity which precipitates his hero into the enchanted Highland world is itself a kind of game. Hunting, of the kind pursued by James V, has the same kind of doubleness as holiday-making. Like tourism, it *denotes* a relationship with the land which is more primitive and immediate than its own: the civilised sportsman, who could go to the butcher's if he preferred to, is in a sense imitating the pre-pastoral hunter for whom it is a matter of survival. But at the same time, hunting as an amusement is not reducible to the category of make-believe: it is a real institution, with a tradition whose length and cultural richness renders it effectively independent of its inherent reference to food-gathering. Besides, the animal really dies. In short, here is one social practice in which the imagined and the actual, romance and materiality, seem to suspend their mutal contradictions and form a single object. A strategy for realising the 'literally poetic' Highlands in practice is afforded by the special fictiveness of sport.

The condition of this reconciliation is of course one which is threatened by Improvement. There must be wild creatures available to hunt, and a sufficiently spacious habitat in which to hunt them without destroying the crops and herds of husbandry. Consequently, as agricultural revolution proceeds and land use approaches totality, hunting tends to be pushed into the margins[24] – geographical margins, certainly, in the sense that the peripheral wilderness, whether it is a primeval relic or an ecological casualty, continues to harbour 'game'; but also cultural margins, as the activity becomes more and more remote from the socioeconomic concerns of actual rural society and makes new connections with myths of wildness and pastness. It's unsurprising, then, that the Highlands should have begun to attract the attention of sportsmen as the region's own agrarian and cultural marginality became more and more pronounced.

The English pioneer was Col. Thomas Thornton, a wealthy Yorkshire landowner and fanatic of gun and rod, whose love affair with the Highlands began in 1784. That summer, he established a camp on Speyside on a military scale, bringing (by two baggage wagons and a sea-going sloop) equipment including boats, fishing-tackle, guns, ammunition, hawks, horses, dogs, furniture, hay and corn, materials for stables and gardens, and a gargantuan quantity of provisions for himself, his retinue, and his numerous guests.[25] Throughout the season he supplemented these resources with a steady haul of fresh fish and game. Thus, interestingly, his overall plan of campaign treated the Highlands as if they were uninhabited: he lived on what he had brought and what he killed. He knew very well that this wasn't necessary: he socialised with the local gentry and made use of local sporting knowledge. His preparations, with their massively practical air, thus have something irreducibly imaginary about them. He appears to be coordinating an ambitious expedition; what he is actually doing is substantiating a fiction. The aim is not only to bag a quantity of game but also to invent a certain primitive and princely style of life – a holiday.

His enjoyment of the result comes freshly off the pages. Sitting on top of the Cairngorms, eating soup made from newly killed ptarmigan and drinking champagne which has been chilled in a nearby snowdrift, he reflects somewhat sententiously that this meal

> was relished with a keenness of appetite that none but those that have been at Glen Ennoch can experience; an appetite, far, very far superior to the palled one, with which the gentlemen at Weltgie's or Lethellier's eat their sumptuous and costly meals.[26]

He is also a partisan of wild scenery, with a contempt for 'beautiful, highly-finished landscapes' which suggests the natural sublime; but this taste is wholly innocent of 'horror'. It is not a question of the spiritual rewards of negativity: Thornton simply likes his views, as he likes his establishment, to be rough and lavish, connoting the adventures of the chase rather than the successes of cultivation. At this point it's clear that the enterprise includes a familiar animus against Improvement: refusing, like Anne Grant's Highlanders, the 'frigid aid' of the butcher and the baker, or rather of the waiter and the landscape gardener, Thornton pours his immense energy into a simulacrum of unalienated and undivided labour. His exertions produce, not exchange value within an abstracting system, but, directly and physically, food and the appetite to enjoy it. Glen Ennoch is his escape from the reifying relations of commodity production – that is, of the sources of his own wealth – 'back' to a means of satisfying needs which is cumbersome, certainly, but feels natural and wholesome.

As the champagne reminds us, though, the escape is a playful one. Thornton is perhaps recreating the enormous hunts and royal hospitality of the old lords of the Highlands, such as the famous stag drive of the Earl of Mar described by an English visitor in 1618.[27] But whereas, historically, such occasions had an intelligible function in the life of the nobility, Thornton's hunting and fishing summer is a private extravaganza, requiring personal inventiveness and disposable income acquired elsewhere. In such a context, the real cost of dining in rude splendour on top of a mountain is much greater than the price of a meal at Lethellier's. Barbarism is more of a luxury than luxury.

In other words Thornton, despite his gentlemanly philistinism, is really an aesthete, going to extraordinary lengths to arrange his life in accordance with a literary conception of beauty. The covert priority of the aesthetic motive is, as we have seen, an Ossianic structure; and Thornton resembles Macpherson's heroes of sensibility, not only by the unconvincing alternation in his behaviour between the earliest and the latest stage of civil society, but also in his devotion to activities which seem functional but aren't. His unremitting pursuit of food *looks* like a productive activity, but actually the product is the pretext for the pursuit. Like the ancient Caledonians, he fights only for fame, disdaining plunder.

In all this he foreshadows the Victorian and Edwardian cult of the Highland stag, which would take his own playacting to extreme heights in the artificiality of its naturalism and the mingled facetiousness and kitsch of its artefacts. He might even be called the father of the sporting Highlands were it not for one omission: as Scott pointed out in a review of his book,[28] Thornton failed to discover deer-stalking. He was a little too early: in his time, the only forms of deer-hunting which were well known in the south were the big traditional drive with hundreds of beaters, and the wild mounted chase using deer hounds, both of which were impractical in modern conditions. Stalking – pursuing the deer alone and on foot by stealth – had been a task or amusement of young Highland men for generations; but it was not until a decade or so after the publication of Thornton's book that it was discovered by Englishmen, such as the Duke of Bedford, who tried it in 1818, and William Scrope, who started stalking at Bruar Lodge on the Atholl estate in 1822, and in 1838 published *The Art of Deerstalking*, thus launching the upper-class English craze which peaked only in 1914.[29]

As the dates strongly suggest, Scott is decisively present at the very beginning of this development. His use of the word 'deer-stalking' in the Thornton review is probably its first appearance in this sense;[30] moreover, the hunt in the *Lady* adumbrates the emotional logic of the whole subsequent enthusiasm. Although the poem's hero doesn't stalk his stag – like Thornton, he doesn't know how to pursue deer in the Highlands, and the quarry escapes once it has crossed the Line – the chase is what leads him to his encounter with the Highland romance. For landscape, as James Holloway and Lindsay Errington have pointed out,[31] the point about deer-stalking is that it makes it impossible to plan your route; it is dictated as you go along by the direction of the wind and the wanderings of the quarry. Attached to the animal as if by a spell, you are led irresistibly into unknown scenes, vast solitudes, immediate and exhausting and possibly dangerous contact with the wilderness. That is, you remake for yourself – disdaining imitation – the predicament of the royal huntsman carried beyond the limits of conventional hunting, standing alone, dismounted, nameless and entranced amid 'the scenery of a fairy dream'.

According to the conventions of the game, then, the pursuit of the deer is the means of entry to a primeval, extra-social world of direct sensations – in short, to nature. Of course, it cannot really produce the transition: rather, the sport is a text which *signifies* it. And in this case, the difference between signified and signifier amounts to a direct incompatibility. Game was in practice a minor issue of Improvement. Alexander Irvine, for instance, a Highland minister and Improving writer, noted in 1802 that

> Some things in the Highlands were not considered by the peasants property till very lately. It was necessary to change their ideas, and teach them to respect the rights of their superiors to game, fish and wood.
>
> The old notions are yet strongly retained in some districts, and not infrequently put into practice; for it is not easy to convince a Highlander, that a landlord has a better right to a deer, a moorfowl, or a salmon, than he has himself, because he considers them the unconfined bounty of Heaven.[32]

According to this, the Highlander shares the romantic view that hunting is a natural activity, and draws from it the logical but inconvenient conclusion that it cannot therefore be private property. Although this 'savage' attitude is one that must appeal to the aesthetics of a Thornton – the last phrase suggests that Irvine himself is not wholly unsympathetic – it's nevertheless out of the question to concede anything to it; for it's the sportsman, precisely, who makes it so necessary to enforce shooting and fishing rights, because of the commercial value his interest confers on the game. By coincidence, it was in Thornton's first season, 1784–85, that a system of game certificates was first introduced in the Highlands,[33] thus formalising the complex struggle between sport and poaching which is still in progress in the region today. The new hunters were hastening the actual extinction of the way of life to which they did imaginary homage. Although the sportsman has succeeded, with great ingenuity, in circumventing the law of diminishing imaginative returns which undermines the satisfactions of

the tourist, he is caught in what is essentially the same trap. Its underlying form is now clearly visible: it is that the holiday escape from
commodification is itself a commodity.

Leisure and industry

The Highland holiday, in other words, is one trace of the complex
process which, around the end of the eighteenth century, was making
leisure into a form of private property.[34] The hunts, fairs and holydays
of traditional British society, both rural and urban, were forms of recreation which were definingly public in their orientation and presence:[35]
they were things which extended communities did, and since they
often included various kinds of production and trading, they represented a sort of 'leisure' which was not wholly separated from work.
The new type of holiday is quite different. By leaving his home area
and going to somewhere he has selected as a holiday place, the
holiday-maker detaches himself completely from his normal social
environment and from the ways in which he makes a living. Instead of
being an expression of society, the holiday becomes a turning away
from it, towards solitude, fantasy, nature, domesticity; we have already
seen how closely adapted the Highland image was to the orchestration
of exactly these themes.

This new practice is associated with the growing strength and universality of commodity production, not only in the sense, exemplified by
Thornton, that the holiday is itself a commodity, privately purchased
and consumed, but also in that it projects an absolute separation of
leisure and work, constituting the two states as mutually exclusive opposites. That's to say, the identification of one's holiday as a finite time
which is 'all one's own' is a reflex of the identification of working time
as belonging entirely to someone else. The logic of political economy,
which requires for its calculation of the costs and productivity of
labour a clear distinction between working and not working, throws
out as the converse and compensation of work the theoretically uncon-
ditioned category of 'spare time'.

For the activists of Improvement, the absence of any such clarity was
one of the main causes of Highland underdevelopment. The two
decades between Thornton's first visit to Speyside and the publication
of his book were dominated by the search for what one influential
pamphlet called 'the means of exciting a spirit of national industry'.[36]
The Highland Society of Scotland and the British Fisheries Society were
both founded with the fostering of such a spirit as one of their explicit

social aims; the 'General View' series of agricultural reports on Scottish counties and Sinclair's *Statistical Account* pursued the same goal in countless local observations.[37] In 1803, the year of the Wordsworths' holiday and of Anne Grant's leisurely pastoral, the Caledonian Canal was begun, partly in the hope of 'improving the Habits of the Country by Teaching Lessons of systematic Industry'.[38] Thus the discovery of the Highlands as a regular location for leisure pursuits went in step with a systematic attempt to control and reduce the irregular leisure of the natives.

Conversely, the pre-capitalist Highlands, considered as a place devoid of the blessings of industry, could also be read as a place free of its pains:

> At two seasons of the year, they were busy; the one in the end of spring and beginning of summer, when they put the plough into the little land they had capable of receiving it . . . the other just before winter, when they reaped their harvest; The rest of the year was all their own, for amusement or for war. If not engaged in war, they indulged themselves in summer in the most delicious of all pleasures to men in a cold climate and romantic country, the enjoyment of the sun, and of the summer-views of nature; never in the house during the day, even sleeping often at night in the open air, among the mountains and woods. They spent the winter in the chase, while the sun was up; and in the evening, assembling round a common fire, they entertained themselves with the song, the tale, and the dance.[39]

Unimproved Highlanders, as here described by Sir John Dalrymple in 1771, do very little work because their primitive husbandry and barren country leave very little work that can be done. Thus, ironically, they derive from their poverty what members of the privileged class in Dalrymple's own society derive from their wealth: the leisure to cultivate their sensibility. Their lives are an undemanding mixture of poetry, scenery and field sports; whatever its accuracy as an account of the Highland past, this was a fairly exact programme for the near future. The original state of society which is projected as the *absence* of Improvement is reproduced as a *holiday* from it. The heir of the carefree savage is the Victorian plutocrat, seeking temporary refuge from his rational and profitable mode of life in a sort of anthropological quixotism. But then the inheritance is inescapably also a falsification: the primitive unity of work and play within a single natural necessity is commemorated in a totally gratuitous form of play which deliberately places itself hundreds of miles away from the scenes of work; and the 'common fire' of the primitive collective is rekindled in a private hearth.

In holiday-making, that is, the aesthetic refusal of Improvement finds a form which is essentially a phase of what it refuses. It was even perhaps the decisive phase. By the time the Caledonian Canal was finished, the sheep were coming under pressure from the spread of sporting estates; the Highlands were attaining new dignity as the summer homeland of royalty; and tourism, rather than trade, was proving to be the beneficiary of the new forms of transport such as steamships and railways.[40] The meagre rewards of crofting were, and are, eked out not by any new dynamic in the real Highland economy but by the expenditure of the consumers of the myth. It had been Thornton and Scott rather than Sinclair or Telford who spoke for the practical future. 'Fancy's Land' imposed itself on the literal territory.

Notes

1. Anthony Champion, *Miscellanies in Verse and Prose* (1801), pp. 72–8.
2. Samuel Johnson, *Idler*, no. 97 (February 1760), in W. J. Bate, J. M. Bullitt and L. F. Powell (eds), *The Yale Edition of the Works of Samuel Johnson*, Vol. II (New Haven, 1963), pp. 298–300.
3. E.g. Edward Young on the 'original' writer: 'on the strong wing of his Imagination . . . we have no Home, no Thought, of our own; till the Magician drops his Pen: And then falling down into ourselves, we awake to flat Realities, lamenting the change' (*Conjectures on Original Composition* (1759), p. 13).
4. Sterne's *A Sentimental Journey* appeared in 1768.
5. James Boswell, *Journal of a Tour*, in *Johnson's Journey to the Western Islands of Scotland and Boswell's Journal of a Tour to the Hebrides with Samuel Johnson, LL.D.*, ed. R. W. Chapman, Oxford Standard Authors (1930), pp. 243, 253, 281, 379, 394.
6. Dorothy Wordsworth, *Recollections of a Tour Made in Scotland A. D. 1803*, ed. J. C. Shairp, reprint of 3rd edn, (Edinburgh, 1974), pp. 103–5.
7. Dorothy Wordsworth, *Recollections of a Tour*, pp. 221–3.
8. William Wordsworth, *Poetical Works*, ed. E. de Selincourt and H. Darbishire, 5 vols (Oxford, 1940–49), vol. III (1946), p. 76.
9. Walter Scott, *The Lady of the Lake* text, and notes in *The Poetical Works of Walter Scott*, ed. J. L. Robertson (1894), Canto I, stanza xxxi; Canto II, stanza ii; Canto III, stanza xxix. For an oddly comparable Highland Elysium, see William Gilpin's 'reverie' of a Loch Lomond inhabited by a group of 'philosophical friends', each with his own island and boat: William Gilpin, *Observations Relative Chiefly to Picturesque Beauty, Made in the Year 1776 on Several Parts of Great Britain; Particularly the High-Lands of Scotland*, 2nd edn (1792), vol. II, pp. 33–5.

10. Anne Grant's phrase: *Memoir and Correspondence of Mrs Grant of Laggan*, ed. J. P. Grant, 3 vols. (1844), vol. I, p. 269.
11. Peter Middleton Darling, *The Romance of the Highlands*, 2 vols. (Edinburgh, 1810), vol. II, p. 134.
12. T. J. H. Curties, *The Scottish Legend: or, the Isle of Saint Clothair, A Romance*, 4 vols. (1802), vol. III, p. 193; Henry Siddons, *William Wallace: or, The Highland Hero*, 2 vols. (1791), vol. II, p. 81.
13. This is not simply an interpretive conceit. Such a relationship between masquerading and literature was realised, in the service of an orientalist myth rather than a Highland one, in the genesis of William Beckford's *Vathek* (1786). See J. W. Oliver, *The Life of William Beckford* (1932), pp. 88–91.
14. This figure was a role-model of sensibility for a few years. 'In truth, I am a strange, and wayward wight, /Fond of each dreadful, and each gentle scene' – Anne Grant, in a letter written in 1778, in *Letters from the Mountains: being the real Correspondence of a lady, between the years 1773 and 1807*, 4th edn, 3 vols (1809), vol. II, p. 32, alluding to James Beattie's poem *The Minstrel; or, the Progress of Genius*, which had appeared in two volumes in 1771/4.
15. Ann Radcliffe, *The Castles of Athlin and Dunbayne. A Highland Story* (1789), p. 8.
16. See Edgar Johnson, *The Great Unknown*, 2 vols. (1970), vol. I, p. 336, and E. Burt, *Letters from a Gentleman in the North of Scotland*, 5th edn, ed. R. Jamieson, 2 vols. (1818), vol. I, pp. 202–3n.
17. Quoted in Scott, *The Letters of Sir Walter Scott*, ed. H. J. C. Grierson, 12 vols. (1932–7), vol. II, pp. 419–20.
18. John Stoddart, *Remarks on Local Scenery and Manners in Scotland during the Years 1799 and 1800*, 2 vols. (1801), vol. II, p. 307. Hence, presumably, the Wordsworths' desire to go there.
19. *Statistical Account*, vol. XII (1977), pp. 137–90 (p. 139). A little contest for precedence between Mrs Murray and the Revd Robertson is recorded in Elizabeth I. Spence, *Sketches of the Present Manners, Customs, and Scenery of Scotland*, 2nd edn, 2 vols. (1811), vol. I, p. 200.
20. See Patrick Graham, *Sketches Descriptive of Picturesque Scenery on the Southern Confines of Perthshire* (Edinburgh, 1806), pp. 10–18.
21. Scott's first publication, in 1796, had included his translation of the Bürger poem. *See Poetical Works*, p. 651.
22. Scott, *Lady*, Canto I, stanzas xi–xiv.
23. Spence, *Sketches*, vol. I, pp. 203–16.
24. The notable exception to this is English foxhunting, the blood sport of the agricultural revolution's heartland, and definitively a local (not a holiday) pursuit. But this is a special case of a peculiar kind: it is extremely stylised, socially and sartorially; and its material base is not food-gathering but pest control. For the story of its regularisation in the period of Improvement, and its grounding in the particular socioeconomic structure of English agrarian capitalism, see Raymond Carr, *English Fox Hunting: A History* (1976), pp. 45–64.
25. Thomas Thornton, *A Sporting Tour through the Northern Parts of England, and great part of the Highlands of Scotland* (1804), 'Advertisement'.
26. Thornton, *Sporting Tour*, p. 93.
27. John Taylor, quoted in Thomas Pennant, *A Tour in Scotland MDCCLXIX*, 2nd edn (1772), p. 108.

28. *Edinburgh Review*, vol. 5 (1804–5), p. 402.
29. Described in Duff Hart-Davis, *Monarchs of the Glen: a History of Deer-Stalking in the Scottish Highlands* (1978).
30. The *OED*'s first reference is from Scott in 1816.
31. James Holloway and Lindsay Errington, *The Discovery of Scotland*, National Gallery of Scotland exhibition catalogue (Edinburgh, 1978), pp. 103–18 (pp. 107–9).
32. Alexander Irvine, *An Inquiry into the Causes and Effects of Emigration from the Highlands* (Edinburgh, 1802), p. 56.
33. *Forest Sketches: Deer-stalking and other Sports in the Highlands Fifty Years Ago* (Edinburgh, 1865), p. xxi.
34. See J. H. Plumb, *The Commercialisation of Leisure in Eighteenth Century England* (Reading, 1973). Plumb's most significant examples, from my point of view here, are the emergence of the spa and the seaside resort as holiday (as opposed to purely medicinal) locations, and the immense growth of light reading which, besides contributing directly to the Highland cult as we have seen, also represented a major domestication of leisure.
35. Hugh Cunningham, *Leisure in the Industrial Revolution c.1780–1880* (1980), pp. 76–84; John Clarke and Chas Critcher, *The Devil Makes Work: Leisure in Cavitalist Britain* (1985), p. 53.
36. James Anderson, *Observations on the Means of Exciting a Spirit of National Industry* (1777).
37. Highland Society of Scotland, 1784; British Fisheries Society, 1786. 'General View' of the agriculture of the Central Highlands, 1794; of the Northern Counties, 1795; of Perthshire, 1799; of Inverness, 1808. *Statistical Account*, 1791–9.
38. Thomas Telford's *Survey and Report*, quoted in A.J. Youngson, *After the Forty-Five: The Economic Impact on the Scottish Highlands* (Edinburgh, 1973), p. 145.
39. Sir John Dalrymple, *Memoirs of Great Britain and Ireland*, 2nd edn, 3 vols. (1790), vol. II, Part II, p. 77.
40. Eric Richards, *A History of the Highland Clearances: Agrarian Transformation and the Evictions, 1746–1886* (1982), pp. 484–5; R. N. Millman, *The Making of the Scottish Landscape* (1975), pp. 168–9.

13
Douglas Oliver, *Poetry and Narrative in Performance* (1989)

Oliver's book is a study in poetics by a distinguished contemporary poet which offers a closely argued theory of how the sound frequencies of a poem can be shown to produce its emotional significance in interplay with its meaning. The book analyses what happens when poems are performed, including in its concept of 'performance' the act of silent reading as well as reading aloud, and develops an account of what a literary performance is. Mechanically recorded traces of different readings of texts are used in the analysis, not to argue for some supposed 'objectivity' but to illustrate Oliver's theory that stress is in practice broadly agreed on and can be productively redefined so as to include its congruence with emotional signification. The possibility of a neutral reading is defended as embodying the idea of a natural and generally intuited music of a line. Restoring the importance of voicing and of pitch is claimed to be essential for understanding the weight of the line as a melodic unit, with a passage of Milton analysed as a case in point. Spatio-temporal paradoxes in the nature of the poetic form are discussed by means of a concentration on the paradoxical 'instant' of poetic time, and on how the 'instant' of a poem relates to its overall form. The effects of poetry and narrative fiction are compared through consideration of Chaucer and Rabelais. Paul Ricoeur's analyses of the relationship between author and reader are extended; with Oliver insisting that a theory of metrics cannot overlook either the meaning or the emotional weight of the poem and that these are not idiosyncratic and 'purely subjective' factors: significance and emotionality can be shown to be performed through the stresses, syllables, voicing patterns, and melody of the poem.

Narrative in performance

In the three chapters that follow I am going to talk of what happens to time, space and the 'I' pronoun in fictional narrative. This discussion will exclude many aspects of prose and poetic writing: for example, I shall not consider genre, intertextuality, or metaphor (unless we take

211

this widely to mean imaginative reconstruction of space and time). My argument continues from my previous analyses of poetic stress and musical form, where I have described the way in which the point-like moment of stress is bound into the overall flow of a poem's music and therefore into its meaning and emotional significance. I now want to show how our perception of form in narrative fiction has essentially the same spatio-temporal dynamic: it, too, involves emotion and meaning and it, too, creates spatio-temporal paradoxes.

The reader will recall that any incorporation of duration into the point-like moment incurs ambiguities of space and time – space because a duration of mental time is necessarily also a spatial extension. In a poem, verbal music is what most immediately binds stress as a tiny artistic form into the overall form of a poem. What plays a similar role in a novel? What is the point-like moment and what is the binding power? The point-like moment is *any* moment when the reader suddenly grasps a formal achievement of whatever size in the novel: it may be an evanescent realisation of part of an event's significance in the plot; it may be a grasp of elements of a character's personality, or of the relationship of that personality to the overall 'poem' of the novel; it could be a host of things, from a formal conception that yields a sudden moral awareness or even a sudden erotic feeling, all the way up to an 'instant-like' appreciation of a novel's whole form. As for the power that binds instant to form, it is a broader concept than 'plot': 'plot', 'character', 'action', 'setting' or 'point of view' can be logically distinguished, but their mental effects upon us are harder to distinguish each from the other. I am calling the binding element narrative 'movement', understanding by that a portmanteau term in which the mental dynamic created by character, setting, action, plot and so on may all play a part. If we can isolate for study a point-like moment when the ambiguity of narrative form is revealed, we shall find comparable ambiguities of space and time to those noticed with the poetic stress. This is simpler to show than might be supposed, because some comic writers, such as Chaucer and Rabelais, have burlesqued the formal processes underlying their own narrative construction; the burlesque therefore exposes exactly what we want to look at: there will be no need to search for more complicated examples.

But before reaching that point I have to interpolate the present chapter so as to acknowledge certain trends in modern literary criticism. I shall only very selectively use any findings of the new 'science' of narratology or of Derridean–Yale 'deconstruction', and shall prefer an ordinary way of talking. It is a necessary difference of procedure, comparable to my distinction in Chapter 1 between rule-governed poetic metrics and poetry conceived as performance: I am to consider narrative as a mental performance of its movement, just as I considered poetry as a mental performance of its musical flow.

But narratology is not a study of performance. As one of the most self-aware critics in that field, Genette, has pointed out (1983, p. 12), two narratologies have developed, one thematic and concerned with analysing the story or the narrative contents, the other formal, or modal, an analysis of the narrative text itself as a mode of representation of stories. Story here usually means the chronological events abstracted from the text's organisation of them. (To illustrate the former, the work of Northrop Frye in categorising story genre is an excellent representative.) Genette reserves the title of 'narratology' proper for the second, modal analysis, and adds: 'The only specificity that a narrative has resides in its mode, and not in its content, which could equally well conform itself to a dramatic, graphic or other representation.' In fact, we have to add that narrative is also specific in its mode of performance *each time it is performed*, which necessarily involves content and extra-linguistic factors such as emotion. The idea that an isolated, individual occasion may have absolutely necessary laws to itself alone is unscientific but is required for a full discussion of art in action.

Story can be studied in isolation from the narrative text, but when considering performance it is not clear we can be so purist, because then we are considering real acts of mind which might both respond to the narrative directly as text and mentally rearrange it chronologically as story. There is a theoretical narrative movement and also what actually happens inside our heads. The reader's reaction has been well described by Wilbur Sanders (1985):

> Just as the author, word by word, sentence by sentence rears *his* structure so, in the reader's mind, a parallel construction is proceeding – experience and intuition racing ahead here in anticipation, pausing to look back there in disapprobation, checking, confirming, collating, dissenting and (most importantly) bringing to bear whatever in our own life seems relevant and responsive to the life the writer is creating.

The rather ill-defined categories of traditional literary criticism reflect this impurity – that something happens between reader and text which is not just responding to the text, straight. Traditional criticism takes the text as a starting-point for a human reaction towards the work, including many extra-linguistic elements such as evaluations of the fictional world in terms of the real world, the critic's emotional response to what he reads, and so on. It is an intuitive art, open to pressures from the social and political position of the critic, which will necessarily be different from that of the author. Then there is the newer study, 'narratology'. It is distinguished by considering the structures of the text or of its relationships to other texts in an abstract way, sometimes by applying methodology drawn from linguistics, analytic logic, mathematics or aid from other disciplines, such as structural anthropology or psychoanalysis. Meanwhile, the Derridean–Yale schools have often concentrated upon the way that all structures seem to disappear in a basic ambiguity when you look closely enough at their points of origin, but then reappear in necessary conjunction with their deconstruction. This essentially mathematical conception has been applied to the study of narrative forms. I do not borrow the complicated language of the deconstructionists because it is too abstract for my purposes and because it is not apt for describing the mental performance by a reader of narrative movement; but ambiguity of structure is certainly supposed in what I write.

One starting-point for narratology, a branch of semiology, was to try to find for the structure of fictional texts a grammar-like set of rules equivalent to those which govern the structure of individual phrases. Narrative was to be treated as a special case of an extended phrase – not that it was to be dealt with as a structure composed of individual phrases (that would be an absurd task) but that the logical structure of its composition was to be found in grammar like rules (see Barthes, 1977, p. 10). The new 'science' began to expand at a time when Chomskyan linguistics had shown that a phrase grammar which dealt only with the surface appearance of language – the normal succession of words – could not explain all the ways that sentences were constructed. Transformational grammar created a deep level of abstract rules and then an intermediate set of rules which, with the realisation into actual words, would transform the deep-level structures into possible sentences.

Some of the narratological methods work in a similar way in this sense: underlying structural principles are sought for narratives, usually by making abstract entities out of the literal surface entities, such as actual characters, events, temporal relations, ways of representing speech, framing and embedding of stories, levels of narrative, different points of view and so forth. Once these features have lost their particularity in a given text – say, Pinkie, his point of view, his level of narrative, his role in *Brighton Rock* – and once they have been assimilated to more general formal entities (x- factor, y-factor, etc.), the underlying structure of the novel can be brought out. To give only one example, one of the clearest and best known: in the extremely abstract early work of Greimas, at the deep level an *actant* is a structural entity to which both human characters and inanimate objects (a magic ring) or abstract forces (destiny) may be reduced Consequently, the rules of their interaction at the deep level of text may be given a wider generality, and so become capable of specifying a greater variety of possible realisations of characters, objects or abstract forces in actual narratives.

If one were to build up these rules from the smallest detail, one would have to find some minimal unit that could be called a narrative. As Genette has shown (1983, p. 14), it is not easy to consider what a minimal phrase, and therefore a minimal narrative, might be: 'I walk' immediately prompts the questions 'Where from?' 'Where to?' He refers to Forster's distinction between story (event in time sequence), 'The king died and then the queen died', and plot (emphasis on causality), ('. . . of grief'); but it seems to me that even 'The king died' obliges us to think of the resulting change to a nation and raises all sorts of causative considerations about what happens next. Also, there are in story already emotional reverberations which plot will mould. In his development of the story, Forster has, interestingly enough, added in more evidently this emotional significance which was, anyway, there in germ. When we read (perform) the actual content even of this simple plot the question of impurity of response immediately arises. This poses the interference of extra-linguistic factors, such as emotional resonance and moral or other evaluation; and these are extremely important in distinguishing the study of narratology from that of narrative performance. Emotion, when referred to in narratological analysis, usually seems such an abstract factor, for example, an 'axis of desire' linking the deep structures to the surface of the actual text; and it therefore lacks fully realised application to the complexity and ambiguity of everyday desire. Rimmon-Kenan (1983, p. 28) says that she as yet knows no real method of crossing from deep abstract narrative structure to the concrete text. It will be argued that activating the temporal relations of the surface text is what makes fictionalised emotion important to us. Activation, I shall show from Ricoeur's work, can best be studied in the light of the Aristotelian Mimesis, or imitation of the characteristic, permanent or universal modes of human thought, feeling and action.

A passage from Todorov (1978, p. 175), another influential early figure in narrative poetics, will help us. Like some more recent theorists he heralded a new age in the study of literary texts by pointing to the decline of old categories: in this case the doomed categories are 'imitation' and 'representation' (presumably in the sense of representation of reality by a 'fictionalised' version). For comparison, the novelist, Ricardou (1978, p. 15) was concerned to develop a left-wing theory of literary production rather than of creation in the traditional sense; Ricardou's doomed categories are the 'expression' of aspects of the Self and the 'representation' of aspects of the World in a novelistic programme.

To interpret a difficult paragraph, Todorov writes that though we may have stopped considering art and literature as *mimesis*, we find it difficult to end our linguistic habit of seeing the novel in terms of representation of a reality which would prexist it. Such a view, even if it only attempts to describe what artistic creation is like, cannot avoid a distortion which is revealed when we apply the description to the text itself. What exists, first of all, is the text and nothing else but that. It is only by submitting it to a particular type of reading that we construct an imaginary universe from it. The novel does not imitate reality; it creates it. This is not just a modification of terminology. Only the perspective that sees the text as constructing an imaginary world allows us to understand correctly the textual function called representative.

On this I have four comments, which I shall summarise and then discuss. It will be seen that often I am not disagreeing with Todorov but merely insisting on a different kind of discussion of the same points:

(1) We cannot so easily do without the notion of imitation because taken in conjunction with plot it permits a necessary temporal dynamism in narrative performance.

(2) Something exists before the text or it would imply creation *ex nihilo*. To experience this 'something' we must respond to the text as Todorov suggests with 'a particular kind of reading', not as a textual entity isolated from the circumstances of its creation and of its being read; instead with an active performance.

(3) To recreate the spatio-temporal world of the fiction, non-linguistic entities must be brought into consideration (I do not suppose that Todorov would necessarily disagree).

(4) 'Expression', 'Mimesis', and 'Representation' in the traditional senses re-enter the discussion whenever we set out to consider the

narrative as a performance and not as a text. This is because the novel, as Todorov himself goes on to argue, exists in a relationship between author, text and reader. I should add here that in the recent reader-response strain in criticism, the concentration is often upon text-reader, and not so much on author-text-reader, so that the study is mainly of communication, as in the so-called 'hermeneutic' study of information gaps in the text. The variety and riches of the reader's response require to be linked more directly to the authorial input of dynamism.

To discuss these points:

(1) Many people have not stopped seeing art and literature as imitative; only some semiologists have. What is mimed in fictional narrative is not just the referential capacity of words to represent reality (or the fantastic), but also their capacity to reawaken, to mime, the temporal movement of thought, along with an imagined emotional movement. Aspects of all this can be redefined into abstract entities, and temporality itself can be reduced to an operator function in a diagram of narrative structure or to a topology in some diagrammatic representation of novelistic structure, whereupon their dynamism becomes potential or immanent and their extra-linguistic, performance aspects are neutralised for the sake of the analytical science. With the neutralism of their dynamic, their true temporality, which has the extra-linguistic, let us say spiritual, effect upon us, retreats also into immanence. This is partly Ricoeur's point (1984, p. 50), for, talking of extracting codes from language, he says that a systematic organisation of linguistic structures can be mastered if the simultaneous (synchronic) aspects of language can be isolated from its successive and historical (diachronic) aspects, providing a finite number of different base units (such as Greimas's *actants*) can be established and combined under rules which generate all the internal relations. Under those conditions, he defines a structure as a closed group of internal relations between a finite number of units. 'The immanence of these relations – that is the system's indifference to any extra-linguistic reality – is an important corollary of this closure rule which characterises a structure.' A result of this isolation of the synchronic axis is the 'achronic' aspect of the deep structures postulated (1984, p. 54). I should only add that if the time relations between author, text, and reader have become achronic, then, although we may draw out the spatial aspects of a text into elegant models, the true nature of spatiality (that it exists in a paradoxical relationship with time which a performance sets in motion) is also held in

immanence. (This is true even if operator functions are included in the formal model of narrative structure which, *if put into action*, would generate the spatio-temporal experience.)

Of course, I do not imply that the narratologists cannot see this: it is a question of critical intention. Genette (1983, p. 105), in his lively way, refers to a criticism by Booth of the former's reading of Proust, in which Booth complains that Genette is too centred on notions of narrative information, of signification, and, as far as the reader is concerned, on the single feeling of intellectual curiosity to the exclusion of all moral and affective solidarity with the characters and especially with the narrator. Genette explains that he does not think the procedures of analysing narrative discourse greatly contribute to determining these affective moments, since sympathy or antipathy for a character essentially depends on the psychological, moral or indeed physical characteristics, and the conduct and discourse which the author attributes to him; they depend very little on the techniques of the *récit* in which he figures. He adds that his earlier work, *Discours du récit* (1972), has to do with the *récit* and narration, not story; and the qualities or faults, the graces or disgraces of heroes, do not essentially arise from the *Récit* or from the narration but from the story, in other words from the content or from the *diegesis* – that is the universe of things signified to which the story comes. He adds:

> To reproach it for having neglected these things is to reproach its choice of object. I otherwise conceive of such a critique very well: why do you talk to me about forms when I am only interested in content? But if the question is legitimate the response is only evident: each one concerns himself with what interests him.

The precision is welcome and makes evident that to consider the effect of content upon us we have to study performance.

(2) What exists first, linguistically considered, is the text: agreed. But the linguist comes to the text after it has been finished. In the author's performance what exists first is *not* the text but the mental tension that creates it. I leave this word 'tension' deliberately inchoate because, at that phase of the creative process, although there is much order already in the tension, it will more fully become this order as it elaborates into text and, finally, into achieved form. From a performance point of view the creation of text is teleological and filled with intention, even if the intention changes as the creation proceeds.

At stake, then, is the familiar linguistic distinction between rule and performance, which comes in various guises: competence-performance (Chomsky); *langue-parole* (Saussure); rule-realisation; or virtual–actual. Temporary forgetfulness of this continues to bedevil interchanges between literary critics and linguists, as the exchange between Booth and Genette illustrates. To study the living art requires a value-laden, extra-linguistic, intuitive criticism; to appreciate its formal relationships one can be aided by narratology. For a fuller philosophical discussion of the issues involved, I refer the reader to a volume edited by Lerner (1983) and to the work of Ricoeur (1983, 1984, 1985).

To make the difference between rule and performance as clear as possible to readers not wholly familiar with the distinction in linguistics, let us make as non-referential a statement as possible: $3 + 7 = 10$. Then we imply an extra-linguistic context for the sum such as (unspoken) ('Dammit, why ask me such a stupid question?'): '$3 + 7 = 10!$'

It has become a conversation, open to extra-linguistic considerations, such as impatience. Whatever structural rules we may create to describe the statement, we still cannot decide when performing this conversation exactly what extra, impatient force to give to the '10'. We need some way of judging the mental field of the speaker in relation to context and in relation to his listener (say, 'ourselves'). In art, we judge such things through the performance of form. This is also the favourite sum of St Augustine, presumably since it puts the Trinity in relation with '10', the number of divine perfection in medieval numerology, via the number of weeks of creation. (It is also the cosmically important sum that governs Boccaccio's *Decameron*, where three men and seven women tell stories for 10 days.) The number '10' could therefore be spoken with utmost reverence if we consider it, intertextually, in relation to St Augustine's other works. But if we try to perform the equation not impatiently but slowly and meaningfully as we guess someone like St Augustine might have pronounced it, we may have to call on our knowledge of the world or of cultural history in order to decide how to emphasise it. It would be fantastically difficult. Suppose St Augustine had set the sum in a poem or into one of his formal rhapsodies to divine creativity, that is into some artistic expression which itself would be a working formal model of St Augustine's own reverence. We should then have better guidance (because repeatable through form) about what emotional emphasis to give it. What semiology does not recreate for us is the drive towards perfection, resolution of tension, or 'truth' of response that creates form. It can only be appreciated in performance.

(3) Non-linguistic entities. Temporal relationships are complex in the average novel and as I have said are only taken out of immanence through performance. For example, there is a play-off between length of narrative passages (number of lines of text, etc.) and the speed of events in the fiction; another between speed of events and descriptive passages; description has its own dynamic; the variety of forms, voices and registers in complex prose has temporal effects, and so on. Despite all this, providing there is a reader to perform the narrative, all the different aspects of temporal experience (ideally) unite into an overall and activated experience of temporal form. Along with this experience necessarily goes a host of extra-linguistic experiences: time passes slowly or quickly according to the reader's aesthetic-emotional response and to his sense of a passage's semantic significance in terms of his own life. Through this experience, the reader brings the fictional text into his own world, where he experiences a tension that answers to the artist's tension that pre-existed the text, changed as it developed, and can be considered as its cause. Here again, Ricoeur is helpful (1984, p. 150). He has been analysing the temporal structure common in semiology between the utterance (*l'énonciation*) and statement (*l'énoncé*) in the *récit*, and studying the doubling-up, parallel to this distinction, between the time taken in recounting a narrative and the time-scale relating together the things recounted. His argument basically continues that only the confrontation between the world of the text and the world of the reader's life will create the true relations of temporality that the text has to offer. This will be more fully understood in terms of Ricoeur's three phases of Mimesis, as described below. (I shall reserve my main analysis to my final chapter.)

(4) The novel, then, does not only create reality: it is born in prospective relationships between the artist and his imaginary world and the reader and his imaginary world. Todorov (1978) has a diagram to show this, that the author's *récit* conducts us to the imaginative world evoked by the author which conducts to the imaginative world constructed by the reader which conducts to the reader's *récit*. 'These two *Récits* bearing on the same text are never identical', he adds (p. 179). He explains this variation by the fact that these *récits* describe not the universe of the book itself but this universe transformed, as it exists in the psyche of each individual. This is accurate. But, as he evidently realises, it remains to bring this relationship alive through a living experience of the text – arrows in diagrams will not do it.

The conjunction author-text-reader creates an active intersubjectivity, relating to the real as well as to the imaginary world. The imaginary only preoccupies part of our minds; we are enabled to grasp form through the difference between the imaginary and the real. Form cannot be fully grasped just from inside the text. If both writer and reader fully entered the imaginary world they would be mentally ill – supposing, which I really do not, that mental illness itself occupied the whole of conscious and unconscious mental life during its apparent empire. (There would be little point to mental illness if it did.)

In Ricoeur's model, this interaction between author, text, and reader depends upon three phases of the Aristotelian imitation. Mimesis 1 exists before the actual act of configuration of the textual world. It has, however, pre-existing 'narrative' characteristics – an action about to be described, for example, may have traditional or situational symbolic significance. Leaving aside (since it belongs to a different method of analysis) many of the hermeneutical aspects of Ricoeur's thinking here, I shall for my own purposes talk throughout this book of a primary tension, meaning by that simply whatever pre-narrative characteristics one might imagine in it for a given work – symbolic, semantic tension, emotional tension, melodic tension, all of various kinds, and so on. Ricoeur's Mimesis II is the configuring activity by which the text itself is created. Mimesis III is the reader's activity in re-configuring the text and therefore carrying into his own world the dynamic effect of the text: it is not quite the same as the first phase of Mimesis (not least because the reader's real life differs from that of the author and readers differ from each other), and Ricoeur compares the two phases as the counter-moving currents that bring the second phase to life. (There is no real English equivalent of the French *amont et aval*, which literally means upstream and downstream.) By such an image Ricoeur no doubt expects us to visualise Mimesis I and III as in a continuously active relationship with the creation (and performance) of the text.

By constructing the interdependence of all the three mimetic modes Ricoeur explains the relationship between time and the *récit*. Unlike Todorov, he starts from a phase preceding the creation of text; and that is very important. He suggests that an Aristotelian activating of the plot (*mise en intrigue*) mediates between a stage of practical experience (Mimesis I) which precedes it and a reader-activity stage which succeeds it (Mimesis III). This presentation of the three phases adds temporality to the Aristotelian model of plot. Talking of the interaction between Mimesis I (the prenarrative phase), Mimesis II (the configuring of the temporal world in the text) and Mimesis III (the reader's own recreation of that configuration), he says: '*We are following therefore the destiny of a prefigured time that becomes a refigured time through the mediation of a configured time.*' In my own view, plot in the novel arises from that drive which shapes the semantic and emotional significance of characters and incident into form: it results from the drive to make things move in time and resolve into unity. 'Movement' (the *'mise'* in the *'mise en intrigue'*) in narrative fiction therefore corresponds to music in poetry (though, of course, many poems also have plots, even if very disguised ones, and are also narratives). I have described poetic stress as unifying into a notional point a content from past and future; and I have compared this with St Augustine's 'triple present'. A moment of formal conception in a novel likewise unifies a content into a point-like awareness and it is the narrative movement which permits this. This may appear odd, but 'setting the plot to work' and 'making the sound flow' are both the moving elements, the media, through which creative tension is resolved, part is related to whole, and the true temporality of the reader's response is awakened. The performance of a fiction by writing or reading it creates a repeatable experience of the Augustinian triple present in which the soul is distended with temporality, discussed in my previous chapter, through a *mise en intrigue*. If I do not specify the Aristotelian *mise en intrigue*, as developed by Ricoeur, but prefer the general conception of 'movement' it is because if we are considering plot in poetry too, it does not do to be too specific. My closing chapter will show that, although I may use a less philosophical language for this process, I am much of Ricoeur's party.

The writer's original creative tension (modifying itself as it goes) exists at every phase of creation if form is to result; and the presumed reader's response is thereby necessarily entrained at every phase too in the creation of the text. All the minor examples of formal achievement along the length of a work also depend upon this mutual presence of all three phases of Mimesis in Ricoeur's theory. Author is already in contact with an ideal reader as he writes; reader recreates author at each stage of reading; the intersubjective temporality is alive at all times of vivid creativity or creative response. It must now be shown how the point-like moment in narrative response exhibits the kinds of spatio-temporal ambiguity we should expect if we compare it with the paradoxes of poetic stress.

References

Barthes, R. (1977) 'Introduction à l'analyse structurale des récits', in R. Barthes, W. Kayser, W. C. Booth, Ph. Hamon, *Poétique du récit* (Paris: Editions du Seuil, Points 78). Originally in *Communications*, 8, 1966.
Genette, G. (1972) *Figures III* (Paris: Editions du Seuil).
—— (1983) *Nouveau discours du récit* (Paris: Editions du Seuil).

Lerner, L. (ed.) (1983) *Reconstructing Literature* (Oxford: Blackwell).

Ricardou, J. (1978) *Nouveaux Problèmes du roman* (Paris: Editions du Seuil).

Ricoeur, P. (1983) *Temps et récit*, t.1 (Paris: Editions du Seuil).

—— (1984) *Temps et récit, t.2, La configuration dans le récit de fiction* (Paris: Editions du Seuil).

—— (1985) *Temps et récit, t.3, Le temps raconté* (Paris: Editions du Seuil).

Sanders, W. (1985) 'Straddling the Criticism and Creativity Border', *The Listener*, 15th August.

14

Laura Mulvey, *Visual and Other Pleasures* (1969)

Visual and Other Pleasures is a series of linked meditations on the politics of representation. Written from the early 1970s to the mid-1980s, the pieces reflect commitments and changes within the Women's Movement during that period: Mulvey's self-reflexive account shows the broadening out of the Women's Movement from a political organisation into a more general framework of feminism, a development that as regards consideration of representation runs from the interruptions of the spectacle of the 1970 Miss World contest to the later elaboration of a fully fledged cultural feminism, responsive to and newly inflecting theoretical trends. The critical appropriation of psychoanalysis, to which Mulvey contributed, was one such crucial inflection and is mapped out by the various pieces as they examine matters of spectacle and melodrama and avant-garde practice, ending with two major reconsiderations – one of which appears below – of the terms and politics and feminist theory. The celebrated essay on 'Visual pleasure and narrative cinema', conceived as radical intervention, used psychoanalytic theory to suggest a complex interaction of different 'looks' particular to cinema, arguing that conventional film establishes, irrespective of the sex of the viewer, a masculine voyeurism that must be refused, 'destroyed'. That idea of the hold of the male gaze fixed to the female passivity it represents was then complicated by subsequent reflections on women's enjoyment as spectators in the cinema, on the possibilities of visual pleasure. Yet how, other than as sexualised images, are women to be represented? This problem is explored by Mulvey through discussion of particular directors and genres, notably the Hollywood melodramas of Douglas Sirk, as well as the films of Fassbinder. *Visual and Other Pleasures* offers, in fact, a history of feminist film theory and culture that is informed and shaped by wider consideration of the politics and aesthetics of representation for feminism. Mulvey is especially alert here to the question as to how the political desire of the seventies for a radical aesthetics might have translated, if at all, to the very different context of the eighties. The question is pursued in reflections on the work of contemporary artists such as Mary Kelly, as well as through examination of Frida Kahlo and Tina Modotti and their presence in Mexican political history. The resulting meditations on change, both historical and conceptual, return always to the insistent problem that is the book's overall concern: how can narrative not end in closure? Problem and concern are the matter of the chapter from the book that follows.

Changes: thoughts on myth, narrative and historical experience

Endings

My work as a film-maker and film-theorist is grounded in the 1970s, particularly in the meeting between feminist politics, psychoanalytic theory and avant-garde aesthetics that had such influence then. After the 1983 election and into 1984, I began to feel that work I considered to be ongoing, in the present tense, had shifted into the past to become identified with the previous decade. My formative experiences, desires and failures that had to do with cultural struggle seemed gradually to be relegated to a closed epoch. The avant-garde was over. The Women's Movement no longer existed as an organisation, in spite of the widespread influence of feminism. And the changed political and economic climate marked the 1980s off from the 1970s. It was tempting to accept a kind of natural entropy: that eras just did come to an end. But then, the sense of *historical* closure recalled the distrust of *narrative* closure that had always been a point of principle for the feminist avantgarde. Once a movement can be reviewed retrospectively its story can be told, but *how* it should be told could still be considered. It seemed as though narrative patterns and expectations of endings had become inextricably intertwined in history as in fiction. We had argued in the 1970s that narrative closure resolves contradiction and stabilises the energy for change generated by a story-line. The same factors seemed to colour my perception of the rhythms and patterns of history. An ending would offer a way out of responsibility, as though one could be indemnified by regret for once-upon-a-time acts of struggle in phrases such as 'the end of an era'. Changes could seem to just happen, the product of a single narrative line under which the minutiae of political struggle were lost. Heterogeneity, discordance and lack of synchronisation between strands of history could be unified.

From parabolas to narrative

> It is out of the question to generalise . . . all the same, the typical pattern of a sharp rise followed by an abrupt fall can very easily be imagined as the probable profile in the pre-industrial economy,

reflecting the brief hour of glory of some city's industry or a passing boom in exports, over almost as quickly as last year's fashions; or competing industries of which one regularly ousts the other; or the perpetual migration of industries which seem to rise from the ashes as they leave their country of origin . . .

All this is quite natural in a period when economies consisted of sectors somewhat disconnected from each other. What is surprising, on the other hand, is that in Walter G. Hofman's book *British Industry 1700–1900* one finds the same kind of parabola.

This must all mean something, but it is not to say we have found the explanation. The really difficult task is to detect the link between the particular industry studied and the *economic context surrounding it* upon which its own career depends.[1]

Parabolic patterns can be applied to the modern avant-garde; a sudden, marked rise into visibility, followed by a downward trend and declining energy, 'over almost as quickly as last year's fashions'. The way that parabolic patterns attract narrativisation became clearly exemplified as the consolidated triumph of Thatcherism was tested by the miners' strike. The strike led me to question the political relevance of my own work; but some of the principles lying behind avant-garde aesthetics and theory seemed applicable to this very different context.

Daily depiction on television turned the strike, in effect, into a 'social drama',[2] moulding events around personality, individualised conflict, and serial-type narrative sequence. Narration is not the same in Downing Street as it is on the picket line, and the roles of villain and victim vary in another set of polarisations. Like the Frankenstein monster,[3] the miners struggled for control of their own story and, like the monster, were cast simultaneously as evil and tragic. At the climactic moment of the struggle inevitably comes *victory* or *defeat*, immediately preceding an ending; and it is in the interests of the one who loses, whether cast as villain or victim, to keep the story open and alive, to resist resolution and closure, to insist that change can continue to happen and take on the surrounding context and its contradictions. But the 'end of an era' opposition conjures up a phantasmagoric polarisation between past and future in which the catastrophic present and the complex processes of class struggle are repressed.

The Conservative government attempted to cash in on the economic parabola, the decline of the old industries, closing down the pits to signal (politically, economically, historically) the 'end of an era', closing off the macro-story of the labour movement, the trade-union movement, even the industrial working class itself. The 'end of an era' was orchestrated around a rhetoric of binary oppositions or polarisations, concealing the processes of history behind the seemingly natural and eternal connotations of technical and economic progress. The old world would give way to a new world, the electronic would replace the mechanical, international would replace national investment, finance capital would overtake industry, the free market would shake off the restraints imposed by labour organisation and, above all, solidarity. This ending could become enshrined in popular mythology by clothing complex political and economic factors in the binarism of a modern/archaic opposition.

Polarisations I: binary patterns and deconstruction

This problem of dealing with difference without constituting an opposition may just be what feminism is all about (might be what psychoanalysis is all about). Difference produces great anxiety. Polarisation, which is the theatrical representation of difference, tames and binds that anxiety. The classic example is sexual difference, which is represented as polar opposition (active–passive, energy–matter, and all the other polar oppositions that share the trait of taming the anxiety that specific differences provoke).[4]

My own work with film theory has been deeply influenced by binary modes of thought. I began to consider the tension between this influence and my desire for change. The problems were epitomised by the place that an article I had written in 1973 (published 1975) had come to occupy in film theoretical orthodoxy. 'Visual Pleasure and Narrative Cinema'[5] was written in the polemical spirit that belongs properly to the early confrontational moments of a movement. The great problem is then to see how to move to 'something new', from creative confrontation to creativity. There had been an enormous sense of excitement in exploring patriarchal myths, analysing images of sexual difference, trying to extract the meanings that lay behind the images of women in popular culture, revealing the 'taming and binding' that seemed to have organised representations of difference for nearly as long as our culture can remember. For all this, the binary mode of thought provided a necessary, dynamic analytical tool. Feminist film criticism took on images as a political issue, exposing the power relations concealed behind the phoney balance between masculine and feminine, drawing attention to the patterns of otherness that flesh out the raw nerve of sexual difference in popular culture and mythology (public vs. private space, nomadic vs. stable, sun vs. moon, mind vs. body, the law vs. the sexual, creator of culture vs. closeness to nature, etc.).

When I wrote 'Visual Pleasure and Narrative Cinema', I was fascinated by the various overlaps and interconnections between the conditions of spectatorship in the cinema and the representations (in story and image) of sexual difference on the screen. The spectacle offers itself to the active gaze of the spectator, but is split, itself, into active or passive elements along the lines demanded by socially established connotations of masculinity and femininity. My argument was influenced by Freud, and looking back, it seems no accident that I drew above all on 'Three Essays on Sexuality' and 'Instincts and their Vicissitudes'.[6] That is, I privileged the Freudian theory of drives as organised around active/passive pairings (named by Freud, metaphorically, as masculine/feminine) giving rise to the sexual instincts: sadism/masochism, voyeurism/exhibitionism. In analysing sexual difference in popular narrative cinema, it seemed as though Freud's metaphoric naming, designed to express the ambivalence within the individual psyche, was doomed to reflect the actual conditions under which masculinity and femininity are depicted and socially understood. I argued that the spectator's position, active and voyeuristic, is inscribed as 'masculine' and, through various narrative and cinematic devices, the woman's body exists as the erotic, spectacular and exhibitionist 'other', so that the male protagonist on screen can occupy the active role of advancing the story-line. There is a sense in which this argument, important as it is for analysing the existing state of things, hinders the possibility of change and remains caught ultimately within its own dualistic terms. The polarisation only allows an 'either/or'. As the two terms (masculine/feminine, voyeuristic/exhibitionist, active/passive) remain dependent on each other for meaning, their only possible movement is into inversion. They cannot be shifted easily into a new phase or new significance. There can be no space in between or space outside such a pairing.

The article wanted to provoke the question, 'So what next, then?' Change seemed to be just around the corner in the mid-1970s, and an article written in a polemical spirit and above all, to precipitate change, loses significance outside historical context and integrated into the timeless body of film theory. To articulate the relationship between cultural forms and women's oppression, to use psychoanalysis in discussing and exposing this relationship, both of these must precipitate a next phase, that will shift the terms and connotations that cluster around representations of sexual difference. But the either/or binary pattern seemed to leave the argument trapped within its own conceptual frame of reference, unable to advance politically into a new terrain or suggest an alternative theory of spectatorship in the cinema.

Polarisations II: conceptual topology

> Outside and inside form a dialectic of division, the obvious geometry of which blinds us as soon as we bring it into play in metaphorical domains. . . . Unless one is careful, it is made the basis of all images that govern all thoughts of positive and negative. . . . Thus profound metaphysics is rooted in an implicit geometry that confers spatiality upon thought: if a metaphysician could not draw, what would he think? Open and closed, for him, are thoughts. . . . And so, simple geometrical opposition becomes tinged with aggressivity. Formal opposition is incapable of remaining calm. It is obsessed by myth.[7]

It is as though the very invisibility of abstract ideas attracts a material, metaphoric form. The interest lies in whether the forms of this 'conceptual topology', as I have called it, might affect the formulation of the ideas themselves and their ultimate destiny. Is it possible that the way in which ideas are visualised can, at a certain point, block the process that brings thought into a dialectical relationship with history? I still stand by my 'Visual Pleasure' article, but it belongs to a particular moment in the history of our particular movement. I feel now that its 'conceptual topology' contributed in some way to blocking advance, although it certainly provoked very rigorous responses that went far beyond its original parameters. But when I looked back at the article after some time, the spatial patterning of ideas caught my attention, how they acquire a metaphorical substance and how this 'conceptual topology' then relates to its historical context. This is the question of *how* ideas are formulated in relation to *when*, the moment in the life span of a political or aesthetic movement that is, itself, subject to a parabolic curve. Just as feminist avant-garde aesthetics has argued that representations must make their formal structures visible (foregrounding signifiers, for instance), so perhaps should the transparency of history and abstract ideas be questioned to reveal their material underpinnings. Then, it could be easier to decipher the constraints that lead to entropy and endings, to build from one historical context to another without the endless loss inherent in the 'tradition of the new'.

Polarisations III: negative aesthetics

> More and more radically Godard has developed a counter-cinema
> whose values are counterposed to those of orthodox cinema. . . . My
> approach is to take seven of the values of the old cinema,
> Hollywood-Mosfilm, as Godard would put it, and contrast these
> with their (revolutionary, materialist) counterparts and contraries.
> In a sense, the seven deadly sins of the cinema against the seven
> cardinal virtues.[8]

'Visual Pleasure and Narrative Cinema' was written as a polemic, a
challenge to dominant cinematic codes. There was a sense of excitement in this negational stance that compensated for such an attack
on a form of cinema, the Hollywood studio system movies, that I
loved and that had taught me about cinematic pleasure. A similar
kind of excitement compensated for the 'difficultness' of the films I
made with Peter Wollen, that could be described as a return to zero, or
an aesthetic 'scorched earth policy'. Our first film *Penthesilea* was
devised very much within this intellectual and aesthetic spirit. We
broke with the codes and conventions of editing that articulate a
flowing, homogeneous, coherent fictional time, space and point of
view, using long 'chapters' made up of sequence shots. The camera
strategy combined with the lack of editing was intended to negate
possible and expected shifts in look, in order to foreground the 'work'
involved in cinematic spectatorship, and undercut the looker/looked-
at dichotomy that fixes visual pleasure. These strategies, however,
depend on acknowledging the dominant codes in the very act of
negation itself; it could only be through an audience's knowledge of
the dominant that the avant-garde could acquire meaning and
significance. A negative aesthetic can produce an inversion of the
meanings and pleasures it confronts, but it risks remaining locked in a
dialogue with its adversary. Counter-aesthetics, too, can harden into a
system of dualistic opposition. But it is also important to acknowledge
that negative aesthetics can act as a motor force in the early phases of
a movement, initiating and expressing the desire for change.

Negation and sexual difference: woman is 'not man'

> Woman is therefore placed 'beyond' (beyond the phallus). That
> 'beyond' refers at once to her most total mystification as absolute
> Other (and hence nothing other but other), and to a *question*, the

question of her own *jouissance*, of her greater or lesser access to the residue of the dialectic to which she is so constantly subjected. The problem is that once the notion of 'woman' has been so relentlessly exposed as a fantasy, then any such question becomes an almost impossible one to pose.

Lacan's reference to woman as Other needs, therefore, to be seen as an attempt to hold apart two moments which are in constant danger of collapsing into each other – that which assigns woman to the negative place of its own (phallic) system, and that which asks the question as to whether women might, as a very effect of that assignation, break against and beyond that system itself. For Lacan, that break is always within language, it is the break of the subject *in* language. The concept of *jouissance* (what escapes in sexuality) and the concept of *significance* (what shifts within language) are inseparable.[9]

Jacques Lacan's ideas and theories of psychoanalysis swept through the extreme theoretical wings of both film and feminism in the mid- to late 1970s. His influence broadened and advanced ways of conceptualising sexual difference, emphasising the fictional, constructed nature of masculinity and femininity, the results of social and symbolic, not biological, imperatives. From a political point of view, this position has an immediate attraction for feminists: once anatomy is no longer destiny, women's oppression and exploitation can become contingent rather than necessary. The Lacanian account of the Oedipus complex pivots on the relation of the Father to law, culture and symbolisation, so motherhood under patriarchy gains an important psychoanalytic dimension. But, in the last resort, the theory and the politics remain in tension. The Lacanian representation of sexual difference (defined by the presence or absence of the Phallus) leaves woman in a negative relation, defined as 'not-man', and trapped within a theory that brilliantly describes the power relationships of patriarchy but acknowledges no need for escape.

The Lacanian 'symbolic order', ruled by the Name of the Father, defines the areas of circulation and exchange through which society expresses relations in conceptual, that is, symbolic, terms beyond the natural and the experiential. Language, the universal, most sophisticated means of symbolic articulation, seals this process. Lacan mapped his concept of the symbolic on to Freud's concept of the Oedipal trajectory: access to the symbolic order is achieved by crossing the frontier, out of the imaginary, the dyadic world of mother and child, into recognition of the Father's Name and his Law. That is, out of a body-based, maternal relationship into one created by social exchange, culture and legal taboos (of which the first, of course, is the incest taboo).

The Oedipus complex is described as a trajectory, a journey or a process. But the doubts, the dust churned up by adventures on the way, the contradictions, are stabilised around a resolution in which the temporal process is split into a spatial opposition, structured around mother/father – a mythic condensation with mother as past and father as future – that suppresses a possible dialectical relationship between the two. In this scheme, any attempt at an exploration of the maternal relationship and its fantasies must appear as a retreat into the body, as a rejection of the symbolic and the Word, into a Utopian quest for a natural femininity, outside the 'tragic and beneficial' experience of castration. But motherhood is overdetermined, the site of imbrication between body and psyche and society. Myth flourishes at the point where the social and psychoanalytic overlap, redolent of fascination and anxiety and generating both creative energy (stories, images) and the 'taming and binding' process through which collective contact with the unconscious is masked. (Feminist film theory and criticism about Hollywood cinema has recognised and analysed this paradox.) The question is whether it is possible to open up the sphere of the pre-Oedipal, to transform its silence through language and politics. 'What escapes in sexuality' must take us back to the Women's Movement in the early 1970s, when the woman's body and motherhood were political issues, in terms of language and representation but also as a site of oppression and thus organisation for struggle. There is a danger that this dimension can be quite simply repressed, so that the relation between *jouissance* and women's oppression becomes again subject to nature, an eternal Idea, outside human investigation. It is here, perhaps, that poetic curiosity, the desire of an avant-garde ('what shifts within language') can contribute as much as convinced theoretical certainty. The destabilising force of negative aesthetics acts as an initial break and starting-point. But desire for an alternative language or symbolic system becomes particularly difficult in relation to the pre-Oedipal, as the child's psychic reality seems inextricably caught up with myths of motherhood. The child's pre- or extra-verbal symbolisations, outside articulated language, can become metonymically associated with the cultural marginalisation of the woman's sphere, epitomised by motherhood and its silence. The individual psyche's complicated and ambivalent journey loses a past and begins its history in language around the terms established by patriarchal value and mythology. The castration complex, initiated by curiosity and questions, is closed by anxiety and polarisations.

Social oppression and the myth of 'otherness'

> In passing from history to nature, myth acts economically: it abolishes the complexity of human acts, it gives them the simplicity of essences, it does away with all dialectics, with any going back on what is immediately visible, it organises a world which is without contradiction because it is without depth, a world which is open and wallowing in the evident, it establishes a blissful clarity: things appear to mean something by themselves.[10]

One way to discover the attributes and self-definition of a 'high culture' is through its opposite, the low culture that represents what the have been presented in a negative relation to creativity and artistic practices.[11] But this polarisation around access to culture is not particular to sex oppression. The mind/body opposition is characteristic of other oppositions of dominance (black/white, colonised/conqueror, peasant/noble, bourgeois/worker) and in each case the oppressed are linked to nature (the body) and the dominant to culture (and the mind). Whatever actual cultural deprivation and economic exploitation may give the myth a historical foundation, it is there to organise 'the complexity of human acts'.

It cannot be easy to move from oppression and its mythologies to resistance in history. A detour through a no man's land or threshold area of counter-myth and symbolisation is necessary. There is an analogy here with the unstable, heterogeneous discourse of Julia Kristeva's semiotic that the symbolic cannot contain within its own order. The pre-Oedipal, rather than an alternative or opposite state to the post-Oedipal, is in *transition* to articulated language: its gestures, signs and symbols have meaning but do not achieve the full sense of language. The lost memory of the mother's body is similar to other metaphors of a buried past, or a lost history, that contribute to the rhetoric of oppressed people, in a colonial, class or even sexual context. When Fr Miguel Hidalgo called on the people of Mexico to revolt against Spanish rule in 1810, he used the image of Our Lady of Guadalupe as the emblem of the uprising and signal for revolt. She had appeared to a poor Indian in a vision near the site that had once been sacred to the Aztec mother goddess, Tonantzin.[12] Guadalupe not only cared for the interests of the poorest people in Mexico, but also forged a link with the pre-Columbian, Indian religion that had been so savagely suppressed by the Spanish conquest. The image of the Black Virgin condenses the metonymic chain that links the 'lower orders', the despised race, to the land, the body, nature, motherhood, the lost past, the pre-Oedipal as Golden Age, the metaphors and emblems that belong to desire rather than reason. This is not to argue that any direct analogy between the loss of the mother and the sense of loss experienced in colonisation exists either in historical or psychoanalytic terms, but rather to emphasise the intermeshing of the two in the rhetoric of the oppressed. It is a rhetoric that takes on the low side of the polar opposition, in order to turn the world upside-down, and stake out *the right to imagine* another.

Kristeva's concept of the semiotic was influenced by Mikhail Bakhtin's work on medieval carnival,[13] For Bakhtin, carnival's strength arose out of its place in class culture: a transgressive space, but acknowledged and permitted by the Law, through which the resentments and envy of class hatred could be acted out in ritual and metaphor. Carnival gloried in the peasant side of the cultural connotations associated with the lower part of the body its functions the earth, the cycles of nature. Carnival inverted the normal experience of daily life, celebrating pleasure and excess in food, drink and sex. Hardship and morals could thus both be mocked. Bakhtin emphasises that the festival also kept alive an ancient tradition that had little place in medieval 'high' culture: the tradition of the comic (the genres of laughter Umberto Eco describes in *The Name of the Rose* as frowned on by the Church as transgressive).

Transgression and the law

If you think that the heterogeneous, polyvalent world is a separate structure in its own right, the law is disruptable. The Carnival can be held on the church steps. But if this is not the case, if the carnival and the church do not exist independently of each other, the pre-Oedipal and the Oedipal are not separate discrete states – if, instead, the Oedipal with the castration complex is what defines the pre-Oedipal, then the only way you can challenge the church is from within an alternative symbolic universe. You cannot choose the imaginary, the semiotic, the carnival as an alternative to the law. It is set up by the law precisely in its own ludic space, its area of imaginary alternative, but not as a symbolic alternative. So that, politically speaking, it is only the symbolic, a new symbolism, a new law, that can challenge the dominant law.[14]

This passage sets out very distinctly the difficulty of envisaging change from within the conceptual framework of a polarised mythology. It is also crucial to this structure that the carnivalesque ludic space, in which the Law allows its own injustice to be represented in a period of controlled disorder, is constructed primarily around rituals of inversion that can very easily be reversed back into 'order' at the end of the day. The problem seems reminiscent of my difficulties with my 'Visual Pleasure' article. Apart from inversion, shifts in position are hard to envisage. And should the system be challenged by 'a new symbolism, a new law', it is equally hard to envisage where that new 'symbolic' would come from. Perhaps the image of carnival can be used to move out of the immediate issues at stake here, the problem of the politics of the Oedipus complex, its relation to women, language and the symbolic order, to extend the argument to the problem of the politics of myth, its relationship to change, language and historical experience. As I argued in relation to the strategies of the avant-garde, a negation or inversion of dominant codes and conventions can fossilise into a dualistic terms of a dialect, an unformed language that can then develop in missing word... missing word...missing word...missing word...its own signifying space.

A spatial structure of inversions is crucial to the symbolic language of carnival, but there is also another, alternative, structure that exists in time, in the process of ritualised change from one state to another, from everyday norm to the licence of disorder and back again. This tripartite structure allows cultural forms and rituals to be used to express disruptive desire, both the desire repressed by a symbolic order and the Law as such, and the desire of the oppressed for change. In this sense it is integrative and arguably conservative, providing, in the last resort, a social safety-valve for the forces of disorder. Disruption is followed by restoration of a *status quo*, in a manner that is reminiscent of narrative patterns. But, more important, the gestures, emblems and metaphors of carnivalesque ritual can provide an almost invisible breeding ground for a language of protest and resistance. Inversion has a central place in the history of transgression within the law, but it is neither the only ritual of carnival, nor is it necessarily simply reversible back into the order of everyday.

I want to argue that the image of the disorderly woman did not always function to keep women in their place. On the contrary, it was a multivalent image that could operate, first, to widen the behavioural options for women within and even outside marriage, and second, to sanction riot and political disobedience for both men and women in a society that allowed the lower orders few formal means of protest. Play with the unruly woman is partly a chance for temporary release from traditional and stable hierarchy; but it is also part of the conflict over the basic distribution of power in a society. The woman-on-top might even facilitate innovation in historical theory and political behaviour.[15]

Narrative and change I: order and disorder

One attribute of myth, according to Barthes, is to impose stasis on history and conceal contradiction. The structure of myth, according to Lévi-Strauss, is primarily spatial rather than temporal, organised around thematic bundles and binary oppositions. Propp emphasises the linearity of the folk-tale, its transformative processes linked like a chain from function to function. From the point of view of envisaging an imaginative framework that can provide a model for conceptualising and offering patterns and expectations to the chaotic experiences of life and history, it is this aspect of story-telling that I want to emphasise here, with the significance of narrative closure still under question.

Gerald Prince gives the following definition of a minimal narrative as having three phases:

> A minimal story consists of three conjoined events. The first and third are stative, the second is active. Furthermore, the third is the inverse of the first. Finally, the three events are conjoined by three conjunctive features, in such a way that (a) the first event precedes the second in time and the second precedes the third, and (b) the second event causes the third.[16]

This definition establishes on a formal and structural level that the opening and closing states of a narrative are static, not subject to change, while the middle section is active and is marked by its difference from the other two. In an article 'Oedipus: Time and Structure in Narrative Form', Terence Turner fills out this basic structure, to give an ideological inflection to the relationship between stasis and event in narrative. He describes the *active* section of narrative as *disruptive* of a given *status quo*:

> The story is bounded at both ends by an implicit or explicit assertion of synchronic order. The narrative itself, however, represents a

complex mediation of this order, necessitated by the eruption of conflict and confusion . . . of the original synchronic order.[17]

In the middle section, the drama and pleasure consist in the eruption of events that disorders the laws of everyday normality. Turner argues that the desire and excess that characterise the middle phase of narrative represent a collectively acknowledged, but unspeakable, conflict with the codes of law that define and contain the normal course of life. This phase celebrates transgressive desire and organises it into a stylised cultural form: narrative. Just as the middle section erupts into action with disorder, so the end must integrate disorder back into stability. The rule of law closes in the space for transgression and disruption.

Turner also argues that this kind of narrative can tell the story of a transitional phase in which social and/or economic change needs to be given the ideological force of order and be integrated into a new expectation of everyday normality. Both he and Propp cite the Oedipus story in this context. There is here, perhaps, some visible link between the parabolic curves of history and economic forces, cited by Braudel, and the structure of stories that must represent, symbolically, moments of social transformation, absorbing the abnormal back into a sense of an order that is altered but still recognisably subject to the law.

Narrative and change II: liminality

Arnold van Gennep analyses the structure of rites of passage also in terms of a tripartite system. These rituals guide an individual through the transitional moments of life, marking the disruption and difficulty of change and the reintegration back into the ordered life of a community. There are rites of separation that initiate the process and put the person concerned into a state of privilege or crisis outside the norms of everyday existence. These are followed by transitional rites, during which the person is in a liminal relation to the world, in a no man's land, that may well be marked literally by a particular relationship to place ('transitional periods that require a certain autonomy'). These rites are followed by those of reincorporation.[18]

The literal representation of transition as movement through a threshold, from one space to another, has a very different mythic connotation from that of a binary opposition. Here it is the possibility of change that is celebrated, and the alteration of status implies movement on a linear model, rather than opposition on a polar model. There is a strong suggestion of *liminality* in the middle phase of a story, very often actually marked by literal movement in space, a journey, an adventure, but certainly by extraordinary events in which the rules and expectations of ordinary existence are left in suspense. Propp's analysis of narrative establishes that a story begins with the disruption of a stable state by 'an act of villainy', that separates out the next phase of the story into crisis and privilege, the hero's exceptional status and his tribulations. Peter Wollen has applied Propp's analysis of narrative structure to Hitchcock's movies; but he has also commented:

> It is appropriate to begin to write about Hitchcock by quoting Buchan: 'Now I saw how thin is the protection of civilisation. An accident and a bogus ambulance – a false charge and a bogus arrest – there were a dozen ways of spiriting one out of this gay and bustling world'.[19]

Hitchcock's heroes are plunged into a world turned upside-down, in which identity and even name become uncertain, in which the logical expectations of everyday life are reversed in a nightmare universe that also celebrates the pleasure and excitement of liminality. But journeys end with safe returns . . .

Although a folk-tale may well deal with social transition, as the hero leaves home to seek his fortune, the symmetry between beginning and end is important. The home that is left at the opening of a story is matched by another home established at the end (as Terence Turner says: 'bounded at both ends by synchronic order') while the shift from poverty to riches evokes the relation of inversion between the first and third states in Prince's minimal story and a return, with stability, to binarism. Significantly, these stories also represent another transition, from immature sexuality to marriage and manhood. Marriage represents the ritual function of reincorporation back into the ordered state of society but also the individual's new status within society.

Narrative and change III: festivals of the oppressed

Edmund Leach has used van Gennep's tripartite phasing of rites of passage in his analysis of carnival. Similarly, a carnival would start with events marking it off from normal life and, particularly, time. It would then proceed to the privileged, liminal phase, with its particular rituals of inversion, and conclude with the process of reincorporation into the normal cycles of life and time. In principle this pattern would be inescapably subject to the Law, as Juliet Mitchell argues for the 'ludic space'. The example of the failed uprising that concluded with the carnival at Romans in 1580, although it confirms an aspect of her argument, also offers another, more complex dimension to the metaphor.

In his brilliant and tragic book *Carnival at Romans*[20] Emmanuel Le Roy Ladurie emphasises the crucial place occupied by the rites of inversion in restoring order in the face of popular revolt. Because these rites depended on a concept of order, temporarily inverted, their reversal in the final phases of the carnival provided the means to restore the dominance of the ruling class. Just as the people had pushed the licence of carnival beyond its normal limits in the middle phase, to express popular unrest and discontent, so the world was turned right side up again with a savage suppression of the revolt. Although the ritual and the narrative structure favoured closure (and the interests of the ruling class) the experience at Romans had another, historical dimension. As intense class conflict and specific struggles had built up during some time preceding carnival, the festival was no longer either a politically neutral expression of individual desire finding collective expression within the law's ludic space, nor was it any longer simply the safety-valve through which class resentment could be graphically acted out and neutralised. The rites of carnival provided a people on the threshold of political consciousness with a liminal moment outside the time and space of the dominant order. Furthermore, carnival provided the people with a primitive but ready-made language of gesture, metaphor, emblem and symbolism at a moment when control over the abstraction of political concepts lagged behind the first inklings:

> Carnival was not merely a satiric and purely temporal reversal of the dual social order, finally intended to justify the *status quo* in an objectively conservative manner. It would be more accurate to say it was a satirical, lyrical, epic-learning experience for highly diversified groups. It was a way to action, perhaps; modifying the society as a whole in the direction of social justice and political progress.

Perhaps it is significant that the next important phase in the peasants' struggle for rights moved into the courts and progress was achieved within the language of lawyer's rationality and control over the processes of the law.

It is clearly impossible to generalise. But the relation between desire, desire for political change and access to language to articulate these desires must be of interest to feminists influenced by psychoanalytic theory. It is also important to see how collective cultural events can act as a spearhead for more organised politics. But to transcend to something beyond a safety-valve for discontent, the political and historical context is crucial. In contemporary society, similar patterns may be perceived in the 'rituals of resistance' associated with sub-cultures. A group can mark out its claim to liminal existence through clothes, music, emblematic loyalty, and so on. In a study of the zoot-suit riots in Los Angeles in the 1940s, Stuart Cosgrove distinguishes between the different levels of catharsis or epic-learning experience involved in a contemporary version of carnivalesque confrontation:

> The zoot-suit was simultaneously the garb of the victim and the attacker, the persecuted, the 'sinister' clown and the grotesque dandy. But the central opposition was between the style of the delinquent and the disinherited. To wear a zoot-suit was to risk the repressive intolerance of war-time society and to invite the attention of the police, the parent generation and the uniformed members of the armed forces. For many pachuchos the zoot-suit riots were simply high times in Los Angeles when they were momentarily in control of the streets; for others it was a realisation that they were outcasts in a society that was not of their making. . . . The zoot-suit riots were not political riots in the strictest sense, but for many participants they were an entry into the language of politics, an inarticulate rejection of the straight world and its organisation.[21]

Collective fantasy: the politics of the unconscious

> In the framework of class and political structure this specific character fragments of crisis of breaking points in the cycle of nature or in the life of society and man) could be realised without distortion only in Carnival and similar market place festivals. They were the second life of the people, who for a time entered the utopian realm of community, freedom and abundance. . . . As opposed to the official feast, one might say that carnival celebrated a temporary liberation from the prevailing myth and from the established order; it marked the suspension of all hierarchical rank, privileges and norms of prohibitions. Carnival was the true feast of time, the feast of becoming, change and renewal. It was hostile to all that was immortalised and completed.[22]

Rather than as a model, an alternative to the Law, I am using carnival as an image to give shape and form to the tension that exists between a conceptual topology that draws its metaphors from space and one that draws its metaphors from time. In the imagery of carnival, the binary, the rituals of inversion, are tied to the spatial, the polarised; and their reversal closes the liminal phase of the festival. It is this liminal phase that suggests imagery of change, transformation and liberation, the burrowing of the old mole rather than the eagle soaring in the sky.

The Oedipus complex shares some of the features of the tripartite narrative of ritual structure. If the dyadic relationship between mother and child corresponds to the initial stative phase, then disrupted by the Oedipal moment, its journey populated by desires, anxieties and contradictions, then the third phase would correspond to resolution and closure around the Law of the Father and his symbolic order. In Freud's version, the Oedipal experience is never perfected, but always remains partial, likely to be deviant and probably never to be completed, especially in the case of women. Rather than dismiss the pre-Oedipal on a binary model, this area between silence and speech, the terrain in which desire almost finds expression, should be taken seriously by feminist psychoanalytic theory, not on the grounds that it presents an alternative symbolic order, but that its imagery, and metaphor, and gesture could provide the basis for change *only* through the fact of feminism's existence as a political context, the expression of revolt against a patriarchal symbolic. That is, the psychoanalytic has to try to take on the political and the historical problems raised by change.

Freud recognised that the actual process of disrupting the dyad transmission of the incest taboo, submission to the father's prohibition, could not be equivalent for male and female if organised around the castration complex. The non-equivalence also implies an imbalance of power, as Althusser acknowledges in his essay 'Freud and Lacan': 'the Oedipal phase is centred and arranged wholly around the signifier *phallus*: the emblem of the Father, the emblem of right, of the Law, the basic model, the problem for the small boy is a simple one of transition, in which he accepts that he will grow up to inherit the 'Right' without any need to switch the gender of his object of desire. The little girl, on the other hand, has to move into masquerade and inversion. In the boy's case, integration and closure are comparatively easily achieved; in the girl's case, as Freud reiterates, they are endlessly postponed. Although each individual lives out the Oedipal trajectory personally and uniquely, patterns of experience, affective structures, language and signs are shared. The problems, contradictions and irreconcilable demands made by the acquisition of sexual identity, family structures and historical conditions surface in collectively held desires, obsessions and anxieties. This is the shared, social dimension of the unconscious, of the kind that Freud referred to in *Jokes and the Unconscious*, which erupts symptomatically in popular culture, whether folk-tales, carnival or the movies. These are temporal forms, narrative forms. If narrative, with the help of avant-garde principles, can be conceived around ending that is not closure, and the state of liminality as politically significant, it can question the symbolic, and enable myth and symbols to be constantly revalued. A feminist perspective should insist on the possibility of change without closure, drawing by analogy on the female Oedipus complex, the crucible out of which sexual identity does not emerge as pure gold.

Departures

'Pleasure becomes a serious matter in the context of innovative change' (Victor Turner).

Notes

With thanks to Ronan Bennett and Kaja Silverman.

A previous version of this chapter appeared in *Discourse*, no. 7, Berkeley, Spring 1985.

1. Fernand Braudel, *Civilisation and Capitalism. Volume 2, The Wheels of Commerce* (London: Fontana, 1985). I chose this particular passage because it uses the word *parabola*, rather than the word *cycle*. For Braudel's discussion of secular and Kondratieff cycles see *Civilisation and Capitalism. Volume 3, The Perspective on the World* (London: Fontana, 1984).
2. Victor Turner, *Dramas, Fields, and Metaphors, Symbolic Action in Human Society* (Ithaca: Cornell University Press, 1974).
3. The analogy between the Frankenstein monster and the industrial working class is suggested by Franco Moretti's essay in *Signs Taken for Wonders* (London: Verso, 1983).
4. Jane Gallop, *Feminism and Psychoanalysis* (London: Macmillan – now Palgrave Macmillan, 1982).
5. Laura Mulvey, 'Visual Pleasure and Narrative Cinema', *Screen*, XVI, 3 (1975).
6. Sigmund Freud, 'Instincts and Their Vicissitudes', *The Standard Edition* (London: The Hogarth Press, 1962), vol. 14; 'Three Essays on Sexuality', *The Standard Edition*, vol. 7.
7. Gaston Bachelard, *The Poetics of Space* (New York: The Orion Press, 1964).
8. Peter Wollen, *Godard and Counter Cinema: Vent d'Est, Readings and Writings*, (London: Verso, 1983).
9. Jacqueline Rose, *Feminine Sexuality, Jacques Lacan and the Ecole Freudienne*, co-edited with Juliet Mitchell (London: Macmillan – now Palgrave Macmillan, 1982).
10. Roland Barthes, *Mythologies* (London: Cape, 1972).
11. 'Women are presented negatively, as lacking in creativity, with nothing significant to contribute, and as having no influence on the course of art. Paradoxically, to negate them women have to be acknowledged; they are mentioned in order to be categorised, set apart and marginalised.' This is

'one of the major elements in of the construction of the hegemony of men in cultural practices, in art'. Rozsika Parker and Griselda Pollock, *Old Mistresses* (London: Routledge & Kegan Paul, 1981).

12. The relationship between the old and new religion is described by Anita Brenner in *Idols Behind Altars* (New York: Biblio and Tannen, 1976): 'Every time the friars razed a teocali they had a church built there with. They buried idols and planted crosses. And again the Indians though this time surely not so innocent, did precisely the same thing. Says Geronimo, rather upset by this discovery: "The friars had many crosses made for them and placed in all the gates and entrances to villages and upon some high hills . . . [The Indians] would put their idols under or behind the cross, making believe they adored the cross, but adoring really the figure of the demon they had hidden there." '

13. Mikhail Bakhtin, *Rabelais and his World* (Cambridge, Mass.: MIT, 1968).

14. Juliet Mitchell, 'Psychoanalysis, Narrative and Femininity', in *Woman, the Longest Revolution* (London: Virago, 1984).

15. Natalie Zemon Davis, *Society and Culture in Early Modern France* (Stanford University Press, 1975).

16. Gerald Prince, *A Grammar of Stories* (The Hague: Mouton, 1973).

17. Terence Turner, 'Time and Structure in Narrative Form', *Forms of Symbolic Action*, Proceedings of the 1969 annual spring meeting of the American Ethnological Society.

18. Arnold van Gennep, *The Rites of Passage* (London: Routledge & Kegan Paul, 1960). Van Gennep's concept of liminality is very usefully developed by Victor Turner, *Dramas, Fields and Metaphors*.

19. Peter Wollen: 'Hitchock's Vision', *Cinema*, 1, 3 (1969).

20. Emmanuel Le Roy Ladurie, *Carnival at Romans* (Harmondsworth: Penguin, 1981).

21. Stuart Cosgrove: 'The Zoot Suit: Style Warfare', *History Workshop Journal*, 18 (1984).

22. Mikhail Bakhtin, *Rabelais and his World* (Cambridge, Mass.: MIT, 1968).

15
Cornel West, *The American Evasion of Philosophy* (1989)

Cornel West's *The American Evasion of Philosophy* is an attempt to bring the full resources of academic inquiry and thought to the specificity of contemporary American experience. West produces a history of pragmatism – the United States's most distinctive contribution to philosophy – which stresses its socially engaged nature and the way in which its development has continually responded to developments in American history. As West remarks in his introduction, 'American pragmatism is less a philosophical tradition putting forward solutions to perennial problems in the Western philosophical tradition initiated by Plato and more a continuous cultural commentary or set of interpretations that attempt to explain America to itself at a particular historical moment.'

West's project locates itself within the American pragmatist tradition, with pride of place being given to John Dewey but with that tradition traced as well through thinkers as diverse as Lionel Trilling and W. E. B. Du Bois up to the work of Richard Rorty today. Pragmatism refuses any epistemological discourse which would seek to provide an overarching correspondence between word and world – this is its 'evasion of philosophy'. Instead of resting on philosophically guaranteed truth, we are engaged with a multitude of practices each of which provides ways in which we can judge the truth or falsity of certain statements.

West cannot remain content with an anti-epistemological position that limits the scope of its critique to the practices of science or the academy. The pragmatist position only achieves its full potential for West when it is actively linked to personal and social struggle in which the aim of creating a more productive self and a more productive society become one and the same. West locates the origin of this 'prophetic' strain within American thought with Emerson, himself then seen in this perspective as an unlikely but crucial pragmatist.

The American Evasion of Philosophy has much in common with Stanley Aronowitz's LDS volume *Crisis in Historical Materialism* in that it poses American historical experience as the starting point, and ultimate testing ground, of intellectual inquiry. The most poweful element of that experience, and the element that immediately links it to global struggles, however, is seen by West as that of race. Indeed, Du Bois functions for West as in many respects the exemplary pragmatist inasmuch as the matter of race forced him to ground his intellectual inquiries in an engagement across the whole political and cultural sphere.

W. E. B. Du Bois: The Jamesian organic intellectual

The career of W. E. B. Du Bois serves as a unique response to the crisis of American pragmatism in the twentieth century. Although he was born nine years after John Dewey (and about a hundred miles away) and died one year after Mills, Du Bois already saw the contours of the 'Fourth Epoch', a period fundamentally shaped by the decolonisation of the third world. As an American intellectual of African descent – the greatest one produced in this country – Du Bois looks at the United States through a different lens from those of Emerson, Peirce, James, Dewey, Hook, and Mills. As one grounded in and nourished by American pragmatism, Du Bois – both by personal choice and by social treatment – allies himself in word and deed with the wretched of the earth. In the United States, this principally takes the form of performing intellectual work within the institutions, organisations, and movements of Afro-Americans or those that focus on their plight.

A New Englander by birth and rearing, Du Bois did not undergo the usual racial discrimination and depreciation during his childhood. He was the only black child in his secondary schools and attended an all-white Congregational church. His family, headed by his mother, was poor, yet not as poor or socially ostracised as the Irish immigrant mill workers in his town. Upon graduation from high school, Du Bois wanted to attend Harvard College, but the poor academic quality of his high school and some white discouragement (though white financial support ultimately allowed him to go) made him settle for Fisk University – the black Yale, as it were. Admitted as a sophomore owing to his excellent record, Du Bois experienced segregation and encountered Afro-American culture for the first time. Unacquainted with the kinetic orality, emotional physicality, and combative spirituality of black music, language, and customs, Du Bois harbored ambiguous attitudes toward this culture. In his graduating class of five in 1888, Du Bois gave a commencement address on his hero, Bismarck, who 'had made a nation out of a mass of bickering peoples'.[1] As he notes in one of his autobiographies: 'I was blithely European and imperialist in outlook; democratic as democracy was conceived in America.'[2]

From Fisk, Du Bois matriculated to Harvard College, entering as a junior owing to the 'lower standards' at Fisk. Despite having no social life at Harvard, including a rejection from the glee club, Du Bois thrived there intellectually. Emotionally sustained by his involvement in the black community, Du Bois was most impressed at Harvard by William James – and his pragmatism:

> I was in Harvard for education and not for high marks, except as marks would insure my staying . . . above all I wanted to study phi-losophy! I wanted to get hold of the basis of knowledge, and explore foundations and beginnings. I chose, therefore, Palmer's course in ethics, but he being on Sabbatical for the year, William James replaced him, and I became a devoted follower of James at the time he was developing his pragmatic philosophy.[3]

Du Bois seems to have been attracted to pragmatism owing to its Emersonian evasion of epistemology-centered philosophy, and his sense of pragmatism's relevance to the Afro-American predicament.

> I hoped to pursue philosophy as my life career, with teaching for support. . . . My salvation here was the type of teacher I met rather than the content of the courses. William James guided me out of the sterilities of scholastic philosophy to realist pragmatism . . .
>
> I revelled in the keen analysis of William James, Josiah Royce and young George Santayana. But it was James with his pragmatism and Albert Bushnell Hart with his research method, that turned me back from the lovely but sterile land of philosophic speculation, to the social sciences as the field for gathering and interpreting that body of fact which would apply to my program for the Negro . . .
>
> I knew by this time that practically my sole chance of earning a living combined with study was to teach, and after my work with Hart in United States history, I conceived the idea of applying phi-losophy to an historical interpretation of race relations.[4]

Du Bois never spelled our what he meant by the 'sterilities of scholas-tic philosophy', but given what we know of James's pragmatism, it surely had something to do with sidestepping the Cartesian epistemo-logical puzzles of modern philosophy. Yet, unlike James and more like Dewey, Du Bois took a turn toward history and the social sciences. In 1890, Du Bois received his Harvard cum laude bachelor's degree in philosophy. Du Bois' move toward history and the social sciences, reinforced by James's candid advice (untinged with racial bias) that there is 'not much chance for anyone earning a living as a philosopher', resulted in his receiving a fellowship to stay at Harvard for graduate work. Since sociology as a discipline did not yet exist at Harvard, Du Bois studied in the history and political science departments. Moreover, the fact that Du Bois 'came to the study of sociology by way of philosophy and history'[5] – that is, primarily James's pragmatism and Hart's documentary approach – put him on the cutting edge of new intellectual developments in late-nineteenth-century America.

Upon the encouragement of his supervisor, Hart, Du Bois spent two years (1892–94) at the University of Berlin. In Germany, Du Bois studied economics, history, and sociology in the seminars of Gustav von Schmoller and Adolf Wagner (both 'socialists of the chair'); and he heard Max Weber lecture as a visiting professor. Yet the heroic romantic nationalism of Heinrich von Treitschke, the famous Prussian historian and political theorist, impressed Du Bois most. Though Du Bois had come far from his uncritical praise of Bismarck, he still was attracted to Treitschke's notion that history was made by the powerful wills of great men who unify and guide their own peoples. Needless to say, Du Bois saw this role for himself in regard to black Americans. On his twenty-fifth birthday he dedicated 'himself as the Moses of his people'.[6]

Du Bois' stay in Europe had a tremendous impact on his view of himself and America. On the one hand, it gave him a way 'of looking at the world as a man and not simply from a narrow racial and provincial outlook'.[7] On the other hand, it provided him with an outlet for his hostility toward America and insight into its provinciality:

> I found to my gratification that they, with me, did not regard America as the last word in civilization. Indeed, I derived a certain satisfaction in learning that the University of Berlin did not recognize a degree even from Harvard University, no more than Harvard did from Fisk . . . 'All agreed that Americans could make money and did not care how they made it. And the like. Sometimes their criticism got under even my anti-American skin, but it was refreshing on the whole to hear voiced my own attitude toward so much that America had meant to me.[8]

In June 1894, Du Bois arrived back in 'nigger-hating' America[9] Sailing aboard a ship full of European immigrants, he noted as it arrived in New York harbor:

I know not what multitude of emotions surged in others, but I had to recall that mischievous little French girl whose eyes twinkled as she said: 'Oh yes the Statue of Liberty! With its back toward America, and its face toward France!'[10]

Since teaching in white universities was unthinkable, Du Bois accepted a job teaching Greek and Latin at a black parochial school in Xenia, Ohio – Wilberforce University. Having shed his dogmatic religious beliefs under James, Du Bois found it difficult to cope with the deeply pietistic atmosphere at the school. For instance, at one gathering it was announced:

that 'Professor Du Bois will lead us in prayer.' I simply answered 'No, he won't,' and as a result nearly lost my new job.[11]

Du Bois quite understandably felt constrained at Wilberforce, though he did complete his Harvard dissertation there on the suppression of the African slave trade. In 1896, it was published as the first volume of the Harvard Historical Studies. As Arnold Rampersad has noted, this work, though full of original and ground-breaking research, is essentially 'a chapter of the moral history of his country' – ethical motives and national conscience are stressed.[12]

Du Bois stayed at Wilberforce for only two years, thanks to an offer to study the black community in Philadelphia (then the largest black community in the North). This offer was a grand opportunity not just to leave Wilberforce with his new wife but also to test his scientific skills and narrow Enlightenment outlook on race relations:

The Negro problem was in my mind a matter of systematic investigation and intelligent understanding. The world was thinking wrong about race, because it did not know. The ultimate evil was stupidity. The cure for it was knowledge based on scientific investigation.[13]

This outlook guided not only his pioneering study *The Philadelphia Negro* (1899), but also the *Atlanta University Publications* (1896–1914) he directed during his thirteen years as professor of economics at Atlanta University. At the first stage of Du Bois' career, he worked diligently as a social scientist and professor gathering the first empirical data on the social conditions of black Americans. Yet as the institutionalized terrorism escalated in the South with tighter Jim Crow laws and more lynchings, Du Bois' moral idealism along with the scholarly strategy of disclosing the facts and revealing the truth of black oppression became less credible:

> Two considerations thereafter broke in upon my work and eventually disrupted it: first, one could not be a calm, cool and detached scientist while Negroes were lynched, murdered and starved; and secondly, there was no such definite demand for scientific work of the sort that I was doing, as I had confidently assumed there would be easily forthcoming. I regarded it as axiomatic that the world wanted to learn the truth and if the truth were sought with even approximate accuracy and painstaking devotion, the world would gladly support the effort.[14]

Du Bois became more and more convinced not only that 'most Americans answer all questions regarding the Negro *a priori*',[15] but also that issues of power, interests, and status played more important roles than he had realised. This recognition led him to put less faith in scientific research as a weapon of social change and to focus more on middlebrow journalism and writing for a general literate public. His American classic, *The Souls of Black Folk* (1903), consisted of eight revised essays already published in leading magazines (mostly *Atlantic Monthly*) and five new pieces. Like Emerson, Du Bois always viewed himself as a poet in the broad nineteenth-century sense; that is, one who creates new visions and vocabularies for the moral enhancement of humanity. This poetic sensibility is manifest in his several poems and five novels. Yet it is seen most clearly in *The Souls of Black Folk*.

Du Bois' classic text can be viewed as being in the Emersonian grain, yet it conveys insights ignored by most of white America. Du Bois attempts to turn the Emersonian theodicy inside out by not simply affirming the capacity of human powers to overcome problems, but, more important, raising the question 'How does it feel to be a problem?'[16] in America – a problem America neither admits it has nor is interested in solving. The aim of his text is to convey and enact 'the strange experience' of 'being a problem: – that is, being an American of African descent':

> The Negro is a sort of seventh son born with a veil, and gifted with second-sight in this American world – a world which yields him no true self-consciousness, but only lets him see himself through the revelation of the other world. It is a peculiar sensation, this double-

consciousness, this sense of always looking at one's self through the eyes of others, of measuring one's soul by the tape of a world that looks on in amused contempt and pity. One ever feels his twoness – an American, a Negro; two souls, two thoughts, two unreconciled strivings; two warring ideals in one dark body, whose dogged strength alone keeps it from being torn asunder.[17]

Du Bois is writing about 'the experience of being a problem' at a time in which discernible signs of the awakening third world appear, such as the defeat of Russia by Japan (1904), the Persian revolt (1905), and the Mexican revolution (1911). And as America emerges as a world power, much of the credibility of its rhetoric of freedom and democracy is threatened by the oppression of black Americans.

Emerson had grappled with the 'double-consciousness' of being an American, of having a European culture in an un-European environment. Yet, for him, being an American was not a problem but rather a unique occasion to exercise human powers to solve problems. Du Bois' 'double-consciousness' views this unique occasion as the *cause* of a problem, a problem resulting precisely from the exercise of white human powers celebrated by Emerson. In short, Du Bois subverts the Emersonian theodicy by situating it within an imperialist and ethnocentric rhetorical and political context.

But, ironically, Du Bois' subversion is aided by his own revision of the Emersonian theodicy. This revision principally consists of exercising his own powers in order to overcome the blindnesses, silences, and exclusions of earlier Emersonian theodicies. The aim remains self-creation and individuality, though with a more colourful diversity; the end is still a culture in which human powers, provoked by problems, are expanded for the sake of moral development of human personalities:

The history of the American Negro is the history of this strife – this longing to attain self-conscious manhood, to merge his double self into a better and truer self. In this merging he wishes neither of the older selves to be lost. He would not Africanize America, for America has too much to teach the world and Africa. He would not bleach his Negro soul in a flood of white Americanism, for he knows that Negro blood has a message for the world. He simply wishes to make it possible for a man to be both a Negro and an American, without being cursed and spit upon by his fellows, without having the doors of opportunity closed roughly in his face.

This, then, is the end of his striving: to be a co-worker in the kingdom of culture, to escape both death and isolation, to husband and use his best powers and his latent genius.[18]

Following his mentor Hart's racialist view of history in which each 'race' possesses certain gifts and endowments, Du Bois holds that those of the Negro consist of story and song, sweat and brawn and the spirit.[19] Du Bois claims that these gifts of black folk have given America its only indigenous music, the material foundations of its empire, and ethical critiques to remind America of its own moral limits. The music expresses the protean improvisational character of America itself, always responding to, adapting, and experimenting with new challenges. Slavery, the foundation of America's power, exemplifies the tragic and usually overlooked costs concealed by American prosperity. Black ethical critiques, themselves often based on American-style Protestantism and US political ideals, expose the hypocrisy of the American rhetoric of freedom and democracy.

As a highly educated Western black intellectual, Du Bois himself often scorns the 'barbarisms' (sometimes confused with Africanisms) shot through Afro-American culture. In fact, I count eighteen allusions to the 'backwardness' of black folk.[20] He even goes as far as to support a form of paternalism that leads toward black self-determination:

> I should be the last one to deny the patent weaknesses and short-comings of the Negro people . . . I freely acknowledge that it is possible, and sometimes best, that a partially undeveloped people should be ruled by the best of their stronger and better neighbors for their own good, until such time as they can start and fight the world's battles alone.[21]

This paternalism fits well with his early doctrine of the talented tenth – the educated, cultured, and refined like himself leading the benighted, ignorant, and coarse black masses out of the wilderness into the promised land. Yet, even in this first stage of his career, Du Bois acknowledges and accents the creative powers of the black masses in the cultural sphere, especially in their music.

Du Bois' stress on black music is significant in that here he sees black agency at work. Like Emerson and other pragmatists, Du Bois posits culture making as the prime instance of history making. He does this not only because for Afro-Americans all other spaces were closed, but also because in every society, no matter how oppressive, human creativity can be discerned in culture making. In good Emersonian fashion, Du Bois' democratic mores are grounded in the detection of human creative powers at the level of everyday life.

Du Bois' departure from Atlanta University and his acceptance of the editorship of the *Crisis*, organ of the newly formed National Association for the Advancement of Colored People, inaugurated a second stage in his career. In the eyes of some black figures like Walker Trotter, the NAACP was too interracialist; in the view of those like William James, it was too militant for the times. Yet Du Bois along with other black and white activists, including John Dewey, pushed on for social reform and civil rights by means of public agitation and political pressure. As director of publications and research, Du Bois was the only black national officer in the organization. The first issue of the *Crisis* was published in November 1910 and consisted of a thousand copies; by 1918 a hundred thousand copies were being printed. He held this position for twenty-four years.

Like Dewey, Du Bois supported Woodrow Wilson in 1912 and American entrance into World War I. Both figures later regretted these decisions and became more radical as a consequence. Du Bois' radicalism principally took the form of an international perspective focused on the decolonization of Africa. As an organic intellectual directly linked to black social agency – and possible insurgency – Du Bois was put at the center of ideological and political debates in America and abroad. He organized the second Pan-African Congress in February 1919 in Paris in order 'to have Africa in some way voice its complaints to the world during the Peace Congress at Versailles',[22] Still under the sway of a talented-tenth doctrine, Du Bois drew up an elitist, neocolonial platform for 'semi-civilized peoples' in Africa; still influenced by a moral idealism with an insufficient grasp of the role of economic and political power, he had great hopes that the League of Nations would curb American and European racism. Regarding the Pan-African Congress, he wrote:

> We got, in fact, the ear of the civilized world and if it had been possible to stay longer and organize more thoroughly and spread the truth – what might not have been accomplished? . . .
> The world-fight for Black rights is on![23]

The Red Summer of 1919 dampened Du Bois' hopes. Southern black migration into northern industries spurred racial competition between black and white workers, and the decoration of many black soldiers back from the war generated white resentment. During that year seventy-seven blacks were lynched, including a woman and eleven soldiers; there also were race riots in twenty-six cities.

With the collapse of the League of Nations, and debilitating ideological strife in the Pan-African movement, Du Bois found himself loyal to a cause with no organization. The tumultuous rise of Marcus Garvey, the brouhaha over the Harlem 'Renaissance', and white racist entrenchment forced Du Bois – now in his late fifties – to re-examine his gradualist perspective. More important, the Russian Revolution, initially held at arm's length by Du Bois, challenged him in a fundamental way. He had considered himself a democratic socialist – a 'socialist of the path' – since 1907 and, in fact, joined the Socialist party for a while. In response to left critiques by socialists such as Claude McKay, A. Phillip Randolph, and Chauncey Owens in 1921, Du Bois replied:

> The editor of *The Crisis* considers himself a Socialist but he does not believe that German State Socialism or the dictatorship of the proletariat are perfect panaceas. He believes with most thinking men that the present method of creating, controlling and distributing wealth is desperately wrong; that there must come and is coming a social control of wealth; but he does not know just what form that control is going to take, and he is not prepared to dogmatize with Marx or Lenin.[24]

Du Bois' basic concern is the specific predicament of Afro-Americans as victims of white capitalist exploitation at the workplace and of white capitalists and workers in the political system and cultural mores of the country.

The major impact of the Russian Revolution on Du Bois was to compel him to take seriously the challenge of Marxism as a mode of intellectual inquiry. Marxist historical and social analysis forced Du Bois to go beyond his moralistic democratic socialism, with its primary stress on 'light, more light, clear thought, accurate knowledge, careful distinctions'.[25] Marxism indeed contained a commitment to scientific knowledge, a crucial requirement for a social scientist with Du Bois' training; but it also highlighted the realities of power struggles in which moral suasion played a minor role, to say the least. In this way, the Russian Revolution for Du Bois was less a historical event and more an intellectual beckoning to Marxist thought, a school of thought that made him see that:

beyond my conception of ignorance and deliberate illwill as causes of race prejudice, there must be other and stronger and more threatening forces, forming the founding stones of race antagonisms, which we had only begun to attack or perhaps in reality had not attacked at all. Moreover, the attack upon these hidden and partially concealed causes of race hate, must be led by Negroes in a program which was not merely negative in the sense of calling on white folk to desist from certain practices and give up certain beliefs, but direct in the sense that Negroes must proceed constructively in new and comprehensive plans of their own. I think it was the Russian Revolution which first illuminated and made clear this change in my basic thought.[26]

On his first visit to Russia in 1926, Du Bois' utopian energies were rekindled. He considered Russia 'the most hopeful land in the modern world'.[27] But he still unequivocally rejected the strategies of the Communist party in the United States. Even after acknowledging the realities of power in America, Du Bois insisted that revolution would be a 'slow, reasoned development' informed by 'the most intelligent body of American thought'.[28]

The most significant product of Du Bois' encounter with Marxist thought was his seminal book *Black Reconstruction: An Essay Toward a History of the Part Which Black Folk Played in the Attempt to Reconstruct Democracy In America, 1860–1880* (1935). This text is seminal not simply because it focused on the postemancipation struggle over the control of black and white labor rather than on the obfuscating racist mythologies of the leading Reconstruction historians, John W. Burgess and William A. Dunning, nor because the book represented groundbreaking research, for it relied exclusively on secondary sources. Rather Du Bois' *Black Reconstruction* is a seminal work because it examines the ways in which the struggle for democracy was stifled at a critical period in American history from the vantage point of the victims (including both black and white laborers).

In *Black Reconstruction*, Du Bois is still exploring 'the strange experience of being a problem', but this exploration has taken a structural socio-economic and political form. Unlike any of the other pragmatists, Du Bois provides an account of the means by which industrial America imposed severe constraints upon an emerging or at least potential creative democracy. The economic power of northern capitalists and southern planters, the racist attitudes of white workers and politicians and the struggles of black freed persons conjoined in a complex way to give initial hope for but ultimately defeat creative democracy in America. And the defeat of any effective movements for radical democracy is inseparable from the lack of even formal democracy for most black Americans.

Du Bois' analysis illustrates the blindnesses and silences in American pragmatist reflections on individuality and democracy. Although none of the pragmatists were fervent racists themselves – and most of them took public stands against racist practices – not one viewed racism as contributing greatly to the impediments for both individuality and democracy. More specifically, neither Dewey, Hook, nor Mills grappled in a serious way, in essay or texts, with how racism impeded the development of an Emersonian culture of creative democracy. By 'racism' here I mean not merely discrimination and devaluation based on race but, more important, the strategic role black people have played in the development of the capitalist economy, political system, and cultural apparatuses in America. To what degree have the demands of blacks fostered and expanded American democracy? In which way is democracy dependent on these demands, given their spin-off effects in demands made by larger ethnic groups, women, gays, lesbians, and the elderly? Du Bois' *Black Reconstruction* implicitly raises these questions in a serious and urgent manner. In graphic and hyperbolic language he writes:

> America thus stepped forward in the first blossoming of the modern age and added to the art of beauty, gift of the Renaissance, and to freedom of belief, gift of Martin Luther and Leo X, a vision of democratic self-government: the domination of political life by the intelligent decision of free and self-sustaining men. What an idea and what an area for its realization – endless land of richest fertility, natural resources such as earth seldom exhibited before, a population infinite in variety, of universal gift, burned in the fires of poverty and caste, yearning toward the Unknown God; and self-reliant pioneers, unafraid of man or devil. It was the Supreme Adventure, in the last Great Battle of the West, for that human freedom which would release the human spirit from lower lust for mere meat, and set it free to dream and sing.
>
> And then some unjust god leaned, laughing, over the ramparts of heaven and dropped a black man in their midst.
>
> It transformed the world. It turned democracy back to Roman imperialism and fascism; it restored caste and oligarchy; it replaced

freedom with slavery and withdrew the name of humanity from the vast majority of human beings.

But not without struggle . . .

Then came this battle called Civil War. . . . The slave went free; stood a brief moment in the sun; then moved back again toward slavery. The whole weight of America was thrown to color caste. The colored world went down before England, France, Germany, Russia, Italy and America. A new slavery arose. The upward moving of white labor was betrayed into wars for profit based on color caste. Democracy died save in the hearts of Black folk.[29]

Du Bois provides American pragmatism with what it sorely lacks: an international perspective on the impetus and impediments to individuality and radical democracy, a perspective that highlights the plight of the wretched of the earth, namely, the majority of humanity who own no property or wealth, participate in no democratic arrangements, and whose individualities are crushed by hard labor and harsh living conditions. James possessed the ingredients for such a view, but he did not see social structures, only individuals. Dewey indeed saw social structures and individuals yet primarily through an American lens. Hook too adopts a cosmopolitan viewpoint, but his cold war sentiments give a tunnel vision of the third world as a playground for the two superpowers. Mills comes closer than the others, yet, for him, postmodern historical agency resides almost exclusively in the Western (or Westernized) intelligentsia. Du Bois goes beyond them all in the scope and depth of his vision: creative powers reside among the wretched of the earth even in their subjugation, and the fragile structures of democracy in the world depend, in large part, on how these powers are ultimately exercised.

Convinced 'that the whole set of the white world in America, in Europe, and in the world was too determinedly against racial equality, to give power and persuasiveness to our agitation,'[30] Du Bois advocated a program of voluntary segregation based on institution building and a separate cooperative economy. This ideological break from the liberal integrationist reformism of the NAACP led to his resignation in 1934. He returned to Atlanta University as head of the Department of Sociology. There he founded and edited *Phylon* and set up a series of conferences on programs to alleviate the economic condition of black people after the war. Yet, unexpectedly, Du Bois was retired by the trustees of the university. Even more surprising, he was asked to return to the NAACP. But after four years of bickering with the NAACP leadership, especially over his support of Henry Wallace in 1948, Du Bois was dismissed.

With the Pan-African movement rejuvenated in 1945 and the peace movement escalating, Du Bois' preoccupation with decolonization found him more and more drawn into the cold war, not only as inter-locutor but also as target. In *Color and Democracy: Colonies and Peace* (1945) he excoriated cold warriors as handmaidens of the American imperial empire. The Marshall Plan was the tool of a new postwar colo-nialism; the containment strategy, a threat to world peace. In 1950, he ran on the Labor party ticket for U.S. Senate, a sure sign of his closer relations with the Communist party. The following February, Du Bois' peace information center, which had disbanded four months earlier, was indicted by a grand jury in Washington, D.C., for 'failure to regis-ter as agent for a foreign principal.' At the age of eighty-three and after over half a century in pursuit of individuality and democracy in America and abroad, Du Bois was an indicted criminal, handcuffed and facing a maximum sentence of five years in prison.

> I have faced during my life many unpleasant experiences; the growl of a mob; the personal threat of murder; the scowling distaste of an audience. But nothing has cowed me as that day, November 8, 1951, when I took my seat in a Washington courtroom as an indicted criminal.[31]

The widespread vilification of Du Bois as a Russian agent in the press – both white and black – left him virtually alone with leftist friends and some black loyal supporters in McCarthyite America. But support overflowed from overseas. And although the government could not prove 'subversion' against him (or his colleagues at the peace center), the stigma stuck for the general populace. He was refused the right to travel abroad and to speak on university campuses (and at local NAACP branches!), his manuscripts were turned down by reputable publishers, and his mail was tampered with.

> It was a bitter experience and I bowed before the storm. But I did not break . . . I found new friends and lived in a wider world than ever before – a world with no color line. I lost my leadership of my race . . . the colored children ceased to hear my name.[32]

Six years later Du Bois' request for a passport was finally granted (owing to a Supreme Court ruling). He traveled abroad for nearly a year to China,

France, England, Sweden, Germany, Russia, and Czechoslovakia. In 1961, Kwame Nkrumah invited Du Bois to Ghana to begin work on the Encyclopedia Africana, a project Du Bois had proposed in 1909. Du Bois accepted, but before he left for Ghana he joined the Communist Party, U.S.A. Locked into the narrow options of American political culture, Du Bois ultimately preferred a repressive communism that resisted European and American imperialism to a racist America that promoted the subjugation of peoples of color. A few weeks before he departed for Ghana, Du Bois wrote to a friend:

> I just cannot take any more of this country's treatment. We leave for Ghana October 5th and I set no date for return . . . Chin up, and fight on, but realize that American Negroes can't win.[33]

After two years of working on the encyclopedia, Du Bois became a Ghanaian citizen. In that same year, 1963, he died – the very day that 250,000 people gathered in Washington, D.C., to hear Martin Luther King, Jr., immortalize the black Emersonian quest for the American dream. Like Malcolm X and later even King himself, Du Bois concluded that this dream was more a nightmare for those whose measuring rod is the plight of most black Americans. For him, an Emersonian culture of creative democracy had become a mere chimera: a racist, sexist, and multinational capitalist America had no potential whatsoever to realize the pragmatist ideals of individuality and radical democracy. Yet Du Bois still encouraged struggle. About a month before leaving America, Du Bois attended a banquet for Henry Winston, a leading and courageous black communist released from prison after losing his sight owing to jail neglect. In words that aptly describe his own life and work, Du Bois quoted from Emerson's 'Sacrifice':

> Though love repine and reason chafe,
>   There came a voice without reply
> 'Tis Man's perdition to be safe
>   When for the truth he ought to die[34]

And though Du Bois may have lost his own ideological 'sight' owing greatly to national neglect and limited political options, there is no doubt that what he did 'see' remains a major obstacle for an Emersonian culture of radical democracy in America.

Notes

1. W. E. B. Du Bois, *The Autobiography of W. E. B. Du Bois: A Soliloquy on Viewing My Life from the Last Decade of Its First Century* (New York: International Publishers, 1968), p. 126.
2. Ibid.
3. Ibid., p. 133.
4. Ibid., pp. 133, 148.
5. Ibid., p. 149.
6. Francis L. Broderick, *W. E. B. Du Bois: Negro Leader in Time of Crisis* (Palo Alto: Stanford University Press, 1959), pp. 27–8; Manning Marable, *W. E. B. Du Bois: Black Radical Democrat* (Boston: Twayne, 1986), pp. 19–20.
7. Du Bois, *Autobiography of W. E. B. Du Bois*, p. 159.
8. Ibid., p. 157.
9. Ibid., p. 183.
10. Ibid., p. 182.
11. Ibid., p. 186.
12. Arnold Rampersad, *The Art and Imagination of W. E. B. Du Bois* (Cambridge: Harvard University Press, 1976), p. 50.
13. W. E. B. Du Bois, *Dusk of Dawn: An Essay toward an Autobiography of a Race Concept* (New York: Harcourt, Brace, 1940), p. 58.
14. Du Bois, *Autobiography of W. E. B. Du Bois*, p. 222.
15. W. E. B. Du Bois, *The Souls of Black Folk: Essays and Sketches* (1903; New York: Fawcett, 1961), p. 81.
16. Ibid., p. 15.
17. Ibid., p. 17.
18. Ibid.
19. Ibid., p. 190.
20. Ibid., pp. 48, 50, 75, 76, 83, 87, 101, 107, 109, 125, 126, 132, 139, 150, 170, 171, 182, 189.
21. Ibid., p. 132.
22. Du Bois, *Dusk of Dawn*, p. 261.
23. W. E. B. Du Bois, 'My Mission', Crisis, 18, no. 1 (April 1919), 9, in *The Seventh Son: The Thought and Writings of W. E. B. Du Bois*, ed. Julius Lester, Vol. 2 (New York: Vintage Books, 1971), p. 199.
24. W. E. B. Du Bois, 'The Negro and Radical Thoughs', Crisis, 22, no. 3 (July 1921), 103, in *Seventh Son*, 2: 264.
25. W. E. B. Du Bois, 'The Class Struggle', Crisis, 22, no. 4 (August 1921), 151, in *Seventh Son*, 2: 265.
26. Du Bois, *Dusk of Dawn*, p. 284.
27. Ibid., p. 290.
28. Ibid., p. 291.
29. W. E. Burghardt Du Bois, *Black Reconstruction: An Essay Toward a History of the Part Which Black Folk Played in the Attempt to Reconstruct Democracy in America, 1860–1880* (New York: Russell and Russell, 1935), pp. 29–30. For the most sophisticated treatment of Reconstruction that builds on and goes beyond Du Bois' classic see Eric Foner's magisterial *Reconstruction: America's Unfinished Revolution, 1863–1877* (New York: Harper and Row, 1988).
30. Du Bois, *Dusk of Dawn*, p. 295.

31. Du Bois, *Autobiography of W. E. B. Du Bois*, p. 379. For more details on this matter, see Marable, *W. E. B. Du Bois*, pp. 182–9.
32. Du Bois, *Autobiography of W. E. B. Du Bois*, p. 395.
33. Quoted from Gerald Horne, *Black and Red: W. E. B. Du Bois and the Afro-American Response to the Cold War, 1944–1963* (Albany: State University of New York Press, 1986), p. 345.
34. W. E. B. Du Bois, *Against Racism: Unpublished Essays, Papers, Addresses, 1887–1961*, ed. Herbert Aptheker (Amherst: University of Massachusetts Press, 1985), p. 320.

16

Stanley Aronowitz, *The Crisis in Historical Materialism* (1990)

Stanley Aronowitz's *The Crisis in Historical Materialism* was first published in the United States in 1981 and then reissued with new material in the LDS series. It is one of the key texts to have come out of the experience of the sixties, a decade marked by a wave of new interest in Marxist thought as the Stalinist hegemony dissolved. Figures such as Korsch and Lukács whose work had been subject to the prohibitions of the Comintern resurfaced and the publication of Marx's own early thinking on the relation between philosophy and economics in the 1844 *Economic and Philosophical Manuscripts* stimulated radical rethinking. Most importantly perhaps, Marcuse's reworking of themes from the Frankfurt School and Althusser's redrawing of the distinction between science and ideology provided many of the emphases that were to issue from the movements of 1968. But if the thinking of the New Left was an essential part of the heterogenous mix of economics, politics and culture which made up the sixties, that thinking was itself fundamentally unaffected by the heterogeneity of which it was a part. The great merit of Aronowitz's book is its sustained attempt to produce a historical and social understanding fully adequate to that experience.

As such, it cannot remain content with a demolition of the theses of Lenin and Stalin. Rather, it takes this as the starting point of a far-reaching critique and recasting of Marx's own categories. The crucial categories recast are those of nature and science. On the one hand, psychoanalysis with its attention to the forms of human sexuality emphasises that there are elements in the constitution of the human which cannot be reduced to history. On the other, the very development of productive forces has reached a point where it is clear that if we leave our understanding of nature as simply material to be refashioned by those forces, we resign ourselves to the death of the world. Nowhere is Aronowitz's book more prescient than in its emphasis on ecology as a necessary reference for any future emancipatory politics.

Indeed, it is perhaps the strongest contradiction of our time that at exactly the moment that the definition of socialism in terms of centrally planned production for defined human needs is most discredited, a new formulation which relates the planning of production to defined ecological needs is most urgently required.

Preface to the second edition

When the first edition of this book was published in 1981, many readers wondered about the title. Shouldn't it be *Crisis* of *not* in *Historical Materialism?* I insisted the difference between the two was significant, that I believed Marx has asked the right questions, but that the tradition his work spawned, Marxism, had failed to carry on his most powerful motto; the relentless criticism of all received wisdom, although unfortunately not of historical materialism itself. This lapse has had the consequence of persuading many that Marxism has been surpassed by other social explanatory modes, and has already suffered its own historicity the more it cannot account for changes, or anomalies in terms of its scientific paradigm; Marxism is most successful, therefore, as a way of seeing the past, although recent developments in historiography tend to refute even the most sophisticated versions, determinations by the infrastructure in the last instance. I argue that despite the tendency of recent marxisms to fuse their tradition with others – phenomenology, structuralism, psychoanalysis of various sorts, and even liberalism – it remains tied to an outmoded conception of agency and has failed to follow the critical side of Marx himself, particularly his dialectical understanding of science. For Marxism has betrayed a tendency to privilege structural constraints over social movements; that is, to submit to a scientism for which 'objective, historical tendencies' allow it to predict and control human action. As the reader will find in the pages that follow, I propose a different conception of agencies, the plural signifying that the proletariat, especially in advanced capitalist societies, no longer, if it ever did, occupies a privileged space in the social formation, and that this space has been radically displaced. This displacement has two distinct dimensions: the historical changes in all advanced industrial countries that have rendered manual labor subordinate to intellectual labour; and, perhaps more importantly, the theoretical displacement whose earliest manifestations were the critiques of Georg Simmel and Max Weber, but have been elaborated and deepened by both intellectuals linked to new social movements and various critiques of 'essentialist' discourse, particularly the post-structuralist repudiation of the Hegelian interpretations of Marxism. My contention is that Marxism retains vitality but is no longer the master discourse about social relations. First, the historical: the working class in all advanced countries is progressively displaced by the globalisation of capital and especially of industrial production which has now been effectively deterritorialised; the concentration of ownership is no longer matched by the centralisation of production. Moreover, knowledge has become the decisive productive force and science the core of technological development. Far from constituting an oppositional social category to that of capital, science (to which Marxism aspires) has been both subsumed under capital and is a new site of power in all industrial societies, including those calling themselves socialist. While the leading capitalist powers still monopolise modern scientific and technical knowledge, the struggle of developing countries for autonomy entails developing their own knowledge centres. The working class of all countries faces not chiefly huge aggregations of physical capital symbolised in huge mills producing means of material production, giant cities that are the centre of these facilities and the visible signs of class power and class struggle, but invisible power congealed in microchips, processed particles and molecules that are produced in the new knowledge factories – the laboratories. The signs of the new power-communications channels funnelling information inscribed on paper and preserved in artificial memory present an entirely new set of problems for those engaged in political and industrial combat. For even as the machines remain in place, they are increasingly driven by programs which occupy an inconspicuous space atop the machine. These programs direct the machine, handle materials and, in many instances, even perform repairs. And the identification of means of production with fixed places has given way to deterritorialisation not only on a global scale but from public to private spaces.

These empirical transformations have had their theoretical counterparts: inspired by semiotics in its Foucaultian formulations, Ernesto Laclau has announced the 'impossibility of the social' and insists that all we have left is discursive formations along which people occupy subject positions. Agency, argue Laclau and his collaborator Chantal Mouffe, has lost its fixed position in history. Even if it once could be said that a working class located in a definite position in something called a social structure, the social as such has disappeared. In any case, even in the nineteenth century it was a system of signs constructed in accordance with definite discursive rules, the totality of which is called historical materialism. For Laclau, interaction is constituted as discourse among shifting signifiers. Classes, social formations, historical agents – these are the categories of an old Hegelian essentialism the validity of which must be denied. A new post-Marxist discourse has emerged to explain the transformations, principally in spatial terms, which have rendered suspect many Marxist: assumptions, especially

Marx's argument that 'we know only one science, the science of history'. Now this tendency proclaims that we know only discourse analysis since language is the only possible object of knowledge. The 'social', like nature, cannot be apprehended without the aid of constructed categories and exists in the interstices of language.

Jean Baudrillard has gone so far as to argue that politics itself, not just particular parties and programs, has been surpassed by the growing mass refusal of participation in elections and civic duties of all sorts. For Baudrillard the power nexus provides absolutely no spaces for interventions of putative agents, except those which he calls a 'silent majority' who have chosen, not only to refuse the rules of the game but to retreat from the simulations of difference upon which the political game depends. Anti-politics is a non-statement assimilated by executive authorities as apathy, a term employed to preserve the legitimacy of the game. So, while others bemoan the separation of the private and public which, for them, signifies an appalling triumph of rulers' economic and ideological hegemony, Baudrillard sees privatisation as the most reasonable form of resistance available to many who will not legitimate the sham of politics in the contemporary era.

It is not difficult to see that in these two variants of post-Marxism, even if influenced by Saussurean linguistics, the historical materialist questions are still present, at least to the extent that the problems of (a) how it is possible to envision agency and (b) how it is possible to overcome the conditions of social domination stay at the core of the discourse. Moreover, even if their conclusions differ from those of Marxism, they are still in dialogue with it if only because there really is no alternative paradigm of capitalist development that embraces the scope of historical materialism. Sartre's remark that historical materialism is the theory of capitalist development, notwithstanding its weaknesses, becomes a late-twentieth century version of the eternal recurrence. Even when sharply criticized, historical materialism remains the referent of all theories and discourses whose object is human emancipation.

It may be safely remarked that unless we renounce metatheory as such, a plausible position, there are no current alternatives to Marxism which match its level of abstraction and historical sweep, only efforts such as Georg Simmel's to 'construct a new storey beneath historical materialism such that the explanatory value of the incorporation of economic forms themselves into the causes of intellectual culture is preserved, while these economic forms are recognized as the result of more profound valuations and currents of psychological or even meta-physical preconditions' (*Philosophy of Money*). Simmel follows this formulation by asserting that the relation between 'ideal structure and economic structure' is dialectically infinite. By refusing the 'economic in the last instance', Simmel inverts Marx's formula of historical causality to be found in the pristine determination in his famous Preface to the *Contribution of Political Economy* but does not thereby propose a new set of categories by which to understand social structure, historically considered.

In this respect, the criticism of Marx advanced by Max Weber argues for the effectivity of ideal structures in historical change and for what Karl Korsch once called the principle of historical specification. In this mode of theorising there are no transhistorical principles underlying social formations; the reasons for the appearance of the capitalist system differ from the transformations of early societies. Early capitalist development was fueled by a new rationality linked to Calvinism. Weber's comparative method distinguished feudal societies by whether the rational structure of traditional religion was displaced or by an ethic that privileged work, the path to salvation, and gave special status to savings/ investment over the use of money for individual pleasure. In contrast his account of transitions in ancient European civilisation depended upon an analysis that focused on different methods of the production of material life: 'The pattern of settlement in the European occident contrasts with that common to the civilizations of East Asia. The differences may be summed up briefly, if somewhat imprecisely, as follows: in Europe the transition to fixed settlement meant a change from the dominance of cattle breeding (especially of milk) to an economy dominated by agriculture, with cattle-breeding continuing as a secondary element; in Asia, on the contrary, there was a shift from extensive, and hence nomadic, agriculture to horticulture without milk-cattle breeding' (*Agrarian Sociology of Ancient Civilizations*).

While capitalism is described as a new system of rational calculation, where instrumental reason replaces substantive reason, the fall of the Roman empire is ascribed to the collapse of its economic basis, particularly the shortages of slave labor upon which the Roman production system had become vitally and fatally dependent. Underlying these differences was, of course, a common thread of power, the appeal to which ultimately marked Weber's developmental history. Yet this hardly qualifies as a metatheory. Weber's whole point is to oppose metatheory as an unwarranted presupposition of historical change which undercuts the referent of empirical evidence as the arbiter of social knowledge. Put another way, Weber joins modern science in which the red thread of methodologies of inquiry replace transhistorical determinations as the common ground of natural and social investigations. On the other hand Weber is still preoccupied with the ramifications of the methodological starting-point of the 'mode of production of material life'. Transcoded into contemporary terms, Weber's theory of modern capitalism privileges the discourses of domination. Religion is a system of shifting signs subject to, but not determined by, 'material' causes. Thus under the sign of 'ideal structures' both Simmel and Weber prefigure later concepts such as episteme (Foucault), discourse (Pècheux, Derrida) and *mentalité* (Annales school). Now, as before, the object of criticism is not necessarily Marx himself, but really-existing historical materialism that has transformed a critical science into dogma.

· Despite Marx's own statements to the contrary, particularly the famous assertion of the *Communist Manifesto* that 'All history is the history of class struggles' and the accusations of commentators such as Baudrillard of Marx's 'economism', his empirically based historical writings are as complex in explanations of concrete events as he was simple in his declarations. The evidence of pamphlets such as *The Eighteenth Brumaire, Class Struggles in France*, and the massive sections in *Capital* on the histories of the labor process, the process of capital accumulation, the history of ground-rent, and so on, show that there is no privileged term in the dialectic of labor and capital accumulation, that the logic of capital is not only mediated but also shaped by the spontaneous and organised working-class resistance to the impositions by capital. Perhaps the most familiar example in Marx is the correlation of the struggle for the eight-hour day by trade unions and the transformation of the form of exploitation from absolute to relative (surplus value), the persistence of parasitism of the *rentier* class, which inhibits productive investment and may overdetermine capital-logic, and the autonomous actions of monarchy and state as well as political intrigues in France. One cannot read Marx without being struck by the variegated character of his historical understanding, one that easily confounded careless critics.

There is the other side, the side pushed forward by Marx's followers, especially in the context of turn-of-the-century Europe when the earlier 'anarchy' of capitalist production seemed to yield to a world capitalism – highly organised, rationalised beyond Marx's expectations and able to offer to the working-class a new deal. As I shall argue in the last chapter, this arrangement was predicated, not on the crisis of the system as later, in the 1930s, but on the halcyon phase of central European capitalist development when, contrary to the 'classical' English model, the integration of state with highly concentrated and centralised German capitalism was able to ameliorate the workers' living standards to an unprecedented level. The power of the economic seemed so absolute that even the anti-reformism of leading German socialists such as Karl Kautsky and Rosa Luxemburg singled out the question of the contradiction between productive forces and production relations as the main dynamic of history. Kautsky, in particular, became the major architect of these conceptions which were, without much amendment, adopted by Marxists the world over, not the least important of which were the Russian Marxists led by Plekhanov and his pupil, Lenin. (Except it is surely unwarranted to call Lenin an 'economist' in the light of his voluntarism, particularly his celebrated theory of the party.) Actually, the charge of determinism, particularly the doctrine of socialist inevitability, is better affixed to the theorists of the Second International than to those of the Communist movement who adapted Kautsky's judgement that the working class by its own efforts could never achieve class-consciousness and required the assistance of revolutionary theory to achieve their socialist destiny. Despite this, turn-of-the-century Marxism was scalded with Kautsky's economism and has not managed to shake it ever since.

Weber, a somewhat younger man than Kautsky, was of the generation that came into its intellectual majority in Germany at the zenith of Kautsky's reputation as the chief legatee of Marx and Engels, the semi-official interpreter of their theory of history and surely the premier theoretician of social democracy. A self-professed bourgeois liberal, Weber could be easily dismissed by orthodox Marxism. But his significance for the further development of Marxism could not be dispensed with so easily. Beginning with Georg Lukács, whose *History and Class Consciousness* attested to the value (or the danger) of merging Marx's analysis of the vagaries of the commodity form with Weber's theory of rationality; and extending to the Frankfurt School for which the category of instrumental reason became the very explanation for emergence of technological rationality and the consequent passing of historical agency as such, a spate of writing has grasped the significance of Weber's contribution to historical materialism, rather than comprehending his work as refutation, despite the many reservations to the universal claims of Marx's followers.

Notwithstanding the obvious linguistic turn in Baudrillard's work especially after 1968, the influence in his writing of his teacher Henri

Lefebvre lingers to this day. Lefebvre's own reading of Marx is a creative combination of Hegelian dialectic and Kantian scepticism mediated by the same German influences that have informed the Critical Theory of Adorno, Horkheimer and Marcuse – not only Weber but also Heidegger and Husserl. For it is the concern with everyday life, with 'lived experience', a category borrowed by the anti-Hegelian Louis Althusser as well, that marks the contrast between the marxisms that took account of the interwar destruction of the once-promising working-class movement and tried to offer an adequate explanation for its defeat, and the triumphalism of the marxisms of the Second and the Third Internationals (of which more below).

I will argue that the crisis in historical materialism is not to be discovered in the so-called failure of Marx's predictions concerning the transition from capitalism to socialism; nor does it consist principally in the economism of the majority of Marx's acolytes, however egregious this misinterpretation may be. What is at stake is the fate of those agents that, in Alain Touraine's terms, struggle over their own historicity and thereby form themselves and social relations. Historical materialism is incomplete, not surpassed. Now, as before, it is obliged to grapple with its own historicity in the wake of the sea-changes that have enveloped the modern world, particularly the fact that the domination of nature which Marx understood as the precondition of human freedom is no longer viable, if it ever was. The emergence of new unexpected agents in the theatre of history which have challenged the old Marxist assumptions have shattered Marxist ideological hegemony even in those countries where Marxism enjoys the status of official ideology. Today, historical materialism is obliged to enter a dialogue with other tendencies which claim theoretical and political validity. It can no longer subsume all competing world views under the rubric of 'bourgeois' to which it counterposes its own, proletarian worldview; it must face ecological, nationalist and feminist world-views, each of which has its own competing camps and whose unity, as in the case of Marxism, is in doubt.

Pluralism has always, for Marxism, been equated with a struggle against liberal ideology. This view is no longer tenable if we understand alternative discourses as neither dominated by liberalism nor socialism. The question is, of course, whether the new discourses can be negotiated with socialist rationality or whether the crisis has gone beyond Marx's own understanding of the term: a profound rupture in the system but not necessarily fatal; in fact, for Marx the crises of capitalism are the necessary condition for renewal. Surely, ecosocialists and Marxist feminists have attempted to find common ground between the ostensibly competing paradigms with only mixed success. Nevertheless, the effort remains crucial, if only to determine whether historical materialism still offers an indispensable dimension.

Finally, I want to report on the progress of historical materialism since the latest crisis; say, the last decade. In general, the record is not particularly encouraging, from a theoretical perspective, although scientific Marxism – the work of historians, social scientists and literary critics influenced by Marxism – has made rapid strides, or to be more precise, continues in paths that were marked by their immediate predecessors. The new social history in the United States and Great Britain continues to contribute to our knowledge of the past, even if, in its desire to resurrect hidden histories of the marginalized, it frequently neglects important elements of economic and political relations. The Marxist hegemony over the study of feudalism and early capitalism has been little disturbed. In some respects, British sociology, including work in Australia and Canada, is marked by the Marx/Weber integration in the entire profession and in the United States Weberian Marxism, particularly in historical sociology, has earned a prominent place in the mainstream. (Although it is often confused with Marxism: I refer to the work of Immanuel Wallerstein and Theda Skocpol.) Although challenged by functionalism on the right and post-structuralism on the 'left', Marxist anthropology in Europe and the United States remains extremely influential. And, largely spurred by Fredric Jameson and Terry Eagleton, Marxist approaches, laced, of course, with both French post-structuralism and German neo-Marxism that owes as much to Lukács and the Frankfurt School as it does to the new democratic movements that sprang up in the 1960s, if not dominant are, at least, respectable in the Anglo-American academy.

The situation is more complicated in economics. For, despite the growth of the political left among professional economists, the serious twenty-year-old crisis of world capitalism, combined with the decline of the hegemony of post-Keynesian doctrine and most importantly, economic policy, has produced a new birth of neo-classical paradigms that seem to have swept all opposition in its path, including Marxism. We discovered that, with few exceptions, notably Michel Béaud in France, the capital-logic school in Germany, James O'Connor and the *Monthly Review* group in the United States among others, that most Marxist economists are really left-Keynesians and have been unable to generate, with the exceptions noted, a coherent theory of the crisis. In any case, Marxist analysis is absent from the public debate, in contrast to the last great depression when, in England, for example, Marxism, despite its painful orthodoxy, enjoyed considerable currency, even in the midst of the implementation of policies of state intervention advised by Keynes.

However, the most serious challenge for Marxist economic doctrine is the discovery, yet again, that socialist models of planning have, for the most part failed, particularly in Eastern Europe, where in the past forty years they have dominated economic activity. In the wake of the world economic crisis, really-existing socialist countries have experienced its effects because, since the 1960s, their economic viability has depended in a large measure on loans procured from Western banks. Enriched with billions of dollars, Eastern European living standards rose, even when productivity slumped. For the joke that travels around the region contains more truth than its leaders care to admit, even in the Gorbachev era: 'How do you like your job?' a visitor asks. 'What job?' comes the reply. 'They pretend to pay us and we pretend to work.'

With the crisis came austerity. Suddenly, almost-forgotten queues formed for meat and many other goods. With the new Soviet regime, the word went out that efficiency criteria might be imposed to determine which enterprises should survive and which should be shut down, an approach that implied possible unemployment. And, for Yugoslavia, the situation was exacerbated by the effects of the crisis on employment in such countries as Germany and Switzerland; emigration was no longer possible on a large scale, a development which revealed the dark side of the country's economic 'miracle'; it simply got rid of one million workers to maintain full employment even as it accumulates $30 billion in debts to western banks. In the wake of these disturbing developments, economists east and west revived discussion of what became known as 'market' socialism. The proposals to reform the economies of Eastern Europe and other countries characterised by central control over most economic activity have, to say the least, spanned the range of possibility. 'Liberals' argue that enterprise managers should have more power to determine a wide variety of functions at the enterprise level including the choice of technology, setting wage and productivity norms, and should have a freer hand to sell products within the framework established by the plan. Further, privately owned peasant plots should be encouraged and the market for agricultural commodities should be expanded. But in no case, according to this view, should central planning be dismantled. The 'market' should be restricted both in definition and scope.

'Radicals', including Alec Nove, echoing the earlier work of Polish economist Oskar Lange, argue that only when consumer choice dictates production decisions can (a) social freedom be guaranteed and (b) efficiency ensured. The function of state planners is to coordinate some decisions in a restricted sector such as utilities, and they may intervene to encourage new types of investment. But, for Nove, 'social ownership' implies neither state ownership nor control, but only that private property is not restored on a large scale. But he does not exclude arrangements that resemble those of Hungary where many enterprises, although state-owned, are leased to private individuals who run them according to (principally) market criteria. Nove's indictment of the stultifying Soviet system of state control over all crucial economic decisions is, to say the least, devastating. However, his idea of consumer-driven rational (i.e. profitability) choices is by no means an inevitable conclusion from his critique. Despite his avoidance of the usual moralising which too often accompanies such critiques, and his willingness to assign to the state considerable power in decision-making, Nove is arguing that the free market is the most effective site for achieving stability and growth, if not equality. On the contrary, Nove implies that democracy and freedom entail surrendering much of the ideology according to which justice is equated with greater equality. For despite the considerable evidence supporting the charge that Eastern European regimes are systems of privilege for party, state and managerial elites, when compared to Western counterparts their allegiance to relative equality is still powerful. However, even with the most stringent state controls, the Soviet Union is far from an egalitarian society; privilege and nepotism are rampant.

That the history of really-existing socialism has been marked by the extreme politicisation of all social and economic functions is beyond question. At its worst, socialism has abolished both the bourgeois public sphere where issues may be debated and the instruments through which some version of the popular will may be felt (such as a freely-elected parliament) and the private sphere where individuals and groups may engage in the exchange of goods and ideas without the threat of surveillance and state intervention. So it has produced the worst of situations. It is neither democratic nor prosperous. And, when civil liberties are not broadly enlarged except for the political and technical intelligentsia, and market relations are severely restricted, we can expect to find a second political sphere where not only dissidence but refusal is rife and where a second economy undermines the official price structure and becomes a challenge to the fundamental premises of the regime. *Perestroika* may be viewed in this light as an intelligent political and ideological accommodation to what is already happening in everyday life, an illustration of the primacy of the social. Of course, restructuration is not so easy, if for no other reason than that the current economic and political system harbors vital interests – of the party elite, the technical and cultural intelligentsia for whom *glasnost* means more openness within and between elites, particularly the scientific and political. In any case, Marxism has been unable to successfully grapple, with some exceptions, with the problems raised by the partial breakdown of socialism as it has historically been constituted. As a result, not only the main features of the liberal state, civil liberties and representative democracy, are being introduced as solutions to the crisis of consent which has produced nationalist turmoil in Yugoslavia and the Soviet Union and profound popular alienation everywhere in socialist countries, but also markets and privatisation are hot issues in the economics debate.

More can be said, and this report is, to say the least, incomplete, but I see no reason to support the view that Marxist 'science' is alive and well. Marxist philosophy has never been more troubled. We are witnessing the palpable decline of Marxist metatheory that filled the intellectual landscape of all countries east and west, north and south, in the 1960s and early 1970s. Superficial judgements would ascribe this outpouring (structuralism, the Frankfurt School, Freud–Marx syntheses, phenomenological Marxism and several others) to the vitality of new student, anti-war, feminist and other social movements. Yet the 1920s produced considerable work of this sort in a period not only of left defeat but of rising right-wing movements that seized power within the decade. I submit that, after the decline of post-structuralism, social and cultural theory is experiencing its own crisis: having renounced master discourses of all sorts, the void is slowly being filled by a new call for ethics or, to be more precise, a drift away from relativism. At the same time, there is a clear 'political turn' to literary criticism parallel to the revival of political theory signified by the slogan 'bringing the state back in' to Marxist theory. Within these rubrics, Marxist criticism and theory are reexamined, precisely because other paradigms offer little more than liberal political ideas when they make room for the political at all. As a consequence, we are currently in the thrall of Marxology, which consists of close readings of classical texts and some of which is excellent intellectual history. Never before have the plots been rendered with such elegance and the preparation of the historians (or philosophers writing summaries and comments) so sophisticated.

Some of these treatments (David Frisby's superb essay on Simmel, Kracauer and Benjamin, Martin Jay's admirable small book on Adorno, and Marshall Berman's discussion of modernity come to mind) are contributions to a Marxist understanding and clarification of the problem of modernity, particularly the sociology and social psychology of the modern world. Similarly, a strong Marxist tendency in feminist literary and philosophical studies has produced significant work. Nancy Hartsock's ambitious and brave treatise for a feminist historical materialism stands out in the American context just as the wonderfully dense essays of Veronica Beechey, Meaghan Morris, and Jacqueline Rose among others, in the British debate. But these are a handful of instances where writers have taken on, from the perspective of a nuanced historical materialism, crucial aspects of contemporary metatheory. In doing so, all of them have been obliged to recognise the structural weaknesses of the Marxist paradigm and have hastened to shore it up rather than dispense with it. This attests to the intellectual power of the questions posed by historical materialism, which remain indispensable for the understanding of the new cultural contradictions of capitalism that seem to have been thrust to the forefront even as states and capital alliances fail to resume a brisk accumulation rate in most countries.

What all of these writers, above all Jurgen Habermas, have grasped is that for which Lukács and Gramsci are attacked: their insistence that the twentieth century has witnessed the persistence of capitalist social relations even in the midst of revolutionary upheaval precisely because they are not merely an economic system but have become a system for organising consent as well, the results of which are not obliterated by changes in the structure of political power. The reproduction of the relations of production by means of cultural hegemony must be seen as analytically separate from the antagonistic production relations, and constitutes the sufficient condition for explaining the survival of capitalism even if the accumulation process exhibits all of the standard features such as frequent breakdowns, stagnation and deformations. However critical I remain of Habermas's solution to the perplexing issues raised by late capitalism, let me hasten to add that he is perhaps singular in attempting to reconstruct historical materialism in the light of some features of modern linguistics, Weber's work and recent history. This singularity only highlights the intellectual crisis. For the fate of historical materialism in the late capitalist epoch is marked by its fragmentation or, to be more specific, a high ratio of absorption by other discourses and paradigms within which Marxism is relegated to one way of seeing among others. In short, nowhere does Marxism retain its status as the master discourse it once enjoyed. Nor are most Marxists concerned with exploring how it may be restored, if not as a master discourse, then as a vigorous theoretical framework for comprehending the novelty of contemporary society and culture. Habermas has felt constrained, not only to return to Weber and Parsons in order to plumb the depths of the legitimation crisis because he has concluded that the sphere of economic relations has transcended ideology owing to the disappearance of class struggles as the structuring principle of capitalism. He has also drawn from developmental psychology and the philosophy of language elements of a new moral theory, just as his studies of modernity have led to the conclusion that historical materialism is not an exhausted paradigm and that post-structuralism and post-modernism are premature if not destructive of the preservation of reason as the regulative principle of human affairs.

Under Habermas's influence, most left post-Marxists, working on the problem of categories rather than time-bound historical or sociological issues, are theorists of modernity. The new rationality suggested by Weber and Marx not only designs and engineers machines and consumer goods, but human souls as well. As Frisby demonstrates, Simmel is the theorist who shows that fragmented snapshots hide a coherent modernity that should be grasped as a unique totality. The problems of modern politics in both the West and Third World societies, are linked to the fact that capitalism, as Marx remarked in the *Manifesto*, not only destroys the old idyllic relations of feudalism, but creates a new world around the permutations of the commodity form where the material and symbolic are to be considered aspects of the totality not arranged in vertical order. This new world is not only a commodity-exchanging universe, but consists in a built environment constituted by the anonymity of its privatized inhabitants. As the production of signs dominates the production of goods, even the old working-class neighbourhoods, from which solidarity was fashioned, disappear or are recast as domiciles for the salariat. The 'inner city' which was once a working-class political and industrial bastion, and even the red suburbs, have been transformed into appendages of the metropolis.

This is the most stunning contribution of recent Marxist and neo-Marxist criticism: to remind us that lived experience is the last frontier of contestation in the wake of the dispersal of the old agents. And this is what the present work is about.

17

Denise Riley (ed.), *Poets on Writing: Britain, 1970–1991* (1992)

Poets on Writing brings together writings about poetic practice by a number of contemporary poets, including those less popularly established and publicly recorded and those associated with innovative or self-consciously vanguardist tendencies or with the supposed 'Cambridge School'. These groupings are neither defined nor revered, and the extracts were not organised according to any predetermined sociologies of their authors. The writers were left free to describe how they worked, or what they understood of the working practices of others by whom they were enthused, as also to indicate what they themselves made of the conditions for writing at the beginning of the 1990s. The aim of the collection was thus to give a number of poets the opportunity to reflect on their working habits and their sense of contexts, and so perhaps to pre-empt thereby the onrush of literary critics bearing categories. If 'the author' has officially died, the suspicion here was that the truth comes closer to cryogenic suspension; while a long freeze is to be sat out, it might nevertheless be entertaining in the meantime to record authors' practices, without in so doing making a fetish of their authority. Sections of the book are concerned with the practicalities of poetic writing, the analysis of influences and contemporary directions and the examination of the histories of small press publication in Britain and of the reader–poet relationship. The collection included pieces by Wendy Mulford, Douglas Oliver, Tom Raworth, Nigel Wheale, and many others. The extract given here is from Veronica Forrest-Thomson's still insufficiently known book *Poetic Artifice: A Theory of Twentieth-Century Poetry*, published posthumously in 1978; in it she argues for an understanding of the force of artifice as a vital adjunct to any reading.

From Veronica Forrest-Thomson's *Poetic Artifice*

The poetry of our century particularly requires a theory of the devices of artifice, such as apparently non-sensical imagery, logical discontinuity; referential opacity, and unusual metrical and spatial organisation, and an account of the relationships between various strata of artifice. The question always is: how do poems work?

'Do not forget', says Wittgenstein, 'that a poem, even though it is composed in the language of information is not used in the language-game of giving information.' It is indeed important to remember this, but simply remembering it is no solution. We must try to describe the language-game in which poetic language is used, and here the initial difficulty is the relationship between the language-game of poetry and what Wittgenstein calls the language-game of giving information. The sentence, 'Pipit sat upright in her chair some distance from where I was sitting' could be used to give information about a state of affairs in the external world: namely, that at a particular time in the past someone named Pipit sat at some distance from the person who is uttering the sentence. But when Eliot begins his poem 'A Cooking Egg' with these lines:

> Pipit sate upright in her chair
> Some distance from where I was sitting;

the function of the sentence, and in particular its relationship to the external world, changes. The statement is altered by its insertion in a poetic context, by its use, shall we say, in this different language-game. It no longer refers to a particular time in the past (it is not simply irrelevant to ask whether the event took place on 3 April 1912 or at some other time: there is no need to suppose such an event at all). Nor need the 'I' be thought of as a particular person. For the purposes of the poem the 'I' is simply a voice.

Every reader of poetry knows that statements are changed by their insertion in a poem, that they no longer mean what they would mean in ordinary speech because of the form in which they appear. To state the relationship between poetry and the external world, however – to show precisely how poetic form and poetic context affect the sentences they include and the non-verbal world which the sentences imply – is difficult. It is the major problem of this book.

But it is not just a theoretical difficulty. It is also the problem of poetry itself. One of the reasons for the general dreariness of English verse in the 1950s and 1960s was the failure of poets and theorists to tackle this problem, to discover or admit what poetry does and how poetic artifice is justified. It is all too easy for poets as well as critics to give in to the kind of reading which criticism often proposes and to assume that the important features of a poem are those which can be shown to contribute to a thematic synthesis stated in terms of the external world. It is easy to treat poetry as if it were engaged in the language-game of giving information and thus to assume that what is important about a poem is what it tells us about the external world. The meaning of the poem is extended into the world; this extended meaning is assumed to be dominant, and if formal features are to become noteworthy components of a poem they must be assimilated to this extended meaning.

Such an approach falsifies our experience of poems, reduces the distinctiveness of poetry, and neglects many of the components of poetic language, but it is an intellectually less taxing approach which triumphs for that reason. Unfortunately, its consequences are not good for poetry. It makes extended meaning the locus of poetic experimentation and poets are expected to explore a new range of extreme external experiences (often with disastrous consequences) in order to earn the title of creative poet. Sylvia Plath and Anne Sexton are praised for opening up new depths of psychological insight; writers with techniques as disparate as Ted Hughes, Charles Olson, Allen Ginsberg, and Robert Lowell are held to combine such insight with a special vision of contemporary society. Whatever technical innovation they display is swiftly taken up and smothered by a critical reading-anxious to convert all verbal organisation into extended meaning – to transform pattern into theme.

This critical process I shall call 'Naturalisation': an attempt to reduce the strangeness of poetic language and poetic organisation by making it intelligible, by translating it into a statement about the non-verbal external world, by making the Artifice appear natural. Critical reading cannot, of course, avoid Naturalisation altogether. Criticism is committed, after all, to helping us to understand both poetry as an institution and individual poems as significant utterances. But it must ensure that in its desire to produce ultimate meaning it does not purchase intelligibility at the cost of blindness: blindness to the complexity of those non-meaningful features which differentiate poetry from everyday language and make it something other than an external thematic statement about an already-known world. There would be no point in writing poetry unless poetry were different from everyday language, and any attempt to analyse poetry should cherish that difference and seek to remain within its bounds for as long as possible rather than ignore the difference in an unseemly rush from words to world. Good Naturalisation dwells on the non-meaningful levels of poetic language, such as phonetic and prosodic patterns and spatial organisation, and tries to state their relation to other levels of organisation rather than set them aside in an attempt to produce a statement about the world.

Contemporary poetry has suffered from critics' disposition to make poetry above all a statement about the external world, and therefore it is now especially important somewhat to redress the balance, to stress the importance of artifice. Poetry can only be a valid and valuable activity when we recognise the value of the artifice which makes it different from prose. Indeed, it is only through artifice that poetry can challenge our ordinary linguistic orderings of the world, make us question the way in which we make sense of things, and induce us to consider its alternative linguistic orders as a new way of viewing the world.

The best way to restore value to artifice is to find ways of discussing it which do not presuppose the subservience of form to extended meaning. And therefore my account of twentieth-century poetry offers a framework of concepts which allow us to dwell at length on the play of formal features and structure of relations internal to a poem. There is, therefore, a proliferation of technical terms which identify various aspects of poetic form and different ways of treating it in the process of reading.

'Naturalisation' I have already defined as the process of rationalising details, making them natural and intelligible in the process of interpretation[. . .]

(pp. x–xi)

[. . .] Eliot also claims that 'only a man of genius could dwell so exclusively and consistently among words as Swinburne.' We can see what degree of truth this comment has: Swinburne is a craftsman of genius but he never lets his form run away with his content. His content is great, spanning almost the whole spectrum of human preoccupations, but it would be nothing if his form were not able to support it. His subtleties of perception, his esoteric sensibility, would be no more use to him than to Ella Wheeler Wilcox if he could not translate them into subtleties of technique by presenting the disingenuous appearance of talking about simple things. This is the essential manoeuvre of pastoral and parody combined: put the complex into the simple and then the complexities will become stylistic and can be dealt with accordingly. The poet will keep, by this appearance of simplicity, some contact with his tribe of readers, while his real complexity will give him contact with the important he – the innovating poet – and with his literary past. This way of dealing with the world may be the difference between life and death to the individual. To Swinburne it was the difference between life and life in the protective seclusion of

Watts Dunton. In the twentieth century the question has been given more immediacy by the suicide merchants who say, in effect, 'no one can become a great poet unless he has at least tried killing himself'. It is obvious that this springs from external expansion and complicity with bad Naturalisation, from an insistence that innovation in 'experience' is the only innovation possible. But people are still taking-off at such a rate. . . . Why, only the other day John Berryman, who was at least enough of a poet to know quite a bit about formal innovation . . .

Swinburne, however, did not dwell exclusively among words; he would not have been a great poet had he done so. Is it necessary to insist on Eliot's 'statements made in dreams' as part of the Surrealist *rêve* – that area of reverse priorities where the looking-glass world transforms our ordinary hierarchies of extended meanings? Is it necessary to recall that Swinburne was for a time stranded in the everyday world of action by his interest in the Italian risorgimento, and produced a lot of bad verse in consequence? Is it necessary to insist that Swinburne knew how to absorb the forms of external discourse and to use these for poetic ends, thus fulfilling Jacob's statement that 'a work is not valuable by what it contains but by what surrounds it'? And what surrounds it is primarily the discourse of the critic who goes between it and other languages in his interpretive reading. It should not, for example, have been necessary to remark, as I did above, that form must support content.

Too many literary theorists, however, have taken this to mean that form and content are fused in such a way as to make it impossible for us to distinguish levels in a poem or to find it good on one level though ill on another. If form must support content, it is no less necessary, as we have seen from the relation between the semantic, the image-complicated, and the thematic levels, that content should support form. There must be as much or as little power in the theme as transmitted through the image-complex – that is, through a mixture of meaning and the non-semantic levels – as is appropriate for the formal convention. In other words, themes appropriate for the villanelle will not suit the sonnet, still less the ode or the epic. This does not imply that form and content are identical, still less that they are fused; on the contrary, it implies that they must be different, distinguishable in order that their relations may be judged.

But let Swinburne himself speak on this topic:

a writer conscious of any natural command over the musical resources of his language can hardly fail to take such pleasure in the enjoyment of this gift or instinct as the greatest writer and greatest versifier of our age must have felt at its highest possible degree. . . . But if he be a poet after the order of Hugo or Coleridge or Shelley, the result will be something very much more than a musical exercise; though indeed, except to such ears as should always be kept closed against poetry, there is no music in verse which has not in it sufficient fullness and ripeness of meaning, sufficient adequacy of emotion or thought, to abide the analysis of other than the purblind scrutiny of prepossession or the squinteyed inspection of malignity.

Precisely. Swinburne is aware that expansion of the level of meaning and imposition of Naturalisation are inevitable constituents of the process of reading poetry and must be allowed for in the process of writing it. He is further aware that in making such allowances one can find ways of making a poem transcend its initial Naturalisation and impose its own world of imaginative possibilities, simply because it has made technical allowance for the reader's initial realistic expansion/limitation.

In a cruder form this may be seen in Lear's 'Akond'. A violent juxta-position of the convention of rhyme and of pseudo-descriptive narra-tive produces an artificial effect, an impression that the whole discourse is governed by the need to find a rhyme, to find the world of Artifice in the nurseries of Victorian England:

> At night if he suddenly screams and wakes,
> Do they bring him only a few small cakes or a LOT
>   The Akond of Swat?
>
> Does he live on turnips, tea, or tripe?
> Does he like his shawl to be marked with a stripe, or a DOT
>   The Akond of Swat?
>
> Does he like to lie on his back in a boat
> Like the lady who lived in that isle remote, SHALLOTT
>   The Akond of Swat?
>
>   . . .
>
> Some one, or nobody, knows I wot
> Who or which or why or what
>   Is the Akond of Swat!

Of course this is less skilful and complicated than 'Faustine', but perhaps, for that same reason, we can see more easily what is going on.

The conventions of pastoral are used with the conventions that parody normal poetic discourse – where poets try to conceal the fact that a rhyme is more important than a philosophy – in order to assert the autonomy poetry grants to the imagination in language. Oddly enough only the difference in subtlety separates Lear's reference to Tennyson and 'The Lady of Shalott' itself: that lady is also a creature of pastoral and inhabits the world of unrealism:

> She left the web, she left the loom,
> She made three paces thro' the room,
> She saw the water-lily bloom,
> She saw the helmet and the plume,
>   She look'd down to Camelot.
> Out flew the web and floated wide;
> The mirror crack'd from side to side;
> 'The curse is come upon me,' cried
>   The Lady of Shalott.

Contact with reality destroys her fantasy world, but not the poem, for she is more than a creature of fiction; she is an organising formal principle, and her abode has been chosen by the need to find a rhyme for 'Camelot'. Like Faustine, she is secure in her internal relations even if her external relations are destroyed. In fact there is a good deal in common between these two ladies – though both their creators would be shocked to be told so. They have been selected for the flexibility in organising rhymes which will feed into the formal level and for their ability as personae to link the formal to the thematic level; while the Akond of Swat with his restriction to hard *k t* and sibilant *s* comes, like Lepidus, a poor third.

I hope I may be excused here for quoting two of my own poems which illustrate how these techniques may be put to use in twentieth-century poetry. The first, called 'The Lady of Shalott', is self-conscious to the degree implied by the choice of such a title and stresses its formal level by having one completely meaningless line, but these sacrifices to parody and disconnectedness enable it to combine pastoral with parody. I quote it here because of its aptness and its illustration of this point.

THE LADY OF SHALOTT

> The child in the snow has found her mouth
> And estate-agents must beware,
> For if what we seek cannot be truth,

And we've only a lie to share,
The modern conveniences won't last out;
Bear tear flair dare
And the old ones just don't care.

Back and forth she moves her arms,
Forth and back, her legs.
No one would care to say:
Her lips are red, her looks are free,
Her locks are yellow as gold.
Whether she's very young or old,
The nightmare life-in-death is she
Who thicks men's blood with cold.

What of the future is in the past
Channels towards us now.
Present and future perfect past
Makes no tracks in the snow
Turn the tap and the water will come
For five seconds.
And then the sand
Flows into our ever-open mouth.
What was it we understand?

She does not stand in the snow; she kneels:
A parody of prayer.
Lucretius said it long ago:
Why think the gods care?
When the telephone goes dead,
The fridge is broken, the light . . .

Why should we think of knowledge as light?
There is enough to see her.
And, having seen, the message is plain
To those who wish to know
(They are not many.):
Run quickly back to darkness again;
We have seen the child in the snow.

Here the poet (having had the effrontery to use my own poems as examples I now hide behind my role) is able to use extremely traditional regular iambic rhymed verse with anapaestic variation (in lines, 1, 3, 7, 16, 20, 23, 25, 28, 37) plus extremely conventional symbolism ('the child in the snow'). He combines this with a traditional use of literary allusion – the title and the Coleridge lines of the second stanza – which is made into the allusiveness characteristic of twentieth-century poetry by the support of specifically twentieth-century conventions: a deliberately extra-metrical line, 'for five seconds', and the ellipsis ('. . .') which stands for 'the light (fails)'.

Thus the conventional and formal levels contribute to a thematic synthesis as old as the hills: 'Fate is against mankind.' Yet it takes on a new aspect when set in relation to poetry as a cognitive instrument: 'It is impossible for poetry to work when we have no standards of knowledge.' The best is obtained from both worlds and the levels of Artifice are restored to their old power by getting new power. The poet is not restricted to the insistence on formal dominance stressed in line 6 – 'Bear tear flair dare' – an insistence that seemed his only resource in other and earlier works. These had the same theme of being unable to escape from language into the 'real' world and they made this imprisonment tolerable only by accepting the non-meaningful aspects of language. Here he can combine strength of content with strength of form given by all the traditional levels of Artifice, as Eliot and Swinburne do; that is, the manoeuvre is similar. I have said it is typical of all twentieth-century poetry written in what is, according to the theoretical position set out in this book, the tradition of innovation.

In another poem, 'Pastoral', I was restricted very much to the stress on non-meaningful aspects of language as the only escape from the intolerable theme:

PASTORAL

> They are our creatures clover, and they love us
> through the long summer meadows' diesel fumes.
> Smooth as their scent and contours clear however
> less than enough to compensate for names.
>
> Jagged are names and not our creatures
> neither in sense or fullness like the flowers.
> Raised voices in a car or by a river
> remind us of the world that is not ours.
>
> Silence in grass and solace in blank verdure
> summon the frightful glare of nouns and nerves.
> The gentle foal linguistically wounded,
> squeals like a car's brakes, like our twisted words

If one writes a line like the first line of this poem one is obviously alerting the reader to the fact that sound resemblance – 'clover' 'love' – is more important than meaning. The second line furthers the process in making it clear that the extension of meaning is less important than the way external contexts – the meadow, the flowers, the cars, the voices, the river – feed back into the thematic synthesis which is given in the fourth line and developed through the other two stanzas. This is particularly noticeable in the last two lines where the 'gentle foal' is important for his *entle oal* sounds rather than for his physical being. For these sounds are taken up in 'linguistically wounded', which is a crucial phrase both for the theme and for the rhythm. That is, the foal's physical being is transferred to the sound of the names we give him. A pretty paradox in view of the poem's theme; since the poet is saying (thematic synthesis) just that: preoccupation with linguistic problems prevents contact with the physical word.

The ninth line provides a linguistic equivalent for the idea of blankness in 'blank verdure'; *b d n*, especially the conjunction of *k* and *u* (which makes the latter almost hard), and the annulment by hard *n* of the *e u* softening vowel sounds all make the verdure particularly blank. The sound pattern of the line thus offers a direct challenge to the dominance of 'abstract' theme and 'concrete' senselessness, but the alliteration and assonance in 'Silence in grass and solace' help to combat any non-poetic extension at this point. The rest of the poem is strong enough on its own to resist such extension. Much of its strength comes from its use of regular metre, half-rhymes – 'fumes/names' – and stanza form. Indeed it is halfway along the path which leads to 'The Lady of Shalott' in its willingness to call on some of the traditional resources of technique; the foal looks remarkably like a traditional symbol used to give the kind of empirical instance in a discursive argument that we saw in Donne and Eliot.

But if 'Pastoral' is halfway along the path to 'Lady of Shalott' it also resembles, in some of its apparent concrete meaninglessness, another form of artifice, whose examples can be grouped under the loose heading of Dada. This is only one incarnation of the perennial god of Artifice, who like other deities, has different names at different places. Whatever the relation of Dada to Swinburne, Lear, Tennyson, and Forrest-Thomson, however, I am not calling them Dadaists in the historical sense. Before expanding Dada to include the central moments in the renovation of Artifice we must turn to the historical Dadaists and their achievement . . .

(pp. 120–6)

We can observe this detached 'I', which is part of an image-complex, a formal pattern, and a thematic synthesis all at once, in a poem famous for the wrong reasons: 'Daddy'. People praise this and other poems, 'Lady Lazarus' for instance, because they present extreme states of mind; unfortunately Sylvia Plath was not able to recognise this as a bad Naturalisation with extended meaning, external limitation/expansion, and devaluation of the non-semantic levels. She was unable to recognise in theory what she knew in poetic practice. We need not to be so blinded, however, and our recognition of the artificial skills in these poems is a tribute (although, like most laurels, it comes too late) to what she has done for this century's poetry.

Daddy

. . . I made a model of you,
A man in black with a Meinkampf look

And a love of the rack and the screw.
And I said I do, I do.
So daddy, I'm finally through.
The black telephone's off at the root,
The voices just can't worm through.

If I've killed one man, I've killed two –
The vampire who said he was you
And drank my blood for a year,
Seven years, if you want to know.
Daddy, you can lie back now.

There's a stake in your fat black heart
And the villagers never liked you.
They are dancing and stamping on you.
They always *knew* it was you.
Daddy, daddy, you bastard, I'm through.

The extreme skill with which the situation of a hysterical woman, enough for the bad naturalisers, is stated and then made symbolic through the traditional level of the vampire image-complex shows 'content as form'. Similarly the implied empirical context of marriage, of the telephone off the hook, of torture, shows how these things are fictionalised by the insistence of rhythm and division into stanzas (formal and conventional level). Just so the 'direct utterance' – 'Daddy, daddy, you bastard, I'm through' – is made part of the rhythm.

I do not mean (and may I say this for the last time) that the 'content' is not important, that Miss Plath's suffering, the invocation of concentration camps elsewhere in the poem, the lack of telephonic connection, even the vampire myth, are of no importance. Certainly they are. A thematic synthesis requires extended meaning, as a stage before it returns to the safe and separate planet of Artifice. I have been at pains to stress that total and irrational discontinuity has no chance of performing the necessary rites of mediation, since no Naturalisation can get near it except the bad kind. Whereas good poetry requires good Naturalisation (good critical reading) as one of its most important external contexts. Without this the telephone will be off the hook. But the reader should not know in advance what message will come through or even in what language it will appear; *a fortiori* the critical reader should not dictate to the poet either the message or the world which it is to concern. The 'message' in the old sense is not what is important; message in the new sense is a product of the recreation of the old orders, primarily through non-semantic levels. The poet as tribal mediator does not himself know what world he is in until the mediation has taken place (the poem is written). The worst disservice criticism can do poetry is to try to understand it too soon, for this devalues the importance of real innovation which must take place on the non-semantic levels. Criticism's function is eventually to try to understand, at a late stage, even Artifice.

That is not easy, as the whole effort of my book has been to show. [. . .]

18
John Barrell, *The Birth of Pandora and the Division of Knowledge* (1992)

A critical history of intense arguments over discursive representations is traced in Barrell's collection of essays on 'the polite culture' of late eighteenth-century Britain. What counts as knowledge and representation in a self-consciously commercial society? This question is the concern of these essays, which include analyses of Thomas Rowlandson's images of the rural poor; of the poetic procedures of William Collins' 'Ode to Evening', of the visual descriptions of divided labour given by William Pyne's 'Microcosm'; of the iconography of Venus in poetic descriptions of statuary; of treason trials; and of landscape art and issues of taste. The title essay discusses neoclassical history painting, looking at James Barry's 'The Birth of Pandora', the aesthetic of which suggests an intimacy between the idea of the monarchy and the depiction of the complete and perfected male body, simultaneously pointing to difficulties in thinking visually the new republicanism. The overall argument of the essays – which cut across the conventionally discrete fields of literary criticism, history of ideas, and art history – is that works of art are embodiments of discursive clashes of interest. Insisting on the volatility of such clashes as those between the languages of political economy and civic humanism, Barrell reads them as a battle between the values of an 'enterprise culture' (in the language of the l980s, the period of these essays' composition) and the older concern for those of 'the public sphere'.

The dangerous goddess: masculinity, prestige and the aesthetic in early eighteenth-century Britain[1]

I

The criticism of the visual arts in early eighteenth-century Britain was largely framed in the terms of the republican discourse we have come to describe as civic humanism.[2] Its founding texts are a pair of essays written around 1710 by Shaftesbury: an account of his design for the painting of *The Choice of Hercules* by Paolo de Matthaeis, and a brief letter on the function of the fine arts; and in addition to these, he wrote an extensive draft of a major treatise on painting which he did not complete.[3] According to Shaftesbury, the primary function of the fine arts was moral and rhetorical: their task was to persuade the citizen to wish to perform acts of public virtue in defence of the political republic. If, and only if, they were successful in this task, were they to aspire to perform the subsidiary but much-valued function, of presenting the civic spectator with images of an ideal beauty by which he might be polished as well as politicised. The fine arts, then, are charged first to produce a citizen with the rough integrity of a Cato, and then to polish him until he shines like Cicero. The danger, of course, is that it may be imagined that this order of priorities could be reversed, and that the beautiful forms displayed by painting and sculpture will be valued more highly than the 'Virtue' and 'laudable Ambition' they should inspire (Turnbull, 1740, p. 128). An art whose first priority is to make Cato fit for the salon may make Cicero unfit for the senate.

It is clear enough, I imagine, that this theory of the fine arts may be regarded in terms of an attempt to legitimate the power of what is conceived of by the discourse of civic humanism as a ruling class.[4] If the primary object of the fine arts is to promote the public performance of acts of public virtue, then they must be thought of as addressing themselves only to those who are imagined to be capable of performing such acts. The qualifications for citizenship in the republic of taste become the same as the qualifications for citizenship in the political republic, and of these the most important is to be a man of independent means, for the best guarantee of political independence is economic independence. It may be, though this is disputed, that those who fail to meet this qualification, and who are thus not acknowledged as citizens and have no opportunity either to exercise public virtue or to understand its nature, are still able to appreciate beautiful forms, but if they are, this is only to say that they are capable of abusing the fine arts, not of using them. For according to George Turnbull, the Scottish critic who was Shaftesbury's most dedicated disciple, if the fine arts display 'merely corporeal Beauty' to the exclusion of 'the Beauties and Excellencies of Virtue, and the Turpitude of Vice', they will 'effeminate the Mind and promote Luxury', and luxury is the prime agent and symptom of corruption, whether in the individual or in the state as a whole; and it follows from this that to display works of art to those incapable of understanding what virtue is, is simply to reinforce their ineligibility as citizens by reinforcing their taste for luxury (Turnbull, 1740, pp. 81, 84, 129).

Thus the civic discourse on the fine arts, in the writings of Shaftesbury and Turnbull seeks to identify those whom it wishes to represent as true citizens – as members of a ruling class, capable of ruling as well as of being ruled – by claiming that only they are capable of profiting by the moral lessons that works of art must teach. More than this, it announces that only the true citizen is capable of being polished, and not corrupted, by the more purely aesthetic characteristics of works of art. Those who are not citizens are excluded as firmly from participation in the republic of taste as they are from the political republic, and they include two groups in particular: the vulgar, and women. The terms of this act of exclusion therefore disclose – as Turnbull has already suggested they do – a politics of gender in the civic discourse, as well as a politics of class.

The discourse of civic humanism was the most authoritative fantasy of masculinity in early eighteenth-century Britain; it was this discourse, above all, which represented public virtue as 'manly' virtue, and which described the corruption of the citizen or the state as 'effeminacy'. It represented civic freedom not only as an emancipation from servility and dependence, but as an emancipation from desire. The ownership of an independent landed estate was curiously but still widely accepted as offering a *prima facie* guarantee that a man was emancipated from the desire for material possessions, but it was no certain test, and it gave no particular guarantee that he was also proof against the promptings of sexual desire. It was thus important to invent narratives of a civic emancipation from sexuality, and for two related reasons. First, because 'manly' virtue, or 'virile virtue' as Shaftesbury termed it, was effeminated as much by submission to 'female charms' as by the rage to acquire and spend; and second, because the vocabulary of the civic discourse, which could describe acquisitive and especially commercial activity in the same terms as it described sexual indulgence – the attractions of both could be termed 'luxury', their effects on men could both be described as 'effeminacy' – enabled emancipation from sexual desire to stand as a mark of emancipation from material desire, and vice-versa (Shaftesbury, 1914, p. 161).

To enable the citizen to triumph over his own sexuality was thus a primary object of civic education, and was to be a primary objective of the fine arts. *The Choice of Hercules* is a case in point. Hercules is represented as choosing whether to accompany Virtue along her steep and rugged pathway, or to linger with Pleasure in the flowery vale.[5] His attitude – turning away from Pleasure to attend to the arguments of Virtue – indicates that he is on the point of making the right choice, the choice that legitimates the claim to exercise political power. But which way will the spectator turn? If the choice of virtue the citizen is obliged to make is to be represented as an act of heroic self-denial, then Pleasure must be made as alluring as possible; and if the fine arts are to be allowed to polish as well as to politicise, this function will – it is universally agreed – be achieved more surely by the exhibition of beautiful forms whose perfection is not too much obscured by drapery. Thus the evident danger of a work like this is not only that the desire of the spectator will be rather inflamed than cooled, but that he will try to claim an aesthetic sanction for preferring the figure of Pleasure to that of Virtue.

Shaftesbury acknowledges that 'effeminacy' may indeed be 'an evil consequent' of the exhibition of nudity, and of the demand that art should exhibit the naked body if it is to make the citizen polite as well as virtuous. But, he argues, the fine arts do not necessarily have this effect, 'if the magistrate provides, without totally banishing, or prohibiting' (Shaftesbury, 1914, p. 104). In the absence of a public official charged with the policing of the fine arts, it falls to the critic to perform that function; and one task of the civic discourse on the fine arts is therefore to produce a theory of art which prescribes not only how images of the naked body are to be produced, but how they are to be consumed, if their didactic and aesthetic functions are to be compatible. And the hardest case the critic-as-magistrate had to confront, was the case of Venus, the goddess whose beauty offered at once the most dangerous threat to manly virtue, and the most perfect polishing agent the fine arts had been able to conceive. Images of Venus, therefore, were thought to be as unstable, as untrustworthy, as the character attributed to the goddess herself; but, like Pleasure, she cannot be left unrepresented; because not to represent her allure is to be incapable of representing her repudiation, one of the most awesome acts of self-denial the civic hero can aspire to.

How then should images of Venus be produced, and how should they be consumed? This essay will examine the attempt made by the civic discourse to find an answer to that question, and the question will turn out to be quite as unstable as Venus herself is claimed to be. Seen from one point of view, it is a question about the value of images of female bodies whose perfection does not seem to fit them for any particularly civic form of action, but only for pleasure. Seen from another, it is a question about whether manly virtue, as defined by the discourse of civic humanism, is not inevitably compromised by the male sexuality it is enjoined to repress. From a third point of view, it is a question which represents Venus as a metonymy for the fine arts themselves, and it asks whether an interest in art is not always, and unavoidably, an unmanly and effeminate interest. It is a question, too, about the feminisation of commerce in the civic discourse, and its consequent difficulty in seeing commerce except as a symptom or agent of corruption. And it is a question, finally, about the viability of the civic discourse itself; about whether it is possible to hold on to an ideal of *virtus* in a society which aspires to be not only civic, but civilised. All these questions will turn out to be implicated in the issue of prestige: the prestige attached to the ability to speak the civic discourse on the fine arts, or rather, the different kinds of prestige attached to it, for these varied according to the position from which the discourse was spoken.

II

Venus, by that account, can mean nothing but trouble for the civic discourse on the fine arts; and indeed, as we shall shortly see, the instability attributed to her could disclose a corresponding instability in the discourse, so profound as to overturn what Shaftesbury announced as the founding doctrine of civic criticism, 'the absolute opposition of pleasure to virtue' (Shaftesbury, 1914, p. 9). But that is not to say that all eighteenth-century critics who consider the problem of Venus seem much embarrassed by it. A number of writers of the generation after Shaftesbury, when they attempt to describe, for example, the Venus de' Medici in the Tribuna at the Uffizi, acknowledge the danger she represents to the integrity of the citizen, but seem rather complacent about it, and are even willing to let on that the pleasure they take in the statue is a sexual pleasure. And they allow this to be disclosed, at the same time as they seem confident that they remain firmly within the orbit of a discourse which claims to prohibit the enjoyment they evince.

We can understand this shift, I believe, in terms of a developing difficulty in the decades after the death of Shaftesbury in conceiving of the republic of taste and the political republic as fundamentally the same constituency. The civic discourse continued, through the middle decades of the century, to provide the only available terms of criticism for the higher genres of the visual arts in Britain, because only in those terms could the claim of painting to be a liberal profession, and not a mechanical and a mercenary trade, be defended. But in those decades, and until the founding of the Royal Academy in 1768 and the attempt then made by Sir Joshua Reynolds to put the relation between the political and the aesthetic on a new footing (Barrell, 1986, pp. 69–162), the civic discourse on the fine arts begins to develop a relative autonomy from the institution it had been developed to define. In Shaftesbury's and Turnbull's writings on art, that discourse had been deployed to empower the institution of aristocracy, and to legitimate it, in the years after the Glorious Revolution, as a republican and a patrician ruling class. It could define the function for the higher genres of art only in terms of their use in educating those who were, or were destined or were qualified to be, members of the visible institutions of government, the Houses of Parliament, or, in the terms of patrician republicanism, the 'senate'. But by the very terms of the civic account of history, this concern with defining the moral qualities of the aristocratic republican hero was almost bound to be attenuated by the mid-century, as Britain became an increasingly commercial society, which offered fewer and fewer occasions for civilian heroism, and which saw little value in an abstinence defined in stoic rather than in Christian terms; and this attenuation was further promoted by the related emergence of the institution of literary criticism, with its own developing autonomy from the institutions of government, and concerned to define the value of literature and the arts for a middle-class audience.[6] Thus there emerged, in the decades after the death of Shaftesbury, a generation of non-aristocratic writers on art (Jonathan Richardson senior and junior, James Thomson, Joseph Spence, Edward Wright) who represent themselves as fully capable of understanding and of defining the function of the visual arts in terms of the discourse of civic humanism, but who write as if the fine arts could be *enjoyed* independently of the possibility of exercising political power, though their value could be *described* only in terms of the effective identity of the political and the aesthetic.

It is this that I have in mind when I speak of the development of a civic discourse on the fine arts which enjoys a relative autonomy from the institution which had produced it; and it is here, particularly, that the appreciation of the fine arts engages with the question of *prestige*. As long as the possibility of appreciating the higher genres of the art was thought of as available only to the aristocracy, it was certainly imagined that an informed concern with painting and sculpture conferred status on the noble or gentle connoisseur; it confirmed his standing as a patrician in the fullest sense of the word, as someone not only born to exercise power, but fit to exercise it. As a result, a form of prestige became attached to the ability to articulate the civic discourse, and that ability could remain to some extent a source of prestige when the discourse came to be spoken by, and addressed to, those with no claim to be regarded as patricians. The kind of prestige it conferred certainly changed: to lay claim to an understanding of the visual arts was now no longer to announce oneself as a true patrician, but as someone who shared something of importance with those who were – something less material than an independent fortune, and less accidental than high birth, but something which was arguably no less valuable for being so.

The developing autonomy of the civic discourse on the visual arts, and the different nature of the prestige it conferred on those who could articulate it, may not at first sight seem to have brought about any very radical change in the discourse itself. Most of what such writers as Thomson or Spence have to say about the function of the visual arts can be read as a repetition or an endorsement of what Shaftesbury had said, and in this paper I shall often be able to draw on their writings in my attempt to illustrate and to amplify the critical and political principles of Shaftesbury. But when such writers consider the representation of the naked female body, and of Venus in particular, this uniformity disappears. All those questions which, I have argued, were entailed in the question of how Venus was to be represented become more apparent, but seem to be suddenly less urgent, when put in the scale with the pleasure which (it is almost openly acknowledged) is to be had from gazing at her nakedness; and in the excited descriptions offered by Thomson, Spence and Wright, of the Venus de' Medici, it seems almost to be implied that the safety of citizen and state alike may be well lost for love.

One way of describing this development would be to see it in terms of the different nature of the prestige which attaches to the civic discourse on the visual arts, as it develops a more attenuated relation to the institutions and the exercise of political power. If the connection between taste and public virtue became a matter of less urgent concern among the followers of Shaftesbury, it also became less important that male sexuality be constituted within the discourse only in order that it might be renounced. And this was not simply a matter, I want to suggest, of a weakening of the old institutional constraints on civic criticism. For the very weakening of the connection between taste and public virtue was necessarily a weakening of the foundation on which the prestige of civic criticism was based. It led inevitably to a tentative valorisation of the aesthetic for its own sake – as connoisseurship, and as a special receptivity to aesthetic form – and as a result the ability to appreciate the visual arts in aesthetic terms began to emerge as a new basis of authority and prestige in the criticism of the visual arts. The discursive strategies by which the aesthetic could begin to be separated from the political are described at the end of this paper. What I want to emphasise here is, first, that within the terms of civic criticism, such a separation was more or less illegitimate, and could neither be argued for nor fully accomplished so long as criticism of the visual arts remained within the orbit of the civic discourse; and, second, that it was nevertheless only by taking advantage of that incipient separation that the sexuality silenced in the writings of Shaftesbury and Turnbull became able to speak itself, and to put in question that ethic of manly abstinence which was so crucial a constituent of the discourse of civic humanism.

Thus, when Thomson and Spence and Wright seem to take a light-hearted and a playful attitude to the threat Venus poses to public virtue, they are producing an account of the aesthetic, and a representation of masculinity, very different from what Shaftesbury had offered: masculinity, in particular, now becomes a matter of virility rather than of abstinence; of the ability to enjoy the pleasures of sexuality rather than to resist them. It is the emergence of this new kind of concern for the aesthetic, and this new representation of what it is to be manly, which establishes the relative autonomy of the civic discourse on the visual arts from the institution of aristocracy; and it is the implicit, the covert, the hesitant form of their emergence which announces that autonomy as relative only. The emergence of a new relation between the political and the aesthetic turns therefore on a representation of woman, and, through that, on masculinity itself.

I shall begin the narrative that follows in the middle of things, with an analysis of a passage by Thomson in which the invocation of Venus disrupts, in a most dramatic way, the connection of taste and virtue; and I shall go on to attempt to demonstrate how Shaftesbury in particular had imagined that the connection could be protected from the threat that Venus posed. In the final sections, I shall attempt a fuller account of how that connection is both affirmed and put in question in the writings of his successors, and of how the civic discourse on the visual arts found a way to accommodate, under the cover of the aesthetic, an account of masculinity as virility which it had earlier been obliged to prohibit.

III

In the second book of his poem *Liberty* (1735–36), Thomson attributes the rise of the fine arts to the liberty enjoyed by the republics of classical Greece. The art of sculpture, in particular, was the result of those civic and public virtues which can develop only in free states, and without which, he tells us, the world would never have seen

> *love*'s awful Brow, *Apollo*'s Air divine,
> The fierce atrocious Frown of sinew'd *Mars*,
> Or the sly Graces of the *Cyprian Queen*.
> (Thomson 1986, *Liberty*, II, lines 304–6)

Why Venus, of all the heathen deities, and why this image of Venus, not merely graceful but sly, should be imagined as an appropriate creation of the civic artist, seems to stand in need of some explanation. And when, fifty or so lines later, the poem does offer something like an explanation, it becomes only too clear how sly, capricious and unstable Venus can be, and how much trouble she can cause the civic discourse on the fine arts. Thomson is describing the function those arts performed in the Greek republics:

> To Public Virtue thus the *smiling Arts*,
> Unblemish'd Handmaids, serv'd; the *Graces* they
> To dress this fairest *Venus* (*Liberty*, II, lines 365–7).

The '*smiling Arts*' were still '*Unblemish'd* Handmaids', of course, because they had not yet prostituted themselves to tyranny and luxury. They were, indeed, '*Graces*', who combined in their efforts to dress 'this fairest Venus', who is now none other than 'Public Virtue' herself. The official argument seems to be that public virtue, though beautiful, can be a brusque, a raw, a naked affair unless clothed by the fine arts: like Shaftesbury, Thomson believes that a degree of politeness can be good for the polity; a '*Venustum*' – the word is cognate with 'Venus' – a 'decorum', can develop in the citizen a pleasing urbanity of demeanour, and allow him to combine, as William Pitt was said to do by his friend James Hammond, 'A Roman's virtue with a courtier's ease' (Shaftesbury, 1727, 1, p. 138; Hammond, vol. 39, p. 333). His virtues will not be corrupted by the luxury of dress, so long as that dress is transparent enough not to conceal his civic character, but only to adorn it. But if that is what Thomson has in mind, he has said something very different, and Venus has evidently exceeded the place assigned to her in and by the civic discourse. Instead of Public Virtue being clothed by Venus, she *becomes* Venus, and it is Venus's body, and Virtue's only in so far as she *is* Venus, that is clothed by the Graces.

This metamorphosis strikes at the heart of civic discourse on the fine arts, because civic iconography defined Virtue, more specifically Public Virtue, as at all points the opposite of Venus. Essential to the accurate representation of Venus, argues Joseph Spence, is her 'indolent character', and 'it is for this reason', he argues, 'that Venus is so often opposed to Minerva, and Virtus; the two deities which presided over an active and stirring life', the *vita activa* to which civic virtue was dedicated (Spence, 1755, p.74). Virtue 'is generally represented', he tells:

> as a military lady. She is sometimes in a coat of mail, or a short succinct vest; with her legs and arms bare, as the Roman soldiers used to be. She has a manly face, and air; and generally grasps a sword, or spear, in her hand. Her dress shows her character, or readiness for action; and her look, a firmness and resolution, not to be conquered by any difficulties or dangers, that may meet her in the way (Spence, 1755, p. 140).

Spence goes on to remark that Virtue is generally opposed to Voluptas, to Pleasure, as she is in accounts and representations of the Choice of Hercules; and he further identifies Venus as the goddess of Pleasure (Spence, 1755, pp. 141, 143). In Shaftesbury's account of *The Choice of Hercules*, he too attributes to Virtue a manliness, expressed in her clothes, which should be those of an Amazon or of Minerva; in her identifying emblem, the 'Imperial or Magisterial Sword', and in the firmness of her posture. 'As for the *Shape, Countenance*, or Person of VIRTUE,' he continues, 'that which is usually given to PALLAS may fitly serve as a Model for this Dame; as on the other side, that which is given to VENUS may serve in the same manner for her Rival,' who should be distinguished from Virtue by a 'Softness', an '*Effeminacy*', and a 'supine Air and Character of Ease and Indolence' (Shaftesbury, 1727, 3; pp. 363–4, 370–1).

Thus when, in *Liberty*, Public Virtue is transformed, by the fine arts, into Venus, she is transformed into her polar opposite, into the other against which her essential character has been defined: in being softened by the 'smiling arts', Virtue is softened up, and feminised. The failure of Thomson's text to deliver up the official civic doctrine, and its transformation of that doctrine into its opposite, can be precisely glossed by Spence's remark that the Romans were 'of so military a turn,' that 'they generally gave Fortitude the name of Virtus, or Virtue, by way of excellence: just as the same nation, now they are so debased and effeminated, call the love the softer arts, Vertu.' A similar point is made by Gilbert West, who notes also that the 'ciceroni', the guides who introduce tourists in modern Rome to the 'gay refinements' which mock the memory of the austere Roman republic, are named after the most eloquent defender of that republic (Spence, 1755, p. 139).[7]

Thomson's substitution of Venus for Public Virtue suggests that his poem, whose entire subject is supposed to be civic freedom, has also been appropriated by a debased and effeminate discourse on the fine arts, associated with the corruption of post-reformation and post-republican Italy, and the appropriation speaks of a difficulty often apparent in civic discourse, a fear that the 'smiling arts' may indeed be the 'softening arts' the product not of virtue but of luxury, of exactly that which most threatens corruption to the state, and moral detumescence to the citizen. That fear is already present in the justification Shaftesbury borrows from Ovid for the representation of beautiful forms: *'emollit mores'* (Shaftesbury, 1914, p. 104).[8] There is a positive and a pejorative sense in the verb 'emollire', to soften: it can mean to make mild or gentle, or to enervate, to render effeminate; and the same ambiguity troubles Spence's account of Venus, who, he says, 'polishes savages, and softens all the world'. George Lyttelton, Thomson's petron, was described, once again by James Hammond, as being 'Firm as man's sense, and soft as woman's love'; we would only have to change that 'and' to 'but' to get a sense of how thin is the film of polish which separates courtliness from effeminacy (Spence, 1755, p. 75; Hammond, Vol. 39, p. 332).

This fear – by the end of the essay it will begin to look more like a desire – is often managed by making a strict distinction between the intellectual pleasures the fine arts are supposed to offer, and the pleasures of luxury which are the pleasures of sense. 'Every-one pursues a GRACE, and courts a VENUS of one kind or another,' claims Shaftesbury, and this is a legitimate and a civic pursuit, provided that this 'VENUS' is a *'moral GRACE'*, a *'Beauty'*, a *'Decorum'*, of the *'inward kind'*, a Venus neutered into a *'Venustum'* (Shaftesbury, 1727, vol. 1, pp. 138, 137).[9] But to pursue Venus in 'an inferior Order of Things', in the mere outward appearance of the human frame, or even in inanimate objects, is another form of effeminacy; it is a characteristic, he argues, of the debasement of the fine arts into objects of luxury, that they cater to 'the whole fantastick Tribe of wanton, gay, and fond Desires', and encourage 'Effeminacy and Cowardice' to such a degree as to ensure that 'the more eagerly we grasp at *Life*, the more impotent we are in the Enjoyment of it' (*Shaftesbury*, 1727, 1, pp. 139, 314).[10] The terms on which the beautiful forms represented by painting and sculpture could be defended as appealing only to the intellect were complicated, at least before Sir Joshua Reynolds put the argument on a new footing, and I shall consider them soon. But earlier in the century, among civic humanist critics, there *does* exist some sort of agreement that, as Shaftesbury argued, if 'ugly' forms 'barbarise' the mind, 'beauteous forms' may 'polish' it, so long as there is no question of 'libidinous representation in plastic art', and flesh is never 'painted as flesh' (Shaftesbury, 1914, pp. 104, 171, 114). The difficulty of this theory, as we shall see, is the difficulty of imagining a painting in which the representation of flesh, however unlibidinous its execution, could not be *seen* as flesh by the spectator.

IV

The embarrassing identification that Thomson has made, between Venus and Public Virtue, is the result, I have suggested, of a discursive slippage, of a kind which the instability of Venus's character both reflects, and is only too likely to produce. Shaftesbury's demand is that the gentleman-citizen should cultivate a courtly lightness of touch, a *Venustum*; and the danger, for Shaftesbury, in that demand – clearly evident in civic reactions to Chesterfield's later version of it – is that the *Venustum* will represent itself not simply as the dress but as the badge of virtue. The demand rests on the possibility of distinguishing between virtue and vertù, between manly politeness and luxurious effeminacy. We have seen that Venus can appear as the agent of both, and one way in which this duality can be sorted out is by appealing to a further distinction, the traditional one between a 'heavenly' and an 'earthly' Venus, between Venus Caelestis or Urania, and Venus Pandemos, who, according to Lemprière's entry on the goddess in his classical dictionary, 'favoured the propensities of the vulgar and was fond of sensual pleasures'. In so far as Venus can slide from one to the other side of the division between the polite and the effeminate, she must herself be divided in two.

But this traditional distinction has itself a long history of instability: Venus is the last deity to entrust with two functions of opposite moral tendency, since it is essential to Earthly Venus that she is deceitful, and can easily conterfeit her heavenly manifestation. Civic humanist theory of the fine arts attempted to confirm the distinction by consigning each Venus to her appropriate discursive site: it defines a public and a private sphere of activity, each with its appropriate aesthetic. The arts have a public function, where they are imagined to operate rhetorically, to persuade us to wish to perform acts of public virtue, and it is here that the Earthly Venus belongs, only ever as the goddess whose designs upon him the civic hero must frustrate. But the arts have also a private function, where they operate in terms of a philosophical aesthetic, appropriate to the contemplative, not the active life, and where the citizen believes he can acquire a polish from inspecting the body of Heavenly Venus, so long as he can regard its form as an object of intellectual, not of sensual delight. The policing of the fine arts that Shaftesbury has called for can of course be a matter of *public* policy only, for he consistently asserts that the freedom of private speculation should be unconstrained; and this seems to amount, in Shaftesbury's writings, to a belief that public images of Venus must always be images of Earthly Venus, and must be enclosed within narratives which leave us in no doubt as to her bad character; images of Heavenly Venus are permitted to be enjoyed, it seems, disjoined from narrative, but only within what is imagined to be a private sphere of the arts.

Thus, as far as painting is concerned, and epic history painting as the most public of all genres. Venus will always be an enemy of the public. We have already seen how, in *The Choice of Hercules*, the hero was required to choose between Virtue conceived of as public virtue, directed towards 'the deliverance of Mankind from Tyranny and Oppression', and Pleasure whose body is modelled on the body of Venus (Shaftesbury, 1727, 3, p. 351). Elsewhere, Shaftesbury considers another possible design from the story of Hercules, where the hero has been seduced by Omphale, and exchanges his club and arrows for a distaff and spindle. The story, explains Shaftesbury, is 'a case of the weakness of human nature, or the virile virtue in opposition to the female charms or those of love'. What kind of a 'machine', what kind of allegorical commentary would such a painting require? Cupids, decides Shaftesbury, insulting the fallen hero, and enjoying their triumph; and a laughing Venus (Shaftesbury, 1914, p. 161).[11]

As far as the public art of history painting is concerned, Shaftesbury is everywhere concerned to point out the dangers of a philosophical aesthetic, if it invites us to take pleasure in mere symmetry of form, in mere beauty, disjoined from purposive action. 'Symmetry', he argues, 'is separate and abstract from the moral part and manners' in painting; 'the moral part . . . lies but little in the forms . . . but is expressed in the air, feature, attitude, action, motion'; 'Characters which in painting are mere forms are not moral' (Shaftesbury, 1914, p. 98). As soon as Venus finds her way into a history painting, she must be shifted therefore from formal to moral, from the body as symmetry to the body as moral tale. The requirement that she *do* something, that she participate in a

narrative, will, or should, immediately betray the kind of moral character she has, and should persuade us, in terms of a rhetorical aesthetic,
not to surrender to her blandishments.

But if Shaftesbury insists on this narrativisation, his contrary insistence elsewhere that the examination of beautiful forms can have a
civilising and a polishing effect has suggested that it might somewhere
be possible to represent a very different image of Venus, whereby her
body could be enjoyed as pure form, precisely because that enjoyment
was not conceived of as bodily; where the perfect unity and proportion
of her form, contained by no narrative, could be understood as the
means by which the civic character can also become civilised and
polite. Such images, as we have seen, would need to be imagined as
occupying a private sphere of the arts, where a contemplative and a
philosophical aesthetic could be allowed to replace the active and
rhetorical aesthetic of public art. The problem for Shaftesbury is that
Venus cannot appear as a visual image in this sphere: there is, for him,
no imaginable private sector in the visual arts. The terms public and
private define, for him, not two different kinds of painting, but the difference between the visual arts and the arts of language. In the literary
arts, he suggests, the beauty of form is a legitimate source of moral
interest; in the visual arts, it can be so only when it is connected with
moral action. Heavenly Venus, the object of the philosophical aesthetic, can be *named*, but she must not be *shown*.

Shaftesbury does not explain why this should be so, but the reason
no doubt lies partly in the intrinsic differences between the literary
and the visual arts, and partly in the differences between the consumers of each. The literary arts, which make use of arbitrary signs, can
offer only mediated representations; because they address the intellect,
not the eye, they do not have the same power to inflame as does the
visual image, and those most easily inflamed, the vulgar, are largely
illiterate and so unable to enjoy them. The 'natural' signs employed by
the visual arts, however, and the immediate representations they offer,
are capable of being enjoyed by all, and what all will enjoy is precisely
their immediacy. It is in vain for Heavenly Venus to invite us to look
beyond the perfection of her body to the perfection of the spirit, for
what lies beyond a natural sign is a natural referent, and that referent
can only be like the sign itself, a thing, something that has mass and
extension – a body. Venus visualised will always be Venus vulgarised,
Venus Pandemos, everybody's Venus.

Had this distinction between the literary and the visual arts been
more fully articulated, it would no doubt have obliged Shaftesbury to

acknowledge a further distinction between public and private, operating within the literary arts themselves. It is in what he describes as 'mere . . . Pieces of Wit and Literature', in the private genre of the letter, the soliloquy, the miscellany, that he himself pursues his contemplations of symmetry and *Venusium* (Shaftesbury, 1727, 1, p. 357). It is perfectly clear, on the other hand, that he regards epic poetry as a public genre, in which the permission granted to the literary arts in general to represent forms which are merely beautiful is overridden by a more urgent imperative to provide lessons and examples of civic heroism (see especially Shaftesbury, 1727, 1, pp. 317–18). In epic, according to the civic humanist critic of poetry, Thomas Blackwell. Venus is the goddess of *'Effeminacy'*, or she should, at least, be represented as such. Thus for Blackwell it is an inevitable but nevertheless an 'unlucky' aspect of the *Aeneid* that its hero is the son of Venus, and that she should therefore be 'the chief Divinity who guides the *holy*, *wise*, and *brave Eneas'*. 'She might well tutor *Paris*,' he writes, 'and favour all the *Trojans* who had their Seraglio's even then', for – as this mention of seraglios suggests – in the *Iliad*, or at least in a civic account of it, the Trojans are defeated as much by their own oriental, and therefore 'effeminate' manners, as by the manly virtue of the Greeks. But in Virgil's epic the Trojans must appear as the originators of that very virtue in the Romans, and 'it was hard,' Blackwell argues, to make Venus appear 'in a *virtuous Cause*', when it was so out of character for her to do so. It was no less hard to allow her to appear in her usual character, which was not to encourage but to destroy civic virtue. Accordingly, Venus was obliged to appear as 'a *mere Person*', with no distinctive characteristics other than her divine power. She exhibits the kind of concern a mother might feel for her son, but not the kind of zeal we might expect from the tutelary goddess of a 'pious hero' (Blackwell, (736, pp. 215, 217, 312). Thomson's failure to distinguish between Venus and Public Virtue is thus analagous to Virgil's inability adequately to characterise Venus: it is the result of a failure to remember that in the public genre of what he described as an 'Epic performance',[12] Venus should always be Earthly Venus, in whatever guise she appears.

It remains true, however, that it is by virtue of the different *nature* of the different arts, disjoined from the particular functiors attributed to their various genres, that Heavenly Venus remains an appropriate object for representation only in writing. It is imagined to be of the nature of the visual arts that they invite us to prefer the sensual to the intellectual, and so transform Heavenly into Earthly Venus, and it is this belief that generates the strange paradox, that a theory of the visual arts which acknowledges, and claims to condemn, the inescapable sensuality of beautiful images of the naked female body, should find itself obliged to permit only such images of Venus as call attention to her sensuality. Thus a civic theory of painting can license the image of what threatens to enervate and undermine the polity, while it denies the possibility that painting could represent an image of Venus which would claim to offer no such threat, and would offer itself, indeed, as the means by which society proceeds from barbarism to civilisation. And it follows from this that if the citizen can indeed be polished without being made effeminate by the supreme image of female beauty, it can only be by images of Earthly Venus, whose body, however, he must be taught at once to admire as form, and to resist as agent. The magistrate who is charged to police, but not totally to banish or forbid, the representation of beautiful forms, can perform that task only by ordaining that visual representations of Venus should be earthly – should be indolent, sensual, and capricious – and by ordaining also that they should be held within, and judgea in terms of, an unambiguous structure of narrative.

V

It is narrative then, that does the police, and licenses the presence of Earthly Venus among the subjects proper to be painted, in a civic society which wishes to become also a civilised society. But where does this leave sculpture – or, more particularly, free-standing sculptures of Venus, which are not apparently, contained, as relief-sculptures, and as sculptured groups such as the Laocoon and the Niobe evidently are, within a narrative structure? Some such statues were positioned within a narrative by their attributes, whether original or acquired during restoration: one of the statues of Venus in the Tribuna of the Uffizi had been given a new hand at the end of the seventeenth century, and an apple to hold in it, to indicate in what contest she had been victorious. And thus she acquired also a name, the 'Venus Victrix', which, however erroneously conceived, served to attach her to a narrative (Richardsons, 1722, p. 57; Haskell and Penny, 1981, p. 332).[13] The name of the most favoured statue of Venus, however, the Venus de' Medici, spoke of her provenance, not of her character or actions; the dolphin which, mounted by a Cupid, supported her on her base, seems not to have been thought to identify her as the Venus of any particular story.[14] It was perhaps this absence of a narrative context, as much as the 'Fleshy Softness' regularly attributed to and admired in her body, which is responsible for the extraordinary fascination the Venus de' Medici exerted over eighteenth-century visitors to Florence, and which blinded them to the other Venuses in the same room. 'when I had spent ten hours in this Gallery', writes the younger Richardson, '. . . 'twas yet impossible to keep my Eyes off of this three Minutes whilst I was in the Room' (Richardson, 1722, p. 56).[15]

The same lack of a narrative context must certainly have been responsible for the regularity with which the Venus de' Medici was regarded as an unstable mixture of characteristics themselves unstable – 'melting', 'dissembled', 'slippery' – and so as an image of Earthly Venus, easily distinguishable from the 'Celestial Venus' which was also housed in the Tribuna. The Celestial Venus was known also as the 'Venus Pudica', because she was holding her drapery so as to make sure that her sexual parts were concealed. By contrast the Venus de' Medici, it seems to have been fairly generally felt, was making only a token attempt to cover her nakedness – was directing attention to what she failed to conceal.[16] Much of Spence's dialogue is imagined as taking place in a temple in the garden of Polymetis 'set apart . . . for the great celestial deities', which houses a copy of the Venus de' Medici. 'It would have been more proper', acknowledges Polymetis:

> to have had a figure of the Venus Coelestis in it: but, to confess the truth to you, I am so much in love with the Venus of Medici, that I rather chose to commit this impropriety, than to prefer any other figure to hers. The thing perhaps is not quite so reasonable, as it should be; but when did lovers act with reason (Spence, 1755, p. 68)?

The Venus de' Medici, by this account, seems to pose a threat to the civic discourse, but she does not do so simply by virtue of the viciousness attributed to her character. For though Venus has always the potential power to conquer and effeminate, and to reduce the free and manly citizen to the sensual condition of the vulgar, it is a power that she has no power to do, so long as she can be trapped in some network of narrative, and so long as that narrative produces a third party, someone other than the spectator himself, who is faced with the choice of conquering or being conquered. It is the fact that sculpture in general, and the Venus de' Medici in general, resists being put into narrative that makes her so much more dangerous

than any historical painting of Venus could be. And the appropriately civic response, therefore, is somehow to overcome sculpture's
resistance to narrative.

One way in which this could be done was by composing epigrams or
inscriptions, to be placed (or to be imagined as placed) beneath the
statue, and with the intention of policing the meanings it could generate. A case in point is the inscription composed by Shenstone to
accompany the copy of the Venus de' Medici in his garden at the
Leasowes. This Venus, Shenstone's 'sober' verses make clear, is *not* the
goddess whose 'amorous leer prevail'd/To bribe the Phrygian boy'
(Paris). Nor is she the 'bold', 'pert', and 'gay' Venus who is worshipped
at Paphos. Her pose, half-revealing and half-concealing her nakedness,
is an emblem of good taste, of taste as absolutely opposed to the luxurious, effeminate, and meretricious display which may be taken to
characterise the goddess in some of her other manifestations
(Shenstone, vol. 2; pp. 318–20).[17] The tourist and connoisseur Edward
Wright composed an epigram on the Venus de' Medici, which
specifically acknowledges, again by reminding us of the fate which
befell Paris, that the statue has the power to make the spectator forget
his civic duty:

> Thus *Venus* stood, and who could blame the Boy,
> For giving Sentence, tho' it ruin'd *Troy*?
> Were they t'appeal, and you to judge the Prize,
> Must not *Troy* fall, were *Troy* again to rise (Wright, 2, p. 409)?

And having made this acknowledgement, the poem can exhort the
spectator to turn away from the image, as Hercules turned away from
pleasure; and so the epigram ends, appropriately, with an admonition:

> Be gone, lest you these naked Beauties view
> So long, you make *Pygmalion*'s Story true.

Whoever speaks this admonition hopes to represent himself as not
himself, in danger of being seduced by Venus. It is someone else, it is
'you', who is at risk. The truly civic spectator is thus constructed as one
who has learned to resist the threat offered to his virtue by Venus's
'Fleshy Softness'; and that lesson safely learned, he can announce
himself as one who, like Shenstone, can be safely trusted to admire,
and to acquire a polish from, the naked stone.

Another way of narrativising sculpture, and sculptures of Venus in particular, was to arrange them in pairs. So different, for Spence's Polymetis, is the Venus de' Medici from Celestial Venus, that he describes the image he so adores as a representation of the 'Vitious' Venus, as the Venus who was brought to 'public shame . . . by her amours with Mars', and was 'caught in the net made by Vulcan'. And 'on account,' he explains, 'of this old story,' he positions his own copy of the statue alongside a statue of Mars, and reproduces the narrative effect of the group sculpture of the two divinities also in the Uffizi (Spence, 1755, pp. 75–6).[18] By this means it is intended that the Venus should be no longer a danger to the civic spectator, but should become, like the story of Hercules and Omphale, a rhetorical exemplum of the danger posed by sensuality to military virtue. In the garden of the great civic palace at Stowe of Viscount Cobham, a copy of the Venus de' Medici was placed in the Rotondo, a structure similar to, and acting, within the garden, as a pendant to, the Temple of Ancient Virtue, so that the goddess is located in a version of the narrative of the Choice of Hercules; and perhaps to make the right choice clear beyond question, the statue was gilded, and thus invited the association of effeminacy and luxury.[19] The practice of pairing copies of antique statues is neither a uniquely British nor a uniquely civic habit; my point is that whatever function it may have served elsewhere, within the terms of the civic discourse on the fine arts it often seems designed to stabilise and so to legitimate the slippery goddess, who, contemplated by herself, would rupture that discourse, and threaten the fantasy of virtuous masculinity it was designed to protect.

VI

Softness, sensuality, indolence, luxury, duplicity, effeminacy – Venus, and the Venus de' Medici in particular – was scribbled over with all the pejorative terms of the discourse of civic humanism. The official civic doctrine, which we came upon most clearly in Shaftesbury's account of Hercules and Omphale, is that the virility of the civic hero is not confirmed but wasted by his sexuality. But as I have suggested, the changing circumstances in which the civic discourse on the visual arts came to be articulated seem to have made it neither necessary nor desirable to end the matter just there, without finding any space for that meaning of virility whereby it denotes male sexuality rather than a manly and therefore asexual virtue. When critics and connoisseurs of the middle decades of the century offer actually to describe the Venus de' Medici, they seem willing to let on that the pleasure they take in her body is a sexual at least as much as an aesthetic pleasure, and they seem somehow to believe that they can allow this to be implied, without forfeiting their civic character.

To attempt to account for this, I need to expand on the account I have so far offered of the opposition that operates in the civic discourse between the private and the public. For the public sphere is involved not in one but in two binary relationships with the private. In the binary I have so far considered, the public is constructed as the *opposite* of a private sphere which is openly theorised by the discourse of civic humanism, and which defines what the citizen *should* do in his private capacity. In the second binary, there is another version of the private, constructed as the *contrary* of the public. This second version of the private is rarely acknowledged and only occasionally visible, for the good reason that it is best left unacknowledged; and it defines what the citizen *may* do in private, so long as he is not thereby disabled from maintaining his public character and performing his public function; and so long as he is not, of course, he may indulge any vice he chooses. 'Publick Virtue' writes John Dennis (2, 1943, p. 113), 'makes Compensation for all Faults but Crimes'.

By this account of the private, there is no question of the enjoyment of images of Venus being pure, spiritual, and aesthetic. Indeed, in this private capacity, the citizen may enjoy exactly those images of Earthly Venus which in public are occasions for moral condemnation; and he may enjoy them for exactly what, in public, he reproves – their sensuality. In the garden at Rousham, the Venus de' Medici appeared at the end of a view which was punctuated, at left and right by statues of Pan and a Faun, and on the garden-front of the house – the private front – she is placed in the company of some entirely uncivic deties, Bacchus among them. In the house at Stourhead she is paired with the narcissistic and exhibitionist Callipygian Venus. In the White Hall at Hagley, the home of George Lyttelton, a copy of the same Venus is paired with the Dancing Faun, also from the Tribuna, as she is also in the entrance hall of the early eighteenth-century house at Towneley in Lancashire (Haskell and Penny 1981, p. 326)[21] These groupings can hardly be read as intending to warn the spectator that sexual indulgence effeminates and brutalises. They seem instead to convert the spaces they inhabit into private spaces, in the terms of this second binary I have been describing; and they seem to say that sexual pleasure does not necessarily effeminate, if it can be sealed within a leakproof private container.

But the container was far from leakproof, and it was always likely that these different notions of the private would invoke and seep into each other, the more so as the civic discourse on the visual arts developed a relative autonomy from the institutions of aristocracy and of aristocratic government, and it became less urgent for it to attempt at every point to define the value of art in terms of its public function, its tendency to promote public virtue. And as the criticism of art became detached from the aristocratic public sphere, so necessarily the notion of the private as the opposite of the public diminished in importance, and the second version of the private, which was altogether more serviceable as an account of the space inhabited by those who enjoyed no opportunity to participate in public life, became, if not more visible, at least closer to the surface of the civic discourse. Because this second version of the private was defined as the contrary of the civic notion of the public sphere, it always offered the possibility of inverting the stoical sexual morality of the public sphere; and because it was, nevertheless, defined in terms of the civic discourse, it was relatively insulated from the protestant code of morality by which middle-class life is more usually imagined to have been regulated. This did not mean, of course, that Thomson or Wright or Spence could now openly, and without qualification, avow that their interest in representations of the female nude was a sensual interest. But it does suggest that the claim made by the civic discourse, that it is possible to subtract the sensual from the aesthetic, or to detach the aesthetic from the sensual, and so to enjoy Venus's body on aesthetic terms while remaining unmoved by her sensuality, may have come to serve some new purposes. It can be understood as providing a justification for the category of the aesthetic as to a degree independent of the political, and as an attempt, also, and a far from whole-hearted one, to mop up the sensual, which, by virtue of that very independence, threatened to become explicit enough to contaminate the aesthetic.

In the process, of course, the mop itself gets saturated. What we have been observing could be redescribed as an attempt to distinguish the aesthetic gaze from the scopophiliac stare, one which seems always to issue in the sensualisation of that gaze, as an unacknowledged sexuality finds eager expression in a concern for the aesthetic, a concern which itself seems to exceed the space it can legitimately occupy by virtue of a prior renunciation of the sexual. The critic who, before he begins to describe the Venus de' Medici, makes a display of his civic credentials, announces himself as one whose aesthetic interest in Venus's body is made possible by virtue of his emancipation from her sexual potency. He is then free to gaze, and gaze, and gaze again; and if he can get close enough to the original, he evinces the innocence of his pleasure by getting out his calipers and footrule. 'Every detail of the goddess's anatomy,' write Haskell and Penny (325), 'was specially examined.' 'The Head,' noted the Richardsons (55), 'is something too little for the Body, especially for the Hips and Thighs; the Fingers excessively long, and taper, and no Match for the Knuckles, except for the little Finger of the Right-hand'. 'One might very well insist,' writes Spence:

> on the beauty of the breasts. . . . They are small, distinct, and deli-cate to the highest degree; with an idea of softness. . . . And yet with all that softness, they have a firmness too. . . . From her breasts, her shape begins to diminish gradually down to her waist . . . her legs are neat and slender; the small of them is finely rounded; and her very feet are little, white, and pretty.
>
> (Spence, 1755, pp. 66–7)

There is more of this kind of thing, by other writers, and it is what passes itself off as an announcement that the threat posed by Venus's sensuality has been safely neutralised by narrative, and is now being seen in aesthetic terms – in terms of the degree of the sculptor's skill, and the pure harmony of proportion. But if that is what these descriptions tell us, as it were, in their official capacity, they seem to take a positive and a playful pleasure in telling us much more besides. In particular there is the repeated refusal of the aesthetic gaze to remain, not merely aesthetic, but a gaze at all: the sense of sight only too eagerly invokes the sense of touch.

This is clear enough in the passage just quoted from Spence; and the Richardsons' careful analysis of the various parts of Venus's body gives way to the observation that the statue 'has . . . such a Fleshy Softness, one would think it would yield to the touch' (Richardson 56). For Thomson, who wrote a lengthy and excited paragraph on the statue, the power of the goddess to displace the visual with the tactile is another aspect of her sly character, her instability, but within the terms of what represents itself as an aesthetic account of the statue this is apparently something to be enjoyed rather than repudiated. He writes:

> The *Queen of Love* arose, as from the Deep
> She sprung in all the melting Pomp of Charms.
> Bashful she bends, her well-taught Look aside
> Turns in enchanting guise, where dubious mix
> Vain conscious Beauty, a dissembled Sense
> Of modest Shame, and slippery Looks of Love.
> The Gazer grows enamour'd, and the Stone,
> As if exulting in it's Conquest, smiles.
> So turn'd each Limb, so swell'd with softening Art,
> That the deluded Eye the Marble doubts.
>
> (*Liberty*, IV, lines 175–84)

'Melting', 'dubious', 'dissembled', 'slippery' – Venus is anarchic and unstable; her swelling body so exceeds the medium in which she is represented and should be confined, that she seems not a woman turned to stone but a stone turning into a woman.[22] But if Thomson evinces no urgent concern to stabilise the statue by containing it within a narrative of repudiation, that is, I suggest, because the passage itself is part of a narrative poem dedicated to recording the triumphs of civic liberty, and thus Thomson's public virtue is already sufficiently on display. With a similar display of his civic character, Edward Wright commands that we should 'Strictly examine every part'; his own examination, however, is less than wholly strict, and by the end of the very first line he is already anxious to touch:

> So just, so fine, so soft each Part,
> Her beauties fire the lab'ring Heart.
> The gentle Risings of the Skin
> Seem push'd by Muscles mov'd within:
> The swelling Breasts, with Graces fill'd,
> Seem easy, to the Touch, to yield;
> Made lovelier yet by a Modesty,
> Forbidding us in vain to see.

– and there follows a lacuna in the poem, which suggests that the sequel was too indecent to be printed (Wright, 2 1730, pp. 407–8).

What I have called this eager invocation of touch by sight suggests that, after Shaftesbury, the civic discourse found a way to have its cake and eat it too. And it could do so especially in relation to the Venus de' Medici, by taking advantage not only of the uneasy senarations of the political from the aesthetic and the aesthetic from the erotic, but of the fact that the statue belonged to no narrative. As we have seen, this absence of a containing narrative could be exploited so as to encourage the critic and connoisseur to provide one for himself, but he did not always provide the kind of story by which Shaftesbury had imagined the body of Venus could be stabilised and made available as a polishing agent. This other kind of narrative could represent itself as the story of an aesthetic response, and so, like the eager descriptions of the various parts of Venus's body, it could pass itself off as of a piece with the aesthetic discourse which the spectator earns the right to speak by resisting the sensuality of Venus; and, like those descriptions, it gives willing utterance to the very sensuality that the aesthetic discourse claims to have displaced.

The standard version of this narrative is recorded by Spence: 'At your first approaching her . . . you see aversion or denial in her look; move on but a step or two farther, and she has compliance in it: and one step more to the right . . . turns it into a little insidious and insulting smile; such as any lady has, when she plainly tells you by her face, that she has made a sure conquest of you.' Spence himself ridicules this account of the Venus: these are 'imaginary beauties', he claims. 'I have paid, perhaps', he writes, 'a hundred visits to the Venus of Medici in person; and have often considered her, in this very view.' But 'I could never find out the malicious sort of smile, which your antiquarians talk so much of' (Spence, 1755, p. 68). But it is a narrative that he records as being common among 'men of taste', at a time when to claim that identity it was necessary to lay claim also to a civic concern for the moral effects of art.

The narrative is as unstable as is the statue itself in Thomson's description: to some, the expression of Venus seemed to change as they approached nearer to her, to others as they moved around her.[23] But, as in Thomson's account of the reaction of the spectator, it always ends in conquest: not in a conquest, by the civic spectator, over his lustful and effeminating passions, such as Hercules achieved when he chose Virtue in preference to Pleasure, but a conquest by Venus over the civic spectator, as Hercules was conquest and effeminated by Omphale, while Venus looked on and laughed. Even Spence is clear enough that the statue had conquered his reason: it was for that reason that he felt obliged to couple Venus with Mars, and it was by doing so, of course, that he was able to continue to indulge the fantasy of coupling with her himself.

Among these writers, then, of the generation after Shaftesbury, the civic discourse appears to have found a way of embracing exactly what it was developed to denounce. The sexuality which is constituted in that discourse, and repressed at the public level of content, of narrative, returns at the private level of aesthetic form and of aesthetic response. It is because, I have suggested, the aesthetic discourse is understood as situated within a private sphere, that it is available to be appropriated by the sexuality that speaks through it. And the return of sexuality is enthusiastically welcomed, in a private celebration of sexual licence, the prior and necessary condition of which is a public renunciation of sexuality. The prestige of a male ruling-class, it is claimed by the civic discourse on the fine arts, has to be earned by that act of renunciation; but the prestige of the middle-class critic and connoisseur comes to be earned in a more complicated fashion. It is won by a public *display* of renunciation, which by granting a legitimacy to an interest in the aesthetic, gives a license to exactly what it appears to have renounced.[24]

Notes

1. This essay was originally written as a paper to be delivered at the conference 'Discursive Strategies and the Economy of Prestige', University of Minnesota, April 1988. It is reprinted from the special issue of *Cultural Critique* (no. 12, Spring 1989) devoted to the proceedings of that conference.
2. The title of this essay has been borrowed from Arthur Young: 'After all I had read and heard of the Venus de Medicis, . . . I was eager to hurry to the *tribuna* for a view of the dangerous goddess. . . . In the same apartment there are other statues, but, in the presence of Venus, who is it that can regard them?' (*Travels in France and Italy During the Years 1787, 1788, and 1789*, quoted in J.R. Hale, 'Art and Audience: The "Medici Venus" c. 1750–c. 1850', 42. This invaluable article deals with (mainly British) resportses to the Venus de' Medici, in the period after that discussed in this essay.
3. (1) 'A Notion of the Historical Draught or Tablature of the Judgment of Hercules', first published in French in 1712, in English in 1713, and included in the second edition of Shaftesbury's *Characteristics of Men, Manners, Opinions, Times* (London, 1714), together with an engraving (see Figure 11) by Simon Gribelin of the painting by de Matthaeis, now in the Ashmolean Museum, Oxford; all references to the *Characteristicks* are to the fourth edition, cited as Shaftesbury 1727. (2) 'A Letter concerning Design', first published in the fifth edition of the *Characteristicks* (London, 1732), and reprinted in Benjamin Rand's edition of the *Second Characters* (hereafter

cited as Shaftesbury, 1914). (3) 'Plastics, or the Original Progress and Powers of Designatory Art', first published in Shaftesbury, 1914.

4. For a fuller account of this matter, see Barrell 1986, 'Introduction', and especially pp. 10–23.
5. On eighteenth-century treatments of the choice of Hercules, see Paulson, 1975, 38–40, 73ff.
6. For an account of this process see Hohendahl, *The Institution of Criticism*, or, for a briefer version, Eagleton pp. 9–43.
7. The thought appears to derive from Plutarch's life of Marcus Cains Coriolanus (Plutarch 4: 120); Gilbert West 'On the Abuse of Travelling', in *The Works of the English Poets*, 1970, 57: 280–3.
8. The phrase is quoted from Ovid, *Tristia*, II, ix, 48.
9. The authority for representing Venus in these terms derives from Horace, *Ars Poetica*, line 42 ('Ordinis haec virtus, erit et venus, aut ego fallor').
10. See also Shaftesbury 1727, 3: 185, where the vice of attachment to the forms of outward beauty prompts the exclamation 'O EFFEMINACY! EFFEMINACY!'
11. See also Turnbull, p. 63, on the painting of Danae by Artemon, in which Venus was represented as smiling at the 'vain Precautions' taken to guard Danae: Turnbull quotes Horace, Odes III, xvi, 6–7: 'Jupiter et Venus/Risissent'.
12. Thomson to Dodington, 1730, quoted by Sambrook in Thomson 1986, p. 39.
13. I am much indebted to Haskell and Penny for information on the Venus de' Medici, and on the other statues referred to in this essay.
14. D'Hancarville (1: 383–4, n. 240) says that the little putti around the dolphin of Venus are often interpreted as 'Amours', and Venus regarded as their mother. But Venus was, according to mythology, the mother only of Cupid, and d'Hancarville points out that the 'amours' are anyway much too small in relation to Venus to be her offspring, so that (he believes) the artist must have thought of them as accessories with at best a very remote iconographical relation to Venus. D'Hancarville does offer to interpret the dolphin, though not according to any mythological narrative: the statue represents Venus as (1: 402, n. 248) the female aspect of the one 'Etre *générateur*', and the dolphin specifies her identity as the mother of marine animal life.
15. See also Turnbull 86. Wright (2: 407) makes an epigram out of the pretence of being unable to tell whether the statue is of stone or flesh:

> Ex Petra num facta Caro est, ex Carneve Petra?
> Credo *Medusaeum* hoc, nullius artis, Opus.

('Is it flesh made of stone, or stone made of flesh? I believe it a work, not of art, but of the Medusa'). And see below, note 21.
16. See Spence, 1755 67: 'if she is not really modest, she at least counterfeits modestly extremely well.' The fact that the Venus de' Medici's left hand was held a little away from her body enabled her to be seen, engraved, and painted, from angles which frustrated her attempt to conceal her sexual parts. Of numerous examples, see the engraving of the statue in Spence 1755 plate V; William Kent's and N. Tardieu's frontispiece to 'Summer' in Thomson 1730; and the painting of the Venus by Sir

Godfrey Kneller presented to Alexander Pope, reproduced in Einberg and Jones plate 21.

17. For a thoughtful account of Shenstone's poem, see Pugh, 1988, pp. 111–12.
18. For copies of the statue in Britain, see Hale, 43n.
19. See Paulson, 1975, pp. 23ff. Gilbert West seems to have regarded the gilded statue as an emblem of modern corruption. He writes:

> Lo! in the *Center* of this beauteous *Scene*,
> Glitters beneath her *Dome* the *Cyprian Queen*:
> Not like to her, whom ancient *Homer* prais'd,
> To whom a thousand sacred Attars blaz'd:
> When simple Beauty was the only Charm,
> With which each tender Nymph and Swain grew warm:
> But, yielding to the now-prevailing Taste,
> In *Gold*, for modern Adoration, drest (West, 1732, pp 13–14).

20. For Rousham see Pugh, 1988, 102–21.
21. In an eclogue by Lyttelton, addressed to Cobham and offered to him as suitable to be read during a perambulation of the garden at Stowe, Venus is narrativised, and sanitised (as is appropriate in a private poem addressed to a relative) by being paired with Hymen:

> Beneath the covert of a myrtle wood,
> To Venus rais'd; a rustic altar stood.
> To Venus and to Hymen, there combin'd,
> In friendly league to favour human-kind.
>
> (Lyttelton, 1790, vol. 64 p. 262)

22. This is not the only occasion where Thomson shows himself unable to distinguish between flesh and marble. Musidora, in 'Summer', bathes in a stream unaware that she is being observed by Damon. He leaves, after a while, but leaves her a note to say that he will enjoy watching her bathe in future, and will protect her privacy from the 'licentious' eyes of others. Musidora is temporarily paralysed, perhaps in amazement at the effrontery of Damon's claim that his own gaze is less than licentious:

> With wild Surprize,
> As if to Marble struck, devoid of Sense,
> A stupid Moment motionless she stood:
> So stands the Statue that enchants the World;
> So, bending, tries to veil the matchless Boast,
> The mingled Beauties of exulting *Greece*.
> Thomson 1981, 'Summer', lines 1344–9)

A footnote by Thomson explains lines 1347–9 as a reference to 'The Venus of Medici'.

23. Compare, for example, Allan Ramsay's circumambulation of the statue, in Spence, 1966, 1, no. 1289.
24. I am most grateful for the advice and encouragement offered by Homi Bhabha and Jacqueline Rose in the writing of this essay.

References

John Barrell (1986), *The political Theory of Painting from Reynolds to Hazlitt: 'The Body of the Public'*, (New Haven and London: Yale University Press).

Thomas Blackwell (1736) *An Enquiry into the Life and Writings of Homer* (1735), 2nd edn (London: (no publisher credited)).

John Dennis (vol 1: 1939; vol 2: 1943,(*The Critical Works of John Dennis*, 2 vols, ed. Edward Niles Hooker (Baltimore: Johns Hopkins Press).

J.R. Hale (1976), 'Art and Audience: The "Medici Venus" c. 1750–c. 1850', *Italian Studies*, vol. 31.

James Hammond (1790), Elegies XIV and XV, in *The Works of The English Poets. With Prefaces Biographical and Critical by Samuel Johnson*, vol. 39, (London: (for J. Buckland *et al.*))

Baron d'Hancarville (1785), *Recherches sur l'Origine, l'Esprit et les Progrès des Arts de la Grèce*, 3 vols (London: B. Appleyard).

Francis Haskell and Nicholas Penny (1981), *Taste and the Antique: The Lure of Classical Sculpture 1500–1900* (New Haven and London: Yale University Press.

Peter Uwe Hohendahl (1982), *The Institution of Criticism* (Ithaca and London: Cornell University Press).

George Lyttelton (1790), 'Possession, Eclogue IV. To Lord Cobham,' in *The Works of the English Poets. With Prefaces Biographical and Critical by Samuel Johnson*, vol. 64 (London: (for J. Buckland *et al.*)).

Ronald Paulson (1975), *Emblem and Expression: Meaning in English Art of the Eighteenth Century* (London: Thames and Hudson) 1975.

Simon Pugh (1988), *Garden–Nature–Language* (Manchester: Manchester University Press).

Jonathan Richardson Sr and Jr (1722), *An Account of Some of the Statues, Bas-Reliefs, Drawings and Pictures in Italy, etc., with Remarks* (London: (for J. Knapton)).

Shaftesbury Anthony, Earl of (1727), *Characteristicks of Men, Manners, Opinions, Times* (1714) 4th edn (London: (no publisher credited)).

Shaftesbury Anthony, Earl of (1914), *Second Characters, or, the Language of Forms, by the Right Honourable Anthony, Earl of Shaftesbury*, ed. Benjamin Rand (Cambridge: Cambridge University Press).

William Shenstone (1764) *The Works in Verse and Prose of William Shenstone*, 2 vols (London: R. and J. Dodsley).

Joseph Spence (1755), *Polymetis: or, An Enquiry concerning the Agreement between the Works of the Roman Poets, and the Remains of the Antient Artists*, 2nd edn (London: (for R. and J. Dodsley)).

Joseph Spence (1966), *Observations, Anecdotes, and Characters of Books and Men, etc.*, ed. James M. Osborn (Oxford: Oxford University Press).

James Thomson (1986), *Liberty, The Castle of Indolence, and Other Poems*, ed. James Sambrook (Oxford: Clarendon Press).

George Turnbull (1740), *A Treatise on Ancient Painting, Containing Observations on the Rise, Progress, and Decline of that Art Amongst the Greeks and Romans* (London: (for the author)).

Gilbert West (1790), 'On the Abuse of Travelling', in *The Works of the English 'Poets.' With Prefaces Biographical and Critical by Samuel Johnson*, vol. 57 (London: (for J. Buckland *et al.*)).

Edward Wright (1730), *Some Observations Made in Travelling through France, Italy etc. in the years 1720, 1721 and 1722* (London: Thomas Ward and E. Wicksteed).

19

Ian Hunter, David Saunders and Dugald Williamson, *On Pornography: Literature, Sexuality and Obscenity Law* (1993)

On Pornography was written in the context of the intense cultural–political debates in the 1970s and 1980s in which pornography was recast as problematic after its neat inclusion in a discourse of sexual liberation and the rights of the private individual (rights to which Clarence Thomas was famously to appeal in the US Senate hearing on his confirmation as Supreme Court Justice when he indicated that he would refuse to answer questions concerning the privacy of his bedroom and so his use of pornography). Decisive here were the debates within and from feminism, one major emphasis of which sharply refocused pornography as a matter not of freedom of expression but of the exercising of a form of power directed first and foremost against women. Perceived as such, pornography raised questions of legal and social control which prompted a variety of reponses, including within feminism (one significant example of which is crystallised in the dual emphasis in the name of the British organisation *Campaign Against Pornography and Censorship*).

The aim of Hunter, Saunders and Williamson's book was to give an account of the policing of – the legal and social controls on – pornography, mainly in Britain and the US, from the eighteenth century through to the present day; this in the interests of demonstrating the historically specific nature of pornography. Their emphasis, resisting all attempts to provide a general statement of the truth of pornography ('whether to discover its origin in the puritanical repression of healthy sexuality, its essence in the patriarchal objectification of women, or its rightful place in the sphere of private morality or in that of literary emancipation'), is on the shifting circumstances in which it emerges as, *inter alia*, an instrument of sexual desire and its gratification, a species of illegal conduct, an ethical failing, a marketable commodity, a legal problem, an aesthetic category, an object of reform campaigns, an issue in medical–pedagogical programmes. What the history of its policing shows is how the various discourses on pornography, in terms of freedom or power, operate with a 'truth' of pornography that brings aesthetico–political conceptions into confusion with legal–governmental ones. The force of this is then not to fall back into a liberal

316

division between law and morality – the philosophical distinction between harmful conducts and harmless representations – but to clarify the range of ethical intelligibility and legal possibility within which the shifting historical field of pornography can better be approached. In the following extract, the authors state this position through a discussion of their assent to, and divergence from, the terms of the work of Catharine MacKinnon and Andrea Dworkin.

Feminism and law reform

No one who enters the debate over pornography gets out unscathed, neither do we expect to be exceptions in this regard. Our historical studies have indicated that the fields in which pornography is discussed are in principle incapable of giving rise to a single unified truth of pornography, in relation to which all individuals could be expected to adjust their thought and conduct. As an eroticising device, a target of medical – pedagogical programmes, a tradeable commodity, an aesthetic category, an object of feminist and governmental reform campaigns, a legal problem – pornography has taken shape differently in different departments of existence. Let those who think that these different constructions of pornography can be reconciled in one overarching philosophical or moral judgement deal with the fact that two centuries of dispute have brought us no closer to this goal. In these studies we have therefore taken the disputes as permanent and philosophically irresolvable. Each of the departments mentioned deploys norms, techniques, conducts and forms of personhood in relation to which pornography can be produced, used, judged, appreciated, pathologised, regulated, and so on. But neither individually nor collectively are they capable of supporting a judgement that might be true of pornography in general, because the norms of judgement reach no further than the sphere in which they are actually deployed.

The one apparent exception is the sphere formed by the institutions of law and government which can, under certain historical circumstances, adjudicate the contending claims advanced by the other departments. This is not really an exception, however. The law does not attempt such adjudication in the name of a philosophical judgement of pornography. In other words, its judgements are neither formal nor empirical as these terms are understood in the epistemological disciplines. Rather, legal judgements are processual, ceremonial, and based on categories informed by specific purposes – the regulation of trade or morality, the proscription of certain behaviours, the facilitation of others. This technical and purposive mode of judgement, coupled with the fact that the law is among other things an institution for settling disputes, is what allows the law to adjudicate in the case of pornography, through the historical category of obscenity. The law adjudicates on pornography not through a universally true judgement but by maintaining a quite narrow set of procedures, categories and purposes that permits a judgement to take place and to be seen to have taken place. The law is the final court of appeal in the dispute and its judgement is binding by virtue of this institutional finality.

We are quite comfortable with this view and role of the law. It is of course compatible with our view of obscenity law as a set of juridical procedures and categories that have been developing in tandem with the governmental 'policing' of modern populations since the early eighteenth century. Moreover, this view of legal judgement – as binding in its social finality – informed our rejection of liberalism's attempt to found and rectify obscenity law in a philosophical analysis of harm. What is to count as harmful, we argued, cannot be decided in advance of the procedures and categories of obscenity law itself and the governmental (medical, pedagogical) programmes with which it is aligned. It will be recalled that at that point we rejected the project to draw a universal boundary between law and morality based on the philosophical distinction between harmful conducts and harmless representations. It became clear that this latter distinction could not be drawn in a uniform and *a priori* manner by presupposing a subject of consciousness able to exercise judgement through given intellectual and moral faculties. And we showed to the contrary that the law in fact draws this distinction in a variable fashion; that it does so relative to medical and pedagogical goals for the conduct of individuals as social types; and that it treats capacities for moral judgement not as given in the faculties of the subject but as acquired ethical abilities or competences, differentially distributed according to age, gender, educational level and social situation.

Feminism is surely right in rejecting the liberal notion of a universal rational subject as the basis of political and social action, although perhaps overly optimistic in thinking that reason is divided along gender lines only, and that the problems associated with constructions of pornography can be solved by removing the distorting effects of patriarchal interest. If the judgements of the law's 'reasonable man' are not the transparent expression of a universal reason, then neither are they duplicitous or botched attempts at such expression – mere distortions of reason open to rectification through exposure of the (patriarchal) 'interests' supposed to inform them. The limits of legal reason are far more varied and far less escapable than any such account can allow. This is because the 'reasonable man' is not the (true or distorted) foundation of legal judgement but a purely retrospective construct, its form and content changing constantly and routinely with changes in the objectives of legal regulation and the forms of calculation informing these objectives.

Our rejection of the project of philosophical liberalism signifies a choice between two different intellectual styles and approaches: the philosophical–aesthetic and the legal–governmental. Under other circumstances it would be possible to explore the historical determination and reality of this dichotomy. Reinhart Koselleck, for example, traces its emergence to the religious butchery and social chaos of the seventeenth century. It was then, in those particular historical circumstances, that legal and political intellectuals detached sovereignty and law from absolute notions of morality and justice and subjected them to a pragmatic and positive reformulation in terms of the needs of the state and the security and well-being of its citizens. These were the circumstances in which philosophical and, later, aesthetic intellectuals defined themselves oppositionally, through the project of subjecting 'positive' law and politics to a higher moral critique – in the name of universal history and its subject.[1] For present purposes, however, it is enough to note that it was just such an attempt to subject positive law to a higher moral critique that was called into question in our critical discussion of philosophical liberalism. That discussion was conditioned by our recognition that the governmental objectives embodied in obscenity law set the parameters within which socially binding judgments on pornography can actually be achieved.

The manner in which our style of analysis problematises philosophical liberalism should, therefore, be reasonably clear. What is perhaps not quite so clear is the coldness of the comfort that it brings to the most widely promulgated feminist analysis of pornography and obscenity law. It is the uncertainty of our relation to this latter analysis that we wish to discuss in these concluding remarks.

It is arguable that the most consistent attempt to translate feminist critique into law reform – the project of Andrea Dworkin and Catharine MacKinnon – is characterised by a blurring of philosophical–aesthetic and legal–governmental objectives, similar to that which undermines the liberal project. If this is so, then we should expect the Dworkin–Mackinnon project to be divided by a radical ambivalence: between the imperative to make feminist objectives socially binding by reformulating them within the categories, procedures and purposes of the law; and the attempt to reconstruct the law from a higher moral position, in the name of universal history and its repressed feminine subject.

Dworkin and MacKinnon drafted a model anti-pornography ordinance and liaised with local government bodies interested in incorporating it in their codes relating to human relations and equal opportunity. A version of this ordinance was passed in Indianapolis in 1984.[2] How does the Indianapolis ordinance (hereafter the Ordinance) enunciate the case against pornography? It defines pornography as a 'practice of exploitation and subordination based on sex which differentially harms women'. It seeks to 'prevent and prohibit' all discriminatory practices of sexual subordination and exploitation operating through pornography (598 F. Supp., p. 1320). The means to do so is to declare pornography unlawful because discriminatory. The Ordinance also provides forms of relief and redress against a range of pornographic practices: trafficking in pornography, that is, the production, sale, exhibition or display of pornography; coercion into a pornographic performance; forcing pornography on a person 'in any place of employment, in education, in a home, or in any public place'; and assault or physical attack due to pornography (pp. 1321–2). The mechanisms for obtaining relief are complaint by persons claiming to be aggrieved by such practices, or by members of a designated board who have reasonable cause to believe that a violation of the law has occurred. In relation to trafficking, a type of class action is provided whereby 'any woman may file a complaint as a woman acting against the subordination of women and any man, child or transsexual may file a complaint but must prove injury in the same way that a woman is injured in order to obtain relief' (pp. 1322–3).

A complaint sets in train an investigation aimed at conciliation and persuasion in relation to the alleged discriminatory practice. If the complaint is not satisfactorily resolved through informal proceedings, the Complaint Adjudication Committee may hold a public hearing. If the complaint is sustained, the relevant party may be ordered to discontinue the unlawful practice and to undertake certain affirmative action including restoration of the complainant's losses incurred as a result of the discriminatory treatment. Provisions for appeal are made. Finally, if it is found that a person engaged in discriminatory practice has failed to correct or eliminate it, the board may file a complaint in the Marion County circuit or superior court for injunctive relief and other affirmative relief or orders 'designed to put into effect the purposes of the ordinance' (pp. 1322–5).

Key themes of a broader feminist critique of pornography reverberate in the finding that is incorporated into the Ordinance:

> Pornography is a discriminatory practice based on sex which denies women equal opportunities in society. Pornography is central in creating and maintaining sex as a basis for discrimination. Pornography is a systematic practice of exploitation and subordination based on sex which differentially harms women. The bigotry and contempt it promotes, with the acts of aggression it fosters, harms women's opportunities for equality of rights in employment, education, access to and use of public accommodations, and acquisition of real property; promote rape, battery, child abuse, kidnapping and prostitution and inhibit just enforcement of laws against such acts; and contribute significantly to restricting women in particular from full exercise of citizenship and participation in public life, including in neighbourhoods (p. 1320).

In line with wider feminist arguments, this finding treats pornography not as some self-enclosed world of representations having no tangible effects in real life but as a 'practice' of sex discrimination. Pornography is a harmful type of behaviour because it reduces the status of women by treating them as 'sexual', where the meaning of this term is wholly imposed by men for their own gratification. In the Ordinance, pornography is identified with various ways of 'presenting' women: as sexual objects who enjoy pain and humiliation, or experience sexual pleasure in being raped; as bodies in bondage, cut up, bruised, physically hurt, fragmented, severed, or in other scenarios of sexual violence and inferiority; as being penetrated by animals; as sexually available for domination, possession, use and the like (p. 1320). This mix of instances is placed under the rubric of 'graphic sexually explicit subordination' of women (although the same ways of presenting men, children or transsexuals are also said to constitute pornography for the purposes of the legislation).

There is a clear difference between the feminist arguments on which the Ordinance rests and the First Amendment absolutist position on pornography examined in the previous chapter. The emphasis has shifted from defending a supposedly inherent right of expression to attacking an insidious form of power. Specifically, it is argued, the pseudo-right of expression relating to pornography should be displaced by recognising the right of women not to be discriminated against on the grounds of sex, a right invoked under the Fourteenth Amendment.

On this account, the abstractness of obscenity and also of free expression as *concepts* is said to have allowed pornographic speech – which is in fact a discriminatory conduct – to be passed off as everyone's speech, a universal value to be protected. Obscenity law, it is said, thus protects the speech of men which 'silences the speech of women', and fends off consideration of the actual harmful conducts involved in pornography. Since the defence of pornography is to male supremacy what its critique is to feminism (MacKinnon, 1987, p. 146), there is little chance of genuine and profound reform being achieved by working within the compromised logic of existing obscenity law and First Amendment 'principles'.

In fact, two quite different political and intellectual styles organise this mix of elements and the argument of the Ordinance. On the one hand, the Ordinance specifies the harm of pornography in legal and governmental terms, as an impediment to women's full participation in civic and economic life. Here the operative term is *discrimination*, and harm is construed as an infringement of civil rights, in turn constructed in terms of governmental objectives associated with equity, efficiency, participation and equality of opportunity.

On the other hand, the harm of pornography is also specified in philosophical and aesthetic terms, as an impediment to the full realisation of women's being. In this regard the key term is *objectification*, and pornography is conceived as a premature fixing of an ideal mode of being in an alien form, the alien form and purposes of the male psyche. The lineage of this conception in Romantic aesthetics and philosophy will be evident from earlier discussion and is clearly signalled in the claims that pornography commodifies, fragments, fetishises and alienates women's bodies.[3] It is this conception that lends a dramatic ambivalence to feminist characterisations of the pornographically represented body as cut up, fragmented, distorted, bound, and so on. Such characterisations hover between an aesthetic repugnance fastidious enough to be applicable to all instrumentalised representation, and a fantasmagoria in which metaphor slides into fact, the Hegelian fragmentation of being finding its lurid correlative in the actual dismemberment of bodies.

Needless to say, we have no interest in the game of accusing and convicting Dworkin and MacKinnon of a philosophical confusion. The ambivalence in question is far more important than that and is historically rather than conceptually rooted. It arises from a radical instability in the forms in which intellectuals may *conduct themselves* in relation to positive law and government. Part of the problem is that there is no way to translate between the philosophical–aesthetic conception of pornography as objectification and the actual operations of legal and governmental institutions. The former conception is a prisoner of the aesthetic dialectic in which a completely developed (women's) being is unfolded from the successive mutual modifications of mind and body, intellect and emotion, the ideal and the real. The law operates quite differently with men, women and children; it constructs their attributes retroactively, in terms of definite and limited legal and governmental norms, objectives and programmes.

What is more, the aesthetic dialectic is actually a means of *withdrawing* from the legal–governmental field and of orienting oneself to another set of concerns: those of the self conceived as the problematic interface of the two sides of the dialectic. In fact, the dialectic is an ethical weapon directed against positive law and government. It aims to problematise their normative regulation of conduct and attributes by picturing 'complete' human development as the dialectical neutralisation of all positive norms and the recovery of 'wholeness' from the fragments. But these of course are precisely the terms in which pornography itself is problematised. For those under the sway of the dialectic, then, obscenity law is just as problematic as pornography, and for the same reasons. The definite and limited (positive) character of legal norms and objectives is treated as a fragmentation of a more complex and organic sphere of women's development (and oppression), it being necessary for society to be totally transformed if full being is to be realised. Once this point has been reached we can be sure that the project to reform the law has given way to an endeavour of an altogether different kind: aesthetic critique and self-refinement.

If our diagnosis of this ambivalence is correct, then there is clearly a danger that the important attempt to construct the harm of pornography as an infringement of civil rights may be swamped by aesthetically conceived rights and harms (the right not to have one's being objectified and misrepresented) whose limitlessness puts them beyond legal claim and redress. More specifically, if the Dworkin–MacKinnon project is indeed torn between legal–governmental and philosophical–aesthetic objectives, we should expect to see it give rise to two interrelated tendencies: first, a tendency to subordinate obscenity law to philosophical and aesthetic critique – to problematise its norms, categories and objectives by showing their inability to realise complete (non-objectified) being; second, the tendency of lawyers to reject the proposed legal enactment of aesthetic imperatives as non-constructable within the technical and normative framework of the law. There is no shortage of evidence for both these tendencies.

Consider in this regard the following remarks by Catharine MacKinnon:

> Feminism doubts whether the average person gender-neutral exists: has more questions about the content and process of defining what community standards are than it does about deviations from them; wonders why prurience counts but powerlessness does not and why sensibilities are better protected from offense than women are from exploitation; defines sexuality, and thus its violation and expropriation, more broadly than does state law; and questions why a body of law that has not in practice been able to tell rape from intercourse should, without further guidance, be entrusted with telling pornography from anything less. Taking the work 'as a whole' ignores that which the victims of pornography have long known: legitimate settings diminish the perception of injury done to those whose trivialization and objectification they contextualize. Besides, and this is a heavy one, if a woman is subjected, why should it matter that the work has other value? Maybe what redeems the work's value is what enhances its injury to women, not to mention that existing standards of literature, art, science, and politics, examined in a feminist light, are remarkably consonant with pornography's mode, meaning, and message. And finally – first and foremost, actually – although the subject of these materials is overwhelmingly women, their contents made up of women's bodies, our invisibility has been such, our equation as a sex *with* sex has been such, that the law of obscenity has never even considered pornography a women's issue (1987, pp. 174–5).

Here feminism is constituted as the higher philosophical and moral prospective from which it is possible to condemn the arbitrariness of the law's categories; the narrowness of its regulatory ambit; its gender blindness; and the absurdity of its attempt to differentiate culture from pornography when – 'examined in a feminist light' – culture itself is pornographic.[4] Indeed, so high is the moral and philosophical ground from which this critique is directed that it risks losing sight of its actual target. It is hardly surprising that the legal categories of prurience and offensiveness 'fail' when they are set a task – the representation of women's invisible being – that only makes sense within the domain of aesthetics.

We are thus given an invitation we may or may not wish to accept: to convert obscenity law into an occasion for aesthetic critique. And the alternative we are offered is to remain with such categories as prurience and offensiveness through which American law has been reconstructing obscenity and defining a programme for the variable pedagogical policing of problem sensibilities. No doubt the extent to which specifically masculine sensibilities to pornography can be affected by such a programme remains an open question, but are we ready to dismiss the question – and the reform opportunities it may afford – by opting instead for the promise of a total aesthetic transformation of masculine being?

With this choice in mind, let us return to the solution proposed in the Ordinance to the perceived problem of sexist bias in the law: the linking of the feminist critique of pornography as objectification of women to the legal-governmental category of a civil right of women, under the Fourteenth Amendment, not to be discriminated against on the grounds of sex.[5] The drafters of the Ordinance deliberately go beyond existing standards in order to make 'pornography', not just 'obscenity', unlawful. They do not attempt to couch the restrictions on pornography in terms of community standards, offensiveness or prurience, nor do they allow for consideration of the literary, artistic or other value of an otherwise 'pornographic' work. The restrictions of the Ordinance would thus extend to soft-core pornography and other materials deemed to be demeaning to women, even though they need not be 'obscene' in the present legal sense (598 F. Supp., pp. 1331–2). The scale of these changes indicates what MacKinnon (1987, p. 195) refers to as an attempt to create an 'affirmative access' to speech for those to whom it has been denied.

There is no denying the uncompromising clarity of this vision. By virtue of a major theoretical intervention, there would be a general jettisoning of the heterogeneous array of thresholds and distinctions which have emerged as the means of achieving and administering a variable dissemination of materials according to legal and pedagogical judgements about kinds of use and kinds of user. As we have demonstrated, legal distinctions between art and pornography or between soft and hard-core inhere neither in sexuality or writing nor in their putative human subject. Rather, they are the particular *instruments* on which a variable obscenity and its administration depend. To abandon them in favour of a global and undifferentiated concept of pornography at the very least must raise the question of the *means* whereby, in practice, distinctions could be drawn between different writings about sex and different uses of such writings. Whatever the preferred thresholds might be, what cultural competences would be required in order to recognise them? Would courts and judges become the agents of what would be essentially an aesthetic judgement?

The courts' reluctance to embark on wholesale change has been taken by some feminists as confirmation that constitutional process has already institutionalised and consecrated a male will to power. Referring to the Supreme Court's affirmation of the decision in *Hudnut*, MacKinnon thus claims that the law continues to make pornography 'available in private while decrying it in public' (1987, p. 211). And Kappeler sees the rejection of the Minneapolis ordinance by liberals and sections of the media as part of a wider defence of patriarchal power, protecting the privileges of men purveying and using pornography and so perpetuating women's oppression (1986, pp. 11–17).[6]

Given the profound ambivalence between principled commitment to an aesthetic conception of recovering the wholeness of women's repressed being and pragmatic embracing of positive legal mechanisms – in this case the constitutional apparatus protecting US citizens against infringements of their civil rights – it is not surprising the law cannot construct an equivalence between the feminist definition of pornography as objectification, and an all-purpose right not to be discriminated against. But is a decision not to validate such a right necessarily to be seen as a failure to recognise and redress the sexist bias of obscenity law?

In relation to this question it is appropriate to recall the manner in which the law recognises and resolves the often intractable disputes and problems presented to it. We can take as an example the process of judicial decision making in this particular case. In doing so, we shall refer to the constitutional calculation of rights in the District Court (598 F. Supp., 1984), although the same general line of reasoning is followed in the Court of Appeals. The District Court sees the litigation as requiring it 'to weigh and resolve the conflict between the First Amendment guarantees of free speech, on the one hand, and the Fourteenth Amendment right to be free from sex-based discrimination on the other hand' (p. 1327), and to establish whether the Ordinance has an unconstitutionally 'chilling effect' on the right to free speech (p. 1328). It is thus a matter of deciding between two legal options. And in fact the Court decides that the state's interest in prohibiting sex discrimination created by pornography as the sexually explicit, graphically depicted subordination of women is not so compelling as to outweigh the constitutionally protected interest of free speech (p. 1326).[7]

Constitutional analysis of the Ordinance is then said to require determination of the following three issues:

[F]irst, the Court must determine whether the Ordinance imposes restraints on speech or behaviour (content versus conduct); if the Ordinance is found to regulate speech, the Court must next determine whether the subject speech is protected or not protected under the First Amendment; if the speech which is regulated by this Ordinance is protected speech under the Constitution, the court must then decide whether the regulation is constitutionally permissible as being based on a compelling state interest justifying the removal of such speech from First Amendment protections (pp. 1329–30).

On the first of these issues, the defendants' premise is that the Ordinance regulates conduct, not speech. They find an analogy for this distinction in the fact that the courts have held that advocacy of a racial segregation doctrine is protected speech under the First Amendment, while segregation itself is not constitutionally protected behaviour (p. 1330). For this analogy to work, it must be accepted that pornography is not only a form of statement or doctrine but also embodies – in its sex discrimination – an equivalent to the category of conduct referred to in the area of racial segregation. The defendants claim that 'the production, dissemination, and use of sexually explicit words and pictures *is* the actual subordination of women' and so constitutes a harmful action, a form of regulable behaviour, not an expression of ideas entitled to First Amendment protection (p. 1330). However, the Court sees this claim as ambiguous and ultimately unacceptable: pornography is acknowledged in the Ordinance to involve 'words and pictures', and although pornography 'conditions society to subordinate women', the means by which the Ordinance seeks to combat this discrimination is 'through the regulation of speech' (pp. 1330–1).

Having found that the Ordinance seeks to regulate speech not conduct, the Court states that pornography as defined therein cannot be held to fall within one of the established categories of speech unprotected by the First Amendment. It rejects the defendant's claim that since pornography is 'nothing more than the infliction of injury on women', it comprises a form of what were identified in *Chaplinsky* as 'fighting words' which can legitimately be regulated because by their very utterance they 'inflict injury or tend to incite an immediate breach of the peace' (p. 1331). The fact that the Ordinance 'sweeps beyond' unprotected obscenity (p. 1326) would normally be enough for it to be overturned as unconstitutional, but the defendants argue that this case raises a new issue for the Court and that while the Ordinance regulates protected speech it does so in a constitutionally permissible fashion (p. 1332).

For all their sweeping character, these claims and counterclaims are in fact conducted *within* the instituted technical procedures of the legal sphere. For instance, and quite predictably, there is the mode of argument from precedent. The defendants claim that the legal category of obscenity has not been the only basis for regulating sexually explicit materials and conducts or for distinguishing the protected from the unprotected, and that the existing variations on *Miller* should be extended to include the newly-defined class of discrimination as a form of unprotected materials (pp. 1332–5). They cite a trio of precedents to make this point, arguing firstly that the interests of protecting women from sex-based discrimination are as compelling and fundamental as those upheld in *New York v. Ferber* (1982) for the benefit of children (pp. 1332–4). In that case, it was ruled that a state interest in 'safeguarding the physical and psychological well-being of a minor' outweighs the interest in upholding guarantees of free speech for child pornography, even despite any literary or other value which the material in question may be deemed to possess. In *Hudnut*, however, the Court holds that the *Ferber* rationale for going beyond *Miller* applies only to minors. The governmental interest in protecting children is not 'readily transferrable to adult women as a class' because the latter 'do not, as a matter of public policy or applicable law, stand in need of the same type of protection which has long been afforded to children'.[8]

The Court also holds that the second case invoked by the defendants, *FCC v. Pacifica Foundation* (1978), is not controlling in the present case (p. 1334). In *Pacifica*, the Supreme Court held that broadcast offensive speech was not entitled to protection. Because the broadcast media have established 'a uniquely pervasive presence' in the lives of Americans, such speech may infringe on the individual's right to be left alone in the privacy of the home. Moreover, broadcasting is 'uniquely accessible to children, even those too young to read'. In *Hudnut*, the Court holds that this precedent, although permitting regulation of the 'content' of speech, specifically involves problems of dissemination. Since the Ordinance does not restrict itself to regulating broadcast media nor to protecting children, the reasons used to justify restrictions in *Pacifica* cannot be called upon in this case.

The Court also rejects the precedent of *Young v. American Mini Theatres, Inc.* (1976) invoked by the defendants (pp. 1334–5). While it notes that in *Young* the Supreme Court upheld a city ordinance regulating the location of cinemas featuring erotic films, it also observes that this was a 'place' restriction, not a complete ban on the pornographic materials. The judgement concerned not the content of the films alone but a type of distribution which, it was considered, would have an effect on the character of the city's neighbourhoods of a kind which justified restrictions on the communications. However, the Indianapolis Ordinance is seen to prohibit the distribution of 'material depicting women in a sexually subordinate role, at all times, in all places and in every manner' and therefore cannot find support from such a precedent.

The argument on these precedents provides an economical and practical reminder of what is meant by obscenity as variable category and of what is involved in its legal administration. The juridical policing of sexual materials and conducts is deemed permissible only when justified by a judicial calculation of governmental interest in relation to particular norms: the welfare of minors, standards of decency in broadcasting, the character of urban spaces. The putative harm of objectification – applicable 'at all times, in all places and in every manner' – is meaningless in a system where harm is variably calculated relative to a diversity of specific social–legal objectives. In each case, what is more, the recourse to legal policing measures has to be balanced with another governmental interest in protecting speech. In its turn, protected 'speech' entails a series of rights and interests exercised by diverse agents of production, distribution and reception. In other words, despite the charge that they simply 'reflect' First Amendment absolutism by misrepresenting harmful conduct as protected speech (MacKinnon, 1987, p. 165), the courts do not enshrine a philosophical-liberal conception of rights, since in delimiting rights of expression they are dealing with the pragmatic question of how particular practices and diverse behaviours associated with pornography are to be regulated. Finally, it is only when practices such as those considered in these precedents pose problems which pedagogic and ethical strategies of management do not adequately resolve, that legal policing measures are seen to be warranted.

Since precedent does not permit the regulation by the Ordinance of otherwise protected speech, the Court then asks whether there is a compelling state interest which would justify a new exception to First Amendment guarantees (pp. 1335–7). Here the Court notes that the premise of the Ordinance is that the discrimination of pornography degrades women as a class, and so does not require specifically defined victims for most of the proscriptions introduced. The reality of this discrimination is not denied. The Court rehearses the arguments that pornography negatively affects those women who suffer the direct abuse of its production or on whom violent kinds of performance are imposed, and that exposure to pornography fosters discriminatory attitudes and behaviours, and causes in its male viewers 'an increased willingness to aggress toward women' (p. 1336). The defendants argue that just as the Supreme Court accepted as constitutional legislation which regulates obscenity as harmful to people, so too should the Court now accept legislation which regulates pornography as harmful specifically to women (pp. 1336–7).

However, the Court distinguishes between judicial and legislative functions. It says that there may be good reason to support legislative action such as the finding on which the Ordinance is based. The Court's own role is not to question the legislative finding but 'to ensure that the Ordinance accomplishes its purpose without violating constitutional standards or impinging upon constitutionally protected rights' (p. 1337). In this framework, the Court reiterates that the Ordinance seeks to regulate protected speech, and states that in its own role it 'cannot legitimately embark on judicial policy-making, carving out a new exception to the First Amendment' for this or some other interest group claiming to be victimized by 'unfair expression' (p. 1337).

Faced with this daunting series of precedential and procedural distinctions, we might well be drawn towards the seeming clarity and directness of a less differentiating and temporising mode of argument and decision-making. Yet, as previously, we would then have to ask: what would be the practical consequences of throwing these legal distinctions away? Would it be feasible to pass the policing of pornography entirely over to a domain other than the law, for instance to pedagogy or to sociology? The Court itself, in fact, acknowledges such an 'alternative' domain when it refers to the discrimination of pornography against women as a class as a 'sociological harm' diminishing the legal and social status of women (p. 1335). However, having admitted the notion of a 'social' judgement and administration of pornography, the Court moves to recognise the limits of its own competence, which reaches no further than the limits of the legal sphere. The Court thus contends that necessary or desirable changes in 'sociological patterns' (p. 1337) are not likely to be brought about by legislative dictate. This is, perhaps, the Court's way of admitting that there is no single or unified truth of pornography, and that the legal definition and management of obscenity is pursued not in some unbounded and undifferentiated space but within the confines of a jurisdiction. This delimitation of institutional competence is in keeping with our argument that the governmental pedagogies by means of which some sectors of the population have learned to problematise their own relation to erotica have not entirely replaced and cannot entirely be replaced by mechanisms of legal policing. A civil right not to be discriminated against by pornography cannot easily be superimposed as a generalised mechanism to police a pornographic field in which forms of self-regulation already play a significant role.

To argue that there are – and in the foreseeable future will need to be – limits on the scope of legal policing is not to imply that an attempt such as that made in the Ordinance to introduce a civil rights law against pornography creates a police state:

> Audiences of lawyers say it is politically naive to rely on courts to administer our pornography law our way. Then they say we should rely on existing law and existing courts for relief of any harms of pornography that they concede are real. Our civil rights law will produce a police state, they say. Then they recommend vigorous enforcement of criminal laws against rapists and batterers, whose victims are conceded to number well over half of all women. When told that they are, in effect, recommending reversing the numbers of those in and out of prisons, they say, do not rely on law at all. Now that we want a law against pornography, they say that law doesn't do anything significant anyway. Rely on the First Amendment – as if that is not a law. Forget law, educate – as if law is not educational. They say that the state is eager for the chance to suppress all sexually explicit materials. They have no explanation – these, the political sophisticates to our political naivete – for the fact that with a tool as vague and discretionary as criminal obscenity statues, this same state has stood by and watched the pornography industry double in the last ten years. Some day try solving a legal problem that has vexed legal minds for decades only to find (or, perhaps, to prove) that many people do not want it solved. And that many of these people are lawyers (MacKinnon, 1987, pp. 222–3, footnotes omitted).

MacKinnon's account of reactions to anti-pornography legislation should also serve to distinguish our arguments from those she attributes to liberal critics. For her, despite the appearance that the law's maintenance of free speech is disinterested, the administration of obscenity law is motivated by the underlying self-interest of those holding power within the patriarchal system. However, we would reject both the notion that the law must recognise an inalienable right of the individual to be free from regulation in the moral domain *and* that it feigns to do so because in reality it expresses an ideological will to power. The issue we have raised concerning the Ordinance is not that governmental regulation of morality is tantamount to censorship. Rather, we have argued that if the ethical problems created by pornography are to be taken seriously, so too are the historical and technical means whereby the 'ethos' of pornography has been produced and may be reformed.

Some form of what the Lockhart Report refers to as 'non-legal' regulation will almost certainly continue to play a crucial role in managing the production, circulation and use of sexual materials. We have shown that to determine where the line should be drawn between legal regulation and self-management the law has had to call on normative and interested knowledges, there being no detached and objective insight into the 'truth' about pornography. When the law calls on such knowledges, it does not act in bad faith or fail to align itself with some transcendent ethical principle of social justice. Sexual aesthetics and sexology are major disciplines of the self which have come to play a role in constructing and governing sexualities; yet their deployment of confessional strategies renders them not clearly distinguishable from a predominantly male auto-erotics. Seen in this light, the *Hudnut* decision is not retrograde. On the contrary, in balancing demands for legal and administrative policing against demands for self-management, it cannot but leave open the question of what are to be appropriate norms for assessing and regulating pornography.[9]

There is no reason to assume that the present ethical forms of regulation are established once and for all. Whilst philosophical liberalism and sexual aesthetics cannot be ignored in current projects of law reform, they might still prove precarious forms of self-management, their practice being always reliant on deployments of particular norms, knowledges and media in a pornographic field which remains constitutively unstable. Evidence of this instability is provided by the marked shift on the question of harm within liberal jurisprudence over the past two decades, under the dual influence of feminist campaigns on the status of women and recurring governmental and familialist concerns with the welfare of children.[10]

Mutation, complexity and disunity continue to characterise the pornographic field. This field now includes a mix of old, modified and nascent communications technologies – print, photography, film, cable television, video, telephone, videophone, computer – whose distributions and uses call for differential regulation according to criteria of reach, age, educational levels, public decency standards and so on. It is also made up of an open-ended series of established and novel interests in criticising, appreciating, regulating, embracing or adapting particular forms of pornography. While we have concentrated in this chapter on a major feminist critique of obscenity law and pornography, other quite different claims are pressed. So, for instance, some groups identifying themselves more or less with feminist or radical cultural politics (and from whose viewpoint the Dworkin–MacKinnon project would doubtless be seen as belonging to a puritanical feminism) have adapted the pornographic repertoire as the basis for an aestheticised and supposedly transgressive and therefore true performance of the self (see, for instance, the treatments of avantgarde erotica by Elinor Fuchs (1989), Linda Montano (1989) and Kate Davy (1989)). Or again, there are various gay and lesbian celebratory uses of pornography to form and intensify sexual identity through the re-functioning of heterosexual pornography. Disregarding their divergent contents and targets, feminist, gay and lesbian pornographies share a common form, now quite familiar to us. In each case pornography structures an exchange in which knowledge of the self is identified with the auto-erotic use of sexual representations and in which pleasure is extracted from the forms of probing the 'true self' beneath its mundane forms.

There is no certainty that affirmative uses of pornography escape or solve the problem of harms. For instance, there are those who contend from their own experience that the use of pornography is destructive, inasmuch as it creates violence in the gay community (*Pornography and Sexual Violence*, pp. 65–6). Surrounded by multiple interests and changes in the pornographic field, the law could not plausibly be expected to realise a single agreed truth of pornography. It has to mediate diverse and often competing interests which may be well-established or, like child rights, still in the process of crystallising. In these circumstances, the law can do no more than continue to treat obscenity as a variable category. By calculating the effects of particular distributions in terms of different audience interests, susceptibilities, competences and patterns of conduct; the law decides where the moveable line should be drawn between legal regulation and the available forms of self-regulation, not to mention regulation by administrative devices such as constraints on public funding of the arts, or the adjudication of legal or other actions generated by the resurgence of conservative campaigns to mobilise 'public opinion' against pornography and to challenge existing aesthetic conceptions of what is to be protected.

To return to our principal example and to clarify the relation between our historical studies and the law reform project of Dworkin and MacKinnon, let us say that we would endorse one element of that project but not the other. This is not a coy reluctance to take sides. It is, rather, a direct response to the fact that the case put by Dworkin and MacKinnon rests on two incommensurate intellectual postures: one concerns objectification and a recovery of repressed being; the other concerns discrimination and an effective administration of a positive constitutional right. In the terms used in this chapter, the former involves an objective in the field of aesthetics, the latter an objective in the field of law and government. Their incommensurability, as suggested in our brief anthropology of the aesthetic personality, is historical and practical not conceptual and theoretical. For a heuristic purpose, the distinction between self-management and legal regulation can be aligned with the distinction between aesthetic and government rationales for defining and dealing with pornography.

This alignment has a definite advantage; it reminds us that however clearly the distinction might be drawn in philosophical terms, in practice there has been no stable boundary between regulation by the criminal law and self-regulation by an aesthetic pedagogy. In both the United Kingdom and the United States, obscenity law has come increasingly to regulate pornography by grounding itself on pedagogic and aesthetic norms for assessing the conduct of individuals and defining what is to count as sexually 'mature' personalities. Even so, Dworkin and MacKinnon's philosophical critique of law as failing to recognise pornography's objectification of women cannot be articulated to legal policing in the form of a civil right. While this critique may, as part of a social *campaign*, have effects on people's attitudes, conducts and manners, its aesthetic components simply cannot be made into law. However, while the law cannot give unified expression to the categories of discrimination and objectification in the form of a global civil right not to be harmed by pornography, it can indeed construct and protect more limited and specific civil rights relating to anti-discrimination objectives. In other words, we see a choice to be decided, not a synthesis to be achieved. The choice is whether to pursue the fundamental transformation of society in order to de-objectify women's being, or to pursue specifically legal and administrative action to promote certain mentalities and behaviours, and to discourage others. The second option includes developing workplace codes of conduct aimed at reducing the incidence of sexual harassment of women and de-eroticising professional relationships and decision-making.[11]

Such action may of course be deemed superficial, a mere masking of the 'fundamental' problem of domination. Between them, in their aesthetic analyses, Dworkin and MacKinnon would reject each of the options. Dworkin has argued that, given existing social and gender relations, the act of sex is the fact of domination of women by men: 'that slit which means entry into her – intercourse – appears to be the key to women's lower human status' (Dworkin, 1987, p. 123). In her account, heterosexual mutuality can only register as a naive contradiction in terms. The evidence is, however, that even this forthrightness will not stop the fashioning of aesthetic images of human emancipation and completeness that are resolutely heterosexual, homosexual, bisexual, pansexual or nonsexual, each of which will claim in the name of a true species to judge the forms of positive law and government as constraining in more or less important respects.

As late in the piece as 1986, it was observed in the Hudson Report (p. 233) that the history of pornography had not yet been written. We hope to have made a beginning to the writing of this history, and to have learned some lessons. The form of erotic sensibility which we have described is an artefact of that particular phenomenon – book sex – whose history is a composite of definite interests and capacities, print and other media technologies, commerce, religion, government, moral and psychological medicine, relations of gender, levels of education and cultural literacy and, not least, the historical interactions of aesthetics, police and law. To attribute an essence to this contingent and mobile amalgam would be to fly in the face of plausibility and the historical evidence. Changes in arrangements for managing pornography cannot be assessed according to whether they promise the complete realisation of our sexual being. What can be achieved is better management – by the legal and ethical means actually available – of the forms of subjectivity which happen to have emerged for and among us.

Notes

1. See Reinhart Koselleck (1988). A parallel account of the emergence of technically and rationally organised forms of law and politics – although one in which the difference between state and civil society is less absolute than in Koselleck – can be found in Foucault (1981).
2. An attempt to introduce a similar ordinance in the City of Minneapolis had been unsuccessful when a Bill introducing an amendment to that city's Civil Rights Code was vetoed by the Mayor after having been passed by the

relevant Council. For a transcript of the first of two ordinances thus vetoed, see *Constitutional Commentary*, Vol. 2, No. 147, 1985, pp. 181–9. The transcript of the Minneapolis public hearing held in conjunction with this ordinance appears in the Everywoman publication *Pornography and Sexual Violence* (1988). Interest developed in other cities, states and countries in developing Bills along similar lines (see Seator, 1987, p. 299 including note 8; *Pornography and Sexual Violence*, pp. 4–5). A version of the Dworkin–MacKinnon ordinance was signed into law by the Mayor of Indianapolis, William H. Hudnut, on 1 May 1984 with amendments on 15 June 1984. It was promptly challenged in the courts on constitutional grounds by various parties including the American Booksellers Association, Inc. and the Association for American Publishers, Inc. – both major representatives of trade interests with elements located in but reaching well beyond Indianapolis – together with other distributional, library, retail, video-rental and reading-public interest groups or individuals. The United States District Court, S. D. Indiana, Indianapolis Division, granting that the action was a justiciable case or controversy under Article III of the Constitution, whereby plaintiffs need not be the subject of an administrative or judicial proceeding at the time the lawsuit is initiated, held that the ordinance was unconstitutional on First and Fifth Amendment grounds (*American Booksellers Association, Inc. v. Hudnut*, 198 F. Supp. 1316 (1984)). The decision was affirmed by the United States Court of Appeals, Seventh Circuit, (771 F. 2d 323 (1985)), whose finding was summarily affirmed by the United States Supreme Court (106 SCt 1772 (1986), rehearing denied 106 SCt 1664 (1986)).

3. In discussing the feminist ideas and goals which underlie the anti-pornography laws, Dworkin identifies pornography's subordination of women with objectification defined in a way that subsumes discrimination as dehumanisation:

> Objectification occurs when a human being, through social means, is made less than human, turned into a thing or commodity, bought and sold. When objectification occurs, a person is depersonalised, so that no individuality or integrity is available socially or in what is an extremely circumscribed privacy. . . . Objectification is an injury right at the heart of discrimination: those who can be used as if they are not fully human are no longer fully human in social terms; their humanity is hurt by being diminished (Dworkin, 1985, p. 15).

4. This critique of law builds upon the feminist idea of a continuum in which pornography both becomes a metaphor for a series of cultural and political practices determined by the same logic of misrepresentation and subordination of women's being and naturalises those practices by eroticising inequality (cf. MacKinnon, 1987, p. 171–4). For a discussion of problems involved in treating pornography as a metaphor for sex discrimination in general, see Lesley Stern (1982).

5. For a historical discussion of sex discrimination and the Fourteenth Amendment, see Morais (1988). On the expansion of interest in the United States in articulating ethical objectives on issues of sexuality and sexual pol-

itics to governmental administration of civil rights and liberties, see Kim Ezra Shienbaum (ed.) (1988).

6. Broadly speaking, we can identify two lines of argument in jurisprudential responses to the Ordinance and *Hudnut*. MacKinnon's negative view of the category of 'speech' in obscenity regulation and her belief that the *Hudnut* decision reveals the sexist bias of the law is shared by several other writers. For example, Penelope Seator argues that in *Hudnut* the courts fail to recognise the reality of pornography as sex discrimination, reinforcing harmful conducts under the guise of defending a right of free expression equally available to all. The social reality of discrimination is thus reduced to a mere idea which, according to the 'liberal, idealistic philosophy reflected in the decision' is sacrosanct under the First Amendment (1987, p. 352). The decision shows that the 'first amendment is a tool of male hegemony' (p. 352). The courts' maintenance of a distinction between obscenity and pornography is seen as a political refusal to recognise women's experience and civil rights. A status quo is thus said to be preserved in which legislation made from the male point of view is not seen as from a point of view; it is only legislation written from the point of view of those injured by pornography rather than those gaining profit, pleasure and power from it that is found to be viewpoint discrimination (p. 354).

In other responses, 'speech' in the context of pornography is not treated as a fundamentally ideological category. Some writers, acknowledging that pornography is problematic or harmful, maintain to a greater or lesser degree a negative conception of free speech as a given right of the individual, such that the Ordinance poses for them a risk of 'censorship' leading onto the slippery slope of loss of fundamental liberties (cf. James Branit, 1986) or, indeed, plays into the hands of a reactionary, antifeminist moral crusade against pornography (Lisa Duggan, 1988). Numerous liberal and feminist writers, while treating the attempt to translate the generalised idea of pornographic 'subordination' of women into law with a degree of scepticism, identify 'speech' positively with processes of educational change (cf. Winifred Sendler, 1985; Geoffrey Stone, 1986).

7. The Court also considers Fifth Amendment due process requirements including overbreadth, prior restraint and vagueness which affects the *scienter* requirement (pp. 1337–41).

8. Of course, the spirit of the Ordinance is to seek not paternalistic protection but redress against sex discrimination. However, the problem encountered in extending the principle of protecting minors to control harms flowing more generally from pornography's subordination of women indicates that the form of governmental 'protection' first associated with medical–moral norms (according to which, as we have seen, women were indeed linked with children as vulnerable subjects) has given way to more sophisticated and differentiated calculations concerning parties affected by pornography. The problems posed by an aesthetic commitment to a universal and undifferentiated subject arise in relation to a lower-level set of discriminations – by gender, age, social situation, level of education and so on – which *for some purposes* women might want to make.

9. To cite the Court of Appeals (771 F. 2d, pp. 329–30), pornography's harms demonstrate pornography's power as speech. In other words, the subordi-

nation and discrimination it creates and maintains depend on particular technologies of media sex, and if the constructions of male sexuality which these involve are to be changed, then this requires forms of intellectual and ethical mediation which, while they may be aligned with the law, are not reducible to it.

10. From this point of view, feminism is clearly the major force contending to redefine the norms operating in what the Court of Appeals refers to as the 'socializing' effects of pornography. We have already seen that the agnosticism professed in the Lockhart Report in support of deregulation does not cut much ice in more recent governmental calculations (cf. the Hudson Report, pp. 299–351). On the shift with regard to harms, see also the *Report of the Special Committee on Pornography and Prostitution; Pornography and Prostitution in Canada, Summary* (1985, pp. 11–13, 45–56) and the recent New Zealand *Report of the Ministerial Committee of Inquiry into Pornography* (1989, pp. 38–47).

11. In *Pornography and Sexual Violence* (pp. 77–9) appears the testimony of a woman employed as a plumber who objected to the display of pornography at her workplace and whose attempts – supported by affirmative rights officers – to have it removed, drew retaliations such that she sought a transfer. Administrative measures to prevent or resolve such situations are inscribed in that part of the Ordinance which makes it actionable to force pornography on a person in employment, education, the home or public places. For such a right to be fully effective it needs to be linked to other economic and civil guarantees of employment, equity, participation and the like. Jeffrey Minson has brought to our attention the promulgation of public service regulations in Australia which include the display of offensive sexual materials in the workplace among those activities which constitute harassment, mentioning for instance 'provocative posters with a sexual connotation. Even works of art may be inappropriate on occasions' (Public Service Board, Australia, 1986, p. 3). It is suggested by William Brigman (1985, p. 501) that the 'forcing' of pornography in the work environment might be treated as a form of sexual harassment and hence as a violation of the United States Civil Rights Act of 1964. Similarly, the sensitisation which has occurred in governmental contexts to problems of prejudicial stereotyping of women, such that it is possible to register and refer to law certain of its discriminatory effects, is arguably related in some measure to campaigns criticising media and other objectification and subordination of women. This is reflected in recent legal decisions such as that made by the United States Supreme Court requiring Price Waterhouse to appoint a women employee to full partnership with back pay because its promotions review system had permitted 'negatively sexually stereotyped comments to influence partnership selection' *The Weekend Australian* 10–11 November 1990, p. 45). We may also note here complex issues surrounding the interests and rights of those harmed in the production of pornography, one of the areas of 'forcing' with which the Ordinance is concerned. The Hudson Report (pp. 595–735) deals with preventions, penalties and remedies specifically in relation to the production of child pornography, including child abuse in this production, and the problem of welfare assistance for runaway or homeless young people.

References

Branit, James R. (1986) 'Reconciling Free Speech and Equality: What Justifies Censorship?', *Harvard Journal of Law and Public Policy*, vol. 9, no. 2 pp. 429–60.

Davy, Kate (1989) 'Reading Past the Heterosexual Imperative: Dress Suits to Hire', *The Drama Review*, vol. 33, no. 1, pp. 153–70 (New York: New York University).

Duggan, Lisa (1988) 'Censorship in the Name of Feminism', in Chester, G. and Dickey, J. (eds) (1988) pp. 76–86.

Dworkin, Andrea (1985) 'Against the Male Flood: Censorship, Pornography and Equality', *Harvard Women's Law Journal*, vol. 8, pp. 1–27.

Dworkin, Andrea (1987) *Intercourse* (London: Secker and Warburg).

Foucault, Michel (1981) 'Omnes et Singulation: Towards a Criticism of "Political Reason" ', in S. McMurrin (ed.) *The Tanner Lectures on Human Values* (Salt Lake City: University of Utah Press).

Fuchs, Elinor (1989) 'Staging the Obscene Body', *The Drama Review*, vol. 33, no. 1, pp. 33–58.

Kappeler, Susanne (1986) *The Pornography of Representation* (Cambridge: Polity Press).

Koselleck, Reinhart (1988) *Critique and Crisis: Enlightenment and the Pathogenesis of Modern Society* (Oxford: New York and Hamburg: Berg).

MacKinnon, Catharine A. (1987) *Feminism Unmodified: Discourses on Life and Law* (Cambridge, Massachusetts: Harvard University Press).

Montano, Linda (1989) 'Summer Saint Camp', *The Drama Review*, vol. 33, no. 1, pp. 94–103.

Morais, Nina (1988) 'Sex Discrimination and the Fourteenth Amendment', *Yale Law Journal*, vol. 97, no. 6, pp. 1153–72.

Seator, Penelope (1987) 'Judicial indifference to pornography's harm: *American Booksellers v. Hudnut* (Women's Law Forum)', *Golden Gate University Law Review*, vol. 17, pp. 297–358.

Shienbaum, Kim Ezra (ed.) (1988) *Legislating Morality: Private Choices on the Public Agenda* (Rochester, Vermont: Schenkman Books).

Stern, Lesley (1982) 'The Body as Evidence', *Screen*, vol. 23, no. 5, pp. 38–60.

Stone, Geoffrey R. (1986) 'Anti-Pornography Legislation as Viewpoint-Discrimination', *Harvard Journal of Law and Public Policy*, vol. 9, no. 2, pp. 461–80.

20

Arjuna Parakrama, *De-Hegemonising Language Standards: Learning from (Post)Colonial Englishes about 'English'* (1995)

If language was one of the main emphases of theory as it developed in the 1960s, whether in theory's semiotic or deconstructionist forms, the 'language' appealed to was remarkably unspecific, lacking both a history (modern linguistics after all was inaugurated by the replacing of the diachronic by the synchronic) and a geography (no attention was paid to the linguistic power relations between centre and periphery either at the national or international level).

While linguistics itself went on to develop specific interests in the sociality of language, in the form of socio-linguistics and discourse analysis, this interest was largely ignored by those concerned with the analysis of literature and culture; as too was the major development of English as a world language. Arjuna Parakrama's *De-Hegemonizing Language Standards: Learning from (Post)Colonial Englishes about 'English'* focuses on both. At the centre of the book is the question 'what is the range of variation within a standard language and what decides that range?' It is a question that no linguistic theory has really begun to pose, despite the fact that it is obvious even from the domestic history of English (where the extent of variation is much greater in Early Modern than in Modern English) that the range is not fixed. For Parakrama, the example of 'Other Englishes' – his particular reference is to Lankan English – makes evident that the standard is always a hegemonic project, to be understood only in terms of the power relations reproduced within educational systems. The study of postcolonial varieties of English makes strikingly clear that the standard is not some 'neutral' description but a deliberate attempt to exclude the speech of those who do not conform. *De-Hegemonizing Language Standards* is an extended argument in favour of a substantial broadening of the standard so as to embrace a much wider variety of social experiences. The argument is prefaced by a demonstration, reprinted here, of just what such a broadening might involve, juxtaposing a 'concrete' piece, written within a utopianly enlarged standard, with an 'abstract' one, written within standard academic English.

Introduction

Concrete

I done shown Standard spoken English as standing up only for them smug-arse social élites. And it ain't really no different for no written English neither. The tired ways in which the standardised languages steady fucked over the users of other forms had became clear when we went and studied them (post)colonial Englishes. Them 'other' Englishes came and made it impossible to buy into sacred cows like native speaker authority because there from the getgo there are only *habichole* users, not natives!

I ask why is it that, say, 'She say I is not good people' and 'She telling I no good fello, no!' are murder to the 'educated' except in the ghetto of 'creative' contexts, whereas something like 'In the conversations that have transpired during our acquaintance, she has intimated to me personally that she cannot bring herself to consider myself to be admirably suitable with respect to my individual character' is only deemed 'wordy', but clearly shows a 'command' of the language? The hegemony of hep standard languages and cool registers which hide where they are coming from, by a shitload of 'arbitrary' rules and 'other-people-in-power-require-'isms is read for points by these non-standard varieties like and unlike the ones I be mixing and jamming here.[1]

If hegemony be maintained through putting up and policing standards, and if a kind of 'passive revolution'[2] manages opposition by allowing for a piss-trickle of the previously non-standard into the standard, then you's resisting when you's refusing the self-evidence of the rules and the proper. Mistakes and bad taste, whether deliberate or not, whether in organised groups or not (as counter-hegemony), is always subversive, though sometimes 'wastefully' so, because they cannot be absorbed into the standard as easily. These non-standard stuff is therefore 'natural' resistance and a sensitive index of non-mainstream against-hegemony. Persistent mistakes and bad taste fuck the system up because they cannot be patronised if you dont accept the explaination, so they fail your ass at the university and say you need remediation like its the pox.

The lastma final word, then, is to go like crazy for the broadest standard and to be psyched up to steady talk in it, teach your head off in it, write like mad in it, despite of its sometime 'oddness' to our ears, refusing of the uncomfortable laughter, inspite the difficulty, paying no mind to some non-standard users and their liberal advocates having an attitude bout it. The ideal, then, is for what is standard now to become contaminated with what is non-standard now, and arse backwards, so much so that everyone will have to know more about what everyone else speaks/writes, and so that not knowing, say, 'black english' will be as much a disqualification as not knowing 'general american'. There should even be room for a certain amount of self-inconsistency as well. Complete intelligibility is a cheap hoax anyway, so it's necessary, yar, to bring this to the up front level, nehi? Alas, putative private languages are the only ones that are out, at least until someone refutes Wittgenstein[3] or until they go public.

All this wont be in place for a long time, and mebbe never, but anything else isn't worth this pul try. As teachers we don't often let blatant sexism and racism get by from our students just because their views are shared by many in power all over the world. Why the hell do we excuse away language values and non-language values hidden within language values, then? All things considered, and *ceteris paribus*, it is my expert and dispassionate opinion, therefore, that, in punishing 'error' so brutally yet so selectively and in laying the blame elsewhere, or in saying in the appropriately subdued tone, 'what else can we do?', the language teacher is pimping with a vengeance for the system while masturbating his/her conscience with this 'empowerment' crap.

Abstract

Champions of the so-called Other [or (post)colonial] Englishes have operated on the basis of the special status of these varieties, thereby justifying the formulation of different criteria for their analysis. A careful examination of the processes of standardization as they affect these 'Others' (particularly 'South Asian English'.) strips the camouflage from standardisation which can be seen as the hegemony of the 'educated' élites, hence the unquestioned paradigm of the 'educated standard'. These standards are kept in place in 'first world' contexts by a technology of reproduction which dissimulates this hegemony through the self-represented neutrality of prestige and precedent whose selectivity is a function of the politics of publication. In these 'other' situations, the openly conflictual nature of the language context makes such strategies impossible. The non-standard is one of the most accessible means of 'natural' resistance, and, therefore, one of the most sensitive indices of de-hegemonisation.

Treating these Englishes as equivalent in every way to their 'parent' forms leads to the re-evaluation of cherished linguistic paradigms such as 'native speaker authority', since hitherto self-evident categories such as this are fraught in the (post)colonial contexts.

Taking the discriminatory nature of the standard seriously and also accepting the necessity of standards, however attenuated, this thesis argues for the active broadening of the standard to include the greatest variety possible; it also holds that the 'acceptable' bounds of general linguistic tolerance will expand with the systematic and sanctioned exposure to such variety.

A case study of de-hegemonisation at work exemplifies this theory of resistance in/through language as it focuses on the Sri Lankan context both in colonial times and today, where the 'English' language is shown to exist in non-standard form, at once theorizable, resistant and innovative. The analysis of written and spoken discourse, supplemented by a historical account of attitudes to English (culminating in a current attitudinal linguistic survey), serves as a prolegomenon to the work that lies ahead for language planners and teachers who wish to widen, strategically, the acceptable range of variation within the standard. This would force (post)-colonial hybridity-as-conflict in the periphery upon the ('western') centre, which will in turn pre-empt 'business as usual' there.

Notes

1. Two observations. This is a mish-mash because the brother wants to show-off essentialist notions of dialect use which ghettoise non-standard forms. Black English is not spoken only by blacks, nor do all blacks speak it, no? This means also that questions of 'authenticity' and 'appropriateness' (semi-literates can only talk in 'vulgarisms') must also be questioned like a mutherfucker. This, of course, does not let whatever dialect or *tuppahi* mish-mash language off the hook if it is racist, regionalist and so on and so forth. Second, why is the 'appropriate liberal response to this *achcharu*, a snicker-giggle? What does this cover-up? At what point in these matters does proving a point become also interventionist practice, not tokenism?

   This operation can then be termed 'strategic de-essentialisation' to parody or upside-downify Spivak's phrase. It attacks notions of (originary) purity even in the oppressed linguistic situation, and confronts the issue of mediated representation through language form. To trash Wittgenstein for a worthy cause, if language be a form of life, then the form of language is telling us nothing epistemologically new about the form of this form of life. What is up for grabs are habits and practices, contextually creative vocabularies and so on, but not systems/possibilities/limits of knowing, because, after all, standard and non-standard forms of language are so differentiated for political reasons, not philosophical ones.

2. *Contra* Gramsci, not merely restricted to relatively weak hegemony, but also strong, pre-empting effective counter-hegemony.

3. This refers of course to the celebrated Private Language Argument, but there is a critique of 'ordinary language' itself embedded here which confuddles the hell out of the 'ordinary' as always-already hegemonic through the collective (mis)use of words such as 'attitude' and 'read' in this piece.

21

Christopher Norris, *Resources of Realism: Prospects for 'Post-Analytic' Philosophy* (1997)

Resources of Realism is concerned with current issues in epistemology and philosophical semantics. It defends a causal-realist approach to theories and explanations in the natural sciences and a truth-based propositional semantics for natural language derived from various sources. Among these sources – unusually in this kind of discussion – is the work of William Empson. Norris argues against various forms of anti-realist (or ontological–relativist) doctrine with regard both to the truth-claims of science and to the construal of intentions, meanings, and beliefs in the process of linguistic understanding. He also offers some incisive criticisms of the 'hermeneutic turn' in the philosophy of language and science, as well as of those kindred schools of thought that would relativise truth to some cultural context or background horizon of consensus beliefs.

In this extract from a chapter entitled 'Complex Words *versus* Minimalist Semantics', Norris makes his strong case for the importance of the contribution that Empson's *The Structure of Complex Words* can make to current issues in linguistics, literary theory and philosophical semantics.

Complex words *versus* minimalist semantics: Empson and Davidson

Empson on truth, meaning, and interpretation

In this chapter I shall put the case that William Empson's *The Structure of Complex Words* (1951) is among the most important and distinctive contributions to issues in present-day linguistics, literary theory, and philosophical semantics.[1] That the book has been largely ignored by philosophers – and received far less than its due share of attention from literary critics – is no doubt the result of its cutting across these conventional divisions of academic labour. Thus the critics have mostly been repelled or mystified by Empson's theoretical chapters (his apparatus of logico-semantic 'machinery') while the philosophers, Donald Davidson among them, have picked up one or two useful ideas but pretty much ignored the way that these ideas are put to work in the close-reading of texts.[2] This seems to me an unfortunate state of affairs since Complex Words is, among other things, the single most sustained and resourceful attempt to bring those disciplines together. In particular it offers a promising escape-route from the dead-end (as I see it) of Davidsonian 'minimalist semantics', that is, the idea that speakers and interpreters can simply get along on 'wit, luck, and wisdom' or with the aid of 'passing theories' that really come down to just intuitive guesswork plus an all-purpose optimizing 'principle of charity'.[3] Such arguments have lately exerted great appeal among post-analytical philosophers and also among a growing number of literary critics in the neopragmatist (or 'against theory') camp.[4] In what follows I shall therefore address myself to both readerships and hope to over-come the various sorts of prejudice that have so far prevented an ade-quate assessment of Empson's remarkable book.

His main purpose in *Complex Words* is to offer some account of what goes on when we encounter certain uses of language – whether in poems, novels, or everyday speech – that are felt to carry implications beyond their normal semantic range. Most often there is a sense, on the reader's or listener's part, that the whole weight of argument is condensed into some particular word in context, thus allowing that word to communicate a kind of 'compacted doctrine', an order of implied entailment-relations between two or more of its possible meanings. Thus Empson devotes the early (and most densely theoreti-cal) chapters of his book to a working-out of the various 'equations' – the structures of logico-semantic entailment – which explain how it is that language can achieve such a variety of subtly suggestive effects. These are all derivatives of the basic structure 'A = B', that is, the stan-dard form of subject-predicate logic which has dominated Western thinking from Aristotle to its latter-day revision and refinement by logicians such as Frege and Quine. On the whole Empson accepts this model as adequate for his own purposes, sometimes alluding to recent work in the field (chiefly by Russell and F. P. Ramsey), but otherwise deploying a fairly traditional range of analytic terms. Where his book does break new ground – and where it should be of interest to philoso-phers – is in its further claim that such modes of logical analysis can usefully be carried over from the level of sentences, statements, or propositions to that of individual 'complex words'. By analysing the various orders of 'equation' or 'compacted statement' carried by certain words in context, the interpreter may avoid having recourse to ill-defined rhetorical terms like 'ambiguity', 'paradox', or 'emotive' meaning. For the effect of such recourse – in literary criticism as in ethics, linguistics, philosophical semantics and elsewhere – is to close off any prospect of improved communicative grasp and thus make language appear more illogical, more prone to forms of irrational mystery-mongering, than is actually (or typically) the case.

This is why, as Empson remarks in a footnote, 'the term Ambiguity, which I used in a book title and as a kind of slogan, implying that the reader is left in doubt between two readings, is more or less superseded by the idea of a double meaning which is intended to be fitted into a definite structure' (*Complex Words*, p. 103n; the reference is to Empson's earlier and much better-known book *Seven Types of Ambiguity*[5]) – Granted there are cases – 'Type IV' equations as he calls them – where it is hard for analysis to get a hold since the implied doctrine is either so vague (as in certain passages of Wordsworth) or so downright and flatly paradoxical (as in various statements of religious faith) that it simply defies rational understanding.[6] But even here, Empson argues, we still do better to assume that 'the human mind is not irredeemably lunatic, and cannot be made so' (*Complex Words*, p. 83n). Which is also to say that we can only make sense of such cases – figure out the deviant 'logic' involved – by seeing how they manage to *exploit or circumvent* the more usual (rationally accountable) forms of logico-semantic equation. For it is against this background of everyday linguistic competence – our ability to assign meanings and motives on a basis of shared understanding – that we can at least grasp the rhetorical gist of such deviant ('Type IV') specimens. Moreover, Empson suggests, '[i]t is because the historical background is so rich and still so much alive . . . that one can fairly do what seems absurdly unhistorical, make a set of equations from first principles' (p. 269). In other words, there is no contradiction – despite some degree of theoretical strain – between Empson's interpreting his various authors always with the *Oxford English Dictionary* to hand (that is, his concern to work within the range of plausible, historically documented meanings) and on the other hand his offering a generalized theory, a logical grammar of complex words with strong universalist claims.

This should really not appear so much of a paradox to anyone familiar (say) with Chomskian linguistics or related developments in cognitive psychology and philosophical semantics.[7] It requires nothing more than the working premise that speakers can produce (and interpreters understand) a vast potentially infinite range of utterances on the basis of a finite – hence intelligible – stock of grammatical ground-rules, transformational structures, logical entailment-relations, and so forth. Indeed I have put the case elsewhere that Empson's approach – or something very like it – is the most promising (if so far neglected) candidate for a theory of semantic interpretation that would meet the requirements laid down by Chomsky in his later writings on the subject.[8] However, my main concern here is with Davidson and his failure to pursue some of these paths opened up by Empson's work. Most important is his distinction between 'head meaning' and 'chief meaning', which I think Davidson must have had in mind when formulating his own (less elaborate) ideas about prior and passing theories.[9] For Empson, the 'head meaning' of a complex word is that which 'holds a more or less permanent position as the first one in its structure' (*Complex Words*, p. 38). There may well be various criteria for deciding on this, such as its 'being the most frequent in use or the one supported by derivation'. Moreover – and crucially for Empson's later chapters of applied literary analysis – 'a word may change from having one meaning as the head to having another, or a writer may impose a head meaning of his own' (p. 38). Nevertheless it is the case – as with Davidson's 'prior theory' – that we are here in the region of a relatively generalised (high-level) order of semantic grasp where communicative uptake depends much more on the interpreter's being 'at home' in the language than on his or her responding to local indications that the word has undergone some semantic shift under pressure of context or speaker's/author's intent. Perhaps, Empson concedes, 'the term is merely a convenience which needs subdividing'; still 'it never refers only to the example of a use of the word which is being considered at the moment' (p. 38). It thus remains distinct from what Empson designates the 'chief meaning' in any given case: that which 'the user feels to be the first one in play at the moment', or which 'the speaker if challenged would normally pick out . . . as "what he really meant" ' (ibid.). And again, by way of helpful analogy: 'if the "chief meaning" is allowed a suggestion of local or tribal chieftains I think it can easily be remembered as applying only to a local occasion' (ibid.).

Empson distinguishes various ways in which a single word can 'carry a doctrine' or be felt to communicate some item of purportedly veridical belief. The first – and most fundamental – is the 'Existence Assertion', that which must standardly be taken to imply that 'what the word names is really there and worth naming'. Of course such assertions may be false, misleading, or fictitious, a point to which Empson repeatedly returns when discussing the more dubious varieties of 'Type IV' equation. For that matter, 'Aristotle pointed out that a syllogism might be regarded as a redefinition followed by a tautology', and something similar might apply to 'the word "electron" in the writings of any one physicist who claimed to put forward a complete atomic theory; all the properties should somehow be included in the idea' (p. 40). But one can best start out, Empson thinks, by adopting some basic formal notation (such as the existential quantifier ∃) which can then most often be taken for granted as a part of the implied background whenever some utterance is felt to carry any kind of assertoric force. This amounts to something very like Davidson's 'principle of charity', that is, the principle that speakers will normally mean what they say, that their meanings can only be construed on a basis of imputed (presumptively true) beliefs, and therefore that we must count them 'right on most matters' if they (and we) are to have any chance of achieving communicative uptake.[10]

The same rule applies – as both Davidson and Empson suggest – to cases where the belief in question may strike the listener/reader as either plain false or in need of further (perhaps more 'charitable') interpretation. Thus, in Empson's words, there is often the sense of an obscure truth-claim 'when really the mental goings-on are more confused'. Even so, 'a "verbal fiction" may need a great deal of looking into, and the full analysis of it may be very complex, but so far as the speaker is wholly deceived by it I think we must accept his own view that he is simply using it for an existence assertion' (*Complex Words*, p. 40). For otherwise – and up to this point he agrees with Davidson – we cannot make a start in understanding what they say on the basis of belief-ascriptions which may diverge widely from our own ideas of rationally warranted belief, yet which none the less enable us to figure out the speaker's gist by a process of (more or less complex) rational reconstruction. In short, we need to count them 'right on most matters' – or wrong only with regard to certain specific items of belief – if we are to see how some localised instance of mistaken reasoning or false analogy has got in the way of our construing their words at face (truth-preserving) value.

So it is, Empson argues, that we are able to interpret even the more irrational ('Type IV') equations as the upshot of obscure yet intelligible processes of thought which can provide a basis for communicative uptake despite all the deep-laid obstacles involved. However, as I have said, there is a crucial difference between Davidson's and Empson's way of applying this generalised principle of charity. For in Empson's case it requires a recognition that some beliefs are indeed false, and that to interpret them properly – that is, against the background of warranted or justified belief – is to see just how far, and in what precise ways, they deviate from the kinds of logico-semantic structure that characterise our 'normal or waking habits of thought'. On Davidson's account, conversely, the principle assumes such a blanket and all-purpose 'charitable' guise that it leaves no room for elementary distinctions between truth and the attitude of holding-true, or veridical belief and whatever lays claim to that title on the say-so of this or that individual speaker, Quinean 'native informant', or local community of like-minded persons.[11]

Newton-Smith makes this point most effectively when he remarks – *à propos* various relativist trends in present-day philosophy of science – that there is something very wrong with a theory where every belief necessarily comes out right just so long as we apply the standard Davidsonian rule. Thus: 'it is fashionable to argue in some quarters that one can transcendentally justify a principle of charity which ordains us to endeavour to maximize the ascription of true beliefs in the interpretation of the discourse of others'.[12] But the effect of this ordinance – if carried right through – is to undermine the very distinction between truth and falsehood by confusing what speakers or thinkers may *truly be held to believe* with what they *rightly or justifiably believe* according to the best available criteria of theoretical consistency, valid argument, evidential warrant, and so forth. Quite simply, 'we do not always want to be charitable', and that for reasons which may indeed dispose us to count other people wrong on some matters, but which thereby promote the shared human interest in advancing knowledge through forms of rational, constructive, truth-seeking endeavour. As Newton-Smith puts it:

[w]hatever plausibility the claim has that the principle of charity is a sort of *a priori* constraint on the interpretation of the ordinary discourse of others, it has no plausibility as a constraint on the theoretical discourse of others. The simple reason is that we well understand how easy it is to have a theory that turns out to be totally incorrect. While it may be hard to see how a group of people could cope with the everyday world in the face of massively mistaken beliefs (this is what gives the principle its plausibility), it is easy to see how a group can be utterly mistaken at the theoretical level.[13]

Thus Davidsonian 'charity' comes out looking more like a vote of no confidence in human reason, or – what amounts to much the same thing – an approach that allows for no adequate distinction between knowledge arrived at through a process of disciplined, self-critical enquiry and beliefs (or attitudes of holding-true) whose warrant is a matter of their happening to fit with other such currently accepted items of belief. Thus a way is left open for cultural relativists or post-modern-pragmatists like Richard Rorty to recruit Davidson in support of the idea that truth *just is* whatever counts as such within this or that interpretive community.[14]

What is needed in order to avoid this unfortunate upshot is a theory of truth (or of validity in interpretation) which conserves the principle of charity up to a point but which doesn't push that principle so far that it collapses into a kind of all-licensing relativist outlook. This is why Empson is so careful to distinguish between, on the one hand, the idea that we should interpret speakers as most likely having reasons (or intelligible motives) for saying and believing what they do, and on the other the equally important principle that those beliefs may on occasion be wrong – products of false analogy and the like – and thus interpretable only by way of a more complex (critical-evaluative) treatment. Thus there are, on his reckoning, five basic 'ways in which a word can carry a doctrine'. The first has to do with existence-assertions – symbolised by Russell's ∃ – whose truth-conditions may well be obscure, or whose analysis may lead rather quickly into regions where there seems little choice but to accept, with Davidson, that 'truth' must be relativized to speaker's belief or the attitude of holding-true. At the limit, Empson thinks, 'the complexity of the word is simply that of the topic', so that (for instance) 'most newspaper headlines . . . must be supposed to make assertions of this sort' (*Complex Words*, p. 40). Such cases are therefore not of much interest for his own purpose, except in so far as 'the feeling [they give] of simplicity and irreducibility is often borrowed by the other types, to make themselves stronger, so that they are easily confused with it'. However, the prospects improve very markedly – so Empson maintains – when attention shifts to the logical 'grammar' (or the structures of logico-semantic implication) whose range is roughly covered by the other four ways in which doctrines are carried by words. For these are less open to the kinds of rhetorical imposition – by false analogy, concealed premises, affirming the consequent and so forth – which can easily work their effects where the whole weight of argument is borne by some strong if obscure use of the existence-assertion.

I had better now offer some sample passages from *Complex Words* in order to convey what Empson wants to do with his pieces of logico-semantic 'machinery'. The first two chapters describe the theoretical scope of his project and – I would argue – suggest just how far short of it Davidson falls by retreating to a minimalist-semantic position where there seems little point in maintaining the distinction between head and chief senses, 'prior' and 'passing' theories, or matters of generalised linguistic competence and matters of local interpretative grasp. First Empson's chart (p. 54) of the five equations according to the implied order of priority between subject and predicate:

The major sense of the word is the . . . Subject			Predicate
The sense demanded by the most			
immediate context is the . . . Subject		II	I
. . . . Predicate		III	V
The order of the two senses is indifferent:		IV	

Type IV would seem to cover existence-assertions of the vaguer, more inclusive or logically recalcitrant kind, as well as 'deep' para-doxical truth-claims or instances (like Wordsworth's pantheistic 'sense') where 'the middle term is cut out' and where 'the whole poetical and philosophical effect comes from the violent junction of sensedata to the divine imagination given by love' (p. 296). But we can get more idea of how the method works from Empson's descrip-tion of the various sorts of equation – or orders of logico-semantic entailment – that are carried by complex words. For it then becomes clear that such 'deviant' (Type IV) cases can best be understood against the normative background provided by Types I to III and V. And this applies even to those puzzling cases where it seems that the whole weight of argument is borne by some paradox or false analogy which must either be taken on its own rhetorical terms (as carrying an obscure but powerful existence-assertion) or else treated as merely 'emotive' and hence beyond reach of rational understanding. In so far as we are able to interpret such instances at all – rather than consign them to some private dimension of associative whimsy, chronic malapropism, linguistic psychopathology, or the like – they cannot be entirely discontinuous with what Empson calls our 'normal waking habits' of logico-semantic grasp. After all, as he says, 'I am trying to write linguistics not psychology; something *quite* unconscious and unintentional, even if the hearer catches it like an infection, is not part of an act of communication' (p. 31).

This may give some idea of how much has dropped out in the passage of translation from Empson's highly elaborated theory to Davidson's minimalist–semantic approach. Of course the comparison would have less point if Davidson had never read Empson or discovered nothing of interest in *Complex Words*; but there is evidence enough to suggest otherwise, both in footnotes and the general drift of his thinking between 'On the Very Idea of a Conceptual Scheme' and 'A Nice Derangement of Epitaphs'. Besides, it seems to me – to strengthen the case – that Davidson's work might have offered more resistance to the current neo-pragmatist/'against theory' trend had he attended more closely to Empson's passages of detailed logico-semantic exegesis. The point is best made in connection with those kinds of obscure existence-assertion that Empson thinks it important to analyse so that we are not too much at the mercy of irrational creeds or doctrines. Thus:

I think that the same feeling of assertion is carried over to an entirely different case, which I shall call an 'equation' and propose to divide into four types. Two senses of the word are used at once, and also (which does not necessarily happen) there is an implied assertion that they naturally belong together, 'as the word itself proves'. . . . The most frequent are 'A is part of B', 'A entails B', and the more peculiar one 'A is typical of B' will have to be introduced. By definition an equation always generalizes, because if it only said '*This* A is B' the effect would only be a double use of the word (which I symbolize 'A.B'), imputing both 'A' and 'B' to 'this', and there would be no compacted doctrine. However it may presume a limited view of 'A', probably one with vague limits, and one could describe this process as saying 'A's *of this sort* are B'. When the sort is clear at the time of speaking the analyst ought to write instead of 'A' the narrower definition, but the speaker may be so vague that this would misrepresent him; for example the sort required may be recognised only as what suits the Emotion or Mood. In particular you can get equations of the form 'a normal A is B', or 'A good A is B', and I do not know that this last has any important difference from 'A ought to be B'. Here we get a case where 'A=B' could apparently be the same as 'B=A', using different interpretations for them; because 'a normal A is B' is the same sort of thing as 'B is typical of A'. I think however that the two orders have different effects, and so are worth distinguishing; the first can be taken very lightly, but the second makes you hold a specific doctrine which you are likely to remember (*Complex Words*, pp. 40–1).

Empson's point, once again, is that we are able to interpret such deviant equations only by analogy with other, more normal or rationally accountable processes of thought, and then (in so far as this 'machinery' comes into play) that we can and should resist their more 'contagious' effects. Such resistance is especially called for, Empson thinks, in cases where the word is held to convey some authentic primordial wisdom or some order of deep paradoxical truth-claim beyond reach of mere analytical intelligence.

Thus Empson cites Archbishop Trench – one of the first editors of the *Oxford English Dictionary* – arguing for the doctrine of Original Sin by way of an appeal to the two senses ('pain' and 'punishment') supposedly conjoined in the Latin *poena* (*Complex Words*, pp. 81–2). And a footnote takes George Orwell more mildly to task for suggesting, in his novel *1984*, that human beings can be made to accept any number of irrational or mindwrenching paradoxes (such as 'war is peace' and the other slogans of Newspeak) once the habit gets a hold through continued exposure. Empson doesn't deny that such cases occur and can sometimes exert a powerful influence through forms of religious or political indoctrination. Thus 'what he [Orwell] calls "double-think, a process of intentional but genuine self-deception, easy to reach but hard to hold permanently, really does seem a positive capacity of the human mind, so curious and so important in its effects that any theory in this field needs to reckon with it' (p. 83n). On the other hand, Orwell was perhaps too quick to generalize from the imaginary 'nightmare world' of *1984* to a gloomy conviction that people could always be swung into accepting any such irrational belief. 'The emotional ground of the process', Empson thinks, 'is a secret but fully justified fear'; all the same 'the case is so hideously special that it seems rather hard to generalize'. And again: 'you can have a usable linguistic theory which doesn't apply to sheer madness, just as you can have a wave theory which doesn't apply to cases of turbulence; but this is not much help unless you have some means of knowing where, and how often, turbulence is likely to occur' (ibid.).

This footnote is important because it shows Empson testing the limits of his theory against an example which might well appear to throw that theory into doubt. His conclusion has the kind of flatly commonsensical tone which may strike some readers as really little more than an evasion of the main issue, a refusal to acknowledge how powerful are the forces that make for unresisting acquiescence in these forms of irrational belief or wholesale paradox-mongering. Such is Empson's final declaration – *contra* Orwell – that 'the human mind, that is, the public human mind as expressed in a language, is not irredeemably lunatic and cannot be made so' (p 83n). But the point of his taking *1984* as a 'hideously special' case is that it offers an extreme (hence untypical) example of one possible way that language or the human mind can go, a case where Type IV equations operate at full paradoxical stretch and where his theory of complex words encounters the greatest challenge to its powers of interpretative grasp. Still there is a sense in which the novel's whole effect comes from its exploiting possibilities of mass-induced linguistic and political 'double-think' which can only be perceived as such against a background of normative (logico-semantic) assumptions.

Thus the Orwell case is not so remote from those poetical uses of paradox or 'Type IV' equations – such as Keats's 'Beauty is truth, truth beauty' – where again 'the assertion goes both ways around' and may well strike the reader as a facile or unearned closing rhetorical flourish. Empson agrees that there is something rather wrong about a statement that bears such a weight of thematic implication while apparently ignoring all the obvious objections (for example, 'ugly truths' like the facts of disease and human suffering) which rise up against it as soon as we ask what the doctrine actually amounts to. Perhaps this is why so many people (Aldous Huxley and Robert Bridges among them) had found Keats's line so offensive: 'there is a flavour of Christian Science; they fear to wake up in fairyland, and probably the country of Uplift' (p. 373). Still it is no answer, Empson thinks, if we take one or other of the currently available lines of least resistance, such as I. A. Richards's talk of poetic 'pseudo-statements' or 'emotive' meaning, or again, Cleanth Brooks's idea of paradox as the structuring principle of all great poetry.[15] For the problem with both approaches is that they rescue Keats from his prosaically minded detractors only at the cost of ignoring his efforts to communicate something of importance in the poem's closing line. Thus one needs to work through all the possible 'equations' involved – the various orders of co-implicated statement carried by the words 'truth' and 'beauty' – before giving up on the attempt to make adequate sense of them. Even then we shall better understand what the poem is about – and not be tempted to dismiss the last line (with Bridges) as a piece of 'flashy' pseudo-philosophy – if we see how hard Keats has worked to bring it around to a conclusion which may not be justified on the strictest (logico-semantic) terms but which yet has considerable power in context. Thus '[t]here should not be a complacent acceptance either of "some indefensible sense" or of a merely emotive stimulus; the thought of the reader needs somehow to be in movement' (*Complex Words*, p. 371).

That is to say, we underestimate the intelligence of poet and reader alike if we take it that analysis has to stop short whenever it is confronted with some instance of paradox or (seemingly) 'emotive' language. The case is much the same for Keats's or Wordsworth's Type IV equations, for Orwell's examples of 'Newspeak' or 'Doublethink', and also – I would argue – for those instances of chronic malapropism which Davidson offers as supporting evidence for his minimalist theory-to-end-all-theories.[16] That is, they each involve a more complex process of thought – on the speaker's, poet's, interpreter's, or theorist's part – than is anywhere provided for in Davidson's account or by literary–critical doctrines of paradox or emotive meaning. Empson-offers various examples of this process at work, some of them – the more extended and elaborate – drawn from literary texts. They include the word 'fool' (or 'folly') as used by writers like Erasmus and Shakespeare with implications varying from 'wise or holy innocence' to cynical self-hatred and disgust; 'honest' as it figures in Renaissance and Restoration usage, again with a wide variety of positive and negative tonings; and 'dog' (like the kindred 'rogue') as a sort of mock-abusive, half-admiring, even affectionate slang-term: 'true to one's instincts (which cannot be all bad), hence trustworthy and reliable in a down-to-earth, doggish, un-self-deluding way'. The point about these words, as Empson interprets them, is that they possess a certain typical 'humour of mutuality', a reflexive or self-implicating tone which also goes along with a decent measure of other-regarding sentiment. This is not to deny that the process can be used to very different, ethically repugnant ends, as with 'dog' in the misanthropic tirades of *Timon of Athens*, 'fool' in some of Lear's more deranged utterances, or Iago's performance with the keyword 'honest' which he uses to snare Othello in the trap of a murderous paranoid delusion. But in these cases, as with *1984*, it can be argued that the whole 'dramatic and psychological effect' results from our sense of how the words have been somehow twisted away from their normal implications and contexts of usage.

To some extent this has to be regarded as an exercise in historical semantics, or a method which finds its preferred home-ground in those periods – like the early- to mid-eighteenth century – marked by the emergence of a secular-humanist ethos. Hence Empson's constant resort to 'that majestic object', the (Oxford) *New English Dictionary on Historical Principles*, as a richly documented source of examples and evidence. But this should not be taken as a limiting judgement on his claim to provide a generalized theory of interpretation, a method that extends beyond particular (period- or culture-specific) examples to the 'logical grammar' of complex words or the means by which communication comes about *despite and across* differences of culture, worldview, or interpretative ethos. For there is no reason – methodological prejudice aside – to suppose (with Davidson) that 'prior' theories' are pretty much useless for interpreting particular speech-acts in particular contexts, or conversely, that such instances can offer no support for anything beyond the most minimal (*ad hoc* or 'passing') theory of what goes on in the process of communicative uptake. Granted, '[the connection between theory and practice, where both are living and growing, need not be very tidy; they may work best where there is some mutual irritation' (*Complex Words*, p. 434). And of course it may be argued that most speakers and interpreters get along well enough without possessing a conscious ('theoretical') grasp of just how the process works. But it is a different matter when Davidson claims that any such project is radically misconceived since philosophy of language (or interpretation-theory) has nothing to explain beyond the mere fact that speakers and interpreters *just do* – for the most part – manage to communicate. For in that case one might as well argue that no theory, whether in the human or the natural sciences, can possibly do more than put itself out of business by confirming what everyone already ('preconsciously') knows as a matter of practical, common-sense, or intuitive grasp.

Not that Empson lacks all sympathy with this line of 'against-theory' argument. After all, as he remarks, '[the] whole notion of the scientist viewing language from outside and above is a fallacy: we would have no hope of dealing with the subject if we had not a rich obscure practical knowledge from which to extract the theoretical' (p. 438). However his target here is the behaviourist approach (represented chiefly by Leonard Bloomfield) which Empson sees as a misguided attempt to emulate the natural sciences in a different field of study, and to do so – moreover – on a narrowly empiricist view of how scientists think and work.[17] This was already Empson's argument in the closing chapter of *Seven Types of Ambiguity*, where he makes the same point by way of an analogy with the current (post-1920) situation in particle physics and the quantum-theoretical domain.[18] But it is well to be clear just what Empson means by drawing this suggestive analogy. He is *not* putting forward an early version of the now fashionable postmodern-pragmatist line, that is, the idea of interpretation – whether in the human or the natural sciences – as observer-relative and hence open to all manner of diverse (incommensurable) claims.[19] Nor is he arguing that there exist no criteria of truth, validity or knowledge aside from those currently adopted by this or that 'interpretive community'.[20] Still less would Empson endorse the radical subjectivist view which exploits all the well-known 'paradoxes' of quantum theory (complementarity, the wave/particle dualism, the uncertainty-principle, the observationally induced 'collapse of the wave-packet', and so on) in order to maintain – in its crudest version – that physical reality *just is* whatever we make of it.[21] On the contrary, he argues: the point of having theories in the human or the natural sciences is precisely to make due allowance for that factor of interpretive or observational involvement which positivism failed to acknowledge. In neither case does this entail a retreat to the sorts of extreme relativist or subjectivist position which were already gaining among literary intellectuals – and some commentators on the new physics – when Empson first addressed these issues in *Seven Types of Ambiguity*.

The best way to understand such attitudes, he suggests, is to see them as a largely reactive or defensive response to the claims of logical positivism in its earliest, most doctrinaire form. For if indeed it is the case – as this programme held – that the only classes of meaningful statements are (1) those that can be verified by experiment or empirical observation, and (2) those whose truth is a function of their purely analytic (hence tautologous) logical structure, then it follows that all other statements – whether in ethics, literary criticism, or the vast majority of everyday social and communicative contexts – amount to no more than a species of 'emotive', 'metaphysical' or strictly meaningless talk.[22] But this doctrine soon ran up against problems, not least the fact that it proved incapable of being stated in a form that satisfied either of its own requirements, that is, the verification-principle or the condition of strict analyticity.[23] Moreover, it was something of an irony that the doctrine should be propounded by philosophers of science at just the time when advances in the quantum-theoretical field were making it increasingly difficult to maintain any such hard-line positivist account of language, truth, and logic. These considerations are all in the background, I think, when Empson puts forward his analogy between the current (late-twenties) situation in particle physics and the question how far we can interpret language – poetic or everyday language – as communicating truth-claims that don't come down to just a matter of 'emotive' pseudo-statement or (what amounts to much the same thing) subjective response on the interpreter's part.

This is why he takes issue with I.A. Richards's claim that 'the function of poetry is to call out an Attitude which is not dependent on any belief open to disproof by facts', and moreover that 'awareness of the nature of the world and the development of attitudes which will enable us to live in it finely are almost independent' (*Complex Words*, p. 7).[24] It is clear, Empson goes on, 'that *almost* might become important here', since it lets in at least the possibility that 'one needs more elaborate machinery to disentangle the Emotive from the Cognitive part of language' (ibid.). *Complex Words* in effect takes up this challenge and offers a full-scale apparatus of interpretive 'machinery' by which to explain how such vague talk of 'emotions' and 'attitudes' might be rendered more precise – more rationally, humanly, and ethically accountable – through a further stretch of logico-semantic analysis. Thus: '[m]uch of what appears to us as a "feeling" (as is obvious in the case of a complex metaphor) will in fact be quite an elaborate structure of related meanings' (pp. 56–7). And again: although 'Emotions and Moods may well be important in calling out and directing the interaction', still 'it seems clear that the first thing to examine is the result, what might be called the logic of these unnoticed propositions' (p. 57). For the trouble with emotivist doctrines, whether in literary criticism or ethics, is their willingness on the one hand to endorse the claims of logical positivism at face value, and on the other, to discount the truth-content of any language – everyday or poetic – that doesn't conform to those same (in any case impossibly restrictive) standards. All of which offers good grounds for supposing that 'the emotions in the words will normally evoke senses that correspond to them (except in swear-words, intensifiers, and for that matter raving), and the structure to be examined is that of the resultant senses' (p. 52). Otherwise – on the emotivist view – there would seem no limit to what 'language can get away with' by imposing false or irrational beliefs, like the paradoxes of Orwellian doublethink, which exploit the presumed incapacity of human thought to muster any defence against them.

It is worth quoting Empson once again to see what is involved in this (sometimes very complicated) process of 'putting emotions into an equation form'. With the simplest cases, he suggests,

> an underlining of the Stock Emotion 'A.A!' may be assertive, as if saying 'A does deserve the emotion commonly given to it', and we could write this 'A = A!'. But I think this can be classed as a kind of existence assertion. In the same way the denial of the stock Emotion 'A. – A!', as in 'jolly lust', can be viewed as a denial of the reality of the supposed 'thing'. Of course the function of 'jolly' is to act as a context which kills the stock emotion, and I agree that the first effect is this and nothing more; but we are at once driven

to look for a new Sense of *lust*, whether successfully or not, which will account for such a use; and people who fail to find one would tend I think to call it a 'cynical denial that there is any such thing as lust'. In any case there seems no great advantage in extending the equation form to this sort of case. The important type would be 'A.B!', and I deny that an equation 'A = B!', without further complications of sense, ever occurs; at any rate without being a recognisable error of a kind very unlikely in a native speaker of the language (*Complex Words*, p. 41).

Without (for the moment) pursuing these complexities any further we can now perhaps see what is involved in Empson's opposition to emotivist doctrines and his general case for this approach to language *via* a logico-semantic theory of complex words. More specifically – and more to the point for my argument – it suggests what is missing from Davidson's under-theorised treatment of related issues. For there is a sense in which Davidson makes the same error as Richards. That is, he assumes that any such theory will encounter all the problems that were faced at an earlier stage by logical empiricism in its failed attempt to demarcate the realms of meaningful and meaningless statement. Just as Richards fell back on an emotivist doctrine through being over-impressed by that programme, so Davidson retreats (in 'A Nice Derangement of Epitaphs') from 'prior' to 'passing' theories, and thence to a notion of communicative uptake in which 'theory' pretty much drops out and interpretation becomes largely a matter of *ad hoc* response to contextual cues and clues.

Notes

1. William Empson, *The Structure of Complex Words*, (2nd edn, rev., London: Chatto & Windus, 1969). All further references given by title and page number in the text.
2. See for instance the passing references to Empson in Davidson's essay 'What Metaphors Mean', *Inquiries into Truth and Interpretation* (Oxford: Clarendon Press, 1984), pp. 245–64.
3. See especially Donald Davidson, 'A nice derangement of epitaphs', in R. Grandy and R. Warner (eds), *Philosophical Grounds of Rationality: Intentions, Categories, Ends* (London: Oxford University Press, 1986), pp. 157–74.
4. See for instance the essays collected in W. J. T. Mitchell (ed.), *Against Theory: Literary Theory and the New Pragmatism* (Chicago: University of Chicago Press, 1985); also S. Pradhan, 'Minimalist semantics: Davidson and Derrida on meaning, use, and convention', *Diacritics*, Vol. 16 (Spring 1986), pp. 66–77 and Samuel C. Wheeler, 'Indeterminacy of French translation: Derrida and Davidson', in Ernest Lepore (ed.), *Truth and Interpretation: Perspectives on the Philosophy of Donald Davidson* (Oxford: Blackwell, 1986).

5. Empson, *Seven Types of Ambiguity*, 2nd edn, rev. (Harmondsworth: Penguin, 1961).

6. Empson, 'Sense in *The Prelude*', *Complex Words* (op. cit.), pp. 289–305.

7. See for instance Noam Chomsky, *Current Issues in Linguistic Theory* (The Hague: Mouton, 1966); *Studies on Semantics in Generative Grammar* (Mouton, 1966); *Language and Problems of Knowledge* (Cambridge, Mass.: MIT Press, 1988); Jerry Fodor, *Representations* (MIT Press, 1981) and *The Modularity of Mind* (MIT Press, 1983).

8. Christopher Norris, *William Empson and the Philosophy of Literary Criticism* (London: Athlone Press, 1978).

9. On this distinction between 'prior' and 'passing' theories, see Davidson, 'A nice derangement of epitaphs' (op. cit.).

10. See especially Davidson, 'On the very idea of a conceptual scheme', in *Inquiries into Truth and Interpretation* (op. cit.), pp. 183–98; also Richard Grandy, 'Reference, meaning and belief', *Journal of Philosophy*, Vol. 70 (1973), pp. 439–52; Colin McGinn, 'Charity, interpretation and belief', *Journal of Philosophy*, Vol. 74 (1977), pp. 521–35; Bjorn Ramberg, *Donald Davidson's Philosophy of Language: An introduction* (Oxford: Blackwell, 1989).

11. On the subject of 'radical translation', see W. V. Quine, *Word and Object* (Cambridge, Mass.: MIT Press, 1960); also Quine, *Ontological Relativity and Other Essays* (New York: Random House, 1966); Davidson, 'On the very idea of a conceptual scheme' (op. cit.); David Lewis, 'Radical translation', *Philosophical Papers*, Vol. 1 (London: Oxford University Press, 1983); Colin McGinn, 'Radical Interpretation and Epistemology', in Lepore (ed.), *Truth and Interpretation* (op. cit.), pp. 356–68.

12. W. H. Newton-Smith, *The Rationality of Science* (London: Routledge & Kegan Paul, 1981), p. 163.

13. Ibid., p. 163.

14. See for instance Richard Rorty, 'The world well lost', in *Consequences of Pragmatism* (Brighton: Harvester, 1982), pp. 3–18; 'Pragmatism, Davidson, and truth', in *Objectivity, Relativism, and Truth* (Cambridge: Cambridge University Press, 1991), pp. 126–50; 'Is truth a goal of enquiry? Davidson *versus* Wright', *Philosophical Quarterly*, Vol. 45 (1995), pp. 281–300.

15. I. A. Richards, *Principles of Literary Criticism* (London: Paul Trench Trubner, 1924); Cleanth Brooks, *The Well Wrought Urn: Studies in the Structure of Poetry* (New York: Harcourt Brace, 1947).

16. Davidson, 'A nice derangement of epitaphs' (op. cit.). His point, once again, is that we interpret malapropisms – along with metaphors, novel turns of phrase, Freudian slips, idiomatic usages, *hapax legomena*, etc. – by application of the standard 'Principle of Charity' plus 'wit, luck and wisdom' eked out (where need be) by contextual cues and clues. Thus for Davidson 'there is no such thing as a language', at any rate not in the sense of that term understood by most linguists, philosophers, and theorists of interpretation.

17. Leonard Bloomfield, *Language* (London: Allen & Unwin, 1935).

18. Empson, *Seven Types of Ambiguity* (op. cit.).

19. See for instance Jean-François Lyotard, *The Postmodern Condition: A Report on Knowledge*, trans. Geoff Bennington and Brian Massumi (Manchester: Manchester University Press, 1984).

20. See Stanley Fish, *Is There a Text in This Class? The Authority of Interpretive Communities* (Cambridge, Mass.: Harvard University Press, 1983) and *Doing What Comes Naturally: Change, Rhetoric, and the Practice of Theory in Literary and legal Studies* (Oxford: Clarendon Press, 1989); also Rorty, *Consequences of Pragmatism* (op. cit.) and *Contingency, Irony, and Solidarity* (Cambridge: Cambridge University Press, 1989).
21. For a strongly argued critique of these notions, see Karl R. Popper, *Quantum Theory and the Schism in Physics* (London: Hutchinson, 1982).
22. See the essays collected in A. J. Ayer (ed.), *Logical Positivism* (New York: Free Press, 1953); also Friedrich Waismann, 'Verifiability' and Isaiah Berlin, 'Verification', in G. H. R. Parkinson (ed.), *The Theory of Meaning* (London: Oxford University Press, 1976), pp. 15–34 & 35–60.
23. See especially Quine, 'Two dogmas of empiricism', *From a Logical Point of View* (Cambridge, Mass.: Harvard University Press, 1953), pp. 20–46.
24. Richards, *Principles of Literary Criticism* (op. cit.).

22

Lyndsey Stonebridge, *The Destructive Element: British Psychoanalysis and Modernism* (1998)

This study of the mutual influences of modernism and psychoanalysis provides a largely missing and much-needed critical dimension for the understanding of British cultural and intellectual history in the war and post-war years. In common with the LDS books of Jacqueline Rose and Denise Riley, *The Destructive Element* moves between intellectual history, psychoanalytic and psychological theory, and feminist thought. The title is derived from Conrad's *Lord Jim*, 'In the destructive element immerse'; an injunction that is here taken up in an examination of how theories of emotional aggression, the death drive and unconscious violence developed within and inflected or reinforced literary, critical and aesthetic directions in the mid-twentieth century.

Stonebridge's book exemplifies an intellectual history which, in its consideration of the ambivalent aesthetics of destructiveness, refuses reductive moves: the psychoanalytical element is not seen as an effect of 'underlying' historical forces nor as radically autonomous and so ahistorical. Shifting between case studies of differing conjunctions of British psychoanalytic and aesthetic practices, Stonebridge examines Kleinian theories of art in relation to Roger Fry's version of modernism, Virginia Woolf's taut engagements with mourning and redemption, and Adrian Stokes's hollowed stones and sculptured maternalism. The idea of destructive phantasy and its accompanying, if troubled, search for salvation through 'values' is traced in the work of the literary critics I. A. Richards and William Empson. Uncertainty is echoed too in the hopes of the saving grace of rhythm, along with a fear of its latent conservatism, to be found in the writings of Woolf and the analyst Ella Freeman Sharpe. For Stokes, the Kleinian trust in art as reparative was never secure, while for the analyst and critic Marion Milner, art again hovered on the exposed frontiers between inner and outer risk.

As the introduction to the book observes: 'At a time when the European theatricals of psychic cruelty which so perturbed both psychoanalysts and writers are once more being played out, and at a moment in contemporary British culture when a politics of reparation (preserving the "good") seems to have acquired a curious new legitimacy, the failures of writers and analysts of the early part of the century to extricate themselves from their own cultural "Kismet" remains as instructive for us now as it was then.'

Sticks for dahlias: the destructive element in literary criticism and Melanie Klein

The waste remains, the waste remains and kills.
William Empson, 'Missing Dates'

'In the destructive element immerse . . . that was the way'. When Richards found the right phrase to describe Eliot's *The Waste Land* in Conrad's *Lord Jim* it was, in part, with reference to psychoanalysis. In 'A Background for Contemporary Poetry' Richards identifies psychoanalysis as one of the causes of the epistemological violence that has been waged upon the 'Magical View of Nature'. Nature, for Richards, is already something like an English suburban garden, as his somewhat breathless indictment of horticultural malaise suggests in the passage which inspires the footnote on Eliot:

> Over whole tracts of natural emotional response we are to-day like a bed of dahlias whose sticks have been removed. And this effect of the neutralisation of nature is only in its beginnings. Consider the probable effects in the near future of the kind of enquiry into basic human constitution exemplified by psychoanalysis.
>
> A sense of desolation, of uncertainty, of futility, of the baselessness of aspirations, of the vanity of endeavour, and a thirst for life-giving water which seems suddenly to have failed, are the signs in consciousness of this necessary reorganisation of our lives. Our attitudes and impulses are being compelled to become self-supporting; they are being driven back upon their biological justification, made once again sufficient to themselves. And the only impulses which seem strong enough to continue unflagging are commonly so crude that to more finely developed individuals, they seem hardly worth having.[1]

Small wonder, perhaps, that it was the footnote and not the main body of Richards' text which acquired such notoriety. ('The answer to that', Stephen Spender ripostes impatiently ten years later, 'is "Don't be a dahlia, and you won't need a stick!" ').[2] The vandal in the garden is psychoanalysis which has removed the stick of belief by uncovering unconscious drive-invested impulses so crude, Richards notes, that 'they seem hardly worth having'.

Where Trilling will later make a virtue out of the fact that psycho-analysis drives us back to our 'biological justification', Richards, who once said that he began his study of physiology with the intention of becoming a psychoanalyst, is more troubled by the cultural implica-tions of desire.[3] Even when psychoanalytic 'stories are duly dis-counted', he argues in 'A Psychological Theory of Value', 'enough which is verifiable remains for *infans polypervers* to present a truly impressive figure dominating all future inquiry into value.'[4] One way to read Richards' footnote, then, is as a possible solution to this threat to value posed, in part, by psychoanalysis. Eliot, says Richards, 'by effecting a complete severance between his poetry and *all* beliefs [. . .] has shown the way to the only solution of these difficulties. "In the destructive element . . . that was the way." '[5] *The Waste Land* offers a 'perfect emotive description' of a crisis of value that psychoanalysis, among other sciences, has laid bare: a 'pseudo-statement' which because it relinquishes any claim to belief, can order and, thereby, transcend the damage that it at the same time diagnoses. To suggest that Richards developed his own theory of value in response to psycho-analysis' threat to value would be to misconstrue his project; yet there remains a noteworthy tension here between psychoanalysis and the construction of Richards' own literary principles which can shed light on how the question of value in each discourse became inextricable from shifting definitions of the destructive element.

Far from overtly inflating the value of art, Practical Criticism prided itself in its attacks on traditional notions of aesthetic value. In *Principles of Literary Criticism* Richards puts paid to the 'phantom of the aesthetic state' by proposing what looks like a thoroughly democratic theory of pleasure and value. Richards wants a psychology of value which will dispense with idealism and offer an alternative to Fry's and Bell's aestheticism. Value, hence, is not to be defined via the category of the aesthetic; rather as with Freud, and similarly following G. T. Fechner, Richards proposes an economic theory that equates value with the reduction of tension: 'anything is valuable which satisfies an appetency'.[6] The key to satisfying an appetency lies in the develop-ment of an organised system that can keep conflicting impulses in balance. Against the implied totalitarianism of an 'aesthetic state' a well-ordered individual psychology acts as a microcosm of the balanced liberal state. Like Freud, Richards recognises that such an organisation of impulses on a cultural level requires a sacrifice on the part of the individual. But where Freud is pessimistic about the exorbitant price to be paid for this entrance into culture (as in *Civilization and its Discontents*), Richards, owing more to Bentham (like his collaborator C. K. Ogden), is more sanguine: 'By the extent of the loss, the range of impulses thwarted or starved, and their degree of importance, the merit of a systematization is judged. That organisation which is least wasteful of human possibilities is, in short, the best'.[7] No use crying over the milk spilt by the *infans polypervers* in its journey, in Richards' terms, to the acquisition of value: waste not, want not.

But phantoms of the aesthetic state are not only illusory; like other ghosts they also have a habit of returning to haunt the site of their supposed exorcism. As Steven Connor has argued, Richards' apparent continuum between disorganised appetencies and aversions, and their development towards equipoise and organisation, quickly hardens into an opposition between good and bad art.[8] While he maintains that aesthetic experiences are 'only a further development, a finer organisation of ordinary experiences, and not in the least a new or different kind of thing',[9] this finer organisation of art also offers an economy that is not available in common experience: 'the experiences which the arts offer are not obtainable, or but rarely, elsewhere. Would that they were! They are not incomplete; they might be better described as ordinary experiences completed'.[10] Art completes, because of its superior organisation of impulses, what ordinary experience leaves unfinished. The value of *The Waste Land*, therefore, lies in nothing so snobbish as its intellectual allusions, but 'in the unified response which this interaction creates in the right reader'.[11] This is the poetically correct reader of *Practical Criticism* (the *bête noire* of anyone who has struggled to demonstrate Richards' point in the course of their literary education). To be immersed in the destructive element in this sense is to subscribe to a view that redeems waste through a critical economy that transmutes conflict into balanced equipoise. Or, as Richards puts it in his revised version of the footnote in his later *Science and Poetry*, Eliot finds a 'new order through the contemplation and exhibition of disorder'.[12]

Dahlias, then, have nothing to lose but their sticks, as *Practical Criticism* begins to put right the damage done by psychoanalysis in the garden of value. But removing the sticks of belief, like banishing the ghost of aesthetic idealism, is easier said than done. Richards bases his claims on a thoroughly modern theory of value: 'The view that what we need in this tempestuous turmoil of change is a Rock to shelter under or to cling to, rather than an efficient aeroplane to ride it, is comprehensible, but mistaken.'[13] But the rhetoric of redemption is never far away. In his appendix to *Principles of Literary Criticism*. 'The Poetry of T. S. Eliot', Richards revises his earlier reading of the poem. Not only does the poem immerse us in the destructive element, here Richards also introduces Eliot's 'persistent concern with sex, the problem of our generation, as religion was the problem of the last'.[14] Perhaps in the light of this new association with sex, Richards, no doubt also responding to Eliot's own corrective complaints, ends with an implicit qualification of his earlier reading:

> There are those who think that [Eliot] merely takes his readers into the Waste Land and leaves them there, that in this last poem he confesses his impotence to release the healing waters. The reply is that some readers find in his poetry not only a clearer, fuller realization of their plight, the plight of a whole generation, than they find elsewhere, but also through the very energies set free in that realization a return of the saving passion.[15]

The rhetoric of redemption here might quite reasonably be said to belong not to Richards but to his – carefully placed – 'some readers'. Notwithstanding, Richards language correlates eloquently with a thesis that sees art as completing experience and as thereby restoring value in a world gripped by a crisis in belief. It is as if, finally, the 'impressive figure' of the polymorphously perverse infant has been promoted to the status of the aesthetically and culturally valuable: the baselessness of contemporary life that this figure signifies is refracted back to us through poetry, not only as a monument to our desolation, but as an icon of possible salvation through suffering. Something, it might be said, has just crawled under a rock; or as Eliot later says of Richards' criticism, drawing the obvious parallel with Arnold, this is ultimately 'salvation by poetry'.[16]

While it is true to say that Richards, in contrast to Eliot and American New Criticism, is reconciled to producing a form of scientific criticism for a secular culture, something perhaps of that unconscious Christianity that Eliot wanted criticism to preserve remains here.[17] This is precisely the point that William Empson, steadfastly opposed to religious criticism throughout his career (particularly in his later work), makes in his astute appendix on value in *The Structure of Complex Words* (dedicated to Richards '[w]ho is the source of all ideas in this book, even the minor ones arrived at by disagreeing with him').

Richards, says Empson, 'need not be as secure against the religions as he intended to be'.[18] It is the lack of qualification in Richards' theory of value, Empson argues, that issues a back-door invitation to the kinds of dangerous idealism that Richards wants to get rid of. Once again this debate about value is caught up in a conversation with psychoanalysis. Empson points out that by defining value as the achievement of equilibrium through the reduction of tension, Richards runs tantalisingly close to reproducing a version of Freud's death drive. As Empson puts it in an apparently un-posted letter to Richards from Peking in 1933: 'Freud's dim but rich concept of death wishes come in here: one sense of it is certainly that all impulses are reactions to a stimulus aiming at the removal of the stimulus'.[19] As long as value is defined solely in terms of the achievement of equilibrium, the democratic balance Richards aims for risks carrying with it a more deathly proposition. And if this is the case, there is nothing to stop the *infans polypervers* from re-emerging as a problem for value. Richards' claims about the sublimatory values of 'balanced' impulses, says Empson, 'still [don't] face the issue that this may be done badly: it is just this process that sends energy into perverse desires that give pain when unsatisfied and no pleasure when satisfied'.[20] As Empson reintroduces psychoanalysis into the debate he also exposes the internal limits of Richards' version of the destructive element: immersing oneself in a world of no belief armed only with a stoically utilitarian theory of value is finally no protection from those other, less civilised, destructive elements identified by psychoanalysis. The waste, that surplus of thwarted and starved impulses that Richards wanted to channel into his version of a useful life, remains.

Far from offering a solution to the crisis of value, Richards leaves us with a question that elsewhere Empson identifies as pertaining to psychoanalysis: 'what version of a perversion is to be admired'?[21] This is the question that Empson addresses to himself in 'Death and Its Desires' which he drafted in the same year as his letter to Richards. It is not (it could hardly be) perversion *per se* that worries Empson here, but the extent to which death wishes in art degenerate into forms of weak mysticism and unwarranted pessimism – corrupted versions of the destructive element which Richards' theory of value, by implication, cannot guard against. Empson finds the purest version of the destructive element, or the death wish, like Eliot before him, in the Fire Sermon of the Buddha, and describes Nirvana in terms which directly recall Richards' praise of Eliot: 'The main effect of the doctrine . . . is to remove *all* doctrinal props about immortality and still claim that death is somehow of the highest value'.[22] Empson particularly relishes the way the Fire Sermon achieves this without Christianity's morbid fascination with spectacles of sacrificial death – his is a dip in the destructive element without a voyeuristic pay-off. Elsewhere Empson thinks of this distinction in terms of the difference between the 'return to a narcissistic state of being' (Nirvana) and 'corpse lust' (voyeuristic sadism) and notes how irritating it is not to be sure which version of the death wish a work of art is offering you – which version of perversion (*The Waste Land* might be a case in point).[23] It is difficult (although probably wrong-headed) not to suspect that Empson is engaged in some irreverent shadow-boxing with Richards here. Where Richards chooses the scene out of *Lord Jim* in which the Bavarian butterfly collector and trader, Stein, lectures Marlow on the ways of non-being ('with the exertions of your hands and feet in the water make the deep, deep sea keep you up')[24] in order to register the profundity of Eliot's disassociation of belief, Empson offers us English pastoral in the form of T. F. Powys ('death like the clown is a sort of perverse figure of pastoral'). In 'John Pardy and the Waves', Powys' Molloy-like tramp character concludes his search for happiness by immersing himself in the waves. Empson paraphrases:

> Passing on to count the waves of the sea he was told by the waves that if he joined them he could not only destroy himself but become one of the great elements of destruction and perhaps take part in a typhoon to destroy a city.[25]

'In the destructive element . . .'. Because it is pastoral, what's important to Empson is the extent to which the genre mystifies or normalises existing social and economic relations. Such is the case with Powys' treatment of death; 'this indefatigable game of talking about death must be a mere blind; the use of death wishes in such literature is only to protect something else'.[26] Powys domesticates the destructive element, and on these grounds Empson charges him with something like bad faith. In the same paper Empson makes a similar charge against R. E. Money-Kyrle, the psychoanalyst who was to become one of Melanie Klein's most trustworthy and steadfast supporters. It is Money-Kyrle, perhaps, who by driving the death instinct to its logical and extreme conclusion, also produces the most grotesque parody of Richards' theory of value: 'the quickest and most final method by which an individual can remove his needs' he advises 'is to put his head in a gas-oven'.[27]

Empson and Richards remind us that while Valentine Cunningham is right to argue that the destructive element is caught up within a general apocalyptic rhetoric of the 1920s and 1930s, the phrase also has a specific theoretical and moral history. For Richards the struggle was to find a model of criticism that could redeem a world out of step with its own values; 'redeem' both in the sense of atone, and in the economic sense of to reclaim what's yours, or to make good the waste. In his 1935 revision of *Science and Poetry*, he increases the political stakes of his theory of value: the Treaty of Versailles, Richards notes, is no longer sustainable, what we need is 'a League of Nations for the moral ordering of the impulses; a new order based on conciliation, not on attempted suppression'.[28] World War Two blasted that illusion apart (notoriously, literary studies took somewhat longer to wake up to the ideological anachronisms of Practical Criticism). Empson, by contrast, cautions against the valorisation of the destructive element, all too aware, perhaps, that the apparent fair-mindedness of a League of Nations, pushed to its conclusion, offers scant protection against the punitive moralities of 1919. As such, Empson moves beyond the impasses of Richards' individualist psychology and shifts to what we could cautiously read as a more 'properly' psychoanalytic critical terrain.

Perhaps the best example of this is Empson's wonderful reading of Herbert's 'The Sacrifice' in *Seven Types of Ambiguity*. Empson's debt to Freud is overt in his chapter on the seventh type of ambiguity. Empson's seventh type bears a mark of repression so that, in his words, the ambiguity both carries the 'notion of what you want and involves the notion that you must not take it'.[29] In Empson's deft hands, Herbert's doctrinal monologue on the suffering of Christ has, thus, to be read double. What emerges in his exemplary reading of the poem is a fusion of both 'the love of Christ' *and* 'the vindictive terrors of the sacrificial idea': Christ's suffering is at the same time the suffering of his betrayers; his agony also translates as a desire for retribution, a wished for agony of his torturers; 'I may *cleave their hearts* with my tenderness or with their despair'; Christ is both sinless and a criminal. In other words the founding act of New Testament law is built upon a love that can barely conceal the hate and vindictiveness that sustain it. It 'is true that George Herbert is a cricket in the sunshine', Empson concludes, 'but one is accustomed to be shocked on discovering the habits of such creatures; they are more savage than they seem'.[30] The idea that civilisation is more savage than it seems was, of course, precisely the point that Freud made in *Civilization and Its Discontents* (published in the same year as *Seven Types*). The command that one should 'Love thy neighbour', Freud points out, is built upon the hostility we feel for our neighbours ('*Homo homini lupus*'). By signing up to Christian ethics, civilisation puts 'a positive premium on being bad'.[31] It is this version of the destructive element, of a violence at the core of culture, that concerns Klein (Freud footnotes Klein twice in *Civilization*), and will later come to dominate debates within British psychoanalysis during World War Two. In 1930 Empson adds a timely literary codicil to Freud's thesis. 'Herbert', he concludes, 'deals in this poem, on the scale and by the methods necessary to it, with the most complicated and deeply-rooted notion of the human mind.'[32] Neither Freud nor Klein would have disagreed.

Empson, on the other hand, would not have agreed that in his reading of Herbert he was moving on to a more 'properly' psychoanalytic domain. In his 1947 preface to *Seven Types* he regrets that 'the topical interest of Freud distracted [him]'. The reading of Herbert, Empson now claims, was not 'concerned with neurotic disunion but with a fully public theological poem'[33] (Freud, for one, might have replied that it was precisely the coming together of personal neurosis and the publicly theological that was at issue). To some extent, Empson's disclaiming caveats are a typical expression of British modernism's tendency to fix psychoanalysis as a form of regressive individualism which must be resisted at all costs. (Wyndham Lewis, for example, discounts Richards on the grounds of this stereotype: 'Mr. Richards is after all a psycho-analyst: and everything in the psycho-analyst promotes self-consciousness.')[34] Writing in 1947, seventeen years after *Seven Types* and *Civilization*, Empson's characterisation of the relation between psychoanalysis and modernist criticism is typical: 'Some literary critics at the time were prepared to "collaborate" with the invading psycho-analysts, whereas the honest majority who were prepared to fight in the streets either learned fire-watching technique or drilled with the Home Guard'.[35] Typically perhaps for Empson, this disclaimer of psychoanalysis is curiously psychoanalytic: compare Freud's description of the ego as 'a kind of frontier-station with a mixed garrison' that may or may not collaborate with the symptom, the 'foreign body'.[36] The passage is also anachronistic: Empson pastes the rhetoric of World War Two over an earlier historical moment (while psychoanalytic ideas invaded the English intellectual scene throughout the 1920s, the psychoanalysts themselves did not really begin to 'invade' until the 1930s). It is as if the in-fighting of modernist criticism can only be couched in the language of war-time

Britain: psychoanalysis is the alien invader, English literary criticism is the plucky Home Guard. The components of England's national culture, one senses, are already beginning to harden. What happens to this picture of modernist criticism and psychoanalysis if, taking a cue from Empson's more pro-psychoanalytic moments, we re-read the aesthetics of the destructive element in collaboration with psychoanalysis? Do the destructive elements of psychoanalysis, as Richards feared, present a threat to cultural value? Or is psychoanalysis too, as Leo Bersani has recently suggested, ultimately complicit with attempts to redeem and transcend the crisis of the modern with a form of aesthetic compensation? These are the questions I want to look at in the rest of this chapter by turning to the work of Klein who, at the same time that Richards was drilling us in the ordering of the impulses, was working her own extraordinary way through the destructive element.

Notes

1. I. A. Richards, 'A background for contemporary poetry', p. 520.
2. Stephen Spender, *The Destructive Element: A Study of Modern Writers and Beliefs*, p. 224.
3. See 'I. A. Richards interviewed by Reuban Brauer' in *Richards on Rhetoric: I.A. Richards Selected Essays 1929–74*, ed. Ann B. Berthott (Oxford: Oxford University Press, 1991), p. 7.
4. I. A. Richards, *Principles of Literary Criticism* (1924) (London: Routledge & Kegan Paul, 1967), p. 34.
5. I. A. Richards, 'A background for contemporary poetry', p. 520.
6. I. A. Richards, *Principles of Literary Criticism*, p. 35.
7. Ibid., p. 39.
8. Steven Connor, *Theory and Cultural Value* (Oxford: Blackwell, 1992), p. 37.
9. I. A. Richards, *Principles of Literary Criticism*, p. 10.
10. Ibid., p. 184.
11. Ibid., p. 231.
12. I. A. Richards, *Poetries and Sciences: A Reissue of Science and Poetry (1926, 1935) with Commentary* (London: Routledge & Kegan Paul, 1970), p. 64.
13. I. A. Richards, *Principles of Literary Criticism*, p. 43.
14. Ibid., p. 233.
15. Ibid., p. 235.
16. T. S. Eliot, 'From the use of poetry and the use of criticism' (1933), *Selected Prose of T.S. Eliot*, ed. Frank Kermode (London: Faber and Faber, 1975), p. 88.
17. For an excellent account of Eliot and New Criticism see John Guillory, *Cultural Capital. The Problem of Literary Canon Formation* (Chicago: University of Chicago Press, 1993), pp. 134–75.
18. William Empson, *The Structure of Complex Words* (1951) (London: Hogarth, 1985), p. 425.
19. William Empson, letter to I. A. Richards, *Argufying: Essays on Literature and Culture*, ed. John Haffenden (London: Chatto and Windus, 1987), p. 552.

Steven Connor draws a similar parallel, see Steven Connor, *Theory and Cultural Value*, p. 39.

20. William Empson, letter to I. A. Richards, *Argufying*, p. 552.
21. William Empson, 'Death and Its Desires', *Argufying*, p. 540.
22. Ibid., p. 536.
23. See Empson's introduction to the Japanese edition of Eliot's essays 'Mr Eliot and the East' (1933) for the significance of Nirvana and Buddhism to Eliot and also for Empson's defence of Richards following Eliot's review of *Science and Poetry* (*Dial*, March 1927) ibid., pp. 566–70.
24. Joseph Conrad, *Lord Jim* (1900) (Harmondsworth: Penguin, 1949), p. 181.
25. William Empson, 'Death and its desires', *Argufying*, p. 542.
26. Ibid., p. 544.
27. R. E. Money-Kyrle, *The Development of the Sexual Impulses* (London: Kegan Paul, 1932), p. 201.
28. I. A. Richards, *Poetries and Sciences*, p. 40.
29. William Empson, *Seven Types of Ambiguity* (1930) (Harmondsworth: Penguin, 1995), p. 226.
30. Ibid., p. 226.
31. Sigmund Freud, *Civilization and Its Discontents* (1930[1929]), The Pelican Freud Library, vol. 12 (Harmondsworth: Penguin 1985) p.301, Standard Edition 21, p. 111.
32. William Empson, *Seven Types of Ambiguity*, p. 270.
33. Ibid., p. 9.
34. Wyndham Lewis, *Men Without Art* (London: Cassell, 1934), p. 87.
35. William Empson, *Seven Types of Ambiguity*, p. 9.
36. Sigmund Freud, *Inhibitions, Symptoms and Anxiety*, (1926[1925]), *The Pelican Freud Library*, vol. 10 (Harmondsworth: Penguin, 1979), p. 251, Standard Edition 20, pp. 98–9.

23

Stanley Shostak, *Death of Life: The Legacy of Molecular Biology* (1998)

There is perhaps no more debilitating feature of modern thought than the almost unbridgeable division in the modern academy between science and the humanities. The dangers that C. P. Snow attempted to indicate in his 1959 Rede Lecture *The Two Cultures* have only increased in the decades since he wrote and no amount of Leavisite fulmination can get over the divide. If the history and philosophy of science can now be considered one of the key disciplines for defining the relations across the disciplines, it is still not the necessary point of reference that it should be. Stanley Shostak takes Cinderella as his muse, when, as a practising biologist, he sets out to describe the historical rise to power and the contemporary inadequacy of molecular biology. He reads the story of the rise to supremacy of the study of the gene as the death of the Cinderella of sciences, biology. His heretical account questions at every level the current dominance of molecular biology and suggests that it depends on a series of factors that have nothing to do with the kind of disinterested inquiry which science is meant to represent. His call for a much richer and more diverse biology makes clear how damaging the current divide between science and humanities is to both parties.

Biology's 'revolution'

A theory is like a historical novel with a cast of characters, some of whom are known to have existed, some of whom are quite different from any known historical personage, but who, if they had existed, would explain history. The scientist proposes such a historical novel in the hope that it will turn out to be accurate history. But if it turns out to be false or nonconfirmable or non-falsifiable, it may be read as fiction; it is not a 'meaningless' story
Kenneth Schaffner, 1993: 132.

The changes in biology wrought by Watson and Crick's discovery of the secondary structure of DNA, the discovery of messenger RNA and Jacob and Monod's elucidation of bacterial induction are frequently characterized as revolutionary. And well they may be, but did biology have a *scientific* revolution?

The late sage of scientific revolutions, Thomas Kuhn,[1] his chief commentators[2] and interpreters[3] agree that a scientific revolution is marked by a change in the paradigm identified with the science. This agreement prevails despite the difficulty Kuhn had defining a paradigm.[4] whether it was a 'disciplinary matrix', 'research programme', 'domain', 'discipline', 'research tradition', etc. Moreover, the idea of a change in paradigms (not necessarily the same as a 'paradigm shift', '*Gestalt* switch', and 'epistemological rupture') survives despite its own ambiguity. A change in paradigms is not a mere slide from what was to what is but an ahistorical (i.e. unrooted), binary and complete departure from a prior paradigm.[5] Furthermore, this change is supposed to be the consequence of the spontaneous eruption of new ideas (not the accumulation of hard-nosed facts) that, by their sheer intellectual power, become inescapable and ultimately triumph over old ideas in biology.

By these criteria, biology did not have a mid-twentieth century revolution. The DNA theory of the gene meets the criteria for a paradigm well enough, but the changes accompanying its promulgation fail to meet criteria for a paradigm change. Notwithstanding widespread opinion to the contrary, the alleged biological revolution is redolent of historical antecedents. The changes wrought in biology following Watson/Crick clearly had roots in the 'old' biology. These were roots concerned with controlling life, human life in particular: from providing health and welfare to manipulating evolution and destiny. These were the same roots tapped by Darwin and Bernard. Watson and Crick's DNA derived its inspiration and sustenance from them, but Watson and Crick's theory did not erupt spontaneously, win converts by 'sheer intellectual power', or even 'triumph over old ideas'.

Watson, Crick and their followers capitalised on the gene (and all overdetermined insistence that everything biological can be reduced to genes), appropriating it completely and modeling DNA to suit it in every way imaginable. Morgan and his followers had demonstrated that the hereditary factors deduced by hapless Mendel were mathematically tractable, hence material. Even Bateson, who opposed Morgan's reductionism, acquiesced in the materialisation of the gene, and when DNA emerged in 1944 as the chemical capable of transforming bacteria from virulence to benignity and back, the possibility emerged for DNA to transform human beings as well. Watson and Crick intended to turn that possibility into an inevitability.

Those arguing the case for a 'revolution' in biology have generally confused a palace coup with a revolution. Biology most certainly experienced a change in the personnel exercising power in the years following Watson and Crick's breakthrough but this was a change from the top down (a coup) not from the bottom up (a revolution). The biologists responding to the call of the gene were armed and trained by physicists and chemists turned biologists. These cadres of molecular biology supplied the tactics and knowhow; vested interest supplied the strategy, government, logistics and tactics. Moreover, the period following World War II was a fortunate time for a coup, since governmental support of science was increasing enormously at the time, and the physicists and chemists turned biologists, fresh from World War II, already had experience placing their expertise at the disposal of national interest.

One argument on behalf of a revolution in biology is rarely heard, although it has merit if revolution is defined by historic consequence rather than method. In revolutions generally, 'everything changes so that everything can remain the same'. Following biology's so-called 'revolution', biology was not ruled by a new class so much as by the same old ruling classes in new alliances: the old eugenicists, striving to control the evolution of human beings like any domesticated animal, had become legitimate as molecular biologists striving to control everything about life through genes. The 'new' biology, like the 'old', derived power from the perception that, somehow, biology was the study of life (not merely of genes). In the popular imagination, biology was still the best chance to save life. The promise of understanding life (not merely genes) was preserved, indeed raised to a new plateau by the 'new' biologists' claim to have wiped away effete notions of life through revolution. The people rallied and unfurled banners for improving life behind a president of the United States calling the nation to wage war on cancer, and interest groups demanding war on AIDS and breast cancer. Molecular biologists, like the natural scientists who came before them, were supposed to rescue us all through further revelations of the 'secret of life'.

What the biologists brought with them into the new biology

At the historical moment that large numbers of physicists and chemists became interested in biology, biology's own brand of reductionism was thriving in several of its subdisciplines. Recognisable as preformation or determinism, the 'old' biology's reductionism posited some form of preformed unit or general principle governing life's processes. In genetics, most of life's properties were reduced to predetermined genes (i.e. 'black boxes' or 'beads on a string'). The new biologists' brand of reductionism easily accommodated to the geneticist's brand and the two contracted to live together under the aegis of molecular biology. The geneticists, who had formerly equated adult characters with genes, easily adopted the new biologists' equation of genes with DNA.

Meanwhile, the materialist conquest of birth had begun with the discovery of experimental parthenogenesis, or artificial activation of eggs, by Jacques Loeb (1859–1924).[6] During its own 'golden years', experimental embryology (the 'molecular biology' of the 1930s) was also liberally infiltrated with the determinism of 'determinants'. Following World War II and the consequent disruption of studies on induction, embryology was an easy target for molecular biologists and quickly became 'developmental biology'. Determinism had also permeated physiology through endocrinology, and even physiology's tradition of vitalism could not save it from the molecular reductionists. Cell physiology was subsumed entirely by 'cell biology', and the rest of physiology became a branch of biochemistry.

Some (weak) resistance to incursions by the new brand of reductionism was mounted in 'old' biology quarters but to little avail. A smattering of embryologists, for example, made a belated effort to stand on their roots in embryology's epigenetic tradition, but these efforts foundered for want of philosophical depth. Chief among the dissidents was Lewis Wolpert who advanced a concept of 'positional information' as a return to Drieschian 'entelechy' and a solution to problems of pattern formation.[7] As it turned out, 'positional information' was a Trojan horse. Disguised beneath rhetorical flourishes, 'positional information' was another determinant, namely 'position', which was somehow supposed to be recognized by genetic mechanisms in otherwise equivalent cells and interpreted for local genomic activation. Hardly dynamic, Wolpert's scheme fell back on genes to specify pattern.

Meanwhile, most biologists found some sort of compromise between the old and new biology and made peace with the molecule. Reduction to DNA would remain an ideal, however, something to be fulfilled in the future. For the time being, the object of biology would be discovering the determinist basis for whatsoever passed as life.

Ironically, the biologists who most earnestly embraced the rationale and objective of the new biology were ethologists, biologists studying animal behavior. The irony is not only that behavior would seem as remote from preformation or determinism as one can imagine, but two of ethology's three founders, Karl von Frisch (1886–1982) and Nikolaas Tinbergen (1907–1988), stayed the course and continued to resist the incursions of reductionism in the study of behavior. The third founder, Konrad Lorenz (1903–89),[8] who had previously found affinities between ethology and the Nazi program of eugenics, was more sympathetic to the idea of genetic determinants of behavior. Ethology was thus set up for takeover by geneticists, and when John Maynard Smith, among others, moved into ethology, the study of animal behavior in the wild and under domestication was quickly replaced by the study of games (game theory). And then came E. O. Wilson (b. 1929), who reified behavior and reduced it to putative genes while turning the study of living things as members of social groups into an exercise in genetic one-upmanship.

Sociobiology: In search of behavioral genes

Edward O. Wilson began his career as an animal watcher and petty animal killer, 'plucking enough pygmy salamanders off bushes to give to museums around the country',[9] and ended as a master exterminator (destroying all arthropods on mango groves in the name of biogeography), a two-time (as of 1996) Pulitzer Prize winning Harvard professor and author of the encyclopedic, block busting, *Sociobiology: A New Synthesis*.[10] Wilson's insight was that genes residing in an organism's cells could influence its life at every level of complexity including behavior in a social environment. It was a modest proposal, and Wilson should not be held responsible for all the excesses of his sociobiology followers.

In the case of human beings, behavior is not only characterized by bodily movement but extends to thought, language, belief systems, truth, knowledge and religion. Sociobiologists place responsibility for any number of phobias and philias, talents and handicaps, likes and dislikes, habits and weaknesses, '-isms' and '-ities' at the doorstep of normal genes or their abnormal mutations. In the 1970s a rash of alleged 'behavioral genes' erupted in research laboratories (Lesch-Nyhan syndrome) only to fade when the aberrant behavior attributed to genes was found to be caused by inborn errors of metabolism leading to biochemical imbalance. The molecular biologists had taken aim on their scientific quarry prematurely: complex behavior was not ready for the slings and arrows of outrageous reductionism. By the 1980s, faith in this research had lapsed, although new methodology spawned by the Human Genome Project led to tracing known hereditarily influenced behavior, for example, so-called Huntington's disease (HD), to regions of chromosomes and occasionally to specific genes (see Chapter 1).

Chastened by their failure to find simple genetic explanations for complex behaviors (but possibly buoyed by the prospects for governmental funding of research employing the new methodology), researchers modified their earlier proposals. This time, they would acknowledge complexity and the variety of influences that shape behavior, but they would hold out the possibility that genes (in addition to the environment) may be one of those influences. Researchers were still thinking of genetic 'traits' but they were talking genetic 'influences', 'trends' and 'potential'. The formula was still wrong.

> People do not understand that if both genes and culture interact – of *course* they do – you can't then say it's 20 percent genes and 80 percent environment. You can't do that. It's not meaningful. The emergent property is the emergent property and that's all you can ever say about it.[11]

The early 1990s continued to be bumper years for alleged citings of behavioral genes not only correlated with particular behaviors but with potential causes of these behaviors (genes for alcoholism, aggressivity, manic depression, schizophrenia). Once again, little has panned out.[12] Conclusions evaporated when more evidence accumulated or original evidence was reanalysed, especially after subjects in the original samples were moved from one category of behaviour to another due to changes in their behaviour. Nevertheless, at the moment (1996), studies are still in progress attempting to correlate dyslexia or reading disability, attention-deficit hyperactivity disorder (ADHD) and autism with chromosomal markers linked to autoimmune disorders and genes ('quantitative trait loci') in the human leukocyte antigen complex and in the major histocompatibility complex of chromosome 6.[13]

Other studies go beyond pathology to link particular patterns of human behavior to genes. For example, some studies claim to have found the gene, or, more precisely, a region of the X chromosome containing the gene, for male homosexuality.[14] Applications to federal agencies for support to study the homosexual 'trait', assert in biologically correct language the same claims and disclaimers heard in bars and bath houses in more mundane binaries ('They're born that way', or, 'I've always known . . .'). The meeting of culture and biology is not too hard to locate. It also occurs in the glare of publicity and the fanfare of news conferences, whenever biologists come out of their laboratories and announce their latest findings. Titillation and voyeurism abound. Even the editors of *Science*, probably the most widely read journal of peer-reviewed scientific research articles and reports in the world, cannot resist the temptation to sensationalise, for example, by accompanying reports on genes for the homosexual 'trait' with an understated accompanying feature.[15]

Overarching molecules and overreaching scientists

The lesson of sociobiology should not be lost in its burgeoning literature: biologists are making enormous and enormously misguided efforts to conform to the reductionist methods of the physicists and chemists turned biologists. At the same time, biologists are turning their back on life, the one thing biologists know something about and could teach to physicists and chemists.

One can excuse physicists and chemists for their ignorance of life. Chances are they have not learned any biology since secondary school (or undergraduate school in the conspicuous case of the ornithologist, James Watson).[16] Like many bright people entering new fields, the physicists and chemists entering biology quickly discover that they have in their hand-baggage the tools for solving problems (naive versions of problems, to be sure). The crunch comes when the same physicists and chemists learn a little biology and confront the more demanding problems of life. Here is where biologists can be most helpful, where they·should keep up their own research and scholarship, and where they should be most generous in teaching their colleagues.[17]

The new biologists' beliefs

The idea, whose eruption was said to have brought about the revolution in biology in the decades after World War II, was that organismic and cellular organisation could be translated into chemistry and physics. This idea was the lightning bolt that was supposed to have electrified the physicists and chemists, vaporized the old biologists and made room for the new. The image of an organism as a civil society coping with an unfriendly environment was transmuted into the model of a molecular society or a 'cellular society wired by communication systems'.[18] DNA could be any part of the system, from hardware to software, from a hard drive's irreducible complexity to the tape for a self-assembling machine.[19] Here was a metaphor that electronic engineers could sink their teeth into; a system made for the likes of Jacob and Monod, equipped with circuits of regulatory elements, some already qualified 'operators', ready for work in the cellular telephone network.[20] Above all, it was an idea that worked, at least at an elementary level: it led to the production of gene products that paid their own way. The biotech industry gushed forth following a ground-swell of venture capital and a surge of molecular biologists into commercial enterprises.

The major problem remaining was to show, in the words of the developmental biologist Walter Gehring, 'how the one-dimensional sequence information stored in the DNA is converted into the three-dimensional structure of an embryo, or four-dimensional formation if we also include time . . .'[21] One hypothetical solution to the problem is 'self-assembly', the automatic fitting together of parts of a thing as a result of their intrinsic properties (and a little kinetic energy thrown in by the environment). Self-assembly was supported by the results of experiments with viruses in which the parts produced at the behest of DNA self-assembled into infectious particles. The parts of a cell, a tissue, organ, organ system and organism, are considerably more complex than a virus, however, and all the environmental shuffling in the world (like shaking a bag of enzymes) would not get these parts into the right place at the right time for self-assembly. Possibly, programs of production, self-assembling 'scaffolds' and preexisting 'templates' provide the framework for the manufacture of building blocks or the insertion of prefabricated parts into the intricate, organismic edifice. Such complexity is a long way from the simple chemistry of DNA, but molecular biologists still speak of DNA as the 'blueprint' for constructing the entire organism as if everything else proceeded automatically.

DNA's ascendance in biology

DNA's meteoritic rise in biology was, in no small measure, due to Watson and Crick's success tying DNA to the gene, whose star had already risen. The importance of genes was already established in biology and society. Eugenics and racism had prevailed on popular consciousness long before Watson and Crick, and the gene was already enshrined as biology's greatest legacy, however sordid, to Western culture.[22]

According to the chronicler of molecular biology, Horace F. Judson, DNA mesmerised biologists and seduced them. In Judson's words:

> The structure of DNA, once known, made its function as a blue-print comprehensible and therefore incontrovertible . . .

Beyond that, deoxyribonucleic acid turned out to be a substance of elegance, even beauty. Structure and those dual functions are united in DNA with such ingenious parsimony that one smiles with the delight of perceiving it. Extreme elegance is almost more convincing to scientists than it should be.[23]

Judson suggests that the transformation of molecular biology from a branch of structural biochemistry to the premier reductionist science occurred because the new biologists preferred the beautiful and elegant DNA to the clumsy and refractory gene.[24]

Alternatively, according to Robert Olby,[25] historian and Watson and Crick apologist, the ascendance of DNA depended on dislodging protein from its reign as the gene. The DNA-as-gene concept acknowledged the centrality of protein in most of life's processes but pushed these processes to the background while bringing encryption to the foreground as life's defining activity. According to Olby, Watson and Crick succeeded in changing a 'central dogma of proteins' to a 'central dogma of nucleic acids' by showing that the physico-chemical properties of DNA could match the biological properties of genes in more obvious ways than could any known physico-chemical properties of proteins:[26]

the change from the protein gene to the DNA gene was brought about by a number of events and not by one or two 'crucial' experiments alone. These several experimental results served to create a climate in which the outcome of the so-called crucial experiments could be interpreted in support of this radical change of view.[27]

The features of genes that could not be duplicated by properties of DNA were ignored or placed on the proverbial shelf for study at some later time.

Olby does not explain, however, what discredited protein's pretensions to the gene's throne.[28] The features of protein that had earlier led molecular biologists to equate genes with protein, especially their specificity and all the activities attributed to proteins in building organisms and working as enzymes, had not gone away or disappeared. Why could not DNA and protein represent different types of genes? Part of the answer is the obsession scientists have with the singular. Another part is purely pragmatic: solutions to the mysteries laid open by DNA's structure were ostensibly solvable with existing or foreseeable technology and provided immediate work for physicists and chemists.

The history of molecular biology since Watson and Crick shows incontrovertibly that the idea of complementarity filled major holes in the concept of the DNA gene. Holes in protein remain gaping.

Philosophers of science, as opposed to historians of science, are less inclined to find DNA's virtue in beauty, elegance or in shifting centers of central dogmas. For philosophers, knowledge of DNA's physical structure allowed biologists for the first time to lay claim to reductionism and to analysis in the tradition of natural sciences. Aside from DNA, the central dogma and natural selection, 'most theories propounded in biology and medicine are not now and will not in the foreseeable future be "universal" theories'.[29] Not even the concept of the gene reached that plateau, and, in any case, the physical language of DNA exceeded anything the concept of the gene had to offer.[30] The personal subjectivity attached to the concept of the gene, in which meaning changes with the discipline or the person using the term, disappears with the 'inter-subjective' physical language of DNA.

This reductionist, neoPlatonic view had as many practical teeth as it had idealist caps. Molecular biologists appreciated that DNA gave them a basis for absolute prediction, since every statement about base pairing would be valid, at least in theory, independently of whosoever was speaking. They also appreciated that absolutes have cultural appeal and are excellent devices of salesmanship and statesmanship. Moreover, in Western society successful prediction derails opposition and rallies supporters. In the view of the philosopher Kenneth Schaffner, DNA won the hearts and minds of biologists through logical pragmatism, according to which: 'both the practices and the results of the sciences [are taken] seriously, as not to be analysed away with neat logical distinctions but rather to be explicated in all their complexity and richness with the aid of both historical and philosophical tools.'[31] to be vulgar, what attracted molecular biologists to the double helix was the power that came from the ability to predict the consequences of experimental manipulations, to launch a new industry, and to ignore anything that does not advance profits.

Notes

1. Kuhn, 1970a,b,c.
2. Lakatos and Musgrave, 1970.
3. Notably, Hoyningen-Huene, 1993.
4. Mastermann, 1970; Horgan, 1996.
5. For a discussion of a historical (rooted), dialectic and incomplete change in a science's method or way of acquiring (epistemological break, rupture and *Gestalt* switch) outside the Kuhnian canon see Bachelard, 1984, and Canguilhem, 1988.

6. Pauly, 1987.
7. Wolpert, 1985.
8. Von Frisch, Lorenz, and Tinbergen were jointly awarded the Nobel Prize in Physiology or Medicine in 1973.
9. Wilson, p. 104, 1984.
10. Wilson, 1974.
11. Stephen Jay Gould, quoted in Horgan, p. 125, 1996.
12. Schizophrenia genes are especially problematic, since their citings jump between chromosomes 5, 6, 9, 20 and 22. For recent 'Research news' on schizophrenia genes see Marshall, 1995a; Holden, 1995; Restak, especially pp. 142–3, 1991, and for manic-depression genes see Morell, 1996. Also see Steen, 1996 for a popular review of genes and behaviour.
13. Cardon *et al.*, 1994; Warren *et al.*, 1995.
14. Hamer *et al.*, 1993. Also Pool, 1993; Marshall, 1995b.
15. LeVay, 1991. Also Barinaga, 1991.
16. For example, Judson, p. 109, 1979, concedes that Crick was 'to an unusual extent self-educated in biology'.
17. Glanz, 1996.
18. Sapp, p. 246, 1985.
19. Hawkins, 1964. Also see Behe, 1996 for other analogues and literature on artificial life, e.g. Levy, 1992.
20. Jacob and Monod, 1963.
21. Gehring, p. 1245, 1987.
22. Nelkin and Lindee, 1995.
23. Judson, pp. 23–4, 1979.
24. Wilson, pp. 60–1 1984, takes the case for beauty and elegance as the basis of scientific epistemology to its logical extreme by basing it on evolution.
25. Olby, 1994.
26. Judson, p. 507, 1979, Attention did not merely move away from protein as a standard for the gene but as a standard for life.
27. Olby, p. 449, 1994.
28. Olby, p. 211, 1994, cites Alfred E. Mirsky (1900–74) and A. W. Pollister (b. 1903) as raising the last serious challenge to a purely DNA concept of the gene.
29. Schaffner, p. 97, 1993.
30. According to Carnap, p. 55, 1934, '[P]hysical language is a universal language, i.e. . . . every statement can be translated into it.'
31. Schaffner, p. 515, 1993.

References

Bachelard, G., *The New Scientific Spirit*, trans. A. Goldhammer (Boston: Beacon Press, 1984).
Barinaga, M., 'Is homosexuality biological?', *Science*, 253: 956–7, 1991.
Behe, M. J., *Darwin's Black Box: the Biochemical Challenge to Evolution* (New York: The Free Press, 1996).
Canguilhem, G., *Ideology and Rationality in the History of the Life Sciences* (Cambridge: MIT Press, 1988).

Cardon, L. R., S. D. Smith, D. W. Fulker, W. J. Kimberling, B. R. Pennington and J. C. Defries. 'Quantitative trait locus for reading disability on chromsome 6', *Science*, 266: 276–9, 1994.

Carnap, R., *The Unity of Science*, trans. with an introduction by M. Black, 1995 (Bristol: Thoemmes Press, 1934).

Gehring, W. J., 'Homeoboxes in the study of development', *Science*, 236: 1245–52, 1987.

Glanz, J., 'Physicists advance into biology', *Science*, 272: 646–8, 1996.

Hamer, D. H., S. Hu, V.L. Magnuson, N. Hu, A. M. L. Pattatucci, 'A linkage between DNA markers on the X chromosome and male sexual orientation', *Science*, 261: 321–7, 1993.

Hawkins, D., *The Language of Nature* (San Francisco: W. H. Freeman, 1964).

Holden, C., 'Who's postdocing now?', *Science*, 269: 1049, 1995.

Horgan, J., *The End of Science: Facing the Limits of Knowledge in the Twilight of the Scientific Age* (Reading, Mass.: Addison-Wesley, 1996).

Hoyningen-Huene, P., *Reconstructing Scientific Revolutions: Thomas S. Kuhn's Philosophy of Science*, Trans. Alexander T. Levine (Chicago: University of Chicago Press, 1993).

Jacob, F. and J. Monod, 'Genetic repression, allosteric inhibition and cellular differentiation', in M. Locke (ed), *Cytodifferentiation and Macromolecular Synthesis*, The Twenty-first symposium of the Society for the Study of Development and Growth (New York: Academic Press, 1963), pp. 30–64.

Judson, H. R., *The Eighth Day of Creation: Makers of the Revolution in Biology* (New York: Simon and Schuster, 1979).

Kuhn, T. S., *The Structure of Scientific Revolutions*, 2nd edn (Chicago: University of Chicago Press, 1970a).

Kuhn, T. S., 'Logic of discovery or psychology of research', in I. Lakatos and A. Musgrave (eds), *Criticism and the Growth of Knowledge* (Cambridge: Cambridge University Press, 1970b, pp. 1–20).

Kuhn, T. S. 'Reflections on my critics', in I. Lakatos and A. Musgrave (eds), *Criticism and the Growth of Knowledge* (Cambridge: Cambridge University Press, 1970c, pp. 231–78).

Lakatos, I. and A. Musgrave, (eds), *Criticism and the Growth of Knowledge* (Cambridge University Press, Cambridge: 1970).

LeVay, S., 'A difference, in hypothalamic structure between heterosexual and homosexual men,' *Science*, 253: 1034–7, 1991.

Levy, S., *Artificial Life: the Quest for a New Creation* (London: Jonathan Cape, 1992).

Marshall, E., 'Dispute splits, schizophrenia study', *Science*, 268: 792–4, 1995a.

Marshall, E., 'NIH's "Gay gene" study questioned', *Science*, 268: 1841, 1995b.

Mastermann, M. 'The nature of a paradigm', in I. Lakatos and A. Musgrave (eds), *Criticism and the Growth of Knowledge* (Cambridge: Cambridge University Press, 1970, pp. 59–89).

Morell, V., 'Manic-depression findings spark polarized debate', *Science*, 272: 31–2, 1996.

Nelkin, D. and S. Lindee, *The DNA Mystique: the Gene as a Cultural Icon* (San Francisco: W.H. Freeman, 1995).

Olby, R., *The Path to the Double Helix: the Discovery of DNA*; unabridged, corrected and enlarged republication (New York: Dover Publications, 1994).

Pauly, P. J., *Controlling Life: Jacques Loeb and the Engineering Ideal in Biology* (Oxford: Oxford University Press, 1987).

Pool, R., 'Evidence for homosexuality gene research news', *Science*, 261: 291–2, 1993.

Restak, R., *The Brain Has a Mind of Its Own: Insights from a Practicing Neurologist* (New York: Harmony Books, 1991).

Sapp, J., 'Concepts of organization and leverage of ciliate protozoa, in S.F. Gilbert (ed), *A Conceptual History of Modern Embryology, Developmental Biology: a Comprehensive Synthesis*, Vol. 7 (New York: Plenum Press, 1985), pp. 229–58.

Schaffner, K., *Discovery and Explanation in Biology and Medicine* (Chicago: University of Chicago Press, 1993).

Steen, R. G., *DNA and Destiny: Nature and Nurture in Human Behavior* (New York: Plenum Press, 1996).

Warren, R. P., J. D. Odell, W. L. Warren, R. A. Burger, A. Maciulis, W. W. Daniels and A. R. Torres, 'Reading disability, attention-deficit hyperactivity disorder, and the immune system,' *Science*, 268: 786–7, 1995.

Wilson, E. O., *Sociobiology: a New Synthesis* (Cambridge: Belknap Press of Harvard University Press, 1974).

Wilson, E. O., *Biophilia* (Cambridge: Harvard University Press, 1984).

Wolpert, L., 'Gradients, position and pattern: a history', in T. J. Horder, J. A. Witkowski and C. C. Wylie (eds), *History of Embryology*, 8th Symposium of the British Society for Developmental Biology (Cambridge: Cambridge University Press, 1985), pp. 347–85.

24

Jean-Jacques Lecercle; *Interpretation as Pragmatics* (1999)

The Language, Discourse, Society series has published several studies of language which have gone far beyond the familiar territory of a professional linguistics – most notably the translations of Jean-Claude Milner's *For the Love of Language* and Michel Pêcheux's *Language, Semantics, and Ideology.* Resembling these in its departures from the customary range of linguists' preoccupations but otherwise distinctive in its detailed and scrupulous iconoclasm, Jean-Jacques Lecercle's *Interpretation as Pragmatics* offers a new account of what it is to interpret a text. Exemplifying a thoroughly Deleuzian stress on the incalculable yet traceable workings of language from the outside, and following on from the author's earlier *The Violence of Language*, with its espousal of the forceful yet fertile seepage of words beyond their commonly supposed bounds, this book proposes that literary interpretations may be sometimes just and sometimes false, while never true. Interpretation here ceases to be seen as a tin-opener and is conceived instead, in neo-Wittgensteinian diction, as a language-game with several players: author, language, text, encyclopaedia, reader. The radiating centrality of the text in this new model does not, however, suppose any radical separability of the fictional from the quotidian, let alone any unique superiority of a literary–critical approach. Rather, the work of literary interpretation proceeds, as Lecercle demonstrates in painstaking detail, in ways closely comparable to what happens in face-to-face dialogue. Because the implications of such a pragmatic account of interpretation also have repercussions for a theory of how the human subject is linguistically installed and pinned in place, Paul Hirst's early commentary on Althusser's concept of interpellation (in his LDS volume *On Law and Ideology*) and Judith Butler's more recent consideration of interpellation (in her *Excitable Speech*) receive an incisive critique and Lecercle develops an empathetic account of inter-pellation's spasmodically emancipating harshness.

The extracts that follow give an indication of Lecercle's argument and his lan-guage-games account of interpretation.

Pragmatics

If our aim is to adjudicate between just and false interpretations, the 'pragmatic contract' that justice in interpretation involves must be defined. The definition and description of such a contract, or 'pragmatic model', is the object of the rest of this book.

In our analysis of interpretation as process and result, we have gradually come within the scope of pragmatics and speech-act theory.[1] Extensions of the tin-opener into translation and intervention, as well as the four theses on interpretation, imply that the link between utterer's meaning (author's intention) and utterance meaning (the meaning of the text) is threatened or severed. This distance between intention and meaning is the specific field of interpretation. And the four moments of interpretation *qua* process involve the actors, or actants (see following chapters) of a pragmatic contract, or of a situation of communication: glossing involves language and encyclopaedia, disclosure or solution the speaker's (the author's) constructed intention, translation the reader, in her relation to both text and encyclopaedia, while intervention lies within the ambit of the reader's powers. What we have here is the five actants of a situation of communication: speaker (author), text, language, encyclopaedia, hearer (reader).

The guiding thread of the book, therefore, will be the following: I mean systematically to operate a metaphorical extension from *speech act* to *text*, from *linguistic interlocution* to *textual interpretation: interpretation is a language-game in which a text is treated as an extended speech act*, involving the five actants already mentioned, and rules or maxims that remain to be formulated.

Such a hypothesis implies a certain critical path, which the rest of the book will follow. I shall attempt to construct a pragmatic model embodying the intuitions the hypothesis evokes, and drawing on precedents in linguistics, the theory of argument, narratology, and pragmatics proper. Thus, interpretation conceived according to this hypothesis may be treated at first as a form of (cooperative?) dialogue. Later it will involve the ascription, and the description, of places within a pragmatic system (the concept of 'place' is developed in Flahault[2]). Lastly, it will involve the question of subjectivity, in Althusserian parlance of *assujettissement*, as the ascription of places implies the interpellation of the various actors caught in the game of interpretation, in order to fill them. The urgent task, therefore, is the construction of a pragmatic model along the lines of my hypothesis.

The language-game of interpretation will be satisfactorily accounted for if I determine the structure of the places or actants involved, and the rules or maxims according to which the game is played.

Notes

1. I use the term 'pragmatics' in the common-and-garden sense in which linguists use it today, even if I draw different conclusions. See S. C. Levinson, *Pragmatics* (Cambridge, Cambridge University Press, 1983); J. L. Mey, *Pragmatics: an Introduction* (Oxford, Blackwell, 1993); S. Petrey, *Speech Acts and Literary Theory* (London, Routledge, 1990).
2. F. Flahault, *La Parole intermédiaire* (Paris, Seuil, 1978).

Language-games

[. . .] Language is encyclopaedic. The language we are talking about, therefore, is like the other elements on the gradient, institutions rituals and practices, material and historical. I have elsewhere attempted such a description of language, centered on the concept of the remainder.[1] This involves a departure from the tradition of 'scientific' linguistics that originates in the work of Saussure. My concept of language is not based on the arbitrary character of the sign, the possibility of formalisation, or the synchronic *coupe d'essence*. It treats language as a social and historical construction, and is more interested in the historical semantics sketched by Raymond Williams than in the centrality of syntax – the history of 'sentiment' and 'Bovril' is of more interest to me than the placement of clitics in Italian. This also involves abandoning the claim that linguistics is a 'hard' science, a model for the rest of the human or social sciences. It involves a research programme incompatible with the Chomskyan research programme. Not so much with the empirical findings (which are, with the development of the theory, less and less compelling) as with the dubious philosophy of language that comes with it. This concept of language (I think this is one of its main advantages) rejects the Chomskyan belief in human nature (where language is an innate competence, inscribed in the hardware of the human brain, not an object of learning), in a psychology of faculties (another regression to the seventeenth or the eighteenth century), and the dissolution of the English, or the French, language as object of study, the Englishness of English being reduced to the switching of a few specific parameters within the array of possibilities provided by universal grammar.

Being passionately attached to the English language, to its grammar, to its stylistics, to its history, I find all this difficult to swallow, and consequently more palatable a concept of language as incarnated (speech acts, as Butler says (op. cit.), are bodily acts – what the construction of meaning is about is the communication of a force), as historical (the systematic aspect is an effect of construction, of the synchronic *coupe d'essence* – but the construction is historical) and cultural (determined by the often mentioned institutions, rituals and practices). In short, I am advocating a Marxist concept of language which, in spite of a few cryptic hints by the founding fathers, the pronouncements of the pseudo-Stalin, and a variegated but fragmented tradition[2] does not yet exist. But that is the subject of another book.

If language is encyclopaedic, the encyclopaedia is linguistic. My thesis in this respect can be formulated simply: *the encyclopaedia is a set of language-games*. I have on many occasions borrowed Wittgenstein's concept, without defining it otherwise than by the simple indication that a language-game involves rules or maxims and participants – in other words a language-game is a game. The time has come to be more specific. By language-game I mean the incarnation of the encyclopaedia-to-language gradient, of the Althusserian chain of interpellation (institutions and so on): the frame within which the force of interpellation circulates, and individuals are captured as subjects and exert their power of imposture.

This appears to be a long way from Wittgenstein: a return to the origins is in order. The concept, as is well-known, has various contents in Wittgenstein, who sometimes speaks of invented, and sometimes of natural, language-games. The first famous passage comes from the *Blue Book*:

> I shall in the future again and again draw your attention to what I shall call language-games. These are ways of using signs simpler than those in which we use the signs in our highly complicated everyday language. Language-games are the form of language with which a child begins to make use of words. The study of language games is the study of primitive forms of language or primitive languages. . . . When we look at such simple forms of language the mental mist which seems to enshroud our ordinary use of language disappears.[3]

This is clearly not the sense in which I have used the phrase – the language-games I have evoked are neither 'primitive' (phrases like 'primitive forms of language' or 'primitive language' are of course highly dubious) nor childish. A language-game as conceived here is a heuristic and a simplificatory device, whereas my examples of language-games have all involved highly complicated (if not always 'everyday') practices. However, Wittgenstein also gives those complicated practices the name of language-games. This occurs, for instance, in *Philosophical Investigations*, in another famous passage where it takes the form of a list:

But how many kinds of sentences are there? Say assertion, question and command? – there are *countless* kinds: countless different kinds of uses of what we call 'symbols', 'words', 'sentences', And this multiplicity is not something fixed, given once for all; but new types of language, new language-games, as we may say, come into existence, and others become obsolete and get forgotten . . .

Here the term 'language-game' is meant to bring into prominence the fact that the speaking of language is part of an activity, or of a form of life.

Review the multiplicity of language-games in the following examples, and in others:

Giving orders, and obeying them –
Describing the appearance of an object, or giving it measurements –
Constructing an object for a description (a drawing) –
Reporting an event –
Speculating about an event –
Forming and testing a hypothesis –
Presenting the results or an experiment in tables and diagrams –
Making up a story; and reading it –
Play-acting –
Singing catches –
Guessing riddles –
Making a joke; telling it –
Solving a problem in practical arithmetic –
Translating from one language into another –
Asking, thinking, cursing, greeting, praying.[4]

So even the tin-opener (in the form of 'guessing riddles') is a 'form of life'. This is a way of pointing out that the list *in nuce* contains most of the analyses I have developed. It appears that interpretation in its four versions of glossing, guessing, translation and intervention is a family of language-games (the two middle versions are explicitly mentioned in the list); that the object of communication is the imposition of a force (some of the language-games mentioned, like 'giving orders', are performative *avant la lettre*); and that not only interpretation but literary production falls within the scope of language-games, from making a joke to making up a story and play-acting: literature is a collection of genres, that is *a family of language-games*. Lastly, it appears that the term 'form of life' covers the whole of Althusser's chain of interpellation as some of those language-games are material practices (constructing an object from a drawing: no one ever managed to construct an air-pump from Boyle's drawings, but many tried), or rituals (play-acting, presenting the results of an experiment, cursing or praying), and some involve institutions (in order to present the results of an experiment, you need an academy).

There is a link between such 'natural' language-games and the language-games Wittgenstein invents as tools for his philosophical method. In a volume of their lengthy commentary on the *Philosophical Investigations*, Baker and Hacker, describing the 'language-game method', give the following seven features as characterising Wittgenstein's invented language-games: (i) they consist of words and sentences – a basic vocabulary and rules or maxims; (ii) they involve extra-linguistic instruments like pictures or gestures (hence insisting on the pragmatic side of language-games); (iii) they imply a context – both a setting for the game, and the meaning-presuppositions generated by the moves in the game, that is the utterances; (iv) they also involve activities that make the point and purpose of the game evident; (v) against a structural concept of language, they insist on the role of use, purpose and function (of the words, of the sentences, of the instruments) in the emergence of meaning – this is the major move away from traditional linguistics into a pragmatics of forms of life; (vi) they need to be learnt: one learns to follow the rules, to bridge the gap between rule and application; and (vii) they are complete: a form of life stands, so to speak, on its own feet – so does a literary genre, or a ritual. A language-game is characterised by its (relative) autonomy.[5]

It seems to me that this array of features accounts not only for the individual components of the encyclopaedia, but for language itself – by operating a shift from language as structure and system to language as institution and practice: what the ALTER model seeks to embody. Which enables me to give a final account of the title of this book in the following three theses:

Thesis 1: A language-game is defined, and developed, as an ALTER structure. Expression and understanding, writing and reading occur within a language-game. They involve a whole form of life and not only utterances and 'ideas': practices, rituals, institutions, extra-linguistic elements, and so on. They involve the action of interpellation and the circulation of the force that it sets in motion – interpellation occurs within the frame of a language-game, and it is the 'point' or 'purpose' of the language-game. And since a language-game is a game, counter-interpellation, or imposture, is not only a possibility but a necessity since a game involves various participants and moves. Even the cooperative Gricean game of understanding an utterance by computing implicatures is based on the activity of flouting the maxims that govern the game. This is the sense in which my theory of interpretation is a 'pragmatic' theory.

Thesis 2: Interpretation is a natural language-game, like guessing a riddle, or translating. It 'comes naturally', it is indispensable even in the most homely of everyday situations. Every time we engage in dialogue we gloss, we guess, we translate and we intervene. And we do this as participants in a game: we play by the rules, otherwise we suffer communicational failure. But interpretation is also the construction of invented language-games, not only in that sophisticated texts require the construction of more and more sophisticated interpretive techniques, but in that it allows, in the guise of the counter-interpellation of imposture, the interpreter a certain latitude to construct the game in which she takes part. On the one hand, she is interpellated at her place by the text, she abides by the rules it imposes on her through an ALTER structure. On the other hand, through imposture, she also constructs those rules, with and against the text – for even the interpellators must be interpellated.

Thesis 3: Literature is a family of language-games (this includes but goes far beyond the traditional concept of genre), sedimented into a canon. I have sketched the concept of canon which this involves elsewhere.[6] Developing this thesis would involve a theory of literature and that, too, is the subject of another book. I shall be content, as a farewell gesture; with a brief excursus into a pragmatic theory of the emergence of literature which I have found in the work of the French classicist, Florence Dupont.[7]

Notes

1. J.-J. Lecercle, *The Violence of Language* (Routledge, 1990).
2. A few names beyond the already cited Bakhtin, Pêcheux, Williams and Tran Duc Thao will suffice: Rossi Landi's Marxist semiotics, Lafont's praxematics, perhaps even Deleuze and Guattari's critique of the postulates of linguistics in *Mille Plateaux*, and Bourdieu's *Ce que parler veut dire*.
3. L. Wittgenstein, *The Blue and Brown Books* (Oxford, Blackwell, 1958), p. 17.
4. L. Wittgenstein, *Philosophical Investigations* (Oxford, Blackwell, 1953), pp. 11–12.

5. G. P. Baker and P. M. S. Hacker, *Wittgenstein. Meaning and Understanding* (Oxford, Blackwell, 1980), pp. 54–5.
6. J. J. Lecercle, 'The Münchhausen effect', in *EJES*, I(1) (Lisse, Netherlands, Swets & Zeitlinger, 1997), pp. 86–100.
7. F. Dupont, *L'Invention de la littérature: de l'ivresse grecque au livre latin* (Paris, La Découverte, 1994).

25

Patrizia Lombardo, *Cities, Words and Images: From Poe to Scorsese* (2003)

Cities are concrete realities. Words and images are used to describe their presence and physical impact on human life. From the nineteenth century on, with the coming of modernity, writers, critics, philosophers, architects and film-makers, among others, have shown conflicting attitudes towards the city, running the gamut from hostility to idolatry. Lombardo's book reflects on the changes in human perception created by urbanisation and the way in which these changes are expressed in the form and content of the various arts. Whatever the particular medium and moving across national boundaries, the urban theme is shown by Lombardo to be fundamental to the understanding of modern art.

The book is wide-ranging in the materials it discusses, taking up *inter alia* the urban fantasies of Poe, Baudelaire's Paris, the Vienna of Hoffmansthal and Musil, Massimo Cacciari's Venice, and New York as conceived by Adolf Loos, Aldo Rossi and Martin Scorsese. In the short chapter reprinted here, Lombardo considers the overwhelming presence of the visual as the sense of the city as icon of the modern world and the terms of an aesthetic resistance to that sense.

The image versus the visible: From Baudelaire's *The Painter of Modern Life* to David Lynch's *Lost Highway*

Human perception in our contemporary world seems to be increasingly visual.[1] The overwhelming presence of the visual calls for a type of experience where physical sensation and the immediate feelings connected with it are constantly solicited. The richness of the visual is boundless: the gaze dominates every human activity. Cinema has magnified the power of the gaze. One need only think of Michael Powell's *Peeping Tom* (1960): the protagonist is obsessed by the camera, and his voyeurism turns him into a serial killer. According to Fredric Jameson in *Signatures of the Visible*, contemporary civilization 'has transformed human nature into this single protean sense, which even moralism can surely no longer wish to amputate'.[2] Media are the instruments of an 'all-pervasive visuality'; films 'are a physical experience, and are remembered as such, stored in bodily synapses that evade the thinking mind'.[3]

The argument developed by Jameson is constructed very generally on the basis of a Marxist approach. On one hand the inescapable presence of capitalism turns the visual into an addiction which bypasses the thinking mind: it is the most contemporary form of alienation. On the other hand, only a historical analysis can help us to resist this process: 'This book will argue the proposition that the only way to think the visual, to get a handle on increasing, tendential, all-pervasive visuality as such, is to grasp its historical coming into being.'[4] Against Jameson's proposition I shall argue that aesthetic experience itself furnishes the resistance Jameson has in mind, and always has done. It is there that we find what Jameson calls 'other kinds of thought' capable of replacing 'the act of seeing by something else'.[5] These different kinds of thought are actually already present in aesthetic apprehension, or more precisely in an aesthetic experience of *high* quality. While considering some of the assumptions of several modern or contemporary critics, this chapter will focus on the analysis of two examples which show an unexpected similarity: Baudelaire's aesthetic principles and David Lynch's aesthetic implications in *Lost Highway*.

It is probably time to rethink the whole problem of aesthetic value and stop being afraid of evaluating works of art as good or bad, even if, of course, in the free-market society under capitalism, the art-object circulates like any other product (as Jameson reminds us in the first chapter of *Signatures of the Visible*, 'Reification and Utopia in Mass Culture'). If production affects aesthetics, this does not mean that the appreciation of aesthetic values has to be completely condemned. High-quality aesthetic experience calls for a type of attention that resists the absolutism of consumption. Historical analysis can indeed get to grips with the increasingly addictive power of visuality as such, but philosophical reflection is equally urgent, reflection which can overcome the simple opposition between the radical consciousness and the so-called 'traditional aesthetic philosophy'.

While emphasising the 'force of application' of the theory of reification so important to Max Weber and the Frankfurt School, Jameson insists on the contrast between this new notion and the traditional definition of art as 'a goal-oriented activity which nonetheless has no practical purpose or end in the "real world" of business or politics or concrete human praxis generally'.[6] But disinterested contemplation is not the sole or even the most important tradition of aesthetics and, crucially, there is more than one traditional aesthetic philosophy. Two contrasting attitudes can be identified in Western thought: one separates the world of emotions from the world of reason (*der Geist*, spirit; *die Vernunft*, the intellect); the other insists that emotions and thought are inseparable, and that both are part of the *Geist*. The first attitude is found in the Kantian tradition and is still popular in philosophy and theories of culture; the second goes back to Shaftesbury and his heirs, and to Austro-German philosophers influenced by Brentano, such as Robert Musil. It is time to consider this philosophical tradition seriously in the field of aesthetics, too. The study of the rationality of emotions has been an important achievement in the last 20 or 30 years within analytical philosophy, political philosophy, ethics.[7] From this perspective, the artistic product can be appreciated as having a critical power comparable to that revealed by historical analysis.

The consequences of Kantian dualism are unfortunately widespread. In philosophy, the irrationality of emotions is often taken for granted; while in literary and artistic works the obsession with feeling and the heart has created, and continues to create, much confusion. Finally, in everyday life the identification of emotion with strong, merely physical impulses (sex and violence) seems inescapable and hides many subtle affective phenomena. The overrating of the sentimental is typical of the nineteenth-century Western romantic attitude (for example, German Romanticism, the English romantic poets, the American Transcendentalists or Chateaubriand[8]). Even the Freudian and post-Freudian concentration on drives and instincts helps to make many affective phenomena invisible, since drives are nothing like as rich as the infinite gamut of emotions.[9] Some contemporary critical fashions which cultivate obscurity, jargon and an overall nihilist flavour also derive from old dualist habits. Postmodern criticism – whether enthusiastic or negative – is often based on an anti-rational impulse, anti-logocentric (to use the canonical term) response, with a simplistic association of reason and bourgeois cultural hegemony. The opposition between low and high culture is often based on the division between the heart and the head, the rational and the irrational.

Against all these sharp, simplistic divisions, the analysis of the work of art, its effects, and its composition as a form, can offer an alternative to the all-pervasive visuality of today's world. The work of art and the aesthetic experience can actually oppose the divorce between body and mind, while revealing the strong link between rationality and emotion.

The Marxist postmodern approach of Jameson simply presupposes the two separate realms: on one side, the sensationalist, addictive, completely physical and totalitarian domination of sight; on the other side, fully rational behaviour within the process of rationalisation in commodification. Here the forms of human activity 'are instrumentally reorganised and "taylorised," analytically fragmented and reconstructed according to various rational models of efficiency'.[10] But a proper understanding of the imagination and its activity through different works of art can clarify the real interrelation between the emotional and the rational. The work of imagination participates in that specific emotion, which is the aesthetic emotion, as well as all the emotions that are represented by the work of imagination itself. A work of art does indeed represent something – a claim all the struggle against representation which has preoccupied avant-garde criticism over the last 30 years has not overturned. The aesthetic approach understands representation not as a way of reinstating the concept of a supposedly stable reality simply reproduced by art, but, rather, as something capable of suggesting models of human mental behaviour.

Imagination, even in its most specific expressions, is a faculty implying human emotions and mental mechanisms that are not separated from the rational, even if they are unconscious (in the sense that they do not depend directly on the will). Imagination can elucidate several aspects of human behaviour in general. Here I would like to draw attention to Gilberto Freyre who, in several of his many editions of *Casa-Grande e Senzala*, talked in a similar vein of the value of art. He speaks of his pioneering work in sociology and anthropology as similar to that of Picasso in plastic arts. He concentrated on the study of 'human behaviour, both the primitive and the civilized, the rational and the irrational'.[11] He mentioned also the examples of Marcel Proust and Henry James whose fiction is 'sometimes the equivalent of a social history that could be also a scientifically psychological history'.[12] Human behaviour is in his opinion both objective and imaginative.

The re-reading of Freyre can help today's theory and criticism to maintain some distance from the approaches of the 1960s and 1970s, and their postmodern re-enactment. The recent massive rejection in European universities of the study of literature and art – as is clearly evident in the treatment by systems of public funding of the humanities – often assumes the uselessness of art. But the analysis of aesthetic experience shows that it is not solely concerned with some supposedly specific and autonomous realm of art. An important assumption of an aesthetic approach, in line with Walter Benjamin's *The Work of Art*

(1936), is the belief that we can understand more about society, contemporary or not, if we look at ways of imagining human behaviour, understanding and feeling. It seems a matter of particular urgency to understand the value of the imagination in today's cyberworld as a conscious resistance against the devaluing of images, since, paradoxically, the effect of the frantic post-capitalist circulation of images is profoundly iconoclastic:[13] images do not mean anything any longer. Understanding works of the imagination can clarify the dangers of complete human catastrophe described by several thinkers, such as Guy Debord or Paul Virilio. In a world of spectacle where images become the ultimate objects of consumption, a reflection upon art should accompany the historical perspective suggested by Jameson.

The main assumptions of postmodern criticism inevitably lead to the complete loss of a structuring principle, for example the assumption that the victory of commodification is total (so total that even the rationalising principle of reification is completely debunked: as in Schumpeter's vision of capitalism, where reification grows beyond any control). But the analysis of aesthetic experience shows that emotional and intellectual life is an open bundle that is nevertheless structured rather than scattered at random – because some artistic objects, while embodying in their form and content the commodification process to which they inevitably belong, nevertheless avoid being entirely dissipated by it, and focus on the interplay between the rational and the irrational, openness and structure, the head and the heart. When Freyre talks about Picasso's unitary art (*'arte unitaria'*), he means precisely such holding together as opposed to all scattering. He finds, in fact, that in spite of the dismembering of human bodies in his paintings, Picasso shows a strong sense of unity.

In the internet age, commodification has reached a level of globalisation that even the most futuristic thinkers of the postmodern condition could not fully foresee. Jameson has suggested, following Guy Debord's *The Society of the Spectacle*,[14] that 'the ultimate form of commodity reification in contemporary consumer society is precisely the image itself. When we buy the new model car, we consume less the thing itself than its abstract idea, open to all the libidinal investments ingeniously arrayed for us by advertising.'[15] But, as we know, along with the negative visions of a society of all-pervasive visuality, there are some thinkers who express enthusiasm for its liberating qualities. Gianni Vattimo, for example, criticised the utopia of a transparent society dear to Jürgen Habermas and Karl-Otto Apel, pointing out the positive values of the *non*-transparency of the society of spectacle. The technological society is non-transparent because it is manipulated by power, since technological development constitutes the object of pro- paganda and of the conservation and enhancement of ideology. But Vattimo's non-transparent society is also a world where reality takes on a soft and mobile character, where experience is marked by constant change and the ludic attitude is pervasive.[16] The chaos of the non- transparent mass-media society, he tells us, is not a phenomenon to be opposed or rejected; on the contrary, such chaos comprehends the very change that makes possible the liberation of minorities. The new form of human experience in the non-transparent society is to be the key to cultural pluralism.

The general aesthetic approach as well as the examples discussed below argue against both the tragic pessimism of Debord and the floating free-associations of postmodern experience. Some artistic pro- ductions involve a critical power which does not correspond to the old-fashioned radical avant-garde hope of total subversion. Some works of art are consciously shaped by the contemporary circulation of images but resist fashionable views of that circulation. They might illustrate what Jameson calls 'the anti-social and critical, negative (although not generally revolutionary) stance of much of the most important forms of modern art'.[17] But these works of art embody the rejection of the Kantian dualism between reason and emotion. They manifest an important affinity with some of Baudelaire's major intuitions about modern art or with some of the main ideas of Robert Musil.

Baudelaire's works obviously furnish the classic example of many modern aesthetic principles; let these illustrate what I have called the 'aesthetic approach'. Baudelaire felt the need for art to respond to the modes of life of the present, which meant metropolitan life and its conse- quences in and for human perception. The conditions of subjectivity and experience in the modern big city are a constant concern in his poems and in his writings on painting. While searching for an art capable of integrating in its own form and content the real conditions of modernity, he insisted on the abstract aspect of art, thus anticipating the contempo- rary idea of the persistence of the vision in the retina and therefore in the mind – as suggested by Paul Virilio. We see, and the image that we see lingers in our memory while other images roll in front of our eyes. In order to be able to see, we must abstract, remember and understand images.

As I have suggested in other chapters, Delacroix's painting was in Baudelaire's opinion the product of thought and intelligence. Memory requires speedy execution, if the artist is not to lose his ideas. Baudelaire had seen the connection between memory and speed already in his *Salons* of 1845 and of 1846, where he comments on the works of Delacroix. Later, *The Painter of Modern Life*, inspired by the work of the painter Constantin Guys, came to be his fundamental text on this issue. Baudelaire's firm belief is that painting needs thought, strength of conception, and the power to express. For him expression becomes more important than the ability to represent. Imagination is that power, and it is based on memory: the recollection of landscapes, of other paintings, and of personal impressions. For the poet of metropolitan life, nature is not a pastoral dream nor the object of imitation, but a *dictionary* which the good painter knows how to consult. The art of painting consists not in copying or reproducing the visible world, but rather in translating mental states onto the canvas.

In *The Painter of Modern Life*, Baudelaire is particularly interested in the need for quick execution in works representing everyday life. Low-cost techniques were crucial: 'For the sketches of manners, the depiction of bourgeois life and the pageant of fashion, the technical means that is the most expeditious and the least costly will obviously be the best.'[18] After pastel, etching and aquatint, lithography appeared the best way for the modern artist to adapt to the 'daily metamorphosis of external things', and to distribute images of 'that vast dictionary of modern life'. Techniques changed the mode of production and circulation of the artistic object, which then ceased to be a *unicum*, something unique and irreplaceable.

But what is most important for my purpose, which is to show the link between Baudelaire's intuitions and film aesthetic, is that imagination is perceived as a moment of struggle between two types of memory: the one would be capable of repeating the entire range of real experience, the other selects its main outstanding features. Imagination does not exist in a sort of *vacuum*; it implies the artist at work with his pencils, brushes and all the other material instruments that should, as Baudelaire suggested with regard to Delacroix, 'translate the idea as quickly as possible, otherwise it fades away'.

In *The Painter of Modern Life*, Baudelaire invents a beautiful story: he imagines Constantin Guys at work. The painter is a real man of the crowd:

The crowd is his element, as the air is that of birds and water of fishes. His passion and his profession are to become one flesh with the crowd. For the perfect *flâneur*, for the passionate spectator, it is an immense joy to set up house in the heart of the multitude, amid the ebb and flow of movement, in the midst of the fugitive and the infinite.[19]

The painter spends every night wandering around Paris in order to observe and absorb with all his senses the external world. Then, at dawn, instead of sleeping, he sets to work, putting down on paper his previous night's impressions, 'skirmishing with his pencil, his pen, his brush, splashing his glass of water up to the ceiling, wiping his pen on his shirt, in a ferment of violent activity, as though afraid that the image might escape him . . .'[20] Memory must work together with imagination, it cannot be reduced to a mere bodily impression. And hence the struggle takes place between the two types of memory, the one capable of recalling the general contour, and the other concerned with capturing details. The only way in which the painter can resolve the tension between the temptation of a total reconstruction and the principle of selection, is to execute the work as quickly as possible.

> Thus two elements are to be discerned in Monsieur G.'s execution: the first an intense effort of memory that evokes and calls back to life – a memory that says to everything, 'Arise, Lazarus'; the second, a fire, an intoxication of the pencil or the brush, amounting almost to a frenzy. It is the fear of not going fast enough, of letting the phantom escape before the synthesis has been extracted and pinned down; it is that terrible fear that takes possession of all great artists and gives them such a passionate desire to become masters of every means of expression so that the orders of the brain may never be perverted by the hesitation of the hand and that finally execution, ideal execution, may become as unconscious and spontaneous as is digestion for a healthy man after dinner.[21]

Time is therefore an essential factor in the relationship between memory and aesthetic experience. But here time is not crucial as existential recollection (it is not Proustian time), since it is the real time of artistic execution; it is the short period in which the artist produces under the pressure of the struggle between the two types of memory. It is the time of the actualisation of imagination. With *The Painter of Modern Life*, art entered the age of speed. Contemplation was typical of a past, agrarian world, while metropolitan life demanded on one hand the slow and solitary accumulation of data, on the other the frantic introjection of various impressions whose rhythm had to reflect that of metropolitan life.

The importance of the time factor in film is obvious: 24 images per second are impressed on our retina, and any movie is divided into sequences lasting for a certain amount of real time. Benjamin defined film as the form of art that corresponds to the ever-increasing danger of losing one's own life – and he would make it clear that film is the form that realizes he essence of any art in the contemporary world. In film, there is no *Geborgenheit*, or security, no reconciliation, but only precariousness, disorientation, in the continuous flux of images, recalling the situation described in the famous poem interpreted by Benjamin, 'A une passante' (which I comment in Chapter 7): the metropolitan passer-by is perceived in a glimpse and then disappears equally quickly. Existence in general is precarious. The aesthetic experience – its frantic absorption of impressions of the external world and its speed – becomes the model for life in general. The extreme solicitation of our senses and an increasing quickness shape our lives and our perception in the cyber-world. From modern art as understood by Baudelaire, to film and to the internet, speed has become the central issue.

Paul Virilio, deeply concerned with the possibility (now already a reality) of technology's tyranny, insists on the question of speed. He reminds us of the totalitarian and military dimension of new technologies since the nineteenth century and of the revolution in transportation. He points to a major feature of our cyber age: speed resembles more and more the speed of light. It has the divine characteristics of ubiquity and instantaneity.[22] Speed can make everything visible – all at once and immediately. Virilio calls speed 'a vision machine'. Photography and cinema in the nineteenth century offered a vision of the world that was objective; television and computers give a vision that is flattened, like the horizon on-screen. The vision of the world today is compressed, crushed in the close-ups of time and space.

Virilio therefore identifies the period of modernity as stretching from the industrial revolution to the contemporary electronic age, and talks about the coming into being, already in the nineteenth century, of 'an aesthetic of disappearance'. This aesthetic can of course be identified with cinema itself and the disappearing of images in the sequences which follow one another. It is the opposite of 'the aesthetic of appearance' in, for example, sculpture and painting, where forms emerge from their supports, while the persistence of what holds the image is essential to its appearance. The snapshot already initiated the aesthetic of disappearance and speed; from the snapshot to the filmic image, human perception has been integrating the response to rapid images. The 24 images per second in film represent a great impact on perception: images disappear in front of us, while they are kept in the retina. An abstract mental activity is substituted for concrete holders. The conditions of seeing have switched from the persistence of marble or canvas or any such-like matter to the cognitive persistence of vision.

Memory, indispensable for the cognitive process, is involved in the process of acceleration. The points made by Virilio were already present in Baudelaire's intuitions, and are manifest in the work of David Lynch, whose film *Lost Highway* (1997) exemplifies what I have suggested about the aesthetic approach.

Speed and vision are but one: at the beginning of *Lost Highway* (1997) the spectator sees for more than three full minutes the tar on a road flashing by, rhythmically lit up by gleams. The dividing yellow line frantically folds in the night up to the point that vision itself becomes difficult. We understand that this two-lane highway is seen from a car driven fast, but neither the car nor the hypothetical driver appear on the screen. The aesthetic of disappearance becomes extraordinarily vivid: nothing but an image running away, which is almost the vision of speed itself materialised on the road's moving surface. The image is forced on our eyes to the limit of the retina's endurance, almost as if the abstraction of the persistence of vision has become tangible. Rather than seeing, our eyes are touching the grey substance of the pavement's tar as it runs away. Speed is described in its totally dehumanised essence: just bare matter hitting the eye and moving beyond the possibility of fixing vision either on a stable object or on a movable one. The traditional technique of representing movement, such as a rapidly travelling camera, is set aside since the point of vision is not really above the road, but inside it – as if it were inside speed itself. Lynch has chosen a magnified close-up on the road. The close-up, the very means used in general to linger on a human face (or on an important object) is used to grasp the ungraspable: speed itself. The Baudelairean passer-by aesthetic has reached the paroxysm of total hallucination. The hallucinatory atmosphere is increased by the violent music which accompanies the cast-list and credits ('I'm Deranged', performed by David Bowle). Hearing and touch are summed up by sight.

After this breath-taking beginning, the visual-auditive-mental hallucination is interiorised in the features of human anxiety: the protagonist's face appears in darkness and in total silence. We can scarcely distinguish the walls of a room, but we can indeed see the expression of suffering, while our brain cannot reconcile itself to the silence of this scene, since the impression of the previous shot and its soundtrack persists in our mind.

A complete reading of many elements of *Lost Highway* would confirm the interpretation of the aesthetic of disappearance: the story of the male protagonist, Fred, is continued by another character, Pete, while the female protagonist splits into two women, Renee and Alice. But, more importantly, already from the very first cut, the overwhelming power of the visual – and the visual as speed – is put in question precisely because of the exaggeration of the image. The 'visible' has, so to speak, such a strong signature that it calls for other senses, highly solicited in our age, such as hearing. But it also calls for an understanding: the utterly physical moment envisioned by Jameson's negative utopia of the visible, is actually the quick shortcut between vision and the mind since the perception of the image is contracted into some inevitable questioning about the events in the film.

The most perfect representation of our cyberworld is not the computer itself, nor a story where some secret file on a drive is the object of dispute, as we have been seeing now for almost 20 years in so many TV series. The most perfect representation of cybernetics is the portrait of its effects on the eyes and the mind. Baudelaire did not so much describe the big city as show its imprint on human perception. In a similar way, almost at the end of the twentieth century, Lynch composes a filmic image, which, without showing any computers, shows the screen-like electronic movements of the greyish particles of a road flattened in such an extreme way that it resembles a TV or a computer screen.

Lynch succeeds in condensing the history of roads and speed into the history of the world of television and computers. At the beginning of *Lost Highway* our eyes are surfing on something that looks like a screen. With that daring, dreadful close-up, Lynch renders the internet in our brains. The film-maker is especially capable of *expressing* the equivalent of its hallucinatory effect on our vision and in our minds. Thanks to this crucial first scene also, the usual contemporary cocktail of sex and violence, so important in this film too, becomes much more than merely physical. The images that we see constantly in all movies here contain a double meaning which challenges the view of them as mere objects of consumption. They are, we may say, therefore presented ironically. *Peeping Tom*, in the early 1960s, hinted at the pornographic and violent aspect of the visual; *Lost Highway*, in the 1990s, sketches a profound meditation on the visual through what might at first appear to be its pornographic and violent essence. Our guts are not solicited *per se*, since the spectator is forced to think through images. Images address intelligence and memory, and become the means to criticize our society of the spectacle. All the elements of a history of the audiovisual appear in the film: videotapes, sound-track, photographs, cameras, portable telephones and portable TVs. They are not simply ornamental, but suggest a reflection on film, in the same way that Baudelaire's lyrics point to a reflection on the very form of lyrical poetry.

If a typical feature of postmodernism is the inclination to quote, Lynch's film is fully postmodern, but with a major difference. Its resistance to the postmodern taste for citations can be retraced in the continuous attempt to recontextualize the world from which quotations come or could come. Many elements – setting, clothes, hair-style etc. – bring into the scene the 1940s and, even more, the 1950s; that is to say the age of the blooming of film and of the spread of television. The two levels of that epoch and our contemporary age blend without nostalgia. The 1950s and the 1990s are periods of major changes in communication techniques, and in the way in which we live and feel. The spectators cannot completely free-float on clichés as if they were empty images of a pure postmodern world. The spectators must be active, must interpret; they have to put their own memory into a historical context, understanding the interplay of different epochs. Lynch's style is indeed postmodern, but not its intention, since he aims exactly to show up the conditions of existence of postmodern style.

As with another major film by Lynch, *Blue Velvet* (1984), which makes use of images and music from the 1950s in the USA, the spectator is led into the world of imagination that the film-maker has made, and comes to grasp what Jameson calls the 'historical coming into being' of the all-pervasive character of the visual. A cultural or social historian would have to write chapters analysing the conditions of communication in the 1950s, and draw comparisons with our present technological revolution; an artist can contract everything into an image.

Let us cast our minds back to the road in the opening sequence. While projecting speed in a most contemporary spasm of vision, this cut alludes not only to the general recurring filmic motif of the road, but to other films. It obviously works as a quotation from Lynch himself, since the frantic road constituted a motif in *Blue Velvet*. Already in that film, he suggests, through the double reading of the present time and the 1950s (songs and images), that we are in the age of the intrusion of film and TV into real life. That is the condition of our mind today. But, in the *Lost Highway* road scene, one can also detect a reference and re-enactment of the first minutes of a famous film of the fifties: *Kiss Me Deadly* by Albert Aldrich. Imagination elaborates elements of memory; it translates, updates them. Road and speed are not the same in the 1950s and in the 1990s: in order to show the jump from one period to the other, the motif needs to be emphasized, accelerated. Aldrich is an acrobat of the camera, Lynch shows a similar deftness, already with the initial powerful close-up, and in quoting and deforming Aldrich's images in several other scenes: the garage, the burning house on a Californian beach, some female voices and tones, the mystery of identities – all these elements recall *Kiss Me Deadly*.

Lynch obviously uses many features of B-movies but his aim is to overcome their addictive, purely physical impact. Through the importance of music and the elaboration of his cuts, he definitely contests the iconoclastic primacy of the purely visual, claiming for the power of the image as an experience of thought. Through cinematic effects he displays the work of artistic imagination intermingled with memory and creates a complex composition that transcends the mere stereotype giving it the depth of film history. Above all, he continues that chapter of modern aesthetics for which art should be a critical response to the demands of its own time.

Lynch, like Baudelaire, shows us how the aesthetic experience is capable not only of placing itself historically but also of displaying what an intelligent interplay of imagination, emotion and thought might be. The image lays claim to more than the merely visible.

Notes

1. A version of this chapter was given as a lecture at the International Colloquium entitled 'Os limites do imaginario', Candido Mendes University, Rio de Janeiro, May 2000.
2. Fredric Jameson, *Signatures of the Visible* (New York, London: Routledge), p. 1.
3. Ibid.
4. Ibid.
5. Ibid.
6. Ibid., p. 10.
7. See Jon Elster, *Alchemies of the Mind: Rationality and the Emotions* (Cambridge, UK; New York: Cambridge University Press, 1999); *Strong Feelings: Emotion, Addiction, and Human Behavior* (Cambridge, MA: MIT Press, 1999). Ronald De Sousa, *The Rationality of Emotion* (Cambridge, MA: MIT Press, 1987); Guy Debord 'Fetishism and objectivity in aesthetic emotion', in Mette Hjort and Sue Laver (eds), *Emotion and the Arts* (New York: Oxford University Press, 1997); Martha C. Nussbaum, *Love's Knowledge: Essays on Philosophy and Literature* (New York: Oxford University Press, 1990).
8. This passage from the *Génie du Christianisme* is eloquent: 'By what incomprehensible fate is man an exception to this law (harmony) which is so nec-

essary for the order, conservation, peace and happiness of human beings? The lack of unity of qualities and movements in man is as striking as their harmony is visible elsewhere in nature. There is a perpetual clash between his intellect and his desire, between his reason and his heart. When he reaches the highest degree of civilization, he is morally on the lowest rung; if he is free, he is coarse; if he refines his manners, he makes chains for himself. If he is scientifically distinguished, his imagination dies; if he becomes a poet, he loses his ability to think. His heart profits at the expense of his head, his head at the expense of his heart.' René de Chateaubriand, *Essai sur les revolutions, Le Génie du Christianime* (Paris: Gallimard, Bibliothèque de la Pléiade, 1978), p. 534.

9. The obsessive use of Freudian categories disturbed Roberto Rossellini. In an essay he wrote a few months before his death in 1977, 'La société du spectacle', the film-maker attacked contemporary society and its use of media. He also meditated on what happened to Freud's discovery of the unconscious, regretting that 'it has been condemned, by means of a huge reduction, to became the sole platform on which is based today's whole intellectual exercise.' (Roberto Rossellini, *Fragments d'une autobiographie* (Paris: Ramsay, 1987), pp. 21–2.)

10. Jameson, *Signatures of the Visible*, p. 10.

11. Gilberto Freyre, *Casa-grande e Senzala* (Rio de Janeiro: José Olympio, 1973), p. 11.

12. Ibid., p. 2.

13. As suggested by Luis Castro Nogueira in his talk at the Colloquium 'Os limites do imaginario'.

14. Guy Debord, *La Société du spectacle* (Paris: Buchet-Chastel, 1971); *Society of the Spectacle*, trans. Donald Nicholson-Smith (New York: Zone Books, 1994).

15. *Signatures of the Visible*, pp. 11–12.

16. See Gianni Vattimo, *La società trasparente* (Milan: Garzanti, 1989), p. 83.

17. Jameson, *Signatures of the Visible*, p. 9.

18. Baudelaire, 'The Painter of Modern Life', *The Painter of Modern Life and Other Essays*, p. 4.

19. Ibid., p. 9.

20. Ibid., p. 11.

21. Ibid., p. 17.

22. See Paul Virilio, *La Vitesse de libération* (Paris: Galilée, 1995).

Series Bibliography

1978

Colin MacCabe, *James Joyce and The Revolution of the Word* (second edition with additional material, 2002)
(An account of Joyce's practice of writing in *Ulysses* and *Finnegans Wake* that is concerned to explore the relations between language, subjectivity and politics)

1979

Paul Hirst, *On Law and Ideology*
(An introduction to and discussion of the theory of ideology developed by Louis Althusser and those around him, followed by a critical consideration of available Marxist analyses of the law of property)

1981

Colin MacCabe (ed.), *The Talking Cure: Essays in Psychoanalysis and Language*
(A collection of essays exploring the relations between psychoanalysis and language through an assessment of the work of Jacques Lacan and its implications for the human sciences)

1982

Jane Gallop, *Feminism and Psychoanalysis: The Daughter's Seduction*
(A study of the relations between feminist theory and the psychoanalysis of Jacques Lacan)

Christian Metz, *Psychoanalysis and Cinema: The Imaginary Signifier*
(An exploration of the psychological anchoring of cinema as a social institution, together with an account of metaphor and metonymy as operations of meaning in film)

Michel Pêcheux, *Language, Semantics and Ideology*
(A critique of the conceptions of language as an object of study in linguistics that develops an analysis of language as a social practice, exploring at once the position of language in ideology and its specific production of individual, subject and society)

1983

Norman Bryson, *Vision and Painting; The Logic of the Gaze*
(A rethinking of art history's familiar tenets, arguing that the predominance of 'realist' visual theories have, in omitting the viewer as anything more complex

than a source of perception, obliterated an awareness of painting in the West as a system of signs)

1984

Jacqueline Rose, *The Case of Peter Pan or The Impossibility of Children's Fiction* (revised edition with new introduction, 1994)
(An examination of the mythical status of the Peter Pan story, considering the terms of our understanding of the child's and our own relationship to language, sexuality and death)

Alan Durant, *Conditions of Music*
(A consideration of the ways in which twentieth-century developments in the technology applied to music-making have altered the performance, reproduction, and hearing of music)

Teresa de Lauretis, *Alice Doesn't : Feminism, Semiotics, Cinema*
(A series of readings of film theoretical and other critical texts, supported by analyses of particular films, that engage with the representation of 'woman' and the understanding of female subjectivity)

David Trotter, *The Making of the Reader: Language and Subjectivity in Modern American, English and Irish Poetry*
(An examination of the kinds of rhetorical address through which poets have identified and consolidated particular readerships, looking at American, English, and Irish poetry from the French Revolution up to 1980s Britain and at ways in which the coming of institutional audiences – made up notably of those who study poetry at school or university – has altered the the 'balance of power' between writer and reader)

1985

Minson, Jeffrey, *Genealogies of Morals: Nietzsche, Foucault, Donzelot and the Eccentricity of Ethics*
(Foucault's thinking, and that of the others named in the book's subtitle, is innovatively applied to a wide set of deliberations about contemporary social questions and related ethical and political positions, including abortion arguments and 'the politics of the personal')

1986

Jean-Michel Rabaté, *Language, Sexuality and Ideology in Ezra Pound's* Cantos
(Drawing on Lacanian psychoanalysis and Heidegger's meditations on poetry and language, Rabaté's study aims at providing a theory of reading adequate to the strategies of writing deployed in the *Cantos* and to the historical and political situations to which those strategies are a response)

Peter Gidal, *Understanding Beckett: A Study of Monologue and Gesture in the Works of Samuel Beckett*
(An analysis of language and sexuality in Beckett's work that seeks to develop an understanding of the radical nature of the political force of his theatre)

1987

Brian Rotman, *Signifying Nothing: The Semiotics of Zero*
(An account of the introduction of the mathematical sign *zero* into Western consciousness as a major signifying event, both as regards the writing of numbers and as the emblem of parallel movements in other sign systems)

Peter Goodrich, *Legal Discourse: Studies in Linguistics, Rhetoric and Legal Analysis*
(An historical and systematic account of the language of the legal institution with the aim of contributing to a theory of legal discourse as a linguistics of legal power)

1988

Teresa de Lauretis (ed.), *Feminist Studies/Critical Studies*
(A collection of essays concerning history, scientific discourse, literary criticism and cultural theory that bear on questions of the relation of feminist politics to critical practice)

Mary Ann Doane, *The Desire to Desire: The Woman's Film of the 1940s*
(A study of a particular genre of film at a particular historical moment that is concerned through that study to shed light on difficulties and blockages in attempts in contemporary feminist theory to conceptualise female spectatorship and subjectivity)

Nigel Leask, *The Politics of Imagination in Coleridge's Critical Thought*
(A study of the genesis of Coleridge's theory of the imagination and of the politics of imagination in his critical thought, offering an account of the relations between criticism and society in the Romantic period)

Andreas Huyssen, *After the Great Divide: Modernism, Mass Culture and Postmodernism*
(A consideration of the challenge to the divide between mass culture and modernism represented by postmodernism, arguing for perception of the latter as neither a radical break with the past nor as a simple continuation of the ever renewed revolt of modernism/avant-gardism against itself)

Michael Lynn-George, *Epos: Word, Narrative and the* Iliad
(Considering theories which have been influential in the recent history of Homeric scholarship, Lynn-George's book proposes new possibilities for reading the *Iliad*, returning it to contexts of Western literature and discourse from which it has been isolated)

David Trotter, *Circulation: Defoe, Dickens and the Economics of the Novel*
(An examination of the use of the metaphor of the circulation of the blood around the body as a way of conceiving social and economic processes in the eighteenth and nineteenth centuries)

Ian Hunter, *Culture and Government: The Emergence of Literary Education*
(A post-Foucauldian argument that the study of English and literary criticism resulted from moral supervision and management intrinsic to the development of popular education, rather than from more elevated but historically inaccurate notions of the diffusion of 'culture')

Denise Riley, *'Am I That Name?' Feminism and the Category of 'Women' in History*
(Riley argues a historically-demonstrable ambiguity and instability of the category of 'women' and examines its different rhetorical deployments and effects, both within and externally to feminist political philosophies and histories.)

Louis Marin, *Portrait of the King* (with a foreword by Tom Conley)
(In a case-study of the role and function of the image of Louis XIV, 'le Roi-Soleil', as it proliferated in seventeenth-century France, Marin considers questions of power and its representations and, inversely, of representation and its powers)

Raymond Tallis, *Not Saussure: A Critique of Post-Saussurean Literary Theory* (second edition with a new preface, 1995)
(Committed to a realist theory of language, Tallis offers a critical analysis of the ways in which Saussure's ideas have been expanded and elaborated into a canonical theoretical orthodoxy rather than understood and used as a particular theory)

Stanley Aronowitz, *Science as Power: Discourse and Ideology in Modern Society*
(Science, Aronowitz argues, has established itself as the only legitimate form of human knowledge; against which, he shows that the norms of science are not self-evident and that science is to be seen as a socially constructed discourse that legitimates its power by presenting itself as truth)

1989

Kristin Ross, *The Emergence of Social Space: Rimbaud and the Paris Commune* (with an introduction by Terry Eagleton)
(An analysis of an oppositional culture related to the Paris Commune, demonstrating that the very notion of 'social space' emerges as one of the by-products of the Commune and leads to a far-reaching rethinking of social and cultural strategies)

Teresa de Lauretis, *Technologies of Gender: Essays on Theory, Film, and Fiction*
(A series of essays linked by an overall concern with questions of gender representation and the theoretical difficulties involved in their understanding)

Michael Ryan, *Politics and Culture: Working Hypotheses for a Post-revolutionary Society*
(An argument for the necessity of formulating alternative institutions to liberalism that will depend on new conceptions of the subject, rights, and the relationship between public and private spheres)

Peter Womack, *Improvement and Romance: Constructing the Myth of the Highlands*
(An account of the construction of the image of the Highlands in the latter half of the eighteenth century, tracing its origins in the economic, military and ideological circumstances of the region's appropriation into the British state)

Mikkel Borch-Jacobsen, *The Freudian Subject*
(A study of identification as an exceptionally problematic psychoanalytic concept, looking at Freud on the question of the desiring subject's emergence)

Douglas Oliver, *Poetry and Narrative in Performance*
(A poet's analytic theory of literary performance, emphasising poetic stress as a delicate yet not reductively 'subjective' balance of meaning and emotional significance.

Laura Mulvey, *Visual and Other Pleasures*
(A reflective and analytic history of feminist interventions in, and conceptualisations of, films and the cinema, set within broader debates on the politics and aesthetics of representation, including problems of 'sexual difference')

Cornel West, *The American Evasion of Philosophy: A Genealogy of Pragmatism*
(A history of pragmatism as the most distinctive United States contribution to philosophy, stressing its socially engaged nature and the way in which its development has continually responded to American historical experience, most crucially the experience of race)

1990

Jean-Claude Milner, *For the Love of Language* (with an introduction by Ann Banfield)
(A linguist's psychoanalytically-coloured reflections on the fate of linguistics itself, its paradoxical claims, its brief modishness in the mid-1960s and its subsequent consignment again to the shadows; in the context of which, the question is posed: what do linguists want?)

Stanley Aronowitz, *The Crisis in Historical Materialism: Class, Politics and Culture in Marxist Theory*
(Aronowitz's examination of historical materialism lays bare the fundamental problems in Marxist theory with repect to nature, gender and race relations, offering an approach to a new way of thinking about these issues)

1991

Lesley Caldwell, *Italian Family Matters: Women, Politics and Legal Reform*
(A study of postwar debates in Italy on the family and the state, involving the Communist Party, Catholicism, and feminist movements, with consideration of the significant resulting changes, including as regards abortion and divorce laws)

Jean-Marie Vincent, *Abstract Labour: A Critique* (with a preface by Stanley Aronowitz)
(A series of five philosophical essays that are linked in their analysis of the conception of labour as a 'real abstraction' and that lead to proposals regarding political action)

Piers Gray, *Marginal Men: Edward Thomas, Ivor Gurney, J.R.Ackerley*
(A consideration of three writers whose imaginations struggled to express their own and others' particularities in the context of a reflection on writing and the self and questions of subjectivity)

1992

Angela Moorjani, *The Aesthetics of Loss and Lessness*
(An exploration of the psychic and social roots of artistic scenarios of loss)

Denise Riley (ed.), *Poets on Writing: Britain, 1970–1991*
(Writings about their and others' working practices, hesitations, convictions, and enthusiasms by contemporary poets, including those associated with innovative or supposedly 'difficult' tendencies)

Barrell, John, *The Birth of Pandora and the Division of Knowledge*
(An analysis of late eighteenth-century works of art as erratic sites of discursive clashes of interest, in essays which cut across the boundaries of literary criticism, art history and intellectual history)

1993

Minson, Jeffrey, *Questions of Conduct: Sexual Harassment, Citizenship, Government*
(An exercise in practical ethics and political philosophy, which unites and re-conceptualises both sexual harassment and the notion of 'citizenship', proposing instead a notion of ethical conduct in the field of social policy)

Ward, Geoff, *Statutes of Liberty: The New York School of Poets*
(A study of the work of the poets John Ashbery, Frank O'Hara, and James Schuyler, looking at their presences among the New York painters and the continuing implications of their work for literary critical theory)

Ian Hunter, David Saunders and Dugald Williamson, *On Pornography: Literature, Sexuality and Obscenity Law*
(A history of the policing of pornography concerned to show the ways in which its legal treatments have functioned as the positive administration of a particular – and historically shifting – sexual practice)

1995

Arjuna Parakrama, *De-Hegemonizing Language Standards: Learning from (Post)Colonial Englishes about 'English'*
(Parakrama's book poses the question: what is the range of variation within a standard language and what decides that range?; answering it with a study of postcolonial varieties of English which, through critical linguistic analysis, makes strikingly clear that the standard is not some 'neutral' description but a deliberate attempt to exclude the speech of those who do not conform)

1996

Alan Hunt, *Governance of the Consuming Passions: A History of Sumptuary Law*
(Examining the functioning of sumptuary laws in late medieval and early modern Europe, Hunt shows how they worked as attempts to stabilise social recognizability in a developing urban 'world of strangers' and explores their connection with specific practices of the governance of cities; the final section of the book is concerned to challenge the view that sumptuary laws simply died and to demonstrate the persistence of forms of the regulation of consumption in the modern world)

Curtis C Breight, *Surveillance, Militarism and Drama in the Elizabethan Era*
(A study of the reshaping of London's social topography in the early modern period, which examines a wide range of places, institutions and social practices in its account of the spaces and identities which characterised the changing metropolis)

1997

Willy Maley, *Salvaging Spenser: Colonialism, Culture and Identity*
(Maley's study places Spenser's writings within a complex cultural and political context, focusing on his formative experiences in early modern Ireland; eschewing both apology and attack, is concerned to salvage Spenser from 'the wreckage of Irish history')

Christopher Norris, *Resources of Realism: Prospects for a 'Post-Analytic' Philosophy*
(A critique of anti-realist trends in philosophical semantics, drawing on Empson's idea of 'complex words' to develop a causal–realist epistemology)

Peter Goodrich (ed.), *Law and the Unconscious: A Legendre Reader*
(A collection of pieces by the French legal philosopher Pierre Legendre whose work confronts law with the teaching and methods of psychoanalysis in order to produce an understanding of the history of legal forms and the role of law today in 'instituting life')

Cowie, Elizabeth, *Representing the Woman: Cinema and Psychoanalysis*
(Cinema is considered in the light of psychoanalytic theory in a discussion of the nature of identification in and across sexual differences and of the production of feminine and masculine spectators)

1998

John Twyning, *London Dispossessed: Literature and Social Space in the Early Modern City*
(An examination of the spaces and identities which characterised London in the early modern period, at a time when the city's Social topography and human landscape was being radically reshaped)

Lyndsey Stonebridge, *The Destructive Element: British Psychoanalysis and Modernism*
(A study of a British psychoanalytic milieu and a related artistic and literary culture; examining Klein's and Winnicott's concepts of an aggressive destruction which might, so Adrian Stokes's writings hoped, be redeemed through the work of art)

Stanley Shostak, *Death of Life: The Legacy of Molecular Biology*
(An account of the historical rise to power and the contemporary inadequacy of molecular biology)

1999

Jean-Jacques Lecercle, *Pragmatics as Interpretation*
(An intervention in the philosophy of literary interpretation, which sets out a pragmatically supported model of the author, the text, and the reader, as an interplay of projected intention, imposture, and interpellation)

2000

Moustapha Safouan, *Jacques Lacan and the Question of Psychoanalytic Training*
(with an introduction by Jacqueline Rose)

(A polemical account of Lacan's attempted transformation of psychoanalytic training, which argues that only a radical reappraisal of the training process will give back to psychoanalysis its true inspirational status)

2002

Piers Gray, *Stalin on Linguistics and Other Essays*
(A posthumous collection of essays by a writer whose early death took away a strongly individual critical voice; the essays range from Wilde to Stalin, Shakespeare to pulp fiction, with an underlying concern for the life and practice of language)

Jean-Jacques Lecercle, *Deleuze and Language*
(Lecercle explores the complex attitude to language in Deleuze's work, arguing that he seeks to replace structural linguistics with a continental form of pragmatics in the development of a new philosophy of language)

2003

Moustapha Safouan, *Speech or Death?*
(An enquiry into what constitutes the unity of a society through a psychoanalytic study of language as social order)

Patrizia Lombardo, *Cities, Words and Images: From Poe to Scorsese*
(Lombardo reflects on the changes in human perception created by urbanization and the ways in which these changes are expressed in the various arts)

James Snead, *Racist Traces and Other Writings: European Pedigrees/African Contagions*
(A wide-ranging collection of essays united in their demonstration of the need to grasp European culture in conjunction with African and African American cultures the better to understand the complexities of modernity, globalisation, and race)

Index